AF594841

REGIME CHANGE

Inside the Imperial Presidency of Donald Trump

Maggie Haberman

Jonathan Swan

SIMON & SCHUSTER

New York Amsterdam/Antwerp London
Toronto Sydney/Melbourne New Delhi

Simon & Schuster
1230 Avenue of the Americas
New York, NY 10020

Portions of this work originally appeared, in different form, in *The New York Times.*

First Simon & Schuster hardcover edition June 2026

Manufactured in the United States of America

7 9 10 8

Library of Congress Control Number has been applied for.

ISBN 978-1-6680-6724-6
ISBN 978-1-6680-6726-0 (ebook)

For Betsy, Esther, Samuel, and my second, unborn daughter, whose name will not be revealed in these pages until the paperback edition. God willing.

—Jonathan Swan

For Dareh, Maximus Atam, Miri Viola Rose, and Dashiell Henry.

—Maggie Haberman

From both of us:

For Pamela Williams.

Contents

Authors' Note *ix*
Note on Sources *xi*
Prologue *xiii*
Introduction *xvii*

PART I: WHIRLWIND 1

PART II: RETRIBUTION 125

PART III: THE ENEMY WITHIN 269

PART IV: PLUNDER 313

Epilogue *407*
Debts *415*
Notes *421*
Index *445*

Authors' Note

We are grateful to the talented journalist and editor Mark Warren. He worked with us for almost a year on this project, contributing to our drafts, research, and editing. He helped us think through the shape and meaning of this work and pushed us to squeeze the very most out of our reporting. We so appreciate his wisdom, loyalty, and friendship.

Another irreplaceable partner was Pamela Williams, one of the greatest journalists that Australia has ever produced and the finest that either of us has ever known. Pam poured herself into this book—guiding our reporting, challenging our thinking, sharpening our prose, and driving us to think even more ambitiously, dig even deeper, make that extra phone call or ten. We love you, Pam.

Note on Sources

The bulk of our reporting for this book took place over a three-year period, from the spring of 2023 until the spring of 2026. During that time we conducted more than a thousand interviews with a wide range of people close to President Trump, including campaign officials, White House staff, officials serving in government departments and agencies, former aides, donors, lawmakers, friends, and business associates. Many of our interviews were conducted on the journalistic ground rule of "deep background," agreed to in advance, which meant we could use the information but not identify who gave it to us.

Throughout the reporting process, we made extensive efforts to contact the individuals named in this book and to give them ample opportunity to offer their perspective. When we use direct quotes in the book, those quotes came either from the person speaking them, someone who heard them directly, or from contemporaneous notes, recordings, or transcripts. When we paraphrase, it's because witnesses or participants in the dialogue cannot recall the precise wording but are confident about the thrust of the message expressed. The book contains detailed scenes in sensitive locations. Where there were discrepancies between the accounts of participants in meetings, we generally erred on the side of removing the disagreed-upon material; in some instances we relied on our own judgment of various sources' reliability, based on our long histories of covering Trump and his inner circle.

Over the course of these past three years, during our daily reporting for *The New York Times*, each of us has spoken to Donald Trump multiple times.

On March 16, 2026, the President sat with us for an hour in the Oval Office and answered our questions. We presented him with accounts of sensitive scenes and private dialogue, including his own interactions with foreign leaders, and he engaged at length—largely without disputing our reporting, though he pushed back on a few specific points. We then sent detailed follow-up emails to his staff that gave the White House extensive visibility into our reporting and every opportunity to respond.

Prologue

Fur stoles swept through the entrance of Mar-a-Lago. An unusual cold front was lowering temperatures into the high forties—enough, in Palm Beach, to justify the parade of mink and sable among the guests arriving to ring in 2026 with the President of the United States. They gathered first around the pool, then made their way along a black carpet, past a cascade of candles and string musicians serenading them as they entered the Donald J. Trump Grand Ballroom. They had come to pay homage. And to party.

When Trump arrived, the music switched from "The Star-Spangled Banner" and "God Bless America" to Rossini's "William Tell Overture," made famous as the theme song of the 1950s TV show *The Lone Ranger*. Trump was in a jovial mood. In the past year—the first of his second term—he had put on a demonstration of raw executive power the country had not seen since the presidency of FDR. He entered the ballroom with Melania, who wore a shimmering silver sequined gown. When reporters asked for his New Year's resolution, the President answered, with apparent earnestness: "Peace on earth."

The crowd of minor celebrities, ball gowns, lacquered faces, and almost unimaginable riches included a familiar crew of MAGA eminences: Eric and Lara Trump; White House advisors like Dan Scavino; the former Fox News host Jeanine Pirro, the U.S. attorney for the District of Columbia; Rudy Giuliani, a ghost from a previous time, in a white dinner jacket.

Marco Rubio, the secretary of state and national security advisor, was there, too. Late in the evening, when the house band launched into a scorching cover of Pitbull's "Fireball," Rubio put on a show for whoever had their phones out, singing along and dancing in his chair.

The display of revelry belied the fact that a major operation—known only to Trump and Rubio, and a few others in the room—was afoot. They had spent weeks planning what promised to be one of the most audacious American military operations in a generation—the seizure of the Venezuelan dictator Nicolás Maduro—and it was now days, possibly hours, from launching.

Nearly three hundred miles away in Ponte Vedra Beach, Susie Wiles had arrived home after five days at Trump's club. Her house had been recently outfitted with a SCIF—a secure space for handling classified information—so that Trump's chief of staff could monitor the high-stakes mission from there. They had been forced to abort several times in the past week, on account of bad weather and Maduro's unpredictable sleeping arrangements due to late-night partying.

Vanilla Ice took the Mar-a-Lago stage, having taken a detour from his "I Love the 90's" tour to entertain the crowd with the song that made him famous thirty-five years earlier. Stephen Miller, in a slim-cut tuxedo, mouthed along to the lyrics, looking stiff and faintly pained, as if caught doing something undignified. He was the architect of so much of what the first year had wrought—the man who forced through executive actions and emergency declarations at a speed that had stunned even some of Trump's other officials, often with little regard for the trail of fallout.

By contrast, Homeland Security Secretary Kristi Noem threw herself into "Ice Ice Baby" with relish, dancing for the cameras, arms pumping. Noem had come to exemplify something central to the Trump presidency: the idea that governing was, above all, a spectacle—a show of strength staged for an audience of one. Online, Noem's critics had taken to calling her "ICE Barbie," a reference to Immigration and Customs Enforcement, which in Trump's first year back in office had been transformed into one of the most richly funded law enforcement agencies on the planet. Noem would last another two months before Trump fired her.

Seated beside the President at the head table was Todd Blanche, Trump's personal lawyer turned deputy attorney general—a living symbol of the way the President had fused his own legal interests with the apparatus of federal law enforcement.

Among the dignitaries present was Israeli Prime Minister Benjamin Netanyahu, who had come with his wife, Sara, to pay their respects. Netanyahu was Trump's indispensable partner in the year's most consequential foreign policy actions, but also a source of significant division and agitation within Trump's inner circle and the broader MAGA movement. Netanyahu had two days earlier privately lobbied Trump for an even more dramatic military intervention that he hoped would remake the entire Middle East.

For the highlight of the evening, Trump took the stage. He called for attention and then introduced a speed painter he described as one of the greatest living artists on earth. As the band slid into a drawn-out rendition of "Hallelujah," the painter took up a position before a large black canvas and set to work furiously, a brush in each hand. Within ten minutes, the visage of Jesus Christ had appeared on the finished canvas. The artist lifted it off the easel and held it up for the crowd.

Trump stepped back to the microphone. "I don't know how you do that," he said. Then, switching to the role of auctioneer, he opened the bidding at a hundred thousand dollars. "These people are loaded with cash, just so you know," he explained to the painter. "Hussain?" Trump called out to the Emirati billionaire Hussain Sajwani, who obliged with $550,000. The price kept climbing. Mid-auction, Trump announced that he would sign the painting of Jesus Christ, thus increasing its value; and within minutes, the winners—a woman in a top hat and her husband all in black—joined the President and the speed painter onstage to claim their $2.75 million portrait of the Prince of Peace. Half the money would go to St. Jude Children's Research Hospital, Trump declared, and half to the local sheriff's department. As the winners claimed their prize, Trump pointed at the husband. "Get this guy's number!"

Earlier, Trump had used part of his remarks from the stage to pivot to a subject that seemed to come from nowhere. He alluded to a fraud scandal among Somali immigrants in Minnesota. "Can you imagine? They stole $18 billion. That's just what we're learning about," he told the glittering room. "It was a giant scam." Then, as if remembering his surroundings: "Other than that, we're going to have a great year."

What almost nobody in the ballroom knew—what even some of Trump's senior officials did not yet fully grasp—was how quickly the new year would test the swagger of the President. In just over forty-eight hours, the United States would seize Maduro, the leader of a sovereign nation, in a covert operation that was an undoubted triumph. But within weeks, federal agents in Minnesota would shoot dead two Americans in separate episodes that would shake the country and lay bare the human cost of the administration's most aggressive domestic policies. And in less than two months, Trump would take America to war in the Middle East, breaking perhaps the most sacred covenant he had made with many of the voters who had helped return him to power.

But all of that was still to come. On this night, in the ballroom that bore his name, the President behaved as though no force could touch him. He swayed occasionally with his familiar closed-fist moves as the First Lady bobbed almost imperceptibly beside him.

The clock struck midnight. The crowd roared.

Introduction

History is full of ironies. For Democrats, there could be no irony more painful than the realization it was their own success in removing Donald Trump from the White House in the 2020 election—and their subsequent determination to ensure he would never return—that has made him the most consequential and feared President of our lifetimes.

Had Trump eked out a victory over Joe Biden in that election, he would have begun his second term in a sorry state. The pandemic was still raging in early 2021, still killing Americans by the thousands, warping the economy, and disrupting global trade. Inflation would soon arrive, as it did across major economies worldwide, dragging down the approval ratings of incumbent leaders in nearly every liberal democracy and fueling the rise of right-wing populists. There is no reason to think Trump would have been the exception. He has insisted that inflation would never have happened on his watch, but that claim, while impossible to disprove, was equally impossible to take seriously. That spring, Trump was set to withdraw American forces from Afghanistan. He had wanted to move much faster than that, and it had required a concerted effort by his military leaders and national security advisor to stop him from initiating a wildly precipitous withdrawal of all U.S. troops from the Middle East and Africa before he left office on January 20, 2021. Who knows whether Trump's withdrawal from Afghanistan would have been smoother, more competent, than Biden's disastrous exit, but the withdrawal was never going to be easy and would have added yet another burden to a consecutive term.

Where Trump envisaged success in a second term, it is not hard to instead imagine him hobbling through those four years, reacting to the pressures that would soon pile up, throwing him off balance and preventing him from ever taking full command of the presidency. Trump had felt stymied for much of his first term, starting with the investigation into Russian meddling in the 2016 election, then impeachment, and then Covid. By the end of Trump's first term he was deeply unpopular, with his approval rating in the thirties. And given the trajectory he was on, it was certainly feasible that he might have finished a consecutive term with an even lower approval—which would have made him an historically unpopular President. Had that happened, Trump's MAGA movement would have been greatly weakened. And the old-line Republican establishment would have had a fighting chance to yank the party away from the populism that Trump had channeled and fueled so masterfully.

All those what-ifs.

Instead, Joe Biden won the 2020 election—a fact Trump would never concede. When, in early 2021, Trump's aides sent out a press release from the office of the "former" President, he made sure it never happened again. For months, he inhabited a fantasy world where, encouraged by oddballs and diehards, he would insist that what he portrayed as the greatest crime in American history—the supposed theft of the 2020 election—would soon decisively be proved and he would return to office as early as August of 2021. To admit he had lost—not to mention that he had lost to an aging politician who struggled on the stairs—would have been psychologically impossible for this New York developer and reality TV star who had spent his life trying to avoid humiliation, trying to brand himself as the world's greatest "winner."

Another irony: Some Trump aides eventually would concede, though only privately, that it was precisely *because of* Trump's unique pathologies—especially a delusional capacity that they thought at the time was entirely self-destructive—that he pulled off the improbable feat of returning to the White House just four years after the infamy of January 6.

The elites of both parties and the national media—and indeed most of Trump's own advisors—considered him dead and buried in early 2021.

Trump himself saw something different, and it wasn't just his typical bluster. He had a feeling that his core supporters were bonded to him every bit as tightly, maybe even *more* tightly, than they were before hundreds of them had stormed the Capitol to try to prevent the transfer of power.

Trump had always endeavored to author his own reality and then force others around him to submit to his version of events. Trump lied, of course, endlessly and preposterously; but what started as fantasies often blurred and morphed into a reality of his making. With jarring frequency, and the help of his devotees, Trump spoke his worlds into existence.

Straight after the 2020 election, Trump embarked on his most ambitious and destructive campaign of reality-bending. Insisting he had won the election—even as nearly all his closest advisors privately accepted he had lost—Trump mobilized his followers in a desperate effort to overturn the results. And even when he left office, he refused to let it go. Whether it was his decades-long adherence to the "power of positive thinking"—a habit, born from the bestselling book of the clergyman Norman Vincent Peale, in whose church the Trump family worshipped for years—or whether it was something beyond that, something that seemed to his closest aides to be a form of mental disorder, Trump refused to accept the title of "loser." By 2023, through the power of repetition he had converted most Republicans to his false gospel. Looking back, many of his allies now concede, it was Trump's adamant refusal to accept reality that laid the foundation of his comeback.

Many of the people in Trump's inner and outer circles have rewritten their own histories since his return to power. Now, they insist, they never left his side; they always *knew* he'd be back. But the truth is very different. Several who had worked for Trump in his first administration kept their distance during his first year out of power. They did so not only to protect their professional reputations; many simply found him impossible to be around. No matter how hard they tried to divert his attention to more productive matters, they could not get him to stop talking about 2020. Trump was so insistent with his stolen-election mantra that time spent with him during his early post-presidency meant nodding along to keep the peace. To suggest, even gently, that he couldn't be reinstated to the presidency, as his former advisor Jenna Ellis did on social media, risked excommunication. There was no point trying to "fact-check" him. "They stole it from us," he would say. And when he sensed he was talking to a skeptic—journalists from any mainstream publication, for instance—he would add, with an insistent edge, "*You do know that, right?*"

Even his voice had been relegated to the outskirts of American life. In early 2021, the social media giants—Twitter, Facebook, and Instagram—had banned the forty-fifth President from posting on their platforms. The most powerful proprietor of conservative media, Rupert Murdoch, had privately told a confidant that Fox News was "very busy pivoting" and "we want to make Trump a non person." Soon, the once-omnipresent Trump was nowhere to be found on the mainstream conservative news channel. When Biden entered the White House, he deemed Trump such a non-person as to publicly refer to him only as "the former guy," refusing to even utter his name.

It was a small and motley crew who stuck with Trump in those dark days of 2021 after he returned to Mar-a-Lago. Most vital was Susie Wiles, a veteran operative and lobbyist from Florida, whom Trump brought in to run his political operation when he was at his lowest ebb. She did more than restore order; she earned Trump's trust and built a team that would be the most stable of any of Trump's three campaigns.

Others had a rockier four years. Some would be indicted, like his body man, Walt Nauta, and his Mar-a-Lago property manager, Carlos De Oliveira, who were both charged with helping Trump obstruct justice. Some would go to prison (Steve Bannon and Peter Navarro) for contempt of Congress. And nearly all would receive subpoenas over the next three years as a bevy of prosecutors, both federal and state, pursued Trump and his businesses, and many of his associates. The allegations ranged from civil to criminal—from the sexual abuse and defamation allegations by a New York–based writer, to the inflation of property values by the Trump Organization, to the hoarding of boxes of classified documents, to engaging in a conspiracy to overturn the results of the 2020 election, all the way to the thirty-four felonies on which he would be convicted. These last charges related to a hush-money payment to a porn actress to buy her silence when her story of their alleged affair could have imperiled his first presidential campaign in 2016.

Just one of those charges would have buried almost any other politician. But by 2024 the public had become desensitized, and Trump, with his preternatural capacities for survival, and for branding, grasped immediately and instinctively that he could repurpose his legal peril as a powerful political asset. He had announced his candidacy earlier than expected, in part because he was under siege and recognized he could use his status as a leading presidential candidate to strengthen his legal defense. Trump spun a story of a grand conspiracy orchestrated by Joe Biden from the Oval Office. And enough voters found it plausible. New York Attorney General Letitia James had openly campaigned on a promise to target Trump, in 2018, and she had delivered on her promise with a civil suit that went at the heart of his self-image and his wealth. Manhattan District Attorney Alvin Bragg tried to avoid the topic of prosecuting Trump, save for an event where he referenced Trump's pattern of criminality during his own campaign in 2021. He later brought a novel legal case that some commentators believed would not have surfaced had the defendant been anyone else. There were weightier cases, of course; it was hard to find anybody in Trump's orbit who would try to argue with a straight face that he hadn't brazenly mishandled classified national security materials or that he hadn't obstructed efforts by the government to get them returned. But the seeming legal pile-on—one case on top of the next, then another, and another, and all within two years—would ultimately prove a gift to Trump, who had spent decades conflating legal problems with public relations. He would crowd the cases together in the public's mind under a single banner: "witch hunt."

To many Democrats, Trump was finally getting some of the accountability he had evaded throughout his life. As Hillary Clinton put it, these prosecutions and civil cases were just the tip of what he should have faced. "I thought they were all well-founded cases," she said. "I can't help it if the guy's a criminal. I mean, that's not my problem. He is a criminal. He has broken the law numerous times and has gotten away with it, and finally somebody was holding him to account."

Trump had learned vital lessons during his years in and out of power. And his second term in office would be nothing like a second term he might have commenced in 2021. In 2025, he wouldn't have to worry about investigations; the Supreme Court that he himself had transformed had granted the President of the United States broad immunity from prosecution for actions taken while in office. He had had four angry years to contemplate what else he would do differently. Some of his key advisors had also spent those years studying the levers of federal power, figuring out how to get Trump exactly what he wanted—from mass deportations to a campaign of retribution unlike anything before directed by an American President. Trump had four years to assemble a team of true loyalists. Most important, the events of the interregnum—the indictments and the conviction, the threat of prison, the two assassination attempts—all served to enlarge the Trump brand and mythology. This was especially true of the shooting in Butler, Pennsylvania. A man who was not known for his physical courage—who was known, in fact, for the opposite, for using his connections to dodge the draft in Vietnam on account of "bone spurs"—had the presence of mind to stand and raise his fist and yell, "Fight, fight, fight!" while blood was trickling down his face, a moment even his enemies were forced to concede was remarkable. Who could stop him now?

Whereas before he had a strong grip on the Republican Party, in the first year of his second term Trump's command would be almost absolute. Congress would be nothing like a coequal branch; its leaders, who once jealously guarded their independence, would effectively serve as Trump staffers. Trump knew that if he returned to the presidency he could get away with so much more than he did the first time. The culture had changed and he had played a big role in changing it. No longer would top Trump officials and donors be routinely chased out of Washington restaurants by protesters with bullhorns screaming about how racist they were. Now they would have their own safe space, the "Executive Branch," a pricey members-only club part-owned by Donald Trump Jr.

Late in the 2024 campaign, the Trump family had gotten started in the crypto industry and now, as President, Trump was set to turbocharge that industry. There were many, many billions to be made, and this time the Trump family seemed determined to realize the vast financial potential it saw in the American presidency.

II

Trump entered his first presidential term as a novice, uncertain of how Washington worked and frightened of a special-counsel investigation whose dimensions he couldn't quite make out. And while much was written about the disruptions of his first presidency, and all the norms he violated, those concerns now seem quaint. He filled his cabinet with well-credentialed strangers, generals like James Mattis and John Kelly, who regarded him and his worldview as dangerous and detestable. When they told him he needed to keep U.S. troops in Afghanistan and off the streets of American cities, he submitted to their counsel. But by the end of his term, he deeply resented the effect they had had on his presidency. He resolved to govern differently the next time, if there was to be a next time.

The faint outlines of Trump 2.0—what his former chief strategist Steve Bannon would call "pure Trump"—had become visible by the end of 2019. Trump had learned vital lessons from his first three years in office—about the degree of loyalty he wanted in his government, about what additional powers he could grab, what norms he could shatter, what laws or institutions he could bend, and what the markets would bear. He was ultimately stymied—by the pandemic, by remnants of Republican resistance on Capitol Hill, by many of his own aides and cabinet secretaries, and eventually by a vice president who refused to abandon his constitutional duty to certify the election—but the trajectory was clear to anyone paying attention.

One private scene that sticks out in our minds: Trump, in November 2019, sitting in the dining room adjoining the Oval Office, watching the televised hearings that would lead to his first impeachment. Aides who wandered in and out of that small dining room described to us at the time a rage that was building inside Trump. They saw that this rage was quickly hardening into purpose—a determination to make drastic changes to his presidency. Trump was being impeached for a phone call that he had branded as "perfect," but that was, in fact, very far from perfect. He had urged Ukrainian President Volodymyr Zelensky to investigate Joe Biden, his possible rival for the presidency in 2020, and Biden's son Hunter. As Trump sat in the dining room, watching a parade of government officials offer damning testimony against the propriety of that call, Trump was almost shouting at the television. *Who the fuck are these people?* he wanted to know. *Who is this guy in the bow tie?* The man with the bow tie was George Kent, a low-profile State Department official who worked on Ukraine policy. The most infuriating witness of all was Lieutenant Colonel Alexander Vindman, the director of European affairs on Trump's own National Security Council, who testified in his dress uniform. "It is improper for the President of the United States to demand a foreign government investigate a U.S. citizen and political opponent," Vindman said.

Trump was incensed. He had long been paranoid about a "deep state" within his own government. For months he had carried around in the breast pocket of his jacket a note card with the names of White House staffers he had been told were "snakes." But now here on the television were the deep staters, finally showing their faces. When the Senate voted to acquit him in early 2020, Trump's advisors smiled and high-fived. But the President did not join them. He sat still and scowling, arms folded, at his small dining table beside the Oval Office. "Never should have fucking happened," he said.

Trump told his aides he wanted to clear these traitors out of the government. "Get rid of them. All of them." He brought his former body man, John McEntee, back into the administration to run the Office of Presidential Personnel—a twenty-nine-year-old former college quarterback with no traditional qualifications for the role, but whom Trump trusted completely.

At the same time, Trump was developing sharper criteria for the types of advisors he wanted around. He was fed up with much of his team, especially with his attorney general, William Barr, and his top military advisors, Defense Secretary Mark Esper and Chairman of the Joint Chiefs of Staff General Mark Milley. He was fed up with them saying it was a bad idea to send troops into American cities to put down protests that had turned into riots. He was fed up with their slow-walking, with his White House lawyers telling him that the demands he was making were illegal, and with the military resisting his requests to remove troops from Afghanistan and Somalia and Syria. He wanted an enforcer at the Justice Department—somebody who wouldn't hesitate to prosecute his enemies: the "scumbags" like James Comey and Hillary Clinton and Barack *Hussein* Obama. He wanted, he would say over and over again, another Roy Cohn—his lawyer and mentor whose motto was "Don't tell me what the law is; tell me who the judge is."

The aides he gravitated to in that final year of his first term were people who would listen to him and then act—immediately and without second-guessing. By the end of Trump's first term, Stephen Miller and Russell Vought had become two of his most critical enforcers. Miller was a White House speechwriter, an ardent culture warrior and anti-immigration ideologue, who had a breakthrough success using Covid emergency powers to essentially shut down the southern border. Vought, who was Trump's budget director, was a fiscally hawkish wonk who, when others had told Trump his requests were unlawful, searched for and often found alternative means. He championed the freezing of congressionally approved funds, diverted Pentagon money to pay for Trump's border wall, and was a key proponent of "Schedule F," designed to make it easier to fire potentially tens of thousands of ostensibly apolitical government workers and replace them with loyalists.

Both would be brought back in the second term—Vought in his former role, but this time with far greater freedom, and Miller with official titles as deputy chief of staff for policy and homeland security advisor that belied his true power.

III

Our book covers the first year of Trump's second presidency, a period that has fully justified that often-misused word: "unprecedented." He has altered the very nature of the presidency and changed what people living in this country and all over the world think of when they picture the American President. He has commanded a display of brute force that has yielded some impressive results on the global stage, as when Trump's strong-arming of Prime Minister Benjamin Netanyahu of Israel led to a major hostage deal and a fragile ceasefire. But his constant threatening and bullying of America's traditional allies—through tariffs, threats to annex the territories of NATO partners, and extrajudicial killings at sea—would finally end any illusions about the viability of the post–World War II order.

By the end of his first year back in office, the institutional architecture that American Presidents had spent eight decades building and maintaining had been, for all practical purposes, dismantled. Trump reduced funding to the United Nations and sought to create his own alternative with what he called a "Board of Peace," stacked with authoritarian governments sympathetic to his agenda. He dismissed international law outright. He hollowed out NATO not merely by questioning Article 5 but by treating its members as adversaries to be coerced rather than allies to be consulted. He eschewed the World Trade Organization in favor of punitive bilateral deals. And the world was adjusting accordingly: America's traditional partners in Europe and Asia, concluding they could no longer rely on Washington, had begun to rearm, cut their own deals with Beijing, and fend for themselves. It was becoming difficult to imagine any future President putting any of this back together.

His biggest early gamble—joining Israel's all-out war against Iran on February 28, 2026—had the potential to be the most consequential decision of his presidency. The Israelis were quick to kill the Ayatollah, but Iran would be no "one-hour war," as Trump would describe his mission to capture Maduro. In launching the war, Trump followed a familiar pattern: overwhelming force first, consequences later.

Domestically, there would be no peace. "I was the hunted, and now I'm the hunter," Trump told reporters on the White House lawn in June 2025. And the hunter didn't think twice about ordering up DOJ investigations of his enemies or using every tool available to get his own way.

Unlike recent Presidents, Trump had shown he was entirely comfortable using extraordinary presidential powers on a whim, to meddle in the private sector, to dictate individual companies' internal policies and decide whether they got a good deal or a rotten one from the federal government. And so it was that in the summer of 2025, the usually self-effacing CEO of America's iconic technology company, Tim Cook of Apple, felt it necessary to present Donald Trump with a 24-karat-gold tribute, in full view of the news media. The tributes came in many forms: a plane from the Qatari royals and hundreds of millions of dollars from America's wealthiest individuals and corporations to fund Trump's political operation, his presidential library, and a giant new ballroom on the grounds of the White House. Foreign investors saw a more straightforward path to influence, putting money directly into the pockets of the Trump family through their crypto ventures. There was so much capitulation, so much conquest, so much corruption, it became hard to follow.

Given his cartoonish persona, his deep orange complexion, and his oversized ties and coiffure, there is often a temptation to cover Trump as if he is a clown. But, as the late Wayne Barrett, one of the first journalists to take Trump seriously, made plain in his 1979 *Village Voice* series about the upstart with a wealthy and politically connected father, Trump was also a decades-long student of power dynamics. He has a feral instinct for power and he is an intuitive reader of people. His son Don Jr. has told associates that his father has a sixth sense for locating a person's weakest point, their hidden vulnerability, and pushing hard on it until he breaks them. And he creates enormous flexibility for himself, thinking nothing of reversing himself entirely and lying brazenly to get out of a tight spot. In this sense, his complete absence of shame—historically unusual among American Presidents—has been a political superpower.

In his second term, President Trump has bent and even broken institutions. No modern President has so quickly reduced his party in Congress to such thorough compliance as Trump did in 2025. And no President in modern memory has so openly used the powers of the office to pressure into alignment the major pillars of civil society and the private sector, from the largest tech companies to the most venerable news organizations to Big Law and the Ivy League universities.

A year into his second presidency, Trump and his admirers had become enamored of the concept of the "Donroe" Doctrine, purportedly Trump's contemporary spin on James Monroe's claims of U.S. dominance in its hemisphere (and a bulwark against European meddling). Much ink was spilled trying to fit his various foreign policy actions into a larger Trumpian vision of America's global role. There was some truth to these assertions, but they are also a trap. Since his first term, Trump has tempted many, from his most devoted supporters to his fiercest critics, to seek out the deeper motivations and ideological underpinnings of his presidency and character.

Time and again, this has proven to be a fool's errand. Trump will often do simply whatever he feels like in the moment, frequently giving in to shockingly impulsive behavior. We have therefore tried to avoid such sweeping generalizations. There are, however, frequent patterns that recur in his life, advisors he keeps returning to, impulses that are predictable, tricks from his playbook that he consistently deploys—and we have tried to draw attention to those.

This book is the culmination of our combined decades of covering Trump, the product of hundreds of interviews with his closest advisors, officials throughout his government, every ring of his networks, past and present. The second Trump White House spent its first twelve months guarding information far more carefully than the first, where leaks out of the Oval Office and Situation Room were near-daily occurrences. This time, rarely have news stories penetrated these rooms. We have made our best efforts to take you inside.

We have been conscious that this story is far from over, and that the shape of this presidency, and the judgments historians will make of it, cannot be adequately understood in real time. This is, therefore, our best attempt at a first draft of the remarkable history we are all living through—a story we intend to cover until the end.

MAGGIE HABERMAN
JONATHAN SWAN
April 6, 2026

Part I

WHIRLWIND

1

"We might not be doing this if you'd stayed in the race, Joe," Donald Trump said after the news cameras had been ushered out of the Oval Office. "You would've been a tougher opponent. They love you in Pennsylvania."

Eight days after the bizarre and rancorous election that would soon return him to power, the once and future President sat by a roaring fire with the incumbent President Joe Biden. This was a traditional show of comity and continuity between administrations. There had been no such meeting four years earlier after an election Trump would not concede and continued to claim he had won. But Biden had made it clear to his senior staff that such traditions were important. He would meet with the President-elect to talk him through significant issues.

Given the ugliness of the recent campaign, Biden was surprised by how solicitous and deferential Trump was during their roughly two-hour fireside meeting. Trump warmly assured Biden that he'd had a successful presidency; he lavished praise on the strength of the economy and complimented Biden's leadership on several thorny ongoing crises, especially the war in Ukraine. "That's really hard," Trump told the President. "You handled it well."

Biden proceeded to walk Trump through a handful of global issues, briefing him on the areas that might be of particular concern to the new administration. Trump had not yet started focusing on policy details, and instead asked questions about the personalities of foreign leaders, interjecting, *What's he like? Can you negotiate with him? What's Putin like these days? What's Xi like these days?*

Trump even steered the conversation onto highly charged terrain, expressing sympathy at the way Biden had been treated by the leaders of the Democratic Party. But if he had hopes of goading Biden into an admission of bitterness about the brutal way he was forced out of the race—or perhaps into disparaging Vice President Kamala Harris, his replacement as the party's nominee—Trump would be disappointed.

"You won fourteen million votes," Trump pressed, referring to the nearly 90 percent of votes Biden had won in the 2024 Democratic primaries. "And they took it away from you."

Biden didn't bite. Then Trump raised the even more painful and delicate subject of Hunter Biden. "It's terrible what they've put your son through," he declared with apparent sincerity and not a word on his own role in savaging the younger Biden over the years. The incoming President assured Biden that he would not do anything to harm his son; and if there was anything that Hunter needed, to please let him know.

"Thank you," was all Biden could muster in reply.

As the meeting wrapped up, Biden turned to Trump's campaign manager and designated chief of staff, Susie Wiles, who had sat quietly in the room to observe the two men. "Where did you get those beautiful blue eyes?" Biden blurted out to Wiles, who responded, "I don't know, because I didn't inherit them from either of my parents."

Trump interjected, "Don't you know who her father was?" Wiles was the oldest child of Pat Summerall, the NFL great who had finished his career with the New York Giants when Trump was a teenager, and who would go on to become a Hall of Fame sports broadcaster. A spirited discussion about the Giants and the value of good genes concluded the meeting.

The scene was so congenial as to be disorienting. Trump had spent the last several years calling Biden a senile and incompetent old man, "the worst President ever," who would never have been President had "they" not stolen the 2020 election. But in their Oval Office meeting, Biden found Trump's warmth disarming.

Trump's sudden graciousness seemed authentic at the time, even to some close aides, but it was also a characteristic move. He had a long history of dramatically changing his tone whenever he believed a different chord could exploit a situation. These shifts were often jarring; the day after he won the 2016 election, Trump had called Bill Clinton, the husband of the woman he had threatened to imprison, for a cordial conversation, as if nothing had happened. Now, offering comforting kindness to Biden, Trump seemed to be seeking the smooth and majestic transfer of power—and the legitimacy the democratic tradition would confer on his presidency—that he had denied Biden four years earlier.

Two weeks after their Oval Office meeting, Trump called to wish Biden and his family a Happy Thanksgiving. Biden told his inner circle that he considered it a nice gesture. Some of them bristled. Could he really be so naive about Trump's intentions? Biden appeared moved by the seeming sincerity. But at the same time, Biden was also weighing a pardon for Hunter, whom he feared might soon be targeted by the Trump Justice Department. His anxiety would only grow as he saw the names Trump was nominating for key law enforcement and national security posts.

In the weeks ahead, Biden would look back at the brief display of civility in the Oval Office and feel hoodwinked. As Trump's old patterns resumed, Biden sank into disbelief and dejection as he and his administration soon found themselves subject again to Trump's daily abuse.

II

The visit to the White House aside, the President-elect had rarely left Florida since the election. He didn't need to, as the world was coming to him. Every day he was receiving obsequious phone calls and visits from world leaders, dignitaries, and business tycoons. They were mobilizing an all-out effort to win his favor or at least to protect themselves—their companies or their countries—from a United States government that would soon be in the hands of a President who had a very long enemies list.

Few things pleased Trump as much as the giants of Big Tech groveling before him, and with his long memory of their supposed treachery, he intended to make a show of it. In his 2024 coffee-table book, *Save America*,

Trump claimed that Mark Zuckerberg, CEO of Meta, had schemed against him during the 2020 election, and he warned the billionaire that he would "spend the rest of his life in prison" if he did it again.

Zuckerberg had banned Trump from both Facebook and Instagram after the riot of January 6. Jack Dorsey of Twitter did the same—spurring Trump to create his own platform, Truth Social. But one by one over the next few years—as he reasserted his hold over the Republican Party and began framing a comeback plan—each tech platform and billionaire warily and then willingly made their peace.

All was not necessarily forgiven, but it could soon be forgotten as the potential for Trump to inflict untold damage on their companies came into focus.

Trump had no intention of letting them off easy. He had long believed in the value of public spectacle, and especially in the power of humiliation and submission. To consecrate their surrender in the weeks before his second inauguration, Trump would welcome the CEOs or founders of the largest tech companies, each making the pilgrimage for dinner on the famed patio amid the tropical gardens of Mar-a-Lago. The guests would include Apple CEO Tim Cook, Amazon founder (and *Washington Post* owner) Jeff Bezos, Zuckerberg, and Sundar Pichai of Google. Zuckerberg would pay a visit right before Thanksgiving, Cook and Bezos later in December.

Some of the billionaires were in for a surprise, with special Trump-style entertainment planned. Often before meals started, the President-elect cued a rousing version of "The Star-Spangled Banner" on his iPad, piped through the club's sound system. Before dinner, Zuckerberg rose to his feet, hand on his heart.

But this was no ordinary national anthem. Not only because Trump's own reading of the Pledge of Allegiance had been spliced into the music, or because the recording ended in a chant of "U-S-A! U-S-A!" but because it was performed by the "J6 Prison Choir," twenty men detained for their alleged involvement in the attack on the Capitol. Here was Trump's pointed way of enlisting some of the country's most powerful business leaders in his campaign to rehabilitate the rioters; to transform them into martyrs and patriots in service to his own holy cause, the 2020 election.

It was also a way to force a master of the universe, who had cited his own principles to punish Trump for threatening the peaceful transfer of power, to tacitly acknowledge—or just give in to—the idea that he was right and Zuckerberg and the others were wrong; that he had won and they had lost. They could eat crow. Early in his new term, the President would exact a roughly $25 million payment from Meta for the indignity of having been banned on Facebook. Twitter had also banned Trump, but the company had since been bought and rebranded as X by Elon Musk, perhaps Trump's most powerful ally. Given the option to allow Musk to settle the lawsuit without a payment, Trump indicated he wanted Musk to pay, too. The settlement was roughly $10 million.

After the Mar-a-Lago dinner, Zuckerberg would speak by phone with Trump. He had smoothly distanced himself from his previous support for a pro-immigration group and had ended his company's diversity, equity, and inclusion policies soon after his Florida visit.

Jeff Bezos, too, sought out a warmer relationship with Trump. Still smarting over *The Washington Post*'s coverage over nearly a decade, Trump told Bezos: "This *Washington Post* is really unfair. You've got to take better care."

Bezos commiserated with Trump over their December dinner, indicating that he, too, was deeply frustrated with the *Post*, though for a different reason. In Trump's telling, Bezos told him he had lost half his friends over the investment. Bezos would tell others that wasn't quite right: He hadn't lost friends, but people close to him had urged him to sell the newspaper.

At first, Trump hadn't believed Bezos when the billionaire told him that he couldn't control the *Post*'s coverage.

As proof, Bezos told Trump that the newspaper's reporters would write negative stories about him, too. "He said they write stories about him. And I didn't believe him the first time, first term. And I hated him for it," Trump recalled. "And then I believed him."

At their dinner after the 2024 election, Bezos described the newspaper that had once brought down a President as his worst financial investment.

"The people there are terrible," he told Trump, complaining about the business side of a storied newsroom he had hoped to make profitable. "They don't listen. My other companies, they listen."

Weeks later, Trump was still regaling visitors with stories of how the tech titans were now "kissing my ass."

"You would not believe the texts I got from these tech guys. I've got to show you," he told some guests as he whipped out his iPhone one morning after Christmas. "Look at this. Here's Zuckerberg."

Trump scrolled through the ingratiating messages he had received from Zuckerberg after their dinner the previous month.

"This is a letter his kid wrote," Trump added, pulling up for guests a photo of a grade-school child's "letter to the President," from one of Zuckerberg's children, who wrote that they looked forward "to the golden age of America."

Trump pulled up another text. "Hold on, hold on. This one's even better," he preened. "Bezos."

One of the guests who viewed the Jeff Bezos text messages recalled a greeting from Bezos, with a smiling selfie of himself and his then-fiancée, Lauren Sánchez.

Later that day, Trump returned to these trophies in a conversation with others, including Elon Musk, who recently had been tapped to lead a cost-cutting pseudo-agency named the Department of Government Efficiency. "Think about where these guys were in 2016," Trump said of Zuckerberg and Bezos. "They hated me. They were doing everything they could to knock me down. And look at them now."

As he boasted to Musk about the texts from Zuckerberg and Bezos, the world's richest man seemed delighted in the humiliation of his rivals. "First-class groveling," Musk called it.

III

Close aides could not recall Trump ever being as contented as he was in those two warm winter months in Palm Beach after the election. His victory was broadly accepted as legitimate—in a way it had never been the first time. It helped that this time Trump had won not just the Electoral College but also the popular vote, something no Republican had done in twenty years, since George W. Bush in 2004.

One close advisor described the President-elect as "zen-like" during this post-election period. Basking in his victory, he would wander around the common areas of Mar-a-Lago, playing deejay on his iPad on the patio after dinner, and meeting donors to raise unprecedented sums for his inauguration fund and political operation. Guests stood and clapped whenever he entered the room.

He marveled in private that the "fake news" had never treated him so nicely—and that this was what it should have been like the first time around. He made it known to his team that he wanted to make Fox News "beg" for their first presidential interview. "At a certain point, they've begged so much they'll let you do whatever you want," he confided to an advisor.

Another aide, who shared a long history with Trump, observed that Trump seemed less competitive with every man around him, even those far richer than he was. Trump was now, indisputably, the significant figure of history he had always wanted to be. And he could see that others thought so, too.

The stakes of this election had been particularly high. He had been indicted in four different cases and convicted in one; that case was still awaiting sentencing. In 2016 and 2020 he had pushed himself hard during the final month of the campaign, but in 2024 aides saw that he was going almost to the brink of physical collapse. He finished the campaign with a sprint of rallies that left him briefly falling asleep on his feet backstage at one of his last events.

There was also the assassination attempt he had survived by just inches in Butler, Pennsylvania, in July 2024, and another close call that September. He began to speak more frequently about his mortality, declaring that his narrow survival must have been divine intervention.

Now he could exhale. He had survived an assassin's bullet and defeated both Kamala Harris and the U.S. justice system. For a few weeks after the election, he lay low, making few public appearances. Aides noticed Trump doing something he had never asked of them in the campaign: For a brief time after the election, he told his press team to dial back the vitriol in their statements. He didn't want them attacking Biden or Harris too harshly.

Trump was also getting something he had never had before: a grudging acknowledgment of legitimacy from the small club of former Presidents. On January 9, he would attend the state funeral for the thirty-ninth President of the United States, Jimmy Carter. Barack Obama was seated next to Trump, and the two avid golfers bantered about Trump's golf courses. Bill Clinton, believing it was the right thing to do, approached Trump at the service and wished him well. Trump appeared grateful for the gesture.

To some aides and allies it seemed as if Trump were about to set aside old grievances and try to unify the country. He had, after all, secured a monumental victory; he was untouchable and could surely afford to be magnanimous.

"This time is about legacy," Trump told one associate. "We're going to do big things. Even the people who don't like me will like it."

When the associate told Trump he had an opportunity to do something different now that he had all the power, Trump replied with apparent earnestness, "You mean rise above?"

Trump was even putting a positive gloss on his political exile, going so far as to muse to one advisor that on balance he was better off to have been out of office for those four years. He was more prepared now, he had a bigger mandate, and he could do things he could never have gotten away with before. And because Biden had been so terrible, he added, the American people had missed him.

"Isn't this better?" he remarked privately. If the Democrats hadn't been allowed to steal the 2020 election from him, he said, "I'd be getting ready to go into retirement."

Trump's bonhomie lasted longer than usual. But few veteran observers of this seventy-eight-year-old man who had thrived on conflict, bravado, vendettas and grievance for most of his career believed he had actually changed. As Inauguration Day approached, the old instincts returned and it became clear that Trump remained fixed on revenge. He told one close ally that the Democrats, with their "Russia hoax"—his term for the investigation into Russia's meddling in the 2016 election—were responsible for the breakdown of his son Don Jr.'s marriage.

He was not about to forget all the slights. He was returning to the presidency with a weaker opposition than ever. Democrats were demoralized. The "fake news" legacy media was struggling financially and discredited in the eyes of most Americans. The Supreme Court had tilted further right thanks to Trump's own first-term appointments—aided by the single-minded campaign of then–Senate Majority Leader Mitch McConnell—and the court had now given him broad protections as President. He was "immune," he would say with relish. The Republican Party was now wholly his possession.

The day before the inauguration, word began to spread among Trump's advisors that he planned to include an especially provocative line in his address, vowing to pardon all the January 6 "hostages." It caused consternation; even if Trump intended to proceed with the plan, there was concern about using his inauguration speech to make the announcement. A group of aides discussed the idea with Trump during preparations for the speech. And one of the group, senior advisor Taylor Budowich, urged caution.

"Mr. President, here's the thing," said Budowich, who had developed a reputation internally for speaking candidly to Trump. "We've got eight hundred people in the Rotunda for your inauguration, and roughly three hundred of them are Democrats. If you announce that you're going to pardon the J6ers, about half the room will get up and leave. It will be remembered as the most divisive inauguration speech in history."

Trump considered the point, and then said, "You know, I never thought of that. Fine. Take it out of the speech."

It would be one of Donald Trump's last concessions to decorum.

2

Donald Trump and his inner circle settled into the Mar-a-Lago tearoom, with its large chandelier and its canopy roof rustling in the ocean breeze. It was November 11, 2024, a week after the election, and the club was filled with aides and advisors as Trump opened discussions on some of the most important decisions he would make: selecting his new cabinet.

The Wall Street hardhead Howard Lutnick, an old associate of Trump's from his New York days, was in charge of the transition. Trump, superstitious as ever, had barely discussed second-term planning before the election. He was seeing the full roster of names for the first time in this room. His top aides, Susie Wiles and Stephen Miller, had added their own suggestions to the list. Vice President–elect JD Vance had given his views as well.

Lutnick had arranged for eight television sets, four lined up on each side of the table. They were all loaded with the same presentation, with stylized photos of the contenders, bullet points of their biographies, and highlight reels of their appearances on cable news shows so that Trump could make his selections.

As Trump chewed on crabmeat skewers served from the Mar-a-Lago kitchens, the slideshow of candidates played before him.

When Senator Marco Rubio was mentioned, Trump said quickly, "Yeah, let's give Marco State," as if his pick for secretary of state had been a foregone conclusion.

"What do we think about Mike?" Trump asked his advisors as they were contemplating the role of national security advisor.

He was referring to Mike Waltz, the former Army Green Beret and congressman from Florida, who had been instrumental in helping the Trump campaign interact with senior officials at the United States Secret Service after the attempt on Trump's life in July.

The reaction from Trump's inner circle was positive. Everyone said they liked Mike.

"Well, good," Trump said, "because I already offered him the job in the hallway outside." The room broke into laughter.

For CIA director, Trump weighed the appointment of John Ratcliffe, a former Texas congressman who had come to the President's attention in the first term by defending him against the Russia investigation. Trump had made Ratcliffe his final director of national intelligence in 2020, but as he prepared to return to the White House, Trump had one lingering question before entrusting Ratcliffe with the Central Intelligence Agency.

"Is he going to shred it?" Trump asked his team.

By "it" he meant the CIA. Once Trump was satisfied that the answer was yes, he gave the job to Ratcliffe. But that wasn't the only thing Ratcliffe had going for him.

"The guy looks like Cary Grant," Trump added. "He's straight out of central casting. If you were going to cast a guy to play CIA director, that's who you'd pick."

So far, Trump was favoring people with traditional backgrounds. But when the discussion turned to the next director of national intelligence, Trump began to toy with more controversial candidates. He pointed to the former Democratic congresswoman from Hawaii turned Trump supporter, Tulsi Gabbard, who had become persona non grata with the establishments of both parties for her jeremiads against the so-called "deep state," and her private meeting with Syria's then-dictator Bashar al-Assad. Roger Stone, Trump's longtime and intermittent political consigliere, had been pushing Gabbard to him privately. Stone thought she had the talent to be President one day, though Trump was skeptical.

"Let's give it to Tulsi," Trump said, adding that he liked her. "What harm could she really do?"

At that moment, his mind skipped over to Robert F. Kennedy Jr., who, like Gabbard, represented a new coalition of anti-establishment former Democrats that Trump had welcomed into the Republican Party.

"You know with Bobby," Trump observed, "when I bring Bobby out to these events it'd be so loud in there you couldn't hear yourself think. And then we bring Tulsi out and people would clap a little bit and it'd be fine. But the difference is, Bobby's a star. And Tulsi? Tulsi *wants* to be a star."

The discussion in the tearoom turned to the Pentagon. Pete Hegseth, the war veteran and Fox News morning host, was a highly unorthodox choice to manage the Department of Defense with its nearly 3 million employees and its global web of combatant commands. But he received Trump's highest form of praise—that he looked good on television.

"Nobody's ever looked better on camera than this guy," the President-elect mused. "He's been so good to me.

"You know what he did?" Trump continued. "They had these three military guys, just killing people. Going around killing people left and right. There's no telling how many they killed. And they're tough guys. And they got prosecuted. And Pete defended them. We've gotta have somebody who's willing to defend our tough guys."

The "tough guys" in question were the Iraq and Afghanistan war veterans Clint Lorance, Mathew Golsteyn, and Eddie Gallagher. Each had faced charges or convictions related to war crimes but had been rescued by Trump in his first term, thanks to Hegseth's sustained advocacy. Trump had granted pardons for Lorance and Golsteyn in 2019 and had restored Gallagher's benefits and rank. The defense establishment was horrified at Trump's meddling in the military justice system, and worried about the message it would send to global allies. But Trump saw these men as heroes, and now he was poised to give their champion, the cohost of *Fox & Friends Weekend*, responsibility for the entire Defense Department.

When Hegseth subsequently faced the threat of being voted down in the Senate over a sexual assault allegation that he denied, Trump briefly considered replacing him with a former bitter rival of his own, Governor

Ron DeSantis of Florida. "We need plot twists," Trump told a startled ally before dropping the thought. Then Trump unleashed JD Vance, his son Don Jr., and the young activist and podcaster Charlie Kirk to bully into submission any Republican who might be tempted to vote against Hegseth. It was just the latest exercise of a guiding principle Trump shared with his mentor Roy Cohn, and with Roger Stone: Never admit to making a mistake.

When the discussion turned to the Department of Homeland Security, every head in the room turned to Stephen Miller. No one in the building was more closely identified with Trump's immigration agenda than Miller, who had been the architect of some of the most contentious border policies of the first term and was expected to reprise that role with even greater ambition. If anyone was expected to have Trump's ear on who should lead DHS, it was him.

The name on the screen was Kristi Noem, the governor of South Dakota. Miller did not hold back. She had given, he told the room, the single worst interview he had ever seen in his life. Full stop. And this was the person they were going to ask to go out and defend the administration's most controversial policy decisions on the border and immigration? She was not, Miller said, a deft-enough communicator to do that. It wasn't clear which interview Miller was referring to, but Noem had given several after publishing a book that had a calamitous rollout.

The conversation went around the room. Then Trump spoke.

"She's been so good to me," he said. "And Corey's been really good to me, too."

By Corey, Trump meant Corey Lewandowski, his first campaign manager in 2016 and a close aide and frequent traveling companion of Noem's. He had remained in Trump's orbit despite a trail of controversy that had seen him fired from the campaign, accused of battery against a female reporter, and later accused by a Republican donor's wife of making unwanted sexual advances toward her at a charity event. Lewandowski—who denied all allegations but agreed to undergo impulse control counseling after charges were filed—was a polarizing figure even among Trump loyalists. But he had never lost the boss's affection.

The sentiment was clear: Trump felt he owed Noem something. "Very loyal," he said. "Very loyal."

Miller did not say another negative word about Noem in the room that day. Once Trump had settled into the idea, there was no point in pushing further—at least not in front of him. On Noem, Trump's mind was made up. Loyalty—to him, and through Lewandowski—had settled the matter.

When Trump had chosen his first-term cabinet, even as he picked some candidates based on their looks, he often suppressed his instincts out of deference to expert opinion. He may have projected bravado back then, but he was overwhelmed by the magnitude of the job, had little familiarity with Washington, and was meeting almost everyone for the first time. Consequently, he would entrust top national security positions to establishment figures.

This time, Trump felt he knew everyone and everything. Now he saw himself as the ultimate expert, smarter and more knowledgeable about every topic than the "stupid people" who had spent decades in Washington destroying the country. And there was something else. Looking good on television was extremely important—that would never change—but a senior role in the second Trump administration required something more. There was a new acid test: January 6.

During job interviews at the transition headquarters in West Palm Beach, several candidates for senior positions were asked what they thought of the events of January 6 and who had won the 2020 election. In fact, officials on the Trump transition team had already searched candidates' social media accounts for any criticisms of Trump after the riot at the Capitol. Former aides who testified in the congressional investigation into January 6 would be divided between those who had shown loyalty to Trump and those who hadn't.

Yet, as always, Trump could be fluid when it suited his purpose. If January 6 was the new threshold, his own interpretation was the final word. Some candidates could be forgiven past insults or slights, while others were sent into permanent exile. Marco Rubio had described the events of January 6 as a national embarrassment. But he would become secretary of state.

Others wouldn't be so lucky.

In the Mar-a-Lago tearoom, Trump startled some with his reaction to a slide displaying the face of one of his first-term national security advisors. Robert O'Brien was assumed by many to have been in good standing with Trump, and with reason; he had interviewed for a top second-term foreign policy or intelligence role and would later be named to a presidential board. Unlike some, O'Brien had never publicly denounced Trump and, in fact, often praised and defended him in media appearances. But Trump had a long memory. After the attack on the Capitol, O'Brien had committed a cardinal sin in Trump's judgment; he had praised Mike Pence after he presided over the certification of Joe Biden's victory. "I just spoke with Vice President Pence," O'Brien said that day. "He is a genuinely fine and decent man. He exhibited courage today as he did at the Capitol on 9/11 as a congressman. I am proud to serve with him."

Now Trump studied O'Brien's face contemptuously. "Hmm. There's a beauty," he said. "You know, he had a problem on January 6. On January 7, he was shaking in his boots. *Shaking.* And now something's happened to the guy. I saw him on camera. He was stiff, like he couldn't move."

One of Trump's advisors chimed in to say that they had heard O'Brien was in bad health.

"I knew there was something wrong with him," Trump said. "Get him off of here," he added, gesturing at the TV screen. "Get him off of here. He's another one like Pompeo. Just get him off of here."

For Trump, there was barely a bigger insult than *He's like Pompeo*. Once held in sterling regard, former Secretary of State Mike Pompeo had briefly considered a challenge for the Republican nomination in 2024; in doing so he had mildly criticized the lack of fiscal discipline during the first Trump administration. To Trump, this was unforgivable.

So what did "loyalty" mean? And when, exactly, did the statute of limitations expire for comparing Trump to Adolf Hitler (as his vice president had done) or calling him a "con artist" (as his secretary of state had done) or mocking him as an "armchair tough guy" (as his secretary of defense had done)? Where the line was drawn was often unclear, but it became increasingly apparent to Trump's inner circle that the key litmus test for these job seekers now was whether they had supported Trump in those early months of 2021. Singed by his experience with staff he saw as "traitors" in his first term, Trump harbored a suspicion and paranoia that could be set off by the flimsiest of accusations. Some candidates had already begun packing for Washington, only to have their offers withdrawn when a stray criticism or guilt by association surfaced.

Most others would never get that far. Allies of Trump had recommended the former Army Ranger Ryan McCarthy for deputy defense secretary. That ended when Pete Hegseth offhandedly remarked to Trump that McCarthy was seen by some as "a Milley guy." This was a reference to General Mark Milley, the recently retired chairman of the Joint Chiefs of Staff, who had been increasingly vocal about his belief that Trump was a danger to the Republic. The mere mention of Milley ended McCarthy's chances. "We can't have that," Trump told Hegseth. "Even if he's *one percent Milley*, we can't have that."

Of all the appointments, there were none more critical to Trump than those at the Justice Department. He believed the first term had in large part been sabotaged by his previous attorneys general, Jeff Sessions (for recusing himself from the Russia investigation) and William Barr (for refusing to go along with Trump's stolen-election conspiracy). Trump initially named then-Representative Matt Gaetz as his attorney general pick on a whim. Given that Gaetz had been investigated on significant allegations, including sexual misconduct, Trump knew this was a test of what he could get away with. He told aides Gaetz had just a 30 percent chance of making it. But after eight days of punishing news stories, Trump had had enough. Gaetz withdrew his name and it would be one of the few times Trump would undo a major cabinet pick.

Trump would soon fill the senior ranks of the Justice Department with his most devoted loyalists—shattering the department's post-Watergate history of independence and effectively turning the DOJ leadership into his personal law firm. He ended up appointing several lawyers who had previously represented him in either government or private life. Among them was Pam Bondi, who would be the attorney general, and Todd Blanche, who would be the deputy attorney general.

The cast was set for an administration that would operate with a unanimity of purpose and payback like no other.

II

Two months later, on January 20, 2025, Donald Trump dressed in a familiar outfit. For his inauguration as the forty-seventh President of the United States, he had selected a suit that followed the cut of his favorite, Brioni; his regular Brooks Brothers shirt; and favored accessories, from his cuff links to his bronzer. A dark overcoat and his famous hairdo smoothed and sprayed in place completed the look.

The day followed a time-honored schedule. Earlier that morning, just after a church service at St. John's Episcopal, the incoming President and First Lady made their way to the White House for the traditional tea reception in the Blue Room. As Trump got out of his car, President Biden—a stickler for custom—greeted him warmly with the words "Welcome home."

The first twenty minutes of the new President's inaugural address was a harbinger of what lay ahead, a new road map for that same vision, but with a darker intensity. *We will be respected by the world. They will envy us. We will annihilate the challenges we face,* Trump declared. *There will only be two genders. The weaponization of the Justice Department will end.*

As many aides before them had done, Trump's new team had built expectations for the speech, saying it would articulate an optimistic vision for the country. But in reality it echoed Trump's 2017 "American Carnage" address: The country was a catastrophic mess, ridden with crime and chaos. His return to the Oval Office, he argued, augured the arrival of a new golden age.

It was familiar Trumpian fare, delivered in as sober and dignified a manner as Donald Trump could muster. Had any other American leader given such an address, announcing his intention to declare multiple national emergencies and deploy American troops to the border, and calmly savaging his predecessor's record to his face and before the world, then "dignified" might seem a stretch. But Trump had already rewritten, profoundly and perhaps irrevocably, the standards that governed how America's leaders were expected to behave.

Good to his word to his aides, though, he would not court controversy in the Rotunda by announcing pardons of the J6 "hostages." The only hostages he did mention were the Israelis held in Gaza by Hamas, one of the few lines in Trump's speech that brought everyone to their feet.

III

On day one of the new term, Trump gathered the press corps assigned to the White House into the Oval Office to watch him sign executive orders.

When the reporters left, the President was finally alone with his senior team. He sat behind the Resolute Desk with his top advisors in a semicircle around him.

"Can you believe what Biden did?" Trump said suddenly to his staff. "Can you believe that crook did it in the middle of my speech?"

He was referring to Biden's flurry of last-minute pardons for his family members, which had occurred while Trump, none the wiser, was preparing to assume power. Biden had agonized over those pardons for weeks. Some advisors had argued for a blanket preemptive pardon of every political employee in the Biden administration; others worried it would look like an admission of guilt for the entire outgoing government. Biden's son Hunter, after receiving his own pardon, took a particular interest in ensuring that other family members were protected from potential retribution. Hunter, who was staying in the White House during the final weeks of the Biden presidency, had participated in several meetings in the Oval Office and the residence to discuss pardons—a move that some of Biden's own staff regarded as inappropriate.

Biden aides said later that the President had been swayed by seeing Trump announce his intention to appoint avenging loyalists like (the ultimately torpedoed) Matt Gaetz and the first-term Trump official and podcaster Kash Patel in top posts at the Justice Department and the FBI.

"I get to the White House, he's so nice to me," Trump continued, recalling his November meeting with Biden. "And then he pardons his own family during my speech."

Trump had told his aides he could not believe how warm Joe and Jill had been to both himself and Melania that morning. Biden, Trump claimed, had repeatedly complimented him, saying he was the toughest political candidate he had ever run against.

After complaining about Biden's pardons, Trump made a sinister-sounding observation. "Biden was the only one he forgot to pardon," Trump told an associate. "It opens up a lot of doors. But I need to move on, right? Maybe I get Congress to do it."

And so, at the end of the frenetic day, before donning his tuxedo and heading out to the inauguration balls, Trump granted clemency to more than 1,500 people charged in connection to the January 6 riot, including those who had attacked police officers.

There had been a review in progress, conducted by the incoming White House counsel David Warrington. It began as a giant list of every case, then morphed into an effort to sort them into clusters—the most pardonable and the least. The general thinking among transition staff was that certainly there would be no pardons for violent offenders. JD Vance had even appeared on *Fox News Sunday* the week before to carefully make that point: "If you protested peacefully on January 6 and you've had Merrick Garland's Department of Justice treat you like a gang member, you should be pardoned.

"If you committed violence on that day," Vance added, "obviously you shouldn't be pardoned."

But Trump had grown impatient. During the transition he informally polled his advisors: Blanket pardon or just a couple of people? The answers would vary, but most were deferential to his view. Susie Wiles told Trump she preferred a narrower set of clemency grants, but she also told him, "It's your decision."

Finally, on the first afternoon of his second term, Trump said: Fuck it. Let's release them all.

Trump's aides felt Biden's sweeping last-minute pardons gave them cover for the blanket clemency grants.

Steve Bannon, who remained one of the leaders of the MAGA movement, had been pounding the case for blanket pardons on his podcast, *War Room*, for weeks. But as word of Trump's decision exploded on Inauguration Day, even Bannon was surprised the President was willing to take the PR hit of pardoning those who beat up cops. Bannon told an associate, "You're getting pure Trump now."

"Pure Trump" also included serious conversations between the President and senior staff in the following days about hosting the J6 "hostages" at the White House. But Donald Trump would privately acknowledge it might be too much of a bad look. He's "aware of the optics," said a senior aide later.

It was the first day of the new administration. There would be a lot of optics to come. Pure Trump was just getting started.

3

It was always understood that Stephen Miller would play a much more expansive role in a second Trump administration—though just how expansive wouldn't become clear for several months.

Miller had carved out two job titles for himself that would give him authority over a wide array of domestic policy and national security issues. He would be the new deputy chief of staff for policy, a position that made him the keeper of all executive orders and put him in charge of all domestic policy. He would also be the homeland security advisor, which gave him reach into the most important agencies across the federal government. The combined portfolio would give him access to nearly any Oval Office meeting and would help him become one of the most powerful policy staffers in the modern history of the White House.

Miller had a well-crafted public image as a meticulous control freak, but some who worked with him described a messier picture—someone who bulldozed through people and process alike, barreling ahead on policy without always paying careful attention to the legal guardrails or procedural steps needed to make things stick.

He had barely settled into his new office—a second-floor spot that would eventually fit a small sofa, two tables, and a bookshelf displaying a photo of his wife, Katie, and their children—when things started to go wrong.

As the second week of the administration commenced, the Office of

Management and Budget (OMB) issued a memo, M-25-13, ordering that federal agencies temporarily pause the disbursement of grants, loans, and other financial assistance, consistent with the law and with Trump's recent executive orders, to allow for spending reviews. The targets of the memo were Biden-era areas of focus, like the Green New Deal, foreign aid, DEI programs, or other areas of "wokeness." The memo was explicit that Medicare and Social Security weren't to be included. But for forty-eight hours, significant blocks of federal funds were indeed frozen, including Medicaid systems—setting off widespread public panic. Federal officials blamed that on a combination of Musk's Department of Government Efficiency indiscriminately yanking the system apart, along with "malicious compliance"—a term White House officials would use to describe what they saw as overly rigid interpretations of the President's directives by career officials in the agencies.

Someone on Miller's team had set the freeze memo in motion, pushing for it to come as quickly as possible. Miller himself defended it the day after it was issued. "I can't help it if left-wing media outlets published a fake news story that caused confusion," Miller told CNN's Jake Tapper, laughing when the host said he didn't know what Miller was referring to. "The OMB guidance memo, if you read it, is as clear as day."

Press Secretary Karoline Leavitt also defended it. "The President signed an executive order directing OMB to do just this," she said.

But the memo prompted a string of emergency lawsuits, and a federal judge would temporarily block it the same day that Miller and Leavitt spoke. Miller would have to contain the frenzy. He soon told colleagues that the OMB crew—namely, General Counsel Mark Paoletta, a close ally of incoming budget director Russell Vought—had sent out the memo without Miller's approval.

Miller was single-minded about the need to break up the power of the federal bureaucracy, but a visibly amateur-hour operation with any connection to him was counterproductive. There was no ideological daylight between Miller, Musk, and Vought's team—they shared the same goals, the same combative instincts, and the same appetite for speed. Where they diverged was on process: how to move the agencies in ways that would produce durable results rather than headlines that dissolved in court.

The rollout of the OMB memo was a mess reminiscent of the incompetent early days of the first Trump administration. Miller distanced himself from the memo so thoroughly that some senior West Wing aides thought he had no idea it was in the works at all. With his new purview firmly established, Miller could scarcely afford any early missteps.

His reach across the government hadn't come overnight.

Few had spent more time preparing for Trump's second term than Stephen Miller, and no one was more ruthlessly determined to cut through traditional obstacles to enact the President's agenda. He had achieved notoriety in the first Trump term, initially as the principal driver behind the sloppily drafted Executive Order 13769, Trump's travel ban on mostly Muslim-majority countries. Back then, as the President's chief speechwriter, he quickly became a favored talking head for the administration on cable news, with menacing, shouting performances that made him a perfect caricature villain for the Left.

Miller was that rarest of species in the Trump orbit—someone who had survived both the first term and the interregnum without ever having had a falling-out with Trump. Almost everyone's influence would wax and wane inside Trump's circle, but never Miller's. He was conscious of this fact—and oddly superstitious about it, too. When he arrived for term two, he had at first wanted his old office back, although he would not ultimately take it. "I'm one of the only ones that made it all four years in the first term. It's my good luck," Miller confided to an associate, referring to the office almost as a talisman.

Trump loved Miller's bulldog mentality, his instinct to turn the dial up on controversy, and his way of framing issues and acting on them with blunt, *Godfather*-inflected language. When Trump wanted something done, Miller would tell the President he could do it immediately, presenting himself as a man of action rather than the traditional bureaucrat consulting with departments and lawyers before coming back to the President with options. Over nearly a decade working for Trump, Miller had earned near-total trust.

Like Trump, Miller reveled in the bitterness of his enemies and relished his own notoriety in the eyes of the Left. He was also a keen observer of popular culture, which he would mine for clues to better understand the changing country.

His wife, Katie Miller, would go on to join Elon Musk at DOGE as a "special government employee." For the time that Musk was in the government, she held a seat on the President's Intelligence Advisory Board, extending the Miller couple's reach even further across the administration. She was a force in her own right, known for getting in people's faces and, particularly in disputes over personnel, invoking Musk's name to get what she wanted.

There was more to Stephen Miller than just his image as a zealot—which he would play up when it suited him. He was constantly monitoring for intimations of trouble, ready to abandon alliances or form new ones in the blink of an eye. Highly selective about what he weighed in on in front of Trump, Miller was much more assertive in front of others. In meetings that Trump did not attend, Miller would often present his own views as representing what the President asked him to convey. Using that tactic, Miller's position would often become the final word.

One senior administration official observed dryly, "Stephen Miller claims outsized credit for everything, and no one ever had a good idea other than Stephen, according to Stephen." The flip side, according to several of his colleagues, was that he would quickly run away from anything that went wrong, even if he had been directly involved. He had perfected the "art form" of being "unaccountable," another senior government official remarked.

But Miller's remarkable longevity in Trump's inner circle—nearly eleven years and counting by 2026, through factional wars that had consumed nearly every other advisor—suggested a more complicated picture. He had maintained the trust not only of the President but of many, though not all, of the various iterations of senior staff, members of the Trump family, and colleagues across the first administration. He often served as a confidant to people who were at war with each other. It required a level of dexterity beyond just behaving as a pure bulldozer.

II

As a teenager in Santa Monica, Miller would stay up late listening to Rush Limbaugh, absorbing the talk radio rhythms that would later sharpen his own instinct for provocation. He was raised in an upper-middle-class Jewish family in a neighborhood whose politics were overwhelmingly liberal, oppressively so in Miller's view. But the conservative movement in California had taken a hard turn to the right on immigration. It was the era of Proposition 187, the ballot measure that sought to deny public services to illegal immigrants, and of Governor Pete Wilson, who rode the issue to reelection. It all left a deep mark on Miller. He styled himself as a contrarian and delighted in antagonizing his progressive classmates at Santa Monica High School.

He gained some prominence on Capitol Hill as an anti-immigration ideologue, working in communications roles. He got in early with Trump when the Republican establishment was still keeping its distance and Trump's staff was tiny. Miller made himself indispensable on the 2016 campaign, pulling all-nighters drafting speeches and policy announcements. He was one of the only people on staff with any experience in policy and he exploited the vacuum.

Miller had told friends he felt a thrill watching Trump's 2015 announcement speech in which the new candidate railed about Mexican rapists and murderers. Miller recognized in Trump the kind of genius for mass communications critical to forcing hard-line immigration restrictionism to the center of the American political conversation. Here, finally, was someone with the force of personality to drive the Bush-era "compassionate conservatives," and the immigration "squishes," out of the Republican Party for good. Miller knew that his boss at the time, Senator Jeff Sessions of Alabama, did not have the charisma for a viable shot at the presidency. Trump gave him the chance to be his key man.

Reporters who had known Miller from his days as a young and somewhat fringe congressional staffer had often underestimated him, and with reason. They would roll their eyes when his name was mentioned, often mocking his skinny ties and a silver pinky ring with tiny black diamonds.

As a teenager, Miller had been a fan of Martin Scorsese's *Casino*; for events with friends he would occasionally dress in the style of Robert De Niro's character, the mobster Sam "Ace" Rothstein, an affectation he would later dismiss to others as youthful enthusiasm. He inundated reporters late at night with emails and phone calls, urging them to amplify stories of immigrant crime, the more lurid the better. Barking orders as if he were their assignment editor, Miller made plain his contempt for mainstream press coverage of immigration. Many journalists who had dealt with him in those years were shocked by his fast rise in the White House.

As his power grew, Miller became more careful about his own habits. As a Senate staffer, he had indiscriminately fired off emails to media outlets; but later, he rarely put anything of substance in writing. One person close to him noted he had never seen someone as cautious with their electronic communications as Miller. He also developed a more polished appearance. In term one, he had once tried camouflaging his receding hairline with spray-on hair in a widely mocked appearance on CBS's *Face the Nation*. He eventually embraced a cleaner, more confident look by shaving his head completely. He had long ago upgraded his suits and ditched the pinky ring when he joined Trump's first campaign. His enduring interest in men's fashion would come out in his frequent and detailed discussions of fabrics, patterns, collars, and lapels.

Miller was not a lawyer himself but he built close alliances with those who were, in the first-term federal and state governments. Not long after Trump left office in 2021, Miller launched a nonprofit called America First Legal; he built on his alliances with like-minded GOP state attorneys general and began thinking about the kinds of lawyers he wanted for a second-term administration. He had learned from term one that finding the right lawyers was the key to everything. He talked in private about hiring and promoting attorneys with "the stiffest spines." No more of what he saw as weak-kneed types who would report back quickly that the President's orders were illegal, or who were unwilling to stretch the law to achieve Trump's goals.

As early as the spring of 2022, he told associates and fellow travelers he intended to wage war on what he saw as the self-perpetuating and largely untouchable power of what he and Trump referred to as the "deep state."

The bureaucrats have been at this for decades, Miller would say to associates. They've got so many moves to throw your way—everything from falsely asserting violations of HR policy, to whistleblower complaints, to writing dissent memos for the purpose of leaking them to the media.

Bring that regime to heel, and it can't defy you, he reasoned. If it can't defy you, then an administration can re-center its power in the Oval Office.

Politicians of both parties had long complained about an intransigent federal bureaucracy obstructing the will of the leader elected by the people. Harry Truman had delivered tirades about the career officials at the State Department and he wasn't the only President to voice such sentiments.

But Trump harbored more innate hostility to the civil service than any recent President. He believed the federal government was dominated by radical Trump haters and Marxists subverting America from within. Miller shared this paranoid vision and became his hatchet man. In the earliest days of the transition, Miller moved to ensure that officials at key agencies would be acceptable to him—and that they understood he was someone to work with willingly, or to fear crossing. That included Hegseth, Kash Patel, and Todd Blanche, among others. He installed his ally, Chad Mizelle, as the DOJ chief of staff. Later Miller would say to others: "I've got enough ideology for everybody. I don't need people to give me more ideology. I need people to get things done."

Despite Miller's concern that Kristi Noem would not convey the gravitas or command of the issues needed to lead a department at the center of Trump's domestic agenda, he had fallen into line. "If I'm nothing else, it is loyal," he would later tell associates of Trump's choice. Soon, Noem had broad support from law enforcement groups, and Miller would pour energy into trying to make her successful. But within months he was telling colleagues that every problem he had predicted was coming to pass.

Miller soon had a second-term remit that sprawled across the government, with the most critical new component his role of overseeing the dozens of presidential decrees the White House would issue in a blizzard of activity in the first week. These included an order to end birthright citizenship that had been dismissed by Trump's first-term attorneys as blatantly unconstitutional. This time, the executive orders would be approved by a new cadre of lawyers—some of whom Miller had personally recruited.

Miller had met every day during the transition with top aides in a conference room in the Trump team's headquarters in West Palm Beach. He grilled the advisors, including May Mailman, a Harvard Law School graduate with experience in the White House counsel's office in the first term, for updates on the progress of dozens of executive actions that would constitute their early-days blitz on the federal bureaucracy. These actions were Miller's highest priority and he made clear he wanted the President to sign as many as possible, as early as possible, to overwhelm the opposition with sheer force and volume. During the transition, Miller, mistrustful of the Biden Justice Department, had refused to send these draft executive orders to the Office of Legal Counsel—a powerful, small, and secretive legal team that acted as general counsel for the entire federal government. Miller did not trust them to fairly review the Trump team's work. Instead, Miller's team formed a trusted core group of MAGA-friendly lawyers—referred to by some transition staff as "fake OLC"—to replace the real Office of Legal Counsel.

Miller's team created a giant Excel spreadsheet tracking more than one hundred executive orders. Each order linked to a campaign promise, a quote from a Trump speech, or a policy statement. They followed up with "table reads" of the executive orders inside the conference room. Miller often harshly critiqued these drafts, anticipating all the ways in which the "deep state" could willfully interpret any poorly drafted language to obstruct or slow-walk the orders. It was clear to those in the room how much his experience from term one would shape their increasingly aggressive tactics going forward.

But the tight control Miller had exercised over the executive order drafts during the transition did not mean he could manage the government itself with the same discipline. Within the first week, after all the long-range planning, the handling of a core issue was being called into question. White House officials later learned that May Mailman had repeatedly reached out to Mark Paoletta, pressing him to speed up delivery of the OMB memo ordering federal agencies to pause certain funding—a push that reflected Miller's own desire for fast action. Paoletta was an outspoken conservative who had served as general counsel of OMB in the first term. Miller would later tell colleagues that the draft was never sent to his team for review, and that his team would have caught language they saw as overly broad.

Now it was Trump who was furious. Not so much about the content of the memo—which tracked with his objectives—but about the bad press it was generating, which he monitored from the television in the dining room off the Oval Office. He was even more upset when he learned that the White House had subsequently rescinded the memo. In Trump's view, this was a sign of weakness; and it looked even more chaotic.

"Who the fuck made the decision to rescind the memo? Why would we rescind the memo?" Trump asked aides. Paoletta had argued for preserving the memo, but the policy and legal teams wanted it pulled back. Some thought that the move could help the administration's standing in court against the onslaught of lawsuits. Trump was not interested in those details.

Somebody's head had to roll for this series of public missteps. Susie Wiles wanted to fire Paoletta, who had not written the OMB memo, but had edited it. JD Vance believed the firing would be a mistake—they shouldn't make it even more of a controversy than it already was. Paoletta's cause was helped when Vought, who was not yet confirmed for his own role, spoke to Trump by phone. "Did Paoletta go rogue?" Trump asked. Vought said no; without mentioning Miller, the OMB director-in-waiting said the West Wing had asked for the document.

Frustrated by the optics, Trump needed to change the subject, and fast. His advisors already had several options in the queue that could be used as distractions. One option was to release the videos of Special Counsel Robert Hur's interview that highlighted Joe Biden's confusion and frailty. Another was to announce that they were going to open camps in Guantánamo Bay to detain migrants. They opted for announcing Guantánamo; there was no better counter for a screwup than an outrage.

III

Foremost among the errors of term one, in Miller's thinking, was the revolving door of personnel. A chaotic transition in 2016 had left the government understaffed and the White House and top cabinet posts filled with people who thought Trump was either dangerous or an idiot, or both. The President's agenda had been hamstrung as a result of cabinet secretaries trying to subvert Trump's desires, or aides who would leak to the press. And the constant shuffling of staff had blunted the first administration's ability to function.

A stable group of trusted staff was vital. And Trump now had a chief of staff who had maintained relative stability in his world. Susie Wiles brought altogether different qualities from Miller, most especially her surprising ease and compatibility with Trump—a sharp contrast from the series of chiefs of staff in term one that Trump had blown through.

She was sixty-seven years old, an arresting figure, standing five feet, six inches tall, with thick silver-blond hair and always immaculately put together. From the first moment of the new administration, Wiles, the first woman to be White House chief of staff, was the person who consolidated the jumble of advisors who existed in factions, keeping them focused on a broader goal. If Trump seemed to be about constant hoopla, Wiles was almost a photographic negative—reflecting as much calm as Trump's noise.

She had worked her way up through Florida's Republican political circles, running Mayor John Delaney's government operation in Jacksonville for years. Developing a reputation as a savvy operative, she went on to manage Rick Scott's surprise gubernatorial victory in 2010, the year of the Tea Party wave and the beginning of the movement Trump would absorb and expand upon. In 2016, Trump had her take over his Florida operation late in the race and then never stopped thanking her for the win there. Any Florida Republican with ambitions either knew Wiles or was forced to reckon with her at some point. Her lobbying work took her constantly between Florida and Washington. And yet, even among her most fervent supporters, few would have anticipated that she would one day become White House chief of staff.

In 2018, at Trump's request, she had helped to save then-Representative Ron DeSantis's flailing gubernatorial campaign, although Wiles and DeSantis eventually fell out. It was a break so bitter that DeSantis had persuaded Trump against hiring Wiles for his 2020 campaign. When some of his advisors protested, Trump changed his mind and brought her back. And in 2021, early in his quasi-exile at Mar-a-Lago, Trump had brought Wiles back once again, to impose order on the shapeless post-presidency that was emerging for the Trumps in Palm Beach.

There had been scant furniture at Mar-a-Lago for any of the staff Wiles brought in to work for the ex-President. A few chairs and tables. No rhythm for each day, nor much of a sense of the future, or of Donald Trump's place in it. Those early days of Trump's post-presidency were largely organized around golf and dinners on the Mar-a-Lago patio, where club members would stand and applaud Trump when he arrived. After several months, Trump would be accompanied on the golf course by Natalie Harp, an aide who supplied him with a fresh stream of positive news stories and social media comments that she would often read aloud and later follow up with copies from the portable printer she carried around. Harp wrote Trump adoring letters that she left in his personal spaces, including one that read "You are all that matters to me." Wiles told others she remembered thinking, *Where am I?*

For the first several weeks of the second term, Wiles had rushed to learn about the federal government. She was a novice when it came to the executive branch, with her experience limited to a short stint working on diaries and schedules in the Reagan White House four decades earlier. She quizzed former chiefs of staff about the West Wing systems and processes. She had not had nearly enough time to study the vast and dizzying array of foreign and domestic policy challenges that would soon pile up on her desk. Still, most figured Wiles would have more staying power than the four chiefs of staff in Trump's first term. She had, after all, run his political operation for years by then, and managed his campaign with as steady a hand as could be expected with such a volatile and self-sabotaging candidate.

Wiles also had good emotional intelligence for reading and handling people. Her staff was treated with respect and in turn were intensely loyal;

many of the key aides around Trump were seen as "Susie's people." When things went wrong, Wiles rarely screamed or shouted, as many others in the job had done. She was warm, charming, and soft-spoken. An advisor to the 2016 campaign once observed that part of Jared Kushner's appeal to Trump was a soothing voice, and Wiles had a similar quality. Trump liked her presence and was comfortable in a way he had never been with her predecessors.

She gave almost nothing away. When Trump was deciding in 2024 between potential vice presidents, people in the President's orbit studied her every word for clues on where she stood, but no one could be sure. Certainly she did not lobby Trump in the direction of a particular candidate in the way his son Don Jr. or the influential conservative commentator Tucker Carlson and others did, pushing for JD Vance.

Years in Florida had given Wiles a fluency in political power that made her well suited for Trump. She had policy interests relevant primarily to issues in Florida, like conservation, and had done work on criminal justice matters. But she was far from a policy wonk. And her relative lack of White House experience risked putting her at a disadvantage for the likely battles ahead over the aggressive agenda spearheaded by ideologues like Stephen Miller and Russell Vought. They had learned during the first term how to operate the machinery of government. Miller, in particular, was almost certain to try to outmaneuver Wiles with his sprawling policy role.

But there was another side to Wiles, too. Those who knew her well attested that underneath the grandmotherly vibes and reassuring manner was an operator who could so deftly wield a knife that her targets rarely saw it coming. Trump had nicknamed her "the Ice Maiden."

4

There was no foreign policy issue on which Donald Trump had staked out a clearer public position than the war between Russia and Ukraine, nearly three years old by the start of his second term. He would repeat his mantra throughout the campaign. The conflict shouldn't have happened; it would never have started had he been President—Vladimir Putin would not have dared. Trump promised he would end the war within twenty-four hours.

Ten days into his presidency, the war had only intensified. Russia had seized new territory in Eastern Ukraine, resulting in more casualties, the combatants heedless to Trump's campaign bluster.

During Thanksgiving week after the election, Trump had announced that retired Army Lieutenant General Keith Kellogg would be his special envoy for the conflict. Kellogg, like several members of Trump's second-term administration, had first come to the President's notice during the 2016 campaign. When Trump was asked at the time whom he was relying on for national security and foreign policy advice, he replied: "I'm speaking with myself, number one, because I have a very good brain, and I've said a lot of things." His campaign soon released a list of businessmen, obscure foreign policy figures, and one retired general—Kellogg—that it named as advisors. At a time when the U.S. foreign policy establishment was shunning Trump, Kellogg was an early validator. He later served in the first Trump administration and had remained an enthusiastic and unwavering booster ever since. With this new and important assignment, perhaps the capstone of Kellogg's thirty-six-year career, Trump seemed to be rewarding his fidelity.

But in the days leading up to the second inauguration, Kellogg grew concerned that the incoming administration was not taking the conflict in Ukraine seriously, or at least was not yet organized enough to take it seriously. He had visited Mar-a-Lago twice during the transition, seeking direction. He received none. Kellogg nonetheless appeared on Fox News before the 2025 inauguration to articulate what he thought was Trump's position on the negotiations to come. "People need to understand, he's not trying to give something to Putin or to the Russians, he's actually trying to save Ukraine and save their sovereignty," Kellogg assured viewers. "And he's going to make sure that it's equitable and that it's fair." He told Fox's viewers that he was not speaking for Trump, but that he wanted to end the war in one hundred days. That timetable corresponded to the last of the Biden aid to Ukraine running out.

But Kellogg was still having trouble finding out what he was supposed to do; he had to resort to asking the newly confirmed Secretary of Defense Pete Hegseth for help getting Trump's attention. Eventually, he got his chance. In a meeting in the Oval Office on January 30, Kellogg's mission was front and center. His purpose in calling the meeting was to determine the "commander's intent," to figure out what actions Trump wanted to commit the United States to in order to end the carnage. He would also present a slide deck, headlined "An America First Plan: Trump's Historic Peace Deal for Russia-Ukraine War."

With Trump reclining at his desk, and others—JD Vance, Marco Rubio, Pete Hegseth, Stephen Miller, Mike Waltz, and Treasury Secretary Scott Bessent—arrayed around him, the President started the meeting: "Okay, Keith, go ahead."

Kellogg opened by describing the current state of the battlefield, a bloody stalemate, with neither side having a clear advantage. He had prepared meticulously, outlining a series of carrots and sticks to get both sides to a permanent ceasefire, and organizing his presentation into six slides that were printed on foam poster boards and propped on an easel to the side of the President's desk. He included a map and a concrete plan of action.

It did not go well.

"Speak up, Keith—we can't hear you," someone said as the eighty-year-old Kellogg ran through his slides.

In his plan, there would be no international recognition of Russia's claims over occupied Ukrainian territory, but it included the significant concession that Ukraine would not try to recapture already-lost territory by force. To enforce a ceasefire, he proposed the deployment of peacekeeping troops in Ukraine from France, Britain, and the Netherlands. As Kellogg made this point, Vance expressed concern that the proposed peacekeepers were from NATO countries. Their presence on Ukrainian soil would surely provoke Russia, Vance argued, and potentially drag the United States into war.

"We'd need to have an Article 5 exemption," Kellogg responded, referring to NATO's collective defense clause stating that an armed attack against one member was considered an attack against all. "It can't be a NATO mission."

"Are there troops from other countries that could serve this purpose?" Vance asked. Waltz agreed with this idea—it would be better to have support from non-Europeans.

Vance suggested Saudi Arabia or India. Trump chuckled. "The Indians won't do that," the President said. "They won't pay for something like that." Prime Minister Modi really liked him and wanted to visit, Trump said, but the Indians don't ever pay for anything. Trump said he was fine with the Brits or the French putting their own soldiers into Ukraine; he didn't care what the other countries did, so long as it didn't involve America.

As Kellogg continued, Trump repeatedly interjected to say just how much he disliked Ukraine's Zelensky. "He's a bad negotiator," Trump said, "and he's destroyed his country. But he was really good at getting stuff from the Biden administration." Kellogg tried to forge on, but Trump kept up a constant stream of digs at Ukraine. It was, he said at one point, the most corrupt country on earth.

"I'm not a big fan of Ukraine," Trump said. "Except their women. They keep winning Miss Universe." The President pointed at his long-serving aide Dan Scavino with a smirk. "Dan knows what I'm talking about."

It was unclear what Trump meant, but Vance and Hegseth suppressed laughter and Rubio looked stunned.

As the meeting progressed, Trump also displayed an essential sympathy for the Russian position, at one point echoing Putin's defense that it was the threat of NATO expansion that had given Moscow no choice but to invade. "This all goes back to NATO," Trump said. "We should've never opened the door to Ukraine joining NATO."

Kellogg proposed that Ukraine could join the European Union instead of NATO. But Trump quickly shut him down, saying that to the Russians "it's the same thing."

Trump declared that he could get Putin to the table. "I've got a great relationship with him," he added, intimating that the two leaders had been in touch. "He's ready to negotiate."

Just the night before, a terrible midair collision had occurred over the Potomac between a military helicopter and an American Airlines passenger plane on final approach into Ronald Reagan Washington National Airport. On board had been an international group of elite figure skaters, including two Russian champions. Kellogg suggested that the tragedy created an opening for Trump to engage Putin, express condolences, and then turn to the war. Trump brushed off the idea, saying, "No, there are other things going on."

Kellogg also brought up the proposal, first presented in October 2024 by Zelensky himself in his "Victory Plan," that the United States could make a deal with Ukraine for billions of dollars' worth of the country's critical resources, including its rich deposits of uranium, titanium, and lithium. Bessent spoke up to say that there could potentially be hundreds of billions of dollars in such a deal for the United States. Trump assigned Bessent to the task.

In Kellogg's thinking, a rare earth minerals deal could have the effect of both financing Ukraine's war effort and vesting the United States in the country's defense.

The minerals deal immediately appealed to Trump, but not because it might bind the two countries together in a common destiny—he was disdainful of that notion, and did not want to offer a security guarantee for Ukraine of any kind. Rather, the President seized on the deal as a way for the United States to recoup the Ukraine military aid that had been approved by the Biden administration. "They owe us," he said. "And they need to repay us. We need to get our money back."

By the time Kellogg reached his fifth slide, detailing "Trump's Truce," establishing pressure points for both the Russians and Ukrainians, it was clear there was another agenda in the room. It was an agenda Kellogg had not been read into. He pressed on, trying to outline the pressure points that would force Russia to negotiate. Kellogg's slide read: "Eliminate Russian oil and gas revenues; cut off China's economic support, incl. sanctions; and work with Europe to demonstrate intent to deploy $330 billion of frozen Russian sovereign assets to rearm and rebuild Ukraine."

Trump abruptly stopped him, telling Kellogg he was not to talk to the Russians. The President's handpicked envoy to the Russia-Ukraine conflict was forbidden by the President from any contact with the aggressor.

"Nobody on your team can talk to these people," Trump added, "because we're working a deal."

Who was the "we"? What was the deal? Trump's special envoy for the conflict had no idea.

The meeting—which made some of Kellogg's colleagues wince over his treatment—made plain how different Trump's second presidency already was from his first. Back then, Trump mostly, albeit at times grudgingly, deferred to the establishment figures that stocked his Pentagon, State Department, and intelligence community—generals, corporate titans, and former senators whom he had empowered to run a fairly conventional interagency policy process, ironing out disagreements and presenting options to the President. Trump had never liked that approach. It was too slow, too fussy. He had little regard for the expertise of his first-term national security officials.

But now, at the start of his second administration, Trump trusted his own gut and would act on it accordingly. And without telling Kellogg, he had already given his job away to somebody else.

Trump had set up a secret back channel with the Russians, an approach that was not without historical precedent. Richard Nixon had entrusted such delicate missions to Henry Kissinger, an expert steeped in diplomatic history and global strategy. Trump had someone quite different in mind. He had quietly assigned this high-stakes mission to Steve Witkoff, a New York real estate investor and an old friend of Trump's who had helped out during the 2024 campaign. Witkoff had no experience in foreign policy, but Trump had already made him special envoy to the Middle East, where Witkoff had a number of business relationships. He trusted Witkoff and believed he could get along with almost anyone. And Trump was becoming impatient; maybe Witkoff could bring home a quick deal with Putin. Trump had told his aides that Putin's economy was in real trouble and that a combination of additional sanctions and lower oil prices—with help from the Saudis—would force Putin to negotiate a speedy end to the war. But Trump also believed Putin was winning, while Kellogg thought Trump was overestimating the strength of the Russian military.

There was yet another angle to Trump's appointment of Witkoff. The Russians had made clear they did not want to deal with Kellogg, a committed Russia skeptic, whose daughter was working with a nonprofit to support Ukraine in the conflict. Replacing Kellogg with Witkoff would serve as a gesture of goodwill to the Russians.

In fact, several days before Kellogg's defenestration in the Oval Office, Trump's top advisors had met in the Situation Room to hash out their Russia-Ukraine policy. The small group included Susie Wiles, Marco Rubio, Mike Waltz, and Witkoff. Kellogg had not been invited.

The meeting ran loosely, with the inexperienced Witkoff talking about how, in his view, the Russians wanted to make a deal. He suggested there would be a lot of upside if the United States could reestablish a normal economic relationship with Russia. The sanctions that could be lifted were enormous. They discussed Witkoff's early conversations with his back channel, Kirill Dmitriev, the head of Russia's sovereign wealth fund.

Rubio, who appeared skeptical, asked Witkoff, "How do we know this guy is the real deal and speaks for Putin?" Waltz also seemed doubtful, cautioning that there were many people coming out of the woodwork claiming to speak for Putin.

A National Security Council staffer at the table weighed in with a proposal to assess whether Dmitriev was the real thing. "Well, sir, we could test him," the staffer said to Rubio. "We could ask him to release a hostage, for example."

Rubio liked the idea. And he said he knew just the guy they could ask for: Marc Fogel, an American high school teacher who had been sentenced to fourteen years in a Russian prison for carrying a small amount of medical marijuana in his luggage.

Witkoff would later tell colleagues that Dmitriev came with the strong endorsement of not only Mohammed bin Salman, the crown prince of Saudi Arabia, but also "TBZ"—Tahnoon bin Zayed Al Nahyan, the high-powered national security advisor of the United Arab Emirates. An endorsement from TBZ seemed to mean a lot to Witkoff. "TBZ is the guy," he told a colleague. "When somebody like that says he's the real thing, then you take that to the bank."

If Kellogg was disappointed when he finally discovered he was shut out, he had, in part, himself to blame. After nearly a decade of association with Donald Trump, Kellogg still seemed oddly naive about his boss. Fundamentally, Trump enjoyed toying with people and operated in a culture of secrecy. There would never be clear lines of authority or command, other than from Trump himself. He often ran different lines in parallel—or even on triple tracks. Even with his closest aides, there were rooms within rooms and no one had entrance to them all.

Trump kept staff, advisors, new acolytes, the faithful in line with this constant instability and keyhole views of what he was up to. Only Trump had the full picture—no one else could know for sure what he'd told the others, or how it differed from what they had been told themselves.

5

During the transition, Donald Trump had accompanied Elon Musk to his SpaceX site at Boca Chica, Texas, to witness the launch of the giant Starship rocket. Trump could not stop talking about it afterward.

He was dazzled by space exploration, and in his eyes, wealth had always equaled intelligence. By that measure, Musk was the smartest man in history. As well, Musk seemed to care deeply about slashing the national debt, and he had just spent at least $300 million to get Trump elected. So why not let him try?

The unlikely alliance between Musk and Trump had begun at a dinner party in Silicon Valley in the fall of 2023.

"I get involved in politics as little as possible," Musk had said back in 2015, when he had a fairly typical businessman's record of contributing to both Democrats and Republicans. Around that time, even though he had described himself as a "moderate" and tended to vote for Democrats, he was already drifting rightward. In 2021, the Biden administration aroused Musk's ire by pointedly excluding him from the White House electric vehicle summit due to Musk's hostility to unions. Within twelve months he had fully switched sides, endorsing Republicans for the first time. Then—much more consequentially—he had bought the booming social media site Twitter and dramatically loosened its rules. He welcomed Trump back onto the platform.

When Musk attended a campaign fundraiser in late September 2023 at the Palo Alto–area home of the technology investor Chamath Palihapitiya, he was already searching for a new presidential candidate. He had previously regarded Trump as a person of low character, and the feeling was mutual. Months earlier, the two had exchanged harsh words online, with Trump calling Musk "just another bullshit artist," and Musk firing back that Trump had no business running for President again, and should "sail into the sunset."

The event that evening in Silicon Valley was a $50,000-a-head dinner for Vivek Ramaswamy, an entrepreneur and long-shot candidate for the Republican presidential nomination. At one point during the night, Musk turned to a favorite topic of Ramaswamy's: dismantling the "fourth branch of government, the administrative state."

Cutting the federal bureaucracy was primarily a technological challenge, Musk declared. And he would know, he said, because he had tackled just such a challenge before. When he took over Twitter, he had quickly gained access to the company's servers and slashed the workforce by around 80 percent. Wouldn't it be great, Musk mused, to have the same sort of access to the computers of the federal government?

"Just give me the passwords," he said half-jokingly, and he would cut the government down to size.

Over the next year, at several dinners organized by Musk and the billionaire investor Nelson Peltz, Musk evangelized about the urgent need for a smaller government. He was chafing at the regulatory oversight of his companies, and was embroiled in bitter disputes with nearly a dozen federal agencies. An estrangement from his transgender daughter was also pulling him rightward, but nothing shaped his politics more than the enormous amount of time he was spending consuming anti-immigrant content on X. By now, he was openly flirting with supporting Trump.

In late May 2024, after Trump's conviction in New York on thirty-four felony counts of falsifying business records, Musk posted, "If a former President can be criminally convicted over such a trivial matter—motivated by politics, rather than justice—then anyone is at risk of a similar fate." Six weeks later, Trump survived a would-be assassin's bullet. Soon after the shooting, Musk took to X to endorse him, posting, "I fully endorse President Trump and hope for his rapid recovery."

And so began the spectacle of Elon Musk's ardent and unprecedented campaign on behalf of Donald Trump. For the next four months he would largely forsake running his own businesses to pour himself into the effort. He spent more on Trump than any single donor was known to have spent to elect an American President.

But Musk would not be satisfied as a mere donor. Weeks later, on the August 2 episode of the Lex Fridman podcast, he would publicly float for the first time the idea that would become the Department of Government Efficiency.

"There has to be a sort of a garbage collection for laws and regulations," Musk told Fridman, "so that you don't keep accumulating laws and regulations to the point where you can't do anything."

"I wish you could just for a week go into Washington and be the head of the committee for making . . . government smaller," Fridman replied.

"I have discussed with Trump the idea of a government efficiency commission," Musk said. "And I would be willing to be part of that commission."

The idea gained steam through the summer. On August 19, it got its name: A meme coin enthusiast on X suggested that Musk's effort should be called the Department of Government Efficiency, or DOGE—an abbreviation referencing the meme cryptocurrency Dogecoin, which Musk had long joked about.

Musk loved it: "That is the perfect name," he replied.

On September 5, Trump publicly incorporated the DOGE concept into his campaign, announcing it as a key component of his economic plans for a second term—one that would "save trillions of dollars."

By late in the election season, DOGE had captured attention like few campaign gimmicks ever had. Howard Lutnick, who had just been appointed chairman of Trump's transition operation, envisioned DOGE as a partnership between himself and Musk. Lutnick told those around him that Musk intended to eliminate a trillion dollars of government waste, while Lutnick personally would bring in a trillion for the country by raising tariffs, sealing tax loopholes, and pursuing a more aggressive strategy around America's natural resources and tangible assets. Together, they would eliminate the federal deficit.

But beyond the bare concept, no actual plans for the department yet existed. Musk carried himself with the bravado of a man accustomed to ruling his companies by fiat, but that was not the way the government worked. He had only the vaguest sense of the mammoth problem that he had set himself to fix. He had little knowledge of the labyrinthine federal system, nor how its budget functioned. And he had even less interest in the Constitution, which could severely hobble the dramatic unilateral reengineering of the government he imagined.

After the election, Musk's team met at Mar-a-Lago to begin planning how to aggressively slash the federal bureaucracy, starting from scratch. If DOGE was to be truly disruptive, they would need to get inside the system. One way to achieve this would come via a little-known agency called the U.S. Digital Service, which had been established in 2014 after the embarrassing launch of the original HealthCare.gov website for Obamacare. DOGE would commandeer the agency, which would then become a temporary standalone entity in the Executive Office of the President.

In a move that critics said shielded him from public accountability, Musk was not named the DOGE administrator. Instead, he would be a "special government employee"—basically a White House contractor, a classification that some allies believed could cocoon him from public records requests. Being a special government employee made him simultaneously an insider and outsider, answerable to the President alone.

At Mar-a-Lago, the planning took on the feel of an engineering sprint. Musk drew guidance on how the executive branch operated from Stephen Miller and his wife, Katie, both veterans of Trump's first term. Stephen Miller had secretly helped to guide Musk's political spending during Trump's years out of power. Following the election, the Millers grew increasingly vital to Musk as he learned to operate within Trump's orbit. He likewise soaked up everything possible regarding the federal budget process and the workings of the bureaucracy from Russell Vought. Vought had been a significant contributor to Project 2025, the blueprint for governing published by the right-wing think tank the Heritage Foundation. It had proved to be so unpopular in general election polls that Trump was forced to publicly disavow it. As a consequence, Vought's prospects for any significant appointment in the new administration were thought at first to be negligible. His name was initially left off the list of prospects to lead the OMB in a second term; Stephen Miller and JD Vance, among others, objected. Miller wanted a like-minded ideologue in the role, and others agreed. Vought's name was added to the roster. When Vought flew to Mar-a-Lago for meetings, he and Musk, a critical voice, hit it off.

Just over two weeks after the election, Trump announced that Vought would return as his director of the OMB.

II

By then, Elon Musk had become a constant presence at Mar-a-Lago, soaking up Trump's time and focus. He was likened by some senior staff, sotto voce, to a bad houseguest who didn't know when to leave. Indeed, he had literally moved into Trump's club, taking residence in a $2,000-a-night cabin on the property called Banyan and irritating the staff by ordering food when the main kitchen was closed.

"He loves it here so much," Trump would say. "I can't get him out."

"He's in every meeting, and at every dinner," groused one aide. "Every discussion with him makes a thirty-minute meeting a ninety-minute meeting."

During the November cabinet selection meetings, Musk had popped in and out of the tearoom as Trump and his team pored over the slides. He was unfamiliar with most of the names under discussion, but he would occasionally chirp in with a question about a candidate.

"Is he a radical reformer?" Musk would most often ask. If the answer was no, then Musk could be expected to have a negative view of the candidate.

Once the inauguration concluded, DOGE staff dispersed throughout the government in short order, gathering intel on personnel, contracts, and computer systems. Within weeks, Musk and his crew of more than forty tried to access some of the government's most sensitive computer systems, including those that controlled government payments. Their list of targets—at least seven government databases in total—included internal systems housed in the Treasury Department, such as those of the Social Security Administration and the Internal Revenue Service.

Musk kept a tiny office on the West Wing's second floor but rarely used it, dismissing the space as a "hovel"—though he'd still slip back now and then to play video games in the dark. He did most of his work instead from the Eisenhower Executive Office Building next door, claiming the Secretary of War Suite, a grand set of rooms named for its former occupants. There, amid the historic decor, he installed a DOGE sign, propped a MAGA hat on his desk, and set up a gaming PC with LED lights and a curved monitor.

"This is our one & only chance to restore democracy from the dictatorship of the bureaucracy," Musk would write in a post on X. "It is now or never. It must be now."

Musk thought nothing of taunting and humiliating people who worked at his companies, and he drove them as relentlessly as he drove himself. He brought the same outlook to DOGE—assuming the federal workforce was, at best, lazy, and, at worst, dead. He believed that wage fraud was rampant, and that the criminal heirs of dead or otherwise nonexistent federal employees were getting fat on regular checks from the U.S. Treasury. He was making wild claims, untethered from evidence, but that mattered little.

Musk would not step away from his companies or take any steps to address his conflicts of interest, but he empowered his cadre of DOGE staffers to delve deeply into the foundational digital architecture of the federal government. For several weeks, most of the White House staff had no idea what he was doing until it was done.

Perhaps most remarkable was how much room Trump was giving Musk to operate.

"Elon is basically running a startup, and we don't have visibility into what they're doing day to day. We learn after the fact," a senior member of the White House staff said at the time. "Elon is figuring out how to do this and shifting his priorities day to day. He doesn't have a boss."

February 2025 would represent the peak of Musk's power in the new Trump administration, power with little precedent in the country's history.

Authorized by the President of the United States but overseen by no one, Musk would momentarily usurp the powers of Congress to control public spending, essentially impound billions of dollars in already-appropriated money, and trample the prerogatives of the President's new cabinet secretaries. All in secrecy and often in the middle of the night.

Within the span of weeks, he would go from being regarded at the top levels of the administration as the greatest "genius" in the world to a "true nut" who was careening out of control. Susie Wiles would start telling people that she was canceling plans because she didn't want to be away from her phone or computer, so she could be prepared for whatever Musk and the DOGE team would do next. "Unaccountable" was how the staff closest to the President would come to think of the eccentric billionaire.

For such a serious undertaking, Musk sometimes appeared unhinged. And he seemed to enjoy scaring people. His essential strangeness was a regular topic of conversation among the White House staff. Musk would show up in the Navy Mess in the West Wing basement at 7 a.m. for coffee and work until midnight. In times past, Trump might have felt insecure about the constant presence of a man so much richer than himself. But after his victory he seemed at ease and more than a little flattered that the richest man in history wanted to work for him.

"You know, he can't be President," Trump would tell others. "He was born in South Africa." Trump could afford to be magnanimous, and enjoy the salutary effects that came with having a disciple who owned one of the most powerful social media platforms in the world and had the spending power of a nation-state.

To some, it appeared Trump had assumed an almost paternalistic regard for his socially awkward charge, as if he were socializing him and easing him into the world. "He used to be a recluse," he'd say of Musk. "He's not anymore."

Musk had asked if he might sleep in the White House residence, and Trump said yes. The First Lady initially objected, but Musk would end up spending several nights in the Lincoln Bedroom. Other nights he stayed with friends, though he also told associates he had taken to using a sleeping bag on the floor of his office in the Eisenhower Building. He would wander into any meeting with the President that he wished, sometimes with his four-year-old son, X, a precocious and highly verbal boy prone to rambunctious behavior, whether in the Oval Office or on Air Force One.

If Elon triggered controversy, all the better, in Trump's view. Let him absorb the bad press—and there was soon to be a lot of it—when someone's cherished program got cut. In one private conversation, Trump commented that Musk's plummeting approval rating made him a useful "heat shield."

It was not unusual for Musk to call Trump directly late at night, tell him of something that he had discovered in the line items of the federal budget, or of his plans to decimate an agency, and Trump would give his blessing, often with only the vaguest notion of what he was actually blessing. One night, Musk described a government body he said was full of lazy Democrats. Let's get rid of them, Musk said. The President said that sounded like a good idea. Soon after, a senior Trump aide would have to inform Musk aides that they could not abolish the Equal Employment Opportunity Commission.

Then came another call. This time the target was USAID.

III

The United States Agency for International Development, founded during the presidency of John F. Kennedy, had been at the heart of American soft power, distributing food and medicine globally and investing in economic development and education. It was a projection of American values that had enjoyed bipartisan support for decades. But even before the Trump era, some members of Congress had raised concerns about the lack of accountability of USAID's "mission directors," who led the agency's in-country operations. Both the Government Accountability Office and USAID's own inspector general had identified issues of corruption and weak governance in recipient countries. But nothing would prepare Washington for the all-out attack on the agency by Musk (or DOGE), an unmistakable warning to the entire federal power structure.

USAID had few natural defenders at home, which made it vulnerable, as the Republican Party had shifted over the course of a decade from Bush-era neoconservatism to a deep hostility to foreign aid. Trump had no interest in funding anything to do with human rights or the promotion of democracy. And many on his team saw USAID as a hotbed of liberal ideology; dismantling the agency became, in their minds, a way of attacking the "woke" Left.

And yet, the vicious terms Musk used to describe USAID—calling it "evil" and "criminal"—mystified even some of the agency's most ardent critics in the administration and on Capitol Hill.

Stop-work orders had arrived at USAID's Washington headquarters on January 24, four days after the President's executive order freezing all foreign spending. The orders—handed down by Rubio—would take a week or so to filter to USAID offices around the world. But by then, Musk and his DOGE team had already gained access to the Treasury Department's payments systems. When Musk discovered that foreign aid payments were still flowing, it emboldened him to hack USAID to pieces.

Caught up in the freeze on foreign aid was spending vital to the national security of the United States. From the moment Trump's executive order on foreign spending was signed, the National Security Council had labored to establish an interagency process to allow for waivers to keep critical funds flowing. At the Defense Department, CENTCOM commander Michael Kurilla was greatly concerned about the Al Hol detention camp in northeastern Syria, which held several thousand ISIS fighters along with tens of thousands of their family members. The camp, run by the Kurdish-led Syrian Democratic Forces, also held many foreign nationals who lacked any clear legal pathways for prosecution or repatriation. The women and children in the camp faced brutal conditions, which brought a high risk of radicalization. It was a complex and precarious situation.

USAID provided food aid and fuel to the camp, and with those programs abruptly shut down, contractors walked off the job, warehouses were looted, and the Kurdish guards faced dwindling supplies. The camp was on the verge of collapse, which meant that thousands of ISIS fighters could potentially escape and threaten the entire region. This was but one example of the unintended consequences of the DOGE approach to budget cutting.

In an attempt to avert such crises, the NSC leadership put together a team to sort and prioritize additional waivers to the freeze. That process seemed to work for a time, as Marco Rubio and his State Department team assumed responsibility for the remaining programs of the decimated agency in early February. But they soon discovered that Musk's team had essentially "pulled the wires out of the wall on the payment system," as one senior official put it. Even when waivers were approved, the money still wasn't moving. Rather than making things more efficient, DOGE had trashed the place.

Rubio was not particularly happy about having to clean it all up. Two days after he had embarked on his first foreign trip as secretary of state, he became administrator of the organization's remnants, which was about 15 percent of what the agency had been just two weeks before.

6

The presidential retreat of Salvadoran President Nayib Bukele, overlooking a lake on the eastern slope of the Santa Ana Volcano in the western part of the country, could not have provided Marco Rubio a more dramatic change of venue from DOGE-consumed Washington. The setting was verdant and spectacular, with Bukele's house nestled among steep hills above the lake. All right angles and large windows, the modernist house would not have been out of place in Malibu. The living room where the delegations met was bathed in natural light and designed with a soft cream palette. Every half hour or so, trays of fruit juices, coffee, and tea made their way through the room.

Bukele was in his second five-year term, having engineered a change to the Salvadoran constitution, which had previously banned successive presidential terms. Before his election, El Salvador was one of the most violent and crime-ridden countries on earth, its violence predominantly driven by powerful gangs, including MS-13 and Barrio 18, which controlled large areas and dominated much of the country's economy. Bukele had made it his mission to crack down on crime and break the hold of the gangs. He built a network of prisons to house the people he was taking off the streets, with the centerpiece a mega-prison dubbed the Terrorism Confinement Center (CECOT). While making his country safer, he had also given El Salvador the highest incarceration rate in the world, sweeping up many innocents in the arrests, and showing little concern for due process or trials. Nodding to his growing reputation as a strongman, he had taken to calling himself "the world's coolest dictator." And on this day, February 3, he dressed the part, clad in khakis, with sunglasses slung just so from the button of his shirt.

Bukele and Rubio huddled close together at one end of the room and spoke cordially in Spanish. They had much to discuss. Before the day was done, the two countries would sign a memorandum of understanding to advance civil nuclear cooperation and outline strategies to counter the influence of the Chinese Communist Party in the Western Hemisphere. But neither of those items was controversial, and neither was the real reason Rubio had come.

In the first Trump term, the United States had negotiated "safe third country" deals with Guatemala, Honduras, and El Salvador, under which those countries would accept asylum seekers who had passed through their territory without seeking asylum before reaching the U.S. border. But the deals had been negotiated relatively late in the administration, and were subsequently stalled by courts and then the coronavirus pandemic. No asylum seekers had been sent to Honduras and El Salvador under the agreements.

Biden moved to undo many of Trump's immigration policies. That, combined with the ebbing of the pandemic, led to a major surge in border crossings. Red-state governors began shipping migrants to so-called sanctuary cities, a gimmick that nonetheless highlighted an untenable situation. The disorder caused considerable handwringing among prominent Democrats, including former President Barack Obama, who believed his party was mishandling the immigration issue and saw the way it was about to be weaponized against Kamala Harris in the general election. At a private Martha's Vineyard fundraiser in August 2024, Obama told guests that while hostility to foreigners was ingrained in America's history, the southern border was undeniably in a state of disorder; when millions of people poured across the border with no orderly process, voters understandably saw chaos. Obama underscored what had been a frequent refrain for him for more than a decade: Democrats should stress the United States was a nation of laws *and* of immigrants. Obama did not mention Biden as he discussed the out-of-control border or the messaging related to it. But it was obvious to some in the room that he was implicating Biden.

Nobody benefited more from that chaos than Donald Trump. The images on television and social media of millions of migrants crossing the border under the Biden administration had widened the Overton window on immigration to just the place Stephen Miller had wanted it, and as Trump prepared to take office for the second time, his team knew that Americans were now primed to accept far more aggressive immigration enforcement.

For several years, Miller had been planning the largest deportation program in American history.

"We climbed Mount Everest in the first administration in terms of shutting off the border to asylum for all of planet Earth and reestablishing the idea that it's your burden to prove to us that you have a right to come to our country if you want a visa—and not our burden to prove to you that you don't," Miller said in October 2023 while mapping out a potential second Trump presidency. "So the next Mount Everest to climb, then, is this process of expelling people from inside the country—but doing it under a completely new system. ICE, under its current parameters, really is only geared toward deporting single adult males and particularly only from a handful of countries. They really don't even have systems in place for minors; they really don't have systems in place for families, as they're constituted currently. So it's about redesigning the whole system."

That redesigned system, which the administration had promised to activate on Inauguration Day, would again require agreements with Central American countries. This was the main purpose for Rubio's visit to Bukele's villa. Rubio broached the subject during their ninety-minute meeting, but Bukele balked. He had just turned his country around, making it a nice place to live, he said. How would he explain to his citizens why he'd allow El Salvador to become a dumping ground for Third World migrants rerouted from the U.S.?

Rubio countered that an agreement from El Salvador to take in migrants from the United States would not result in a flood of deportees. The point was simply to force migrants to choose between staying in their home countries or traveling to the U.S. and risk being sent to a Salvadoran prison. The migrants would likely choose to stay home, Rubio argued.

But Bukele wouldn't budge. With immigrants journeying up and down Central America—including a historic flight from crisis-stricken Venezuela—he had done a good job keeping migrants out. And when they did manage to cross his border, his internal security service was effective at finding and removing them. He would look like a hypocrite if he turned around and opened the country back up.

But then, unexpectedly, Bukele made a tantalizing counteroffer: What if the United States sent him its migrant criminals to be detained in the crown jewel of the Salvadoran prison system, CECOT? The idea was perfectly calibrated to Trump's campaign promise—to get the "worst of the worst" rapidly out of the United States, including members of organized crime gangs like Tren de Aragua of Venezuela. And then Bukele went even further. He told Rubio that if America's jails were overcrowded, he could send even American citizen criminals to CECOT.

Rubio and his entourage knew immediately that sending U.S. citizens to a Salvadoran prison for terrorists was a nonstarter, and that any judge in the U.S. would stop it. But he appreciated the gesture.

That day would mark the genesis of a deal between the two countries that would shock the world.

II

Marco Rubio was an unlikely front man for sending migrants to a terrorist prison in El Salvador; and he was an even unlikelier face of Donald Trump's overall foreign policy.

The two men had faced off against each other for the Republican nomination in 2016, a contest that had devolved into an exchange of schoolyard taunts, with both Rubio and Trump trading crude quips about the size of their hands. Trump would later boast to advisors that he "broke" Rubio in that race, and those close to the Florida senator did not exactly disagree. Throughout 2016 and 2017, some in Rubio's circle believed he had lost his bearings, stumbling to find his place in this new and bewildering era of Trump.

Until 2016, Rubio's career had been defined by an astonishingly rapid rise up the ladders of society and power—from the son of a Cuban bartender and hotel maid, to law school at the University of Miami, to city commissioner, state representative, Speaker of the Florida House of Representatives, and then United States senator elected in the Tea Party wave of 2010.

Clever, young, and handsome, with photogenic children and a beautiful wife, Rubio dazzled many conservative elites as something of a Cuban Jack Kennedy. But unlike Kennedy, raised in privilege and the scion of a powerful political family, Rubio's background was cut from the cloth of immigrants with big dreams. It was no small part of his identity. He had a deep connection to South Florida's exile community, where his parents had made a home after immigrating to the U.S. in 1956. The corrupt American-backed Fulgencio Batista—known for his relationships with American mobsters—was still in power and the revolution that ushered in the communist regime of Fidel Castro was more than two years away. It was a classic migrant story of the opportunity that lay ahead in a new land, and the emotional tug of the old. For the Rubio family, visits to Cuba would end soon after the 1961 Bay of Pigs fiasco and the U.S. embargo that followed. Rubio's grandfather had gone back and forth, but had then been detained as an illegal immigrant on his return to America; the decision was reversed and he later became a permanent resident of the United States.

Rubio viewed the Castro regime as pure evil and he dreamed of liberating the country of his parents' birth. In his memoir he recalled a boast, made as a young boy to his grandfather, that he would "someday lead an army of exiles to overthrow Fidel Castro and become president of a free Cuba."

Rubio carried a grand vision for regime change in Latin America throughout his surging career. He traced the political networks that saw the leftist regime in Venezuela playing a key role in propping up the Cuban government, providing cheap oil in exchange for security services. If the United States could force regime change in Venezuela, Rubio believed, it could create a domino effect, toppling other leftist leaders in Latin America, including in Cuba.

Even before he arrived in Washington, conservative opinion makers were hyping Rubio as the future of the party. In 2009, the conservative publication founded by William F. Buckley Jr., *National Review*, cast him as the Right's answer to Barack Obama, putting Rubio on the magazine's cover with the title "Yes, He Can."

For a time, Rubio seemed to be doing everything right to position himself to lead the modern GOP. He built relationships with donors who had supported the Iraq War, building a national reputation as an advocate for American military power, a fiscal hawk, and a compassionate voice on immigration. But Rubio had made one costly mistake. In 2013, he became a key member of the "Gang of Eight," a bipartisan group of senators who had drafted an overhaul of immigration laws. The bill passed the Senate, but would never be given a vote in the House as an angry Republican base turned against it, seeing the legislation as a betrayal of their interests in favor of big corporations wanting to replace them with cheap immigrant labor. Stephen Miller, then an aide to Senator Jeff Sessions of Alabama, helped to engineer its defeat. The rout of the Gang of Eight was an early precursor to the Trump revolution. Rubio became the face of that failure and as he prepared to run for President, the hard-liners worked to ensure he paid for it. In an email to a Breitbart reporter in December 2015, Miller called Rubio "pathological."

After the 2016 election, Rubio remained wary of Trump, but over the course of the first term edged his way into the President's corner. He praised Trump on television, collaborated on policy, and began to refashion his own views. He was now in lockstep with Trump on immigration and was working on trade and spending policies that appalled traditional fiscal conservatives. It was only in foreign policy that the updated version of Rubio retained some vestiges of the original. This was especially the case on Latin America, where he had been an outspoken advocate in Trump's first term for toppling the Venezuelan dictator, Nicolás Maduro.

By 2024, Rubio had so successfully worked his way into Trump's good graces that he was under serious consideration for vice president. A key to this was his relationship with Susie Wiles. They had known each other from the relatively small circle of Florida politics; Rubio was first elected in 2010, on the same successful statewide ticket as both Rick Scott and Pam Bondi. More important, Wiles had not forgotten that Rubio refused to join the scrum of people attacking her when Ron DeSantis tried to end her career in 2019. Rubio had made a great impression on Trump during the VP selection process in 2024; unlike his rivals, he did not press his own case aggressively with Trump, and he was gracious when he was passed over. Throughout the campaign, Trump aides often talked about Rubio's ease playing the role of ally to Trump and doing everything asked of him. When the time came, his appointment as secretary of state surprised only those who had not paid attention to his transformation.

III

Rubio's newfound closeness to the President added two new twists to the dynamics of Trump's inner circle. He would always be seen by some as Susie Wiles's man, a willing ally for her interests and agenda in the power struggles around the President. And Trump would constantly pit him against JD Vance.

While Rubio had told Vance he had no interest in running for President in 2028, and soon became personally close to Vance, that had not stopped the media murmurings that he would eventually challenge Vance for the nomination. And as the year progressed, Trump seemed to delight in making ambiguous statements over who would be his designated successor, asking aides and advisors from time to time who they liked better, "JD or Marco?"

Trump treated Rubio as first among equals in his government. White House aides would observe that Rubio had a nice way with Trump, and that he quickly developed a comfortable rhythm with the President. Unlike some of Trump's first-term advisors, such as his first secretary of state, Rex Tillerson, Rubio never lectured the President or flaunted his own knowledge. He waited until Trump asked his opinion and then he gave it, deferentially. He saw his role as an implementer of Trump's will and rarely sought to push his own views on Trump. The President found him fun to be around. Where others seemed anxious in Trump's presence, Rubio was constantly cracking jokes and putting the President at ease.

Nowhere was his presence more greatly felt than on the Latin America desk. While Trump had handed off parts of Rubio's responsibilities to others—most notably to Steve Witkoff, who was now handling the Middle East and Russia-Ukraine portfolios—Rubio made it known that he wanted to help execute the nascent Trumpian vision of reorienting America's foreign policy in the Western Hemisphere. On this he made a compelling point: For the past quarter of a century, Washington's foreign policy elites had spent far more time worrying about the Middle East than America's own backyard. It was a given therefore that Rubio's first trip abroad would be to Latin America.

Soon after his return from travels to El Salvador, Panama, Costa Rica, Guatemala, and the Dominican Republic, Rubio's diplomacy was about to pay off in a different arena. The back channel between the Russians and Steve Witkoff had become a reality; and Rubio's idea of a particular hostage to release had come to pass.

On the night of Tuesday, February 11, Witkoff had returned home with Marc Fogel, the American schoolteacher who had been held captive in Russia. Waltz, Rubio, and hostage negotiator Adam Boehler greeted him at Andrews Air Force Base. Fogel bent down and kissed the snowy tarmac. At the White House he gripped the President's hand as they stood at the side entrance. "President Trump is a hero," Fogel said later. Trump, true to form, criticized the Biden administration for not securing Fogel's release sooner.

"To me you look damn good," he told Fogel before taking him and the others on a tour of the White House residence. A day earlier, Fogel had awoken in a Russian prison. Now he was touring the Lincoln Bedroom—emotional and at a loss for words.

7

By all accounts, Steve Witkoff was a very nice man, affable and outgoing, the kind of guy who never met a stranger.

As one of Donald Trump's lawyers in the 1980s, he had watched his client become a household name in New York real estate, and he found it irresistible. Rather than continuing to represent developers, he decided instead to become one. Like Trump, he would buy buildings with borrowed money to become rich in his own right. He, too, was from the outer boroughs (Queens for Trump, the Bronx for Witkoff), but he was self-made. When he started in the business, Witkoff would drive around uptown Manhattan in an unassuming '78 Buick looking for cheap apartment buildings to buy. And when the rents were slow to come, he would sometimes dig his own trenches and do his own plumbing. When he collected rent at his properties, he would keep a pistol in his sock. After the stock market crash of 1987, when others were timid, he made his move downtown, branching out to buy landmark buildings, eventually expanding his holdings to Philadelphia and Dallas, Los Angeles, Miami, and London.

Witkoff had also been indelibly scarred by a personal tragedy he spoke of often: the 2011 lethal OxyContin overdose of his twenty-two-year-old son, Andrew, who was living in a sober house at the time. He would tell people how kind the Trumps had been to him, consoling him, and even hanging one of his son's guitars at Trump's Doral golf club in Miami.

Before Trump appointed him special envoy to the Middle East in November 2024, Witkoff's only diplomatic experience had been as Trump's intermediary with his toughest rivals for the GOP nomination—arranging a meeting with Ron DeSantis, forging a truce with Nikki Haley, and trying, unsuccessfully, to broker a peace with Mike Pence. That last one was beyond even his grasp.

Over the years, Witkoff had developed his own significant relationships in the Middle East and some of the region's wealthiest countries would invest in and ultimately purchase the debt-heavy Park Lane Hotel in New York. Witkoff's company had been the minority stakeholder when he bought it in 2013 with the Malaysian businessman Jho Low, who became mired in a corruption scandal. With a viewfinder focused on Washington, senior Qatari officials were anticipating that Witkoff would be named secretary of state.

In advance of the new administration, Witkoff threw himself into his new role, joining negotiations with the outgoing Biden team that had resulted in a six-week ceasefire in Gaza, followed by a hostage exchange. He built a close working relationship with Biden's lead negotiator, Brett McGurk, a veteran diplomat who had served the last four Presidents and had spent months in the region putting together the potential deal. The two men began speaking several times a day, encouraged by both Trump and Biden. It was an unusual example, in such a polarized moment, of an outgoing Democratic administration and an incoming Republican one working together on a high-stakes deal.

"He brought no baggage from Middle East policy disputes or prior negotiations," McGurk said later. "He could care less what so-called experts said we should do. Let's get this done and bring people home."

Witkoff also sought advice from Trump's son-in-law Jared Kushner, who had worked on Middle East issues in the first term and had helped negotiate the breakthrough Abraham Accords, to normalize relations between Israel and several Arab states. Kushner mostly kept a low profile, still burned by biting criticism of his first time in Washington. He would help guide Witkoff, but only behind the scenes, at least for now.

Two weeks before the inauguration, Witkoff joined McGurk in Doha, where talks were well underway. There were two issues left to close and both sides had dug in. "Steve told everyone to shut up and do the deal," McGurk recalled, "and if they refused, they'd have a big problem with Trump."

Witkoff flew next to Jerusalem to keep up pressure on the Israelis, while McGurk stayed behind in Doha to push Hamas through talks with the Qataris, who had for years provided a base for Hamas's external leaders. When they reached the moment for a final agreement, McGurk dialed into a meeting with Netanyahu and Witkoff. He conveyed the Hamas positions, Netanyahu agreed, and the deal for a ceasefire was made.

"He gets shit done," McGurk remarked later, offering praise for a diplomatic novice. "And that's the point of diplomacy. I know career diplomats who have never closed a deal in their life. Steve closes deals."

II

Witkoff's portfolio quickly expanded from the Middle East to the Russia-Ukraine war. Marc Fogel's release had been a test of good faith. The back channel that made it possible had come together during the Gaza negotiations. As Witkoff was talking to the Qataris, the Emiratis, and the Saudis, the Saudi crown prince, Mohammed bin Salman, known as MBS, had offered to facilitate talks with the Russians.

MBS had maintained a neutral stance on the war. But the Saudi sovereign wealth fund was very interested in investment opportunities in Russia—critical minerals, uranium, and oil and gas. In short order, MBS had directed Witkoff to Kirill Dmitriev, the head of the Russian sovereign wealth fund, and between them, the two established the back channel that brought Witkoff to Moscow in February.

On February 11, as he waited for Fogel to be released, Witkoff spoke to Putin for nearly three hours. What seemed especially astonishing was how he did it. Witkoff had gone to meet Putin alone—no entourage of advisors, just the blessing of the President of the United States. The next morning he briefed Trump on the dialogue, telling the President that he and Putin had "hit it off."

"He wants to make a deal," Witkoff assured Trump, who then boasted to aides about the bond his envoy had formed with the mercurial Russian leader.

"Putin doesn't meet with anybody for three hours," Trump kept saying. As always, he took credit for the casting. He later told an ally, perhaps with a mix of seriousness and jest, "I sent Steve to Moscow because he's the same height as Putin."

Some of the more seasoned national security professionals in the administration worried that Witkoff, lacking historical knowledge of the issues and with no experience in statecraft, was no match for Putin—a legendary manipulator who had spent more than fifteen years in the KGB. How Witkoff could handle such a meeting on his own was a very big question.

Putin struck up a warm rapport with Witkoff, charming the special envoy. Witkoff reported back to Trump that Putin had said he had been so upset on the day of the attempt on Trump's life that he had gone to Mass to pray. Whether it was all window dressing and string-pulling from the Russian end, it was the kind of message Trump appreciated. As a gift, Putin had commissioned a portrait of Trump from that day in Butler—his face streaked in blood, his fist raised. Trump and Witkoff were both delighted by the kind gesture from the former KGB officer. And it was not all that Putin had sent home with Witkoff.

When he returned to the United States with Fogel, on February 11, Witkoff also brought a "term sheet" outlining a range of U.S.-Russian business opportunities, many in the energy sector—critical minerals, uranium, oil and gas. As it happened, this was precisely the sort of arrangement Trump had in mind—a grand bargain with Russia, a historic deal that would open up both countries to each other's banking and business, a values-neutral, all-business reset, a relationship unencumbered by the ideological struggles of the past, or by the more recent territorial ambitions of Moscow—or by the America-led order that had for decades aimed to hold the Russians in check. Others on the team saw an opportunity to pull Russia away from China and Iran. In conversations with Republican senators who were worried about Trump's emerging Russia strategy, Mike Waltz told them that he was very concerned about the growing cooperation and sharing of technology between Russia, Iran, and China. Russia was the lesser threat, he believed, and they needed a mix of carrots and sticks to pull it away from the two other adversaries.

These were monumental plans. There was just the obstacle of Ukraine, a struggling democracy in a fight for its life—the country that Putin had invaded and intended to conquer.

Flush from the success of Witkoff's mission, Trump was eager to get the Russian President on the phone. Despite media reports of secret phone calls between the two leaders—reporting that Trump himself had ginned up—the ensuing conversation indicated this was the first time they had spoken in more than four years. In their ninety-minute call on February 12, they spoke through translators, but referred to each other as Vladimir and Donald.

Putin began by praising Witkoff and thanking Trump for sending such a wonderful man to meet him. The Russian President then confessed his surprise that Trump had won the election, an admission that brought a flash of annoyance from Trump, who told Putin he couldn't believe that.

Putin asked Trump not to be angry and quickly made amends for the slight, lavishing praise on the President.

Top aides had noted that Trump sometimes would wonder out loud whether Putin really even wanted a deal to end the war. "Or does he just want the whole thing, and he's going to keep going?"

He now put the question to Putin directly, asking whether he wanted the whole of Ukraine or just some of it.

Trump would later tell others that Putin assured him he didn't need all of Ukraine.

Twice on the call, Trump broached the subject of a ceasefire, and of finding a way to stop the carnage. Trump told Putin—"Vladimir"—that even he must be sick of all the killing.

Putin professed that he wanted peace and invoked the cooperation between their countries during World War II. We know how to work together, he told Trump, because we worked with Franklin Roosevelt to defeat the Nazis. This was a standard Russian talking point, but it seemed to resonate with the President. Trump noted to Putin that while Russia was America's ally in World War II, guess who wasn't? *Germany.*

Trump spoke of all he wanted in terms of opening the Russian market to American oil and gas companies. And he put it to Putin that Ukraine pushing for NATO membership had taken things too far. It was a concession Putin surely appreciated, given it was part of the Russian grievance list.

Putin returned the gesture. Keenly aware of Trump's antipathy for his predecessor, and his insistence that the war simply would never have happened on his watch, Putin told Trump that Biden wouldn't speak with him and had therefore missed potential partnership opportunities between Russia and the United States.

Maybe now, Putin said, there are things that we could do that the Biden regime couldn't. It seemed almost too easy to impress Trump.

Trump was freshly excited about the potential for U.S. businesses in Russia, especially in the energy sector. But he told Putin the fighting would have to be over before they could make any deals.

After hanging up, Trump turned to his aides: "Okay, let's call Zelensky."

The two back-to-back calls were a study in contrasts.

I just talked to your best friend, Vladimir Putin, Trump began, when Zelensky came on the line. It was an especially cruel greeting, given that Putin had been bombing Ukraine for nearly three years. Immediately, Trump pressed Zelensky to concede his country's fate. And he made clear that he intended to recoup America's investment in the war effort. Your people are dying, Trump told him, you've got no money left. Trump was the only one offering him a way out.

Zelensky had no interest in talk of surrender. He told Trump they had fought too long and hard to give up so much. But Trump continued to work him over, telling Zelensky he was broke, his country was destroyed, and that he needed to make a deal.

After hanging up, Trump muttered to his aides that Zelensky was "not very smart." He had already posted on Truth Social that his negotiating team for the Russia-Ukraine conflict would be Rubio, Waltz, Witkoff, and CIA Director John Ratcliffe. He made no mention of Keith Kellogg.

III

Zelensky's sour mood was no doubt colored by a visit from earlier that day. Scott Bessent had arrived in Kyiv bearing his own "term sheet" on the minerals deal between the two countries and he wanted Zelensky to sign it.

Bessent had been a surprise choice as treasury secretary; many in Trump's orbit had not heard of him in the first term. But Bessent was a talented macro investor who had made his name working for George Soros, helping him break the Bank of England with a massive short bet in 1992. Over four decades in the business, he had traveled to some sixty countries and built relationships with central bankers and government leaders around the world. He had run an aggressive campaign to put himself on Trump's radar. He had donated more than $1 million during the 2024 cycle and recruited the help of key figures such as Steve Bannon and the Fox Business host and former Trump aide Larry Kudlow, who understood how to appeal to the President.

Trump was impressed by the South Carolinian, who—with his silver hair, imposing height, broad shoulders, and stylish suits—merited the President's favored epithet of "straight out of central casting." But Bessent's veneer of a courtly southern gentleman masked a fiery side. Trump would describe him to others, approvingly, as "financially violent."

Bessent's proposal would require Ukraine to pay the United States 50 percent of future revenue from state-owned natural resources, including hydrocarbons and rare earth minerals. The document prescribed very specific commitments from Ukraine, but offered no security commitments from the United States. Even though the minerals deal had been Zelensky's idea, part of the "Victory Plan for Ukraine" he had recently unveiled, he was shocked by Bessent's terms.

Zelensky explained that he was leading his country through a particularly violent phase of the three-year-old war, and insisted that he and his staff needed more time to consider the proposal. Bessent saw things very differently. He had traveled nearly five thousand miles to an active war zone to obtain Zelensky's signature, and now Zelensky was telling him no.

"You need to sign this," Bessent urged. "The purpose of this is to show that there is no daylight" between the U.S. and Ukraine.

Zelensky, furious, replied that the document was an attack on Ukraine's sovereignty. This was not the way international agreements worked—this was a shakedown. He told Bessent the deal, as proposed, was not enforceable under Ukrainian law.

For forty-five minutes, the men berated each other. Bessent had only been on the job for a few days, and already he had gotten into a shouting match with the leader of a country in the middle of a war. Finally, he looked at Zelensky and said, "What the fuck do you want to do? You've got fifty reporters out there, and I don't think we want to go out there and blow this thing up, so what are we going to tell the press?"

Stalling, Zelensky indicated—at least to Bessent's ears—that he would be willing to sign the deal in Munich. Their teams agreed to keep talking through the terms in the meantime.

The Munich Security Conference was just two days away, but that wouldn't prove to be enough time for Zelensky, either. In Munich, he would meet with Trump officials on the state of the Washington-Kyiv relationship, and he would repeat his insistence that the United States provide a security guarantee for Ukraine, in exchange for the minerals deal.

Keith Kellogg, who had a title, but no clearly defined job, lurked in Munich, picking up any information that he could on the subject that was supposed to be his brief. Kellogg privately thought NATO membership for Ukraine was a nonstarter, but he intimated to European counterparts that it was still on the table. He was aghast when he heard about Bessent's encounter. He told associates later that the whole confrontation with Zelensky was ill-conceived and ill-prepared. But the person whose view mattered most had a very different opinion; Trump wanted Bessent to squeeze Zelensky and squeeze him hard.

From there, the deterioration of Washington's relationship with Kyiv continued apace. Or, more accurately, Donald Trump's relationship with Ukraine continued to spiral.

On February 17 and 18, peace talks aiming to end the Russia-Ukraine conflict were convened in Riyadh, Saudi Arabia. The Ukrainians were not invited. Instead, MBS hosted the Russians and a delegation from Washington headed by Rubio. Russian Foreign Minister Sergey Lavrov insisted on grinding through old grievances and root causes of the conflict, while Rubio and Waltz tried to establish a reset. Their message to the Russians was succinct: *The past is the past. We can have a much better bilateral relationship. There is a lot of upside to this relationship, if only we could stop this fighting. Do you want twenty more kilometers of Ukraine, or do you want a better relationship with the United States?*

When Zelensky expressed concern at being excluded from the talks, saying, "We don't want anyone making decisions behind our backs," Trump lashed out. He called Zelensky a "dictator" and blamed the Ukrainians for starting the war in the first place.

The table was set for a very public showdown in the Oval Office.

8

Bibi Netanyahu arrived bearing gifts.

There were few regions that posed such challenges to the incoming administration as the Middle East, and few world leaders as challenging to Trump personally as the Israeli prime minister, Benjamin Netanyahu. The two had been strong allies in the first term, but fell out when Netanyahu made the crucial mistake, in Trump's eyes, of congratulating Joe Biden on his 2020 election victory. Netanyahu had grown frustrated with the Biden administration and had made amends with Trump during the 2024 campaign, paying court at Mar-a-Lago.

Trump confidants had been telling Netanyahu since 2021 that Trump was convinced—wrongly, as it turned out—that Netanyahu was the first of all the world leaders to congratulate Biden. Trump had been stewing on this false impression for three years. To smooth things over, when the Israeli prime minister visited Trump in July 2024, he brought along a list showing the large number of foreign leaders who had congratulated Biden before he did. It was the sort of detail that Trump found irresistible. Netanyahu's wooing of Trump then went into overdrive after he won the election.

As soon as the 2024 results came in, Netanyahu posted a social media message that was so over-the-top that even some of his closest allies cringed. "Dear Donald and Melania Trump," he wrote, "congratulations on history's greatest comeback! Your historic return to the White House offers a new beginning for America and a powerful recommitment to the great alliance between Israel and America. This is a huge victory! In true friendship, yours, Benjamin and Sara Netanyahu."

On February 4, 2025, Netanyahu would become the first head of state to visit Trump in the second term, a meeting where Trump would encourage him to extend the ceasefire Witkoff had helped negotiate and to complete a deal for the release of all Israeli hostages held by Hamas. Netanyahu in turn would discuss with Trump the need to deal "with the Iranian terror axis in all its components," as the prime minister put it. His main objective was to destroy Iran's nuclear enrichment facilities, and he wanted American help. Netanyahu had prepared a presentation in the Oval Office, narrating the various Iran nuclear sites, warning the President that if they didn't act imminently, Iran would soon have enough highly enriched uranium to make a bomb.

Trump was well primed for Netanyahu's message. He had been enthralled by a spectacular military operation that Israel had recently pulled off against its archenemy, the Iranian proxy force Hezbollah. The episode had given Trump renewed confidence in the Israeli military's capabilities, which would be a prerequisite for convincing him to join Netanyahu in a risky war.

The mission was like something out of a spy movie: In Lebanon, on September 17, at three thirty in the afternoon, thousands of pagers assigned to Hezbollah members had exploded simultaneously. The next day came the exploding walkie-talkies. The blasts had killed at least thirty-seven people, including children, and injured nearly three thousand. The backstory of this attack soon emerged: Israeli intelligence had created shell companies to dupe a Taiwanese business into selling compromised pagers and radios to Hezbollah. They would conceal an explosive substance inside the batteries, waiting for the right time to trigger them. A former Mossad agent told CBS later that Hezbollah had bought the devices at "a good price."

To commemorate the success of the operation, Netanyahu brought a gift for Trump: a gold-plated pager.

Already, the issue of how to deal with the Iran nuclear threat was creating tensions among the President's advisors. Mike Waltz and Marco Rubio were seen as Iran hawks. They had made numerous statements over their years in Congress to declare that Iran's nuclear program posed a serious and imminent threat to both Israel and the United States. Waltz had warned colleagues that once Iran tested a nuke, the entire region—Saudi Arabia, the UAE, Turkey—would race to develop nuclear weapons of their own. That possibility, he said, should petrify every American.

Susie Wiles and JD Vance, however, were deeply wary of the Israeli pressure campaign. Both worried that a "limited" U.S. military intervention in Iran could spiral into an Israeli regime-change war.

After the meeting, and just before the two leaders were to speak to the press, Trump informed Netanyahu that he planned to announce a proposal for the United States to simply take over the Gaza Strip once the war was over.

This was a surprise. No discussions had taken place with the Pentagon or State Department, the typical starting point for any major foreign policy initiative, much less one of this scale. No working groups had been convened. The Defense Department had not generated projections regarding how many troops it would take to remove 2 million Palestinians from Gaza and handle the wreckage. No cost projections existed—not even a basic sketch of the logistics behind how it might function.

Trump had been spitballing the idea privately during intelligence briefings as a CIA briefer showed him images of the devastation in Gaza. But nobody imagined he would announce it as a fully formed proposal.

Shortly before bringing in the press, he asked the staff members whose job it would be to explain this bombshell to the world—Press Secretary Karoline Leavitt, Communications Director Steven Cheung, and Waltz—what they thought. The strong suggestion was that they should like it.

"What if we own it?" Trump said. "That's a good idea, right? We'll just own Gaza."

It was a bizarre real estate play if ever there was one. In a radio interview the previous fall, referring to Gaza's twenty-seven miles of Mediterranean coastline, Trump had claimed it had "the best water, the best everything," adding, "It could be better than Monaco." His stunned advisors didn't know what to say. Would this require American troops? What did "owning" one of the most densely populated and bitterly contested territories in the world even mean?

Waltz spoke first. "Mr. President, we have to make it clear you're not suggesting U.S. troops when you say we'll own Gaza."

Waltz, a former special operator trained in urban warfare, had spent weeks alongside Steve Witkoff in a series of discussions with Netanyahu's top aide, Ron Dermer, about the supply of munitions for Israel's war in Gaza. The two Americans had asked the Israelis why they needed so many heavy artillery and tank rounds from depleted U.S. stocks. "Ron, you don't have to fire a salvo of artillery at every damn sniper in Gaza," Waltz had quipped during one session, according to a staff member who was present. Waltz understood, perhaps better than anyone else in Trump's orbit, what "owning Gaza" would actually entail.

Trump, brimming with excitement, turned to Cheung. "You like this idea, right?"

After a beat, Cheung replied, "It's a strong move."

Both Jordan's and Egypt's leaders had rejected Trump's weeks-long public campaign pushing them to take in Gazans. Such a forced displacement of Palestinians would amount to ethnic cleansing on a historic scale and run afoul of international law. But standing before the cameras with a very pleased Netanyahu at his side, Trump said he thought Gaza's 2 million residents would be happy to evacuate their "uninhabitable" homeland. They could return eventually, he suggested, once the war-torn strip was transformed into the "Riviera of the Middle East."

"The U.S. will take over the Gaza Strip, and we will do a job with it, too," he announced. "We'll own it and be responsible for dismantling all of the dangerous unexploded bombs and other weapons on the site. Level the site and get rid of the destroyed buildings. Level it out."

"Legitimately nutso," one senior aide said later. "But very on brand."

How any of this squared with an "America First" foreign policy was a head-scratcher. Staff immediately feared the President's impulsiveness might blow up the ceasefire—or worse.

After the press conference, Trump turned to an aide. "So, what do you think?"

"Well, sir," the aide replied, "I think there's going to be cars burning on Pennsylvania Avenue tomorrow."

This was clearly not the response Trump had expected. He paused and stared out the window, then allowed a faint smile.

No cars burned on Pennsylvania Avenue the next day. Perhaps because the idea was so obviously fantastical, the reaction was bewilderment rather than rage. And as in his first term, when Trump followed his impulses and the worst failed to materialize, he felt validated. He was a real estate man. War-torn waterfront property suggested a simple solution. He would improvise the details.

II

The Gaza idea represented the spur-of-the-moment nature of Trump's foreign policy that many had feared.

Two days after the Netanyahu visit, Trump began a meeting with Elon Musk and the influential podcaster and former Fox News host Tucker Carlson by showing them what the Israeli leader had brought him. "Don't push the button," Trump joked as he pulled the gold pager from his desk and handed it over. Musk was transfixed by the device, staring at it intently, silently working it between his fingers like a Rubik's Cube.

Trump then regaled them with horror stories of the destruction that the explosions had wrought. He had seen pictures, he said. Mutilated genitals and missing hands. He was horrified by the injuries, but fascinated as well, lingering on the scenes and the details. One survivor, he said, "looked like a great white came and just took a chunk out of him. It was like a shark bite. It was horrible." He grew voluble, repeating, "It's horrible, horrible!"

And there was something else that captivated him. Many of the devices had detonated in public, and it was hard to know who was holding a pager when it exploded. The indiscriminate nature of the killing and maiming had shocked Trump, and while he was taken by the ingenuity, he showed a measure of disbelief at its recklessness. He seemed at once enthralled and horrified.

As Musk continued to fiddle with the pager, Carlson got to the subject he had come to talk about. He was afraid Trump might be persuaded to go to war with Iran, especially in the wake of Netanyahu's lobbying mission, and Carlson intended to exert every ounce of his influence on Trump to ensure it didn't happen. The two men had had an up-and-down relationship over many years. Trump had respected Carlson's star power when he hosted the highest-rated show on Fox News, but it was not all smooth sailing. In text messages that were released during a defamation case between Dominion Voting Systems and Fox News over coverage of 2020 election conspiracies, Carlson had written that he hated Trump "passionately," that he was a "destroyer" and a "demonic force." Trump was said to have been upset by this, but the two quickly made up and Carlson went all in for Trump's 2024 campaign, even speaking on his behalf at the Republican convention. Trump continued to solicit Carlson's advice, believing he still had sway over a significant portion of the base.

Carlson had previously criticized Trump for refusing to knock Netanyahu over the Gaza carnage; now he would make clear to the President that a broader war would be his ruin.

"They want you to go to war with Iran," Carlson said.

"We're not doing that," Trump answered.

"Good, because the only thing that can blow up your administration is if you get into a war with Iran," Carlson said. "Your voters don't want any more wars. You ran on that. That's the main reason people voted for you in 2016. That's what set you apart from the pack. You changed the Republican Party. And the people who didn't want to change are now trying to lure you into a trap. This is a trap set by your enemies. These people fucking hate you. And once you get in, it's very hard to get out of it. And that'll wreck your presidency. That'll wreck everything. You won't be able to do anything."

"I don't think there's ever been an American President as powerful as I am," Trump said later in the conversation.

Struck by this hubris, Carlson replied, "Certainly not since FDR. Really, the only thing that could wreck it is war with Iran."

III

Trump, however, was consumed with other matters. He was about to embark on a major redecoration of the Oval Office and renovation of portions of the presidential residence, and he would not be satisfied until he had rubbed out even the tiniest remnants of his most recent predecessors.

The White House staff had been told after the election that both the Oval Office and the First Family's private living quarters, known as "the residence," were to be returned to exactly what they had been four years earlier. Several carpets in the bedrooms and some common areas were replaced from the time the Bidens and their dogs had lived there, which had left the carpets covered in dog hair and stains. This was done in the few hours between the departure of one First Family and the arrival of another.

The staff soon faced a bigger conundrum. How, they wondered, would they re-create the five silver-plated figurines of Greek gods kept on the Oval Office mantel during Trump's first administration? The President had first come across these figurines in the Paris embassy during a 2018 visit, along with some artwork he liked, including a portrait of Benjamin Franklin. Trump had immediately ordered them to be packed up and brought back to the White House, where he would install them in the Oval Office. It soon came out that the statuettes were twentieth-century copies of sixteenth- and seventeenth-century sculptures. Copies or not, Trump liked the pieces, which included the trident-wielding god Poseidon, and they stayed on the mantel. When he left the White House in 2021, the staff had returned them to the embassy in France. Shuttling them back across the Atlantic seemed too onerous, so the staff replaced them with silver-plated eagles.

But even restoring the decor to its term-one state would not prove enough. It soon became clear Trump had ambitions for a broader redecoration of the living and work spaces. He instructed staff to bring various items from the second-floor residence to the Oval Office. Among these was a set of gold epergnes—decorative, tiered centerpieces suitable for serving macarons or small fruits at a table. They had previously been used by Melania Trump to serve cookies or madeleines alongside tea when hosting the visiting spouse of a head of state. The epergnes were soon whisked away to the Oval Office and added to the fireplace mantel.

Trump had done less redecorating of his bedroom during the first administration and his living quarters back then were often chaotic. His bedroom carpet was regularly covered in piles of bankers boxes, where he stashed documents. First-term aides would privately refer to them as his *Beautiful Mind* boxes, a sardonic reference to the biopic of the schizophrenic math prodigy John Nash. The boxes were sometimes stacked so high that they left impressions in the carpet when moved. A nighttime snacker, the President would frequently leave an array of empty potato chip bags, Starburst wrappers, and ice cream cartons in the trash, or on the floor. The staff had to begin monitoring the trash after it was discovered he was sometimes throwing out White House sterling silver utensils.

The Bidens had made remarkably few changes to the Trump family's first-term decor. But for his second term, Trump wanted to spruce up his bedroom with gold and other flourishes. In the early weeks of the new administration, items were spirited from the second-floor corridor into the President's bedroom. Sometimes Trump carried the objects in himself, rearranging things across the private quarters on a whim. A massive mirror framed in gold leaf—one Melania had made the centerpiece of a first-term redesign of the Queens' Bedroom—was relocated to the White House colonnade, where it became known as the "selfie" mirror.

The President's redecorating generated such a flurry of activity that staff often felt caught between the two Trumps, who were the only presidential couple to regularly use and maintain separate bedrooms since Richard and Pat Nixon. (Bill and Hillary Clinton were said to have slept in separate bedrooms for a period of time after his affair with Monica Lewinsky became public.) Trump would let his wife use the master bedroom, known inside the White House as Room 219, and its dressing room; the President took Room 220, next to the Yellow Oval. Melania spent little time at the White House in the early weeks after the inauguration and was not around to consult as various objects vanished into the Oval Office or her husband's bedroom on his say-so. Once, when staff gently reminded the President that he was taking things from the Center Hall his wife had personally selected, he made clear he didn't care. He seemed almost to be competing with her—determined to have the better room. The staff resorted to photographing potential substitutes and sending the images to Mrs. Trump for approval.

Trump, a television addict, had three sets installed in his personal quarters, just as he had in his first term: two for the bedroom and one for the bathroom. New carpet was laid in the bathroom on Inauguration Day, as before. Trump's preference for a fully carpeted bathroom had posed a challenge for the residence staff during his first term. The portion nearest the shower would often be soaked through; the staff was never quite sure why, but they worried about mold growing underneath. The solution was to lay a small piece of the same carpet—never an actual bath mat—over the larger one. Several of these pieces were kept in rotation, swapped out and dried.

Trump's obsessive focus on interior decorating made the staff yearn for the First Lady to return and hopefully rein him in. This became an especially pressing matter when the President turned his attention to the Rose Garden. The garden, whose redesign was overseen by the Kennedys in 1962, had been updated by Melania during Trump's first term. She considered it one of her proudest achievements. So when early talk made the rounds that Trump now intended to turn the garden into a version of the Mar-a-Lago patio, word came back from the First Lady's team that she was very unhappy. The compromise solution was to pave over the grass with white stone; the rosebushes would remain intact.

Mrs. Trump would soon lose a larger battle over what would become the President's signature project, which he announced in July: a White House ballroom that, like a sponge in a glass of water, continued expanding until by early 2026 it was expected to be larger than the White House building itself. It would involve something else, too: tearing down the entire East Wing. Trump had previously said the new ballroom would be "near" the East Wing, "but not touching it." The public would only learn about the demolition after photos of the construction site emerged, taken by onlookers at a nearby building.

For several weeks in early 2025, White House aides had tried accommodating the couple's competing desires about the future of the complex. Mrs. Trump, who preferred a quiet environment with minimal disturbances and objected to living in a construction zone, had repeatedly expressed concern about the size and location of the ballroom.

It was not that a ballroom on its own was a bad idea; in the past, Presidents held state dinners in tents on the South Lawn and had to bring in portable toilets for guests. But beyond the startling size of the new building envisioned by Trump, the White House grounds also sat above hidden spaces, among them the Presidential Emergency Operations Center. Located below the East Wing, this was where Vice President Dick Cheney and senior Bush administration officials had helped respond to the September 11 terrorist attacks, and where Trump himself was taken when protesters breached a barricade around the Treasury Department building in late May 2020.

Several people tried to persuade Trump to build a smaller ballroom and to place it somewhere that would not be so disruptive to sensitive operations. But Trump was insistent: The East Wing location was what he wanted. If it meant building an entirely new bunker, several stories below ground, then so be it.

9

It was an email, sent from the government's HR department, the Office of Personnel Management, to hundreds of thousands of federal workers on Saturday, February 22, that marked the beginning of the end of Elon Musk's reign.

Earlier that morning, the President had posted on Truth Social that he wanted Musk to "GET MORE AGGRESSIVE." Three hours later, Musk replied: "Will do, Mr. President!"

Soon after, an email landed in the inboxes of federal workers. Carrying the subject line "What did you do last week?," it delivered a bracing message to an already beleaguered workforce. Employees of the federal government were ordered to document, within forty-eight hours, five things they had accomplished in the previous week. And every week thereafter. Responses were due by 11:59 p.m. every Monday. A lack of response, Musk posted on X, "will be taken as a resignation." The email's author at least had the presence of mind to ask workers to refrain from sending any classified information.

Senior White House staff were in the dark about what Musk was doing. Word of the email quickly reached Susie Wiles, who was livid. She tried repeatedly to call Musk, and got no response. So she called Stephen Miller's wife, Katie, who was Musk's key aide. Miller told Wiles that the chief of staff needed to call Musk.

By then, agitated or enraged cabinet members were calling. The across-the-government blast was gratuitous, Wiles told an associate. Not all federal employees were bad, she added.

Musk had even started homing in on the cabinet secretaries. The President and several of his staff—including Wiles and Musk—were on Air Force One returning from Florida, when the head of presidential personnel, Sergio Gor, hurried to get Wiles. He told her she better get up to the front cabin because Musk was trashing Rubio. In Musk's view, Rubio wasn't doing enough to gut USAID, and Trump was listening.

The confrontation on Air Force One was just a preview of what was coming.

II

Meanwhile, the Ukraine minerals deal was also causing considerable internal dissension in the administration, along with rivalry and backbiting at senior levels. Howard Lutnick had told the President that Scott Bessent had "screwed up" the deal. Not only had Bessent failed to get Zelensky to sign it when he was in Kyiv, Lutnick explained, but Bessent had also made a hash of its terms. Lutnick asked Trump's permission to fix things and the President gave his blessing.

With Zelensky due at the White House in less than a week for his first official visit, Lutnick presented Trump with his newly negotiated deal. "I've saved it for you," he told the President. "I made the deal binding and made it for five hundred billion. So much better than what Bessent did."

"Great," Trump replied.

At a meeting of top officials in the Situation Room later that day, Lutnick sat down across from Bessent and slid his new deal across the table. The two men's natural antipathy toward each other was further exacerbated by the fact that Lutnick had originally wanted Bessent's job and had had to settle for commerce secretary instead.

Bessent looked at Lutnick's proposal. "This is a shitty deal. You're an idiot," he told Lutnick. "I don't know who told you my deal wasn't binding, but it is, and the reason the Ukrainians are so excited about your version is because you capped it at five hundred billion and we could've made one to two trillion from the deal. So of course they're excited to sign it."

"Well, that was what I was told," said Lutnick, taking an uncharacteristic step back. "I was trying to save it. But if that's not right then we won't do it."

Another key difference between the competing draft deals was that Bessent had negotiated his deal based on a percentage of revenue, while Lutnick's was for a percentage of earnings. Under Bessent's version, the United States would receive 50 percent of the revenues involved, not the earnings. Lutnick told others the Bessent version was absurd and would never be fulfilled by the Ukrainians because it would cripple them financially. Lutnick said to associates that Bessent didn't understand how deals worked.

If anything, Bessent's estimation of Lutnick's abilities was even lower. "Do you know how an airplane flies?" he would ask associates in private. "So there's a formula for the wing, and the wing has a series of stalls that we never see. So it's constantly stalling, recovering. Howard lives in a series of fifteen-minute increments. And he moves like he just needs to get to the next fifteen minutes—to keep the plane from stalling." Bessent would tell others to "remember that" when they were dealing with Lutnick.

The two men were primed for a clash. If Lutnick had developed a reputation as a commerce secretary who would rather be treasury secretary, and who spent little time in the Commerce building and a lot of time in the Oval Office and on cable television, Bessent was becoming known as something of an office pugilist. He had risen on Wall Street with a cerebral buttoned-up persona, but he surprised people when he quickly and aggressively escalated.

Bessent went right back to the President and said, "Howard's fucked up the deal. I had an uncapped deal and we're getting revenues not earnings."

"Is that right?" Trump said. "They gave you that?"

"Yes."

At that, Trump started mocking Lutnick, sometimes in front of others, enjoying the sport. On one occasion he turned to Bessent and asked, "Scott, where are you from?"

"South Carolina."

"So," Trump said. "A WASP from South Carolina." He turned to Lutnick. "I thought you Jews from New York were supposed to be tough, Howard."

III

The meeting in the Oval Office between Trump and Zelensky on February 28 began cordially enough, with the President of the United States lauding the President of Ukraine and the deal they were about to sign. But as cameras flashed and reporters asked questions, Trump demurred on specific security guarantees for Ukraine.

"I don't think you're gonna need much security," he said. "Once this deal gets done, it's over."

At that, Zelensky shook his head.

Normally, by the time such a deal was to be signed, all the staff work had been done, disagreements bridged, details worked out, drafts finessed. All that should be left was the ceremony to unveil the agreement before the world. But it was clear that many issues were still unresolved. During negotiations, the Ukrainians had asked for continued assistance from the United States at a rate similar to the previous three years under Biden. They wanted ironclad security guarantees: If NATO membership was out of the question, then perhaps a new alliance that would be like NATO in all but name—not far from what Keith Kellogg had proposed back in January. And they had asked for a commitment that the United States would not recognize any Russian-controlled territories. They had gotten none of those things. Trump had asked JD Vance's wife, Usha, also a Yale Law School graduate, to review the Ukrainian edits to the minerals deal. She declared the document "awful" and had taken a heavy pencil to it.

In the Oval Office, even as Trump declared it a "fair deal," Zelensky harbored doubts not just about its fairness, but about America's commitment to upholding what he saw as its end of the bargain. And in spite of the air of ceremony, Zelensky could hide neither those fears nor the rawness of his rage at the man who had invaded his country and killed his people.

"He is a killer and terrorist. But I hope that together we can stop him," he said of Putin. "He hates us," he continued. "He wants destroy us." The minerals deal, Zelensky added, was a "very good start," but "not enough to stop this person."

As Zelensky savaged Putin in front of the cameras, Trump in turn savaged Biden. "The United States should not have allowed this to happen," he said. Biden didn't know "what the hell he was doing." He again trumpeted his recent election victory, briefly doglegged into all the red states on the electoral map, and declared that if he hadn't been reelected the brutal conflict in Ukraine may well have devolved into World War III.

This free-form press conference in the Oval Office—a room that had borne witness to such moments as a joint press conference after Pearl Harbor in 1941 between President Franklin Roosevelt and Winston Churchill—would continue for forty-nine agonizing minutes. The longer the two leaders talked, the more their voices were raised, and the more the scene spun out of control.

Several Trump aides had been worried about something like this. Mike Waltz had tried—unsuccessfully—to get the message across that Zelensky should come wearing a suit. Bessent had strongly recommended to Trump that he not even allow Zelensky into the White House before he had signed the minerals deal. "I've dealt with this little fucker," Bessent would say to associates about Zelensky. "He's tricky. He's like the special-needs child for the Europeans. And he's acting like Mr. Bean on crack."

As the meeting unwound, the true feelings of all involved came to the surface—Zelensky's existential mistrust, Trump's disdain and impatience. It began to seem like a meeting of adversaries. Others present could see that Vance was steadily turning red. Just five weeks into his vice presidency, Vance had mostly adopted a low-key approach. His plan was to pick his opportunities and over time emerge as a voice in his own right. He knew the next four years came down to one thing: securing Trump's blessing as his successor.

If for Trump "America First" was more slogan than coherent governing philosophy, for Vance it was a worldview to which he wholeheartedly subscribed. This worldview meant a complete reappraisal of America's commitments, particularly in Europe. And so Zelensky's insistence on pushing for American security guarantees, live on camera from the Oval Office, began to sound to Vance like impertinence and ingratitude.

The vice president had not planned to speak that day in the Oval Office, but as Zelensky refused to yield, Vance's temper got the better of him. There was no such thing as a ceasefire with Putin that could be trusted, Zelensky insisted. The only thing that would restrain the Russian dictator was an American security guarantee. After a Polish journalist cut into the noise, telling Trump that Polish people were worried the President was too close to Putin, Vance had had enough.

"I will respond to this," the vice president said. "So look, for four years, the United States of America, we had a President who stood up at press conferences and talked tough about Vladimir Putin, and then Putin invaded Ukraine and destroyed a significant chunk of the country. The path to peace and the path to prosperity is maybe engaging in diplomacy. We tried the pathway of Joe Biden, of thumping our chest and pretending that the President of the United States' words mattered more than the President of the United States' actions. What makes America a good country is America engaging in diplomacy. That's what President Trump's doing."

After going through a decade's worth of ceasefires and other negotiated agreements that Putin had blithely violated, Zelensky said, "What kind of diplomacy, JD, you are speaking about? What do you mean?"

"I'm talking about the kind of diplomacy that's going to end the destruction of your country," Vance said. "Mr. President, with respect, I think it's disrespectful for you to come into the Oval Office to try to litigate this in front of the American media. Right now, you guys are going around and forcing conscripts to the front lines because you have manpower problems. You should be thanking the President for trying to bring an end to this conflict."

"Have you ever been to Ukraine that you say what problems we have?" Zelensky asked. "Come once."

"I've actually watched and seen the stories," Vance said. "And do you think that it's respectful to come to the Oval Office of the United States of America and attack the administration that is trying to prevent the destruction of your country?"

"During the war, everybody has problems, even you," Zelensky said. "But you have nice ocean and don't feel now, but you will feel it in the future."

Trump had sat silently watching the exchange, but at this last comment he snapped. "You don't know that," Trump said.

"God bless," Zelensky said, "you will not have a war."

"Don't tell us what we're going to feel," Trump said, voice rising, as the two leaders talked over each other. "We're trying to solve a problem. Don't tell us what we're going to feel, because you're in no position to dictate that. You're in no position to dictate what we're going to feel. We're going to feel very good. We're going to feel very good and very strong. You're right now not in a very good position."

Trump continued: "You don't have the cards right now. With us you start having cards—"

"I'm not playing cards—" said Zelensky, who was not using his translator and seemed to be struggling with the fast pace of the dialogue.

"You're playing cards," Trump said. "You're gambling with the lives of millions of people."

"I am the President in war—" Zelensky said.

"You're gambling with World War Three," Trump said, cutting him off. "You're gambling with World War Three, and what you're doing is very disrespectful to the country, this country, that's backed you far more than a lot of people said they should have."

"Have you said thank you once, this entire meeting?" said Vance, twisting the knife.

"A lot of times," Zelensky said.

Trump was visibly angry. "It's going to be a very hard thing to do business like this," he warned.

But while Vance had twice encouraged Zelensky not to "litigate this in front of the American media," Trump savored the confrontation. As he wrapped the meeting up, he noted the dramatic scene that had just unfolded was going to make for "great television."

A sort of pandemonium then set in. The press was asked to leave. The Ukrainian delegation left the Oval Office, gathering across the hall in the Roosevelt Room to figure out what to do next. The President, vice president, and members of the cabinet huddled and agreed on one thing: There would be no signing, no deal. In the Oval Office, Trump told his inner circle,

"I don't think that guy wants peace. Just have him leave." The Ukrainians, desperate to salvage the meeting, offered to continue talking. They asked if they might still sign the deal. But that window had closed. There was later talk among Trump's cabinet of the growing fear that Zelensky was not rational.

But as evidenced by the despairing reactions from America's European allies, many thought Zelensky was quite rational. European ambassadors were texting and talking among themselves, many describing the day as a "turning point" that cemented a profound loss of trust in America. "It is over and we are alone," texted one senior European official to another.

Almost an hour after the clash in the Oval, Rubio and Waltz crossed the hall and told Zelensky and his party that there would be no lunch to follow, as had been planned. The Ukrainian ambassador, Oksana Markarova, looked distraught.

But Trump thought the confrontation was great. "Better," he would tell an advisor, "than *The Apprentice*."

It was playing well outside the building, too. A jubilant Don Jr. told an associate that the Vance-Trump smackdown of Zelensky was "maybe the best thing that's ever happened in the Oval Office."

Moscow, too, reveled in the blowup. Russian Foreign Minister Sergey Lavrov praised Trump's "common sense." Kremlin spokesman Dmitry Peskov declared that America's "rapidly changing" foreign policy "largely coincides with our vision." And the deputy chair of Russia's security council, Dmitry Medvedev, said that "the insolent pig finally got a proper slap-down in the Oval Office."

It had not been a setup. Not an ambush. But the antipathy between Trump and Zelensky had exploded into view all the same, capturing the attention of the world. The embattled Ukrainian President had been belittled as an ingrate and ordered off the premises. And given Trump's new transactional order, that suited the White House just fine.

10

One morning, Press Secretary Karoline Leavitt entered the Oval Office to find Donald Trump clutching a tube of superglue and attempting to affix gold decorations to the marble fireplace mantel. As he was known to prefer his own aesthetic handiwork to anyone else's, the sight of the President squeezing glue onto gilded appliqués and mounting them on the wall himself surprised no one in his inner circle.

Trump's first wife, Ivana, the vice president of interior design at his company, had had a penchant for gilding everything. It was Ivana who was said to have first encouraged the gold obsession that soon became a hallmark of her husband's properties. Gold projected the ostentation that would be Trump's brand and he reveled in its glow. His signature New York City building would bear the words "TRUMP TOWER" in gold letters and boast gold-hued elevator doors and escalators; gold silk lined the walls of the bedroom on his private plane, he draped himself in bling for the cover of *Esquire*, and he would eventually sell gold sneakers.

The Oval Office had always been deliberately understated—a reminder that the United States was a republic, not a monarchy, and the President's office was not a palace. Trump had gone along with that tradition in his first term. In his second term, he would unleash his inner Louis XIV.

Every President had put his own stamp on the White House. In 1909, William Howard Taft bathed the original Oval Office expansion of the West

Wing in olive green. Some critics at the time imagined that Taft's greenery was an homage to the natural beauty of America, but in fact Taft just liked green. Similarly, Trump now brought gold. Golden urns and chalices would replace the tufty green Swedish ivy on the mantelpiece—which had graced the Oval Office for many decades before Trump. As the year progressed, he kept jamming more gold pieces onto the mantel. When Trump asked White House residence staff what they thought of the glittering display, most responses were muted, but his devout aide Natalie Harp would gush with delight.

Gold cherubs flitted about in the pediments above doorways. Golden molding encircled the room, a golden presidential seal beckoned like heaven from the recessed ceiling above, and golden appliqués festooned the hearth and walls, alongside ornate gold-framed paintings from the vast art collections of the federal government. Trump called the antique golden urns plucked from the White House collection "cash," and would tell people: "See that cash? People look at it, all they see is cash."

II

Trump's attachment to gold wasn't merely cosmetic.

During the previous year's campaign, Trump had often invoked what he described as his economic ideal—the Gilded Age tariff policies that fueled America from the end of the Civil War to the turn of the twentieth century. This would be his model for national prosperity. "In the words of a great but highly underrated President, William McKinley," he declared in a speech on September 5, 2024, to the Economic Club of New York, "the protective tariff policy of the Republicans has been made—and made—the lives of our countrymen sweeter and brighter."

Mark Twain had coined the term "Gilded Age" satirically; for this was also an era of rapid industrialization, vast wealth for the few, widespread poverty for the masses, and rampant political corruption; all concealed beneath the thinnest veneer of gold. But for Trump, gold was gold. He would continue to cite McKinley as his economic lodestar. "I am a Tariff Man, standing on a Tariff Platform," McKinley had declared during the presidential campaign of 1896. And so, too, would Trump declare himself a Tariff Man. McKinley had come by his attachment to tariffs honestly, having passed what became known as the McKinley Tariff into law as chairman of the House Ways and Means Committee in 1890, a policy meant to punish foreign imports and foster "infant industries" domestically. McKinley's bill set import duties to an average of nearly 50 percent, raising consumer prices and resulting in retaliatory tariffs, weakening the American economy and contributing to the Panic of 1893.

And yet the allure of tariffs as a trade barrier, a source of revenue and, above all, a tool of power remained irresistible to Donald Trump. Eleven days after his return to office, on January 31, 2025, Trump would say, "We were at our richest from 1870 to 1913. That's when we had, we were a tariff country. And then they went to an income tax concept." The very next day, he signed three documents—Executive Orders 14193, 14194, and 14195—invoking emergency powers under the International Emergency Economic Powers Act (IEEPA). The White House asserted that due to "the extraordinary threat posed by illegal aliens and drugs, including deadly fentanyl," Trump was imposing tariffs on imports from America's three top trading partners—25 percent for Canada and Mexico, and an additional 10 percent tariff on imports from China. It would be the opening salvo for the global trade war he would wage in the spring.

The early tariff announcement came faster than some of Trump's most senior aides had wanted. No meaningful staff work had been done at the Commerce Department and there was little clarity on just what the President hoped to achieve. Those working outside his immediate circle were forced to guess about his intentions. Neither fentanyl nor illegal immigrants were crossing the northern border in significant numbers, and Mexico was cooperating with Trump's efforts to shut down illegal border crossings. Recently elected President Claudia Sheinbaum had dispatched thousands of troops to Mexico's borders to better manage the flow of migrants. At a meeting in the Oval Office on January 31, the day before Trump signed the executive orders, Stephen Miller had argued against the 25 percent tariff on Mexico. "They've done everything we've asked them to do regarding immigration," he told the President. Miller had no objection to tariffs on

Mexico if they were part of a global tariff regime, but he did not think singling Mexico out for punishment before formulating a broader approach made sense. Marco Rubio concurred. Scott Bessent suggested that Trump hold off on implementing the tariffs until March 1, saying it would be better to run some Treasury analysis on the potential impacts on the U.S. and the global economy. But Trump dismissed these concerns and the tariffs would go into effect immediately.

Underscoring just how ad hoc the plan was, at one point in the meeting Trump realized that he had forgotten to include China. "Where are they?" he asked. Off the top of his head, he added, "Put them in for ten."

Trump's concept of the global economy and America's place in it was encased in the amber of his youth, and it remained largely uninfluenced by the dramatic changes in the decades since. In his mind, America should always be the manufacturing behemoth it had once been, consuming mostly what it produced and dictating terms to the world for the rest.

The fall of the Iron Curtain had ushered in the third wave of globalization, offshoring manufacturing jobs and spurring the creation of complex supply chains that had integrated the global economy to a profound degree. The American economy was transformed at an almost molecular level to one no longer dominated by manufacturing and heavy industry. Instead it was a services, information, and tech economy, with the financial sector constituting an increasingly significant share of the economy. Many factories went to China and the jobs went with them.

In response to the displaced workers and abandoned towns that had little to show for globalization, both parties in Washington had offered much talk about training for the jobs of the future, but little action. While still the world's largest economy, the United States consumed more and made less. This struck to the core of both Trump's appeal to working people and his frozen-in-time concept of America's economic role in the world. He would "bring back" jobs that had left. He rhapsodized about the return of bygone industries like coal. He promised the roaring return of America's manufacturing base. It was, in part, why he loved tariffs.

Trump now was promising to do nothing less than reindustrialize the

United States, forcing foreign businesses or American businesses operating offshore to either move their production back to the U.S. or face heavy duties on their products. Free trade had become a core principle of American conservatism and, in his first term, those whom Trump called "globalists" had hoped his protectionism was just a passing fad. But by the time he returned to office, resistance to tariffs had collapsed along with all other resistance from Republicans, and the free traders who remained in Trump's party mostly kept it to themselves.

A shift so transformational usually required more than back-of-the-envelope planning, and the first shots of Trump's second-term trade war were aimed at some of America's closest friends and neighbors. This was more than unnerving to some members of Trump's own team. The markets convulsed. *The Wall Street Journal* was withering in its criticism. *Bloomberg News* described Trump's tariffs as "the most extensive act of protectionism taken by a U.S. President in almost a century," a reference to the Smoot-Hawley tariffs of 1930, *the* cautionary tale for those who favored trade barriers. But in the White House it was said there were now two types of people: those who loved tariffs and those who had lost the will to fight.

III

Corporate America had spent fortunes on consultants trying to decode Trump, and the familiar advice about taking him "seriously but not literally" had perhaps outlived its usefulness. Still, many executives clung to the hope that he viewed tariffs primarily as leverage. Trump didn't truly love tariffs, they reassured themselves—what he loved was the deal-making power that came from dangling the threat of imposing them.

In an early March call with three titans of the American auto industry—Stellantis chairman John Elkann, Ford CEO Jim Farley, and General Motors CEO Mary Barra—the President broke some tough news. Auto executives, echoing leaders across other sectors, had been making the case that the supply chains underpinning their industry would be thrown into chaos—and the industry itself crippled—by Trump's 25 percent tariffs on vehicles from Mexico and Canada. The President's agreement to a one-month pause offered slight relief.

But now they all needed to buckle up, Trump told them. The full tariff regime would be going into effect on April 2, or as he would take to calling it as the day drew nearer, "Liberation Day." It was time for everyone to get on board.

According to Barra, Elkann, and Farley, billions in new costs would be heaped onto their companies—wiping out profits entirely—if tariffs hit cars and parts coming from Mexico and Canada. "Liberation Day" for General Motors, Ford, and Stellantis (whose brands included Chrysler, Dodge, Fiat, Jeep, Ram, Alfa Romeo, and Maserati) could well mean liberation from making profits.

Trump was unmoved. His convictions of four decades seemed genuine after all: America was getting fleeced by foreign nations, and the cure-all for the country's troubles could be found in tariffs. But acceding to his reality didn't solve the seismic problems that the tariffs would cause. Was there anything that might dissuade him?

On March 6, the Mexican President made her own appeal. Claudia Sheinbaum had initiated a call with Trump, requesting a delay on the fentanyl tariffs until April 2, to bring them into line with the tariff program Trump had in mind for the rest of the world. Sheinbaum had a distinct advantage in her dealings with Trump; he liked the way her voice sounded.

"You've got an elegant voice," Trump told the President of Mexico. Sheinbaum thanked him and turned the conversation to business.

Her dilemma—the dilemma of all of North America, really—was that imposing the planned tariffs on Mexico and Canada a month earlier than the rest of the world would put products made under the United States-Mexico-Canada Agreement at a terrible disadvantage. Even in just one month, the results could be significant. The big three automakers had told Trump the same thing.

Sheinbaum emphasized how helpful she had been to Trump on immigration. Trump relented finally, agreeing to the delay. As their conversation was wrapping up, he handed the phone off to Howard Lutnick. Just before he ended the call, Trump, in the background, declared, "But no more! We're not doing any more exceptions anymore. Once April 2 comes, that's it—no more exceptions."

During his first term in office, Wall Street served as both Trump's compass and constraint, and anti-tariff advisors would exploit the fact that any downturn in the markets would deter him from tariffs. In that way, the markets would act as a shock collar to limit the damage.

But not even that could be counted on anymore. The Dow Jones Industrial Average had shed more than 600 points since his new tariffs hit China, Mexico, and Canada—but neither the market free fall triggered by his initial tariffs, nor the unflattering headlines, which would have sent first-term Trump scrambling to reverse course, had managed to rattle the President. None of it appeared to matter to Trump.

In the lead-up to the 2024 election, Trump's new economic team had sent reassuring signals to Wall Street. That September, Lutnick had characterized tariffs as a "bargaining chip" that would eventually lead to more open trade. From his hedge fund perch at the time, Bessent sent investors a letter declaring, "The tariff gun will always be loaded and on the table but rarely discharged." But six months later, as Liberation Day approached, many of these same advisors had to backtrack, spreading word to foreign officials and chief executives like Barra, Elkann, and Farley that the President would not be restrained.

Of all the things that tariffs could be—bargaining chips, sources of revenue, tools of raw power—it was the last of these that Trump savored most. Tariffs were the perfect blunt weapon to bully foreign leaders over matters that had nothing to do with economics or national security.

Of course, sweeping tariffs also came with the potential to do great harm, and that was what scared Trump's advisors. And the more they heard about Liberation Day, the more scared they got.

11

Franklin Roosevelt's ninety-nine executive orders during the first hundred days of his presidency in 1933 set a record that stood for nearly a century until Donald Trump's second term. While only signing a record low five bills into law during his first hundred days, Trump issued more than 140 executive orders in a frenzy of unilateral action, defining the philosophical contours of his presidency, presuming to nullify certain features of the Constitution, and expanding executive authority as never before.

Like Roosevelt, Trump claimed emergency powers. But unlike the objective disaster of the Great Depression, Trump's emergencies were far more debatable. When the coronavirus pandemic hit American shores during Trump's first term, he and Stephen Miller had learned that an emergency—in that case, an undisputed one—unlocked immense new powers that could be deployed with great speed. Using a once-obscure federal statute known as Title 42, they were able to seal the border during the pandemic. And now, in term two, Trump and Miller decided to redefine the very concept of an "emergency."

In addition to what some senior staff referred to as the "fentanyl tariff" emergency, Trump declared a national energy emergency, citing "inadequate energy supply," even though the United States was energy independent when he returned to office, with domestic oil production at a record high. He declared that America's trade deficit was an emergency, even though the United States had been running a trade deficit constantly since 1976. He also declared the situation on the southern border to be an emergency, due to an "invasion" of illegal immigrants. If a border emergency had been declared in December 2023, at the peak of the crisis due to the Biden administration's lax border enforcement, few would have argued. But following Biden's June 2024 executive order cracking down on asylum seekers, border crossings had dropped 77 percent. No matter. Trump would seize on the broadest definition of emergency powers to reverse what he saw as the excesses and neglect of the previous administration.

Along with this would go the President's crackdown on American civil society. He would threaten private businesses that embraced diversity, equity, and inclusion in hiring practices and company culture; and he would issue an executive order describing government DEI practices as "illegal and immoral discrimination." He would sic the Justice Department on his enemies, whom he called "scum." And even as the President and vice president boasted that they were restoring free speech, the administration moved to stifle dissent.

In March 2025, after a former Columbia University student named Mahmoud Khalil was arrested and detained with intent to deport him, Trump's "border czar," Tom Homan, would say, "Freedom of speech has limitations. We consider him a national security threat." Khalil, a legal permanent resident of the United States with no criminal record, had been a student leader of the pro-Palestinian campus protests the year before. The threat he posed was holding views the government had deemed dangerous. On Truth Social, the President posted that Khalil's detention was "the first arrest of many to come."

And sure enough, suddenly, from coast to coast, masked agents from Immigration and Customs Enforcement seemed to be everywhere, and a new phenomenon emerged: Unsuspecting targets were being snatched from sidewalks and during traffic stops and removed to federal detention facilities in distant states, their whereabouts sometimes unknown even to their families and attorneys. The U.S. had always carried out deportations, but never quite like this: It was a spectacle, captured on video, and that was key to the strategy. Viral videos made for viral fear—a powerful deterrent to migrants who might consider coming to the U.S.

II

During the first term, the focus had been on securing the physical border rather than deportations. There had been some discussions of scaling up operations targeting families in blue-state cities, but that plan met with widespread criticism when it became public. This time, however, with the border essentially sealed within two months of Trump taking office, interior enforcement became the top priority. Immigration and Customs Enforcement was the focus. Right away, the agency developed a fearsome persona—armed, masked, and menacing—and began to post daily arrest numbers. Stephen Miller was applying immense pressure on the agency to keep up the pace of mass deportation and hit a 3,000 daily-arrests target. The number had not been plucked from thin air: Miller and others across the administration had converged on a round target of 1 million arrests per year, which worked out to roughly 3,000 per day. The previous daily average had been less than a third of that, but Miller made no apologies for the pressure, telling officials that the President had campaigned on the largest deportation operation ever, and they were not even approaching Obama-era numbers. Miller wasn't interested in lengthy deliberations. He wanted real-world results.

Tom Homan, an ICE official under Obama and during Trump's first term, would partner on the deportation agenda with Miller, whom he called in an interview in the autumn of 2025 "probably the smartest man I ever met."

"He's brilliant," Homan raved. "I've done it for forty years, he hasn't. And he comes up with some ideas and he can reiterate a lot of immigration law that sometimes I even forgot. I come to the table with experience; he comes with a lot of knowledge." The two would meet at the White House every weekday morning at ten o'clock, and over a secure phone line on Saturdays.

Originally from a small town in upstate New York, Homan had been a cop like his father and grandfather before going to work in immigration enforcement, spending years as a uniformed agent on the southern border. He later joined ICE, becoming acting director, and he was an architect of the family separation strategy to discourage border crossings, although it would not come into practice until the first Trump administration.

When Homan and Stephen Miller joined forces again, in 2025, mass deportation became a whole-of-government effort. Miller drove the policy; Homan made it happen. At first, Miller was pleased by the sharp reduction in migrant encounters at the border, but he grew quickly infuriated by what he saw as the slow pace of deportations. On a call in late February with all the agencies involved in border enforcement, including Defense, Justice, and Homeland Security, Miller warned that those incapable of meeting the President's demands would soon find themselves without a job. One of the senior officials got off the call and told a colleague, "Stephen lost it. He's threatened to fire all of ICE and DHS, and said they're not moving fast enough. He's about to lose it on all of us."

Miller's eruptions became legendary across the government. On the conference calls, he would often berate Department of Homeland Security personnel, with much of his frustration directed at the different rules and standards each agency had for detaining illegal immigrants.

But the calls were not merely exercises in intimidation. Much of the time was consumed by operational problem-solving—finding planes to move deportees, securing legal opinions agencies needed before they could act, determining which level of official needed to lean on a foreign government that was refusing to cooperate. It was granular, tedious work, and Miller believed it only yielded results when there was a competent chain of command at agencies capable of translating his directives into action.

Miller saw the signing of an executive order not as the culmination of the policy process but as its beginning. What mattered was whether an order on paper translated into handcuffs on a subject, a migrant on a plane, a smuggling network disrupted. It was this obsession with real-world execution that drove his relentless pressure on the interagency discussions. But those on the receiving end of his barrages described them as often unhinged and needlessly abusive. And there were limits to what pressure from the West Wing could achieve from afar.

"We need a hundred thousand beds," Homan would say. This was a number almost twice the available ICE bed space. "And we've got to get there. Because—I've been doing this for a long time; we need a hundred thousand beds to get what we want to do on this deportation operation."

Homan was further driven by what he saw as a wider conspiracy. Having carefully evaluated the Biden administration's performance on the border, he believed Biden had purposely slowed the processing of migrants in the hope that he would be succeeded by another Democratic President, and "all of a sudden there's an amnesty."

"And that's why they're so upset right now," Homan said. "Because we're making arrests in record numbers. We're spoiling their game plan."

Homan was initially seen as vital to the administration's immigration enforcement efforts—so vital that Trump would shrug off news reports that Homan had accepted $50,000 in 2024, a literal bag of cash, in exchange for promises to help secure contracts for favored companies in a future Trump administration. The Biden Justice Department had been investigating Homan's activities, but the Trump DOJ swiftly called off the dogs, describing the investigation as part of Biden's "weaponization" of justice.

A large part of Miller's authority stemmed from the perception that he, more than any other White House staffer, spoke for the President. Miller fostered that perception, and often used it to his advantage. One colleague later described the way Miller would sometimes arrive midway through meetings: "He basically states what he believes to be the President's intent. And he says, 'Well, I've spoken to the President,' or 'I've heard the President say this about this issue.'"

Some may have rolled their eyes, but few would challenge Miller directly. The larger question in all this was just how closely aligned he was with Trump on immigration. Trump had long demagogued the issue of immigration, but he was also an instinctive showman who could read a room—and when the press coverage turned ugly enough, he had a history of backing down. Miller was different. He was a true believer, more hard-line than the President he served, and he didn't flinch. Trump would acknowledge that difference and joke about it in private. In a 2024 campaign meeting, Trump remarked that if it were left to Miller there would be only 100 million people in the United States and they would all look like Stephen Miller.

But Miller's relentless pressure from the West Wing ran headlong into a problem he could not solve from there: The department responsible for carrying out his vision was completely dysfunctional. The chaos at DHS under Kristi Noem had become one of Miller's frustrations. He had urged the department to expand the detention facilities that already existed along the border—sites the Biden administration had built out during the migrant surge, already connected to water, electricity, and heat, and close to entry ports and supply lines. Instead, Miller would later tell associates he had discovered that DHS had purchased Amazon warehouses to use as detention space. No one had consulted him and he could not fathom the logic: The warehouses were not coded for habitation, would require enormous investment to convert, and solved a problem that existing infrastructure had already addressed. He told a colleague he had traced the decision to a Noem ally who had been installed as a senior official at DHS and who, in Miller's view, had no business making such major operational decisions.

Miller would tell associates that the chain of command at ICE had broken down, with leaders unable to execute on his directions, and Noem compounding the problem with her public messaging. Early on, she had branded the mass deportation campaign as ICE arresting "the worst of the worst"—hardened criminals, gang members, the most dangerous offenders. It played well on television and it was accurate that the administration was targeting violent criminals. But Miller had a broader vision; they were also targeting hundreds of thousands of other immigrants, and, in Miller's view, the phrase boxed them in. Now when ICE arrested a family that fell into one of those other categories—as the agency inevitably would—the White House would have to spend days explaining why. Had Noem been able to articulate the broader scope of the mission from the outset, Miller told colleagues, the public would have better understood. But, in his view, she was not fluent enough with the substance to have that conversation.

The contrast between the bungled handling of mass deportations with the successful management of essentially sealing the southern border was maddening to Miller. At the border, the interagency process was working as intended—by turning nearly every person arriving at the border away and essentially ending asylum. But none of that level of effectiveness translated to the interior enforcement operations led by DHS. The same administration that was carrying out a militarized border operation was now facing court challenges over how it engaged with arresting people, including protesters. And from his perch in the West Wing, Miller could give all the advice he wanted—run his daily calls, send his directives, deliver his warnings—but the follow-through could only happen inside the department. And in the view of Miller and other senior West Wing staff, the department, under Noem, was broken.

III

Miller's ambitions went well beyond just shipping migrants out of the country. Nowhere was his newfound authority more clearly on display than during a March 19 meeting with the most powerful fossil fuel CEOs in the United States.

Trump himself was running ninety minutes late.

"This is my favorite industry," he said breezily as he entered the Cabinet Room and took his seat.

If there was a constituency that Trump would move heaven and earth for, it was the executives in this room. Chevron. ConocoPhillips. ExxonMobil. From the moment the meeting began, the deference paid to the companies that would make good on Trump's *Drill, baby, drill* promise was remarkable. Their wishes were Trump's command. There was no regulation he wouldn't overturn, no law he wouldn't challenge, if doing so would accelerate their pursuit of hydrocarbons. Even though the United States had been the world's top crude-oil and liquefied natural gas producer for several years, on Inauguration Day Trump had declared an "energy emergency," saying, "We have something that no other manufacturing nation will ever have—the largest amount of oil and gas of any country on earth—and we are going to use it."

The administration was determined to use it *now* and placed a premium on projects that would yield measurable results during the second term, delivering Trump the credit. If a project was going to take six years, it was much less interesting. There was no bigger evangelist for this gospel of now than Stephen Miller, who had no patience for the legal and environmental regulations the large oil companies had to deal with.

Around the table, a complaint arose about the Climate Superfund bills that had recently passed in New York and Vermont, which aimed to hold major fossil fuel companies financially responsible for climate change-related damages. The executives considered it to be a tax on the industry for climate sins over the decades, and the room wasn't having it.

"It's just a new way to fund new social programs in New York and Vermont," complained one executive. "And we sued them as soon as they passed these laws last year."

As they were speaking, Miller was already texting the attorney general, Pam Bondi, asking her to sue Vermont and New York. "I'm on it," he told the group at the table. More than six weeks later, the administration would sue both states, seeking to block enforcement of the laws.

Darren Woods, the CEO of ExxonMobil, raised a regulatory issue from the European Union. He wanted to know if anything could be done about a law called the Corporate Sustainability Due Diligence Directive (CSDDD), which mandated that big corporations detect, avert, and reduce negative environmental and human rights consequences across their entire global "chains of activities." As if that were not enough of a red flag for an oil CEO, the law also required companies to develop a "climate transition plan" to align their business with the Paris Agreement. There would be penalties for noncompliance.

"We need to do something about this EU reg," said Woods, "because it will basically shut us down in the EU."

Trump looked at Howard Lutnick and said, "Well, we'll just tariff them. Howard, add ten more percent to whatever we were going to do to the EU; actually, add twenty percent. Make it twenty percent more, until they fix this regulation."

The executives were incredulous. The Cabinet Room was like a fun house; regulatory regimes could disappear at a simple request.

Miller gave the room an assignment, asking for a list of ten projects the White House could help fast-track. And he wanted them to highlight how much more energy the projects would produce in the United States during the Trump presidency.

This was not typical. The fifteen CEOs in the room had done a lot of business in Washington, having extensive experience with the Presidents and the policy shops of both parties. In any other White House, there would be a detailed policy process before a decision was made—a deputies meeting, an assistants meeting, economic analyses, environmental impact statements—and only then would the President look at options. Now a CEO could simply ask for something and it was granted.

"He has a better sense of his executive authority than anybody else we've ever dealt with," said one executive who attended the meeting. "Now, I would never want a Democrat to have that same sense of executive authority. But this guy fucking does."

Trump was always open to the idea that regulations or laws were unfair to private businesses. The Trump family's real estate company had a long and scarring history of legal battles with federal and state governments, dating back to the 1950s in the case of Trump's father. Now Trump *was* the government.

"I want to talk about Venezuela," Trump suddenly announced to the group out of nowhere. "Who's the Venezuela Guy?"

IV

The Venezuela Guy was Mike Wirth, the CEO of Chevron, the last major American oil company still operating in Venezuela after Hugo Chávez's left-wing government asserted state control over foreign companies in 2007. That wave of nationalization had led ExxonMobil and ConocoPhillips to leave the country, unwilling to keep investing in a place where the government might seize their assets at any moment. After they left the country, Chávez did exactly that, with both companies losing billions of dollars' worth of assets. Chevron had made a different decision. The company's leaders decided to place a long-term bet on Venezuela—accepting lower profits and majority state control—in order to keep a foothold in the world's largest-known oil fields. Chevron had been in Venezuela for more than a century; when Venezuela was run by U.S. allies, it had been a booming country with a thriving oil industry. Why not again?

Trump had long been obsessed with Venezuela's enormous oil reserves. In term one, he had mused about "taking the oil" from Venezuela, just as he had toyed with taking the oil from Iraq, Syria, and Libya, to bring vast riches into the United States. He had also mulled over a "military option" to replace Chávez's successor, dictator Nicolás Maduro, but his military advisors had counseled against an invasion. Instead, Trump's first-term aides talked him into supporting the opposition movement against Maduro. Trump declared the opposition leader at the time, Juan Guaidó, Venezuela's legitimate leader, and he had backed a protest campaign to remove Maduro from power. But Maduro's forces crushed the 2019 uprising and Trump quickly lost confidence in Guaidó, describing him as "weak."

Now in his second term, Trump had a new leader at the Pentagon—Pete Hegseth—who was far less cautious about the use of American force than Trump's first-term defense secretaries, James Mattis and Mark Esper. As he reviewed maps of the lands near the United States, Trump was thinking more seriously about several countries he could annex. Publicly, he talked about taking over Greenland and turning Canada into America's fifty-first state—an idea the Canadians rejected out of hand—but privately, he was zeroing in on Venezuela as a potential new American territory. He told several associates that Venezuela could be America's fifty-first state and that he would appoint a governor to run it. He gave no indication that he was joking. Whatever happened, he wanted total control over Venezuela's oil fields and to kick China, Iran, and Russia—who were all doing business there—out of America's backyard.

By March, Trump was still trying to figure out what to do about Maduro, who had proven surprisingly resilient. Over the previous twelve years he had survived many challenges to his rule, including mass protests. He had stolen elections and presided over an economic disaster of such epic proportions that close to a third of all Venezuelans, around 8 million people, had fled the country. More than 600,000 had migrated to the United States.

The Venezuelan exodus to the U.S.—and especially the Venezuelan gang Tren de Aragua—had been a key talking point for Trump during the 2024 campaign. But Maduro was still there, still in power, and defiantly in charge.

Trump started by playing nice; instead of applying maximum pressure, as Marco Rubio would have preferred, Trump empowered his special envoy, Richard Grenell, to negotiate directly with Maduro. Grenell had served as acting director of national intelligence during the first administration and was one of the President's fiercest loyalists. Trump had given him the mission of securing the release of American hostages and pressuring Maduro to accept deportation flights of Venezuelan migrants.

He also wanted preferential treatment for America and access to Venezuela's oil. Grenell made some progress, with Maduro provisionally agreeing to Trump's objectives.

But Rubio was not buying it, and he warned Trump that Grenell was getting played. Rubio expected Maduro to give Trump some short-term "wins" by releasing hostages and accepting some migrants back into Venezuela, but after that he predicted Maduro would string Trump along, waiting him out until Trump left the White House in 2029. Grenell might have been on the cusp of a deal, but Rubio regarded any deal with Maduro as worthless.

Rubio's arguments were bolstered by Republican members of Congress from South Florida. Dubbed by some in the White House as "the Cuban Caucus," Mario Díaz-Balart, Carlos Giménez, and Maria Elvira Salazar had been urging Trump to take a harder line against Maduro. Their immediate ask was to stop Chevron's oil operations in Venezuela as a way to tighten pressure on the regime. These South Florida Republicans were given privileged access to an administration run at the highest level by Florida GOP luminaries: Rubio, Susie Wiles, Pam Bondi, and James Blair, a Wiles ally who oversaw the White House's political and legislative affairs operations as deputy chief of staff.

With a tight Republican majority in the House, the three Cubans knew they had tremendous leverage; they could threaten to block Trump's major piece of domestic legislation, the One Big Beautiful Bill, if the President didn't take a tougher stand on Maduro.

Caught in the middle of this mess was Mike Wirth. The Chevron CEO had spoken to Trump during the transition to argue for his company's continued presence in Venezuela. Chevron was the last big American firm still there; if Venezuela were ever to be liberated from its leftist dictatorship, the United States would want at least one company still in position, to ensure that Venezuela's $17 trillion oil reserves didn't fall to China.

And now, once again, in the Cabinet Room on March 19, Wirth calmly repeated his arguments to the President. Warning of the dangers of ceding this vital country to China, Wirth pushed for an extension of Chevron's license to operate in Venezuela. Trump appeared to hedge; he told Wirth that what he was saying sounded reasonable, but Venezuela is "a tough issue for us." Little did Wirth know just how tough it would soon get.

Having heard from Wirth about Venezuela, Trump wanted to know more about America's own oil reserves—specifically Alaska's.

Seated across the table from Trump was Ryan Lance, the CEO of ConocoPhillips, who ruled the roost in Alaska. Since 2020, ConocoPhillips had been heavily invested in the Willow project in a wetlands area on the North Slope of Alaska, which had received final government approval during the Biden administration in 2023. Once construction was completed in 2029, the site was expected to yield 576 million barrels of oil over thirty years, with a peak of 180,000 barrels of crude a day. But its wetlands location presented great challenges. There were no roads, so it was only possible to work on the site during winter, once the area was frozen and workers could build ice roads. The conditions were harsh.

Lance explained this to the President, who wanted details. "Don't the trucks slip off the road?" Trump asked.

"No," Lance said. "At a very low temperature, ice actually isn't slippery." And then, to unintentional comic effect, the petroleum engineer explained that "the coefficient of friction at a certain temperature makes the ice not slippery—it's like driving on a regular road." Which struck some around the table as an amusingly wonky detour for a meeting with the President.

Stephen Miller, though, was not amused. After the meeting, he approached Lance with an air of urgency.

"We'll do anything you want us to do to get this construction going," he told the CEO. "But we want this oil produced during this administration."

Lance was not receptive. As gingerly as he could, he conveyed to Miller that the reality at Willow was not subject to any authority he might have to offer. Unfortunately, the White House could not rewrite the laws of physics. There were also legal considerations.

But Miller was insistent. "I'm *giving* you the authority to do this," he replied.

12

The cabinet meeting for Thursday, March 6, had been called abruptly, just the night before. Tensions between DOGE and the rest of the administration had reached a boiling point. "Why isn't Elon letting these people manage their own departments?" Trump asked his aides, as if surprised by the conflict he had set in motion. Susie Wiles encouraged the officials who were concerned about Musk's tactics to speak up in the meeting so that the President could hear.

At long last, they would duke it out. There was room for Elon Musk or an executive branch full of cabinet officials. But not both.

Musk was letting Rubio have it. Why, he demanded, hadn't Rubio slashed his staff yet?

And Rubio wasn't going to take it anymore. He was the U.S. secretary of state—seated beside the President in the Cabinet Room, and being subjected to an attack from the richest man in the world, who was growing increasingly hysterical.

"You haven't fired anyone!" Musk barked, scornfully adding that perhaps the only person Rubio had fired was a staff member from Musk's own Department of Government Efficiency. Rubio had been angry with Musk since the mess at USAID. But now the enmity was erupting in full view, and Rubio would have his say.

Musk was lying, Rubio retorted. What about the more than 1,500 State

Department officials who took early retirement in buyouts because they didn't like the direction Trump and Rubio were steering the administration? "They retired early," Rubio snapped. "If you'd like, I can rehire all of them and fire all of them if it makes you feel better?"

"How many people have you fired, then?" Musk persisted. "Tell me. Give me the names."

"You want me to produce all the names right now?" Rubio asked, incredulous. "Like, every single person?"

"Yeah, that's proof," Musk said. "If you have the proof, give me the names right now in front of everybody."

"This is ridiculous," Rubio replied.

To show he was in command of his department—and demonstrate to Trump that he was up to the task—Rubio then carefully laid out his plans for reorganizing State.

Musk was unimpressed. "You're good on TV," he told Rubio, implying that he was not good for much else. The spat continued for fifteen minutes, but seemed much longer. The atmosphere in the room was equal parts absurdity and futility, and while Rubio held his own, arguing with Musk was like walking into a lawn mower blade, and it was not clear who would prevail.

Throughout this pitched battle, the President sat back in his chair, arms folded, taking it all in. After an uncomfortably long time, Trump finally intervened to defend Rubio, who he said was doing a "great job." Marco has a lot to deal with, the President said. He is very busy, he is always traveling and on TV, and he has a department to run. So everyone just needs to work together, he added.

Rubio wasn't the only cabinet secretary to have it out with Musk that day.

Musk went at it, too, with Sean Duffy, the transportation secretary. Duffy argued that Musk's team was trying to lay off air traffic controllers just as he was dealing with fatalities attributed to mixed air traffic around the Washington airport named for Ronald Reagan. What am I supposed to do? Duffy said, noting there had been a yearslong shortage of people manning the towers. I have multiple plane crashes to deal with now, and your people want me to fire air traffic controllers.

That's a lie, Musk shot back.

It's not, Duffy replied. I've heard it from them directly.

Musk asked who on the DOGE staff had been pushing to fire air traffic controllers. Give me their names, he demanded. Tell me their names.

It doesn't matter what the names are, Duffy said. Because I stopped them from being fired.

Musk claimed that Duffy had hired people under DEI programs who were still working in control towers.

No we don't, Duffy snapped. Give me names. Who? Duffy demanded.

Musk did not provide any.

Suddenly alert to the mention of the air traffic controllers, Trump told Duffy he should hire people from MIT, the elite research university in Boston. These air traffic controllers need to be "geniuses," Trump said, as if he were taking part in an entirely different conversation.

Veterans Affairs Secretary Doug Collins had faced what may have been the most politically delicate task among Trump's cabinet members. The workforce reductions driven by Musk stood to impact thousands of veterans—a group that carried significant political clout and represented a key segment of Trump's supporters. Collins argued for a targeted approach rather than sweeping, indiscriminate cuts across the VA. Trump expressed agreement, saying they should retain the smart ones and get rid of the bad ones.

At the peak of the tension, EPA administrator Lee Zeldin chimed in. "I don't know about everyone, but I'm pretty happy!" he chirped. "I've got no problems." Zeldin drew some dirty looks.

Cabinet officials all liked Musk's mission—reducing waste, fraud, and abuse in government—but they had been outraged by his haphazard cuts and impossible demands. And they were starting to suspect that he might not know exactly what he was doing. Running a cabinet agency was a heavy-enough lift without Musk's chainsaw hacking off their limbs. It had put them in an impossible position. Republican members of Congress had begun to call the White House to complain about the impact of DOGE on jobs in their districts.

Throughout the meeting, Musk repeatedly sought to assert his dominance by invoking his wealth. He stressed that he had multiple companies with market caps in the billions. I know what I'm doing, he said. My results speak for themselves, he crowed.

But perhaps there were differences after all between how a business was run and how government was meant to function. "You know," one witness to the meeting would say later, "there are laws, there are constituencies, there are politics. We're not just juicing shareholder value here. You know, different deal."

"Look," observed a cabinet official who was at the meeting, "it's not the President who gets hauled before the Senate and it's not the White House staff. Who is it? Me. And other cabinet members."

Trump tried to conciliate finally, praising the efforts of both Musk and the cabinet secretaries. But from then on, he pronounced, the secretaries would be in charge. Musk and his team would only advise.

Musk, who had been furious since the reaction to his "What Did You Do Last Week?" email, did not initially appear to grasp what had just happened. The shockingly rancorous meeting had exposed the depth of the animus DOGE had created among Trump's team. After the meeting, Trump went to his Truth Social account and posted that the next phase of his plan to cut the federal workforce would be conducted with a "scalpel" rather than a "hatchet."

Elon Musk had roared into the new administration, just six weeks earlier, as a self-styled demolition man. A guy with a chainsaw. What was he supposed to do with a scalpel?

"We saw another side of Elon today," said a senior aide soon after the meeting. "He was nasty."

In reasserting the authority of the cabinet secretaries over DOGE, Trump was clipping Musk's wings. At the next cabinet meeting, Trump told Musk that they had an election coming up the following year, and we can't keep firing all these people. You can get rid of waste, fraud, and abuse, Trump said, but you can't fire anybody else. Privately, Trump was already telling associates Musk's time in the White House would soon end. But winding Musk down would have to be done carefully. For a while yet he would remain a perpetual presence in the West Wing, often still at the center of critical conversations.

II

Just days after Musk's blowup with the cabinet secretaries, the White House hosted the Technology CEO Council. Gathered in the Roosevelt Room on March 10 were the leaders of some of the world's most iconic tech firms—IBM, Dell, HPE, HP Inc., Qualcomm, and Intel.

"I'm shitting bricks about our vulnerability to China," Musk announced. He had built Tesla with China's help, and he'd paid for it with flattery—praising the Communist Party's leaders and waving off concerns about authoritarianism. But Musk had grown increasingly alarmed in recent years, especially over the threat of a Chinese invasion of Taiwan, which would jeopardize the supply of high-end chips that Musk's companies depended on. And now, with these CEOs as his audience, Musk was frantically sounding the alarm about the fact that an island country roughly the size of Maryland, floating eighty-one miles off mainland China, produced around 70 percent of all the semiconductors on earth and 90 percent of the most advanced chips. He was lecturing a gathering more familiar with this problem than perhaps any other group of people in the world.

But Musk kept banging away. "If we don't start building chips outside the zone of confrontation," he said, "we are headed for disaster." He reiterated the point: "Somebody's got to build the damn fabs [fabrication plants] outside the battle zone!"

The President interjected, saying that Xi Jinping had assured him that "China won't invade Taiwan while I am President. Could be lying," Trump added. "Taiwan is the apple of Xi's eye, just like Ukraine was for Putin."

Howard Lutnick added that the President was focused on semiconductor manufacturing and the supply chain coming to the U.S. "Taiwan is eating our lunch, how do we bring the supply chain home?" That steered the group conversation to how American companies had fallen behind on EUV—extreme ultraviolet lithography—the high-tech process used in semiconductor manufacturing to etch intricate patterns on silicon wafers. A single Taiwanese company, TSMC, accounted for more than half of the global EUV system installations to make the most advanced chips.

"The U.S. gave it all away," Trump said. "Ninety-nine percent of the business is in Taiwan."

"Chip fab capacity in the U.S. is weak," Musk said. "Especially for the most advanced chips. The United States will only have thirty percent of TSMC's capacity in 2029. If China invades Taiwan," he said, "the entire economy crashes."

"What keeps the Taiwanese ahead?" Trump asked.

It was a good question—it was *the* question. TSMC, the world's largest chipmaker, had pioneered a model that separated chip design from manufacturing—allowing it to make chips for other companies without competing with them, and creating a global market virtually from scratch. No one had caught up. In an effort to try, Congress had passed the CHIPS and Science Act in 2022, providing billions in subsidies and tax credits to incentivize companies to build new fabrication plants in the U.S. In his address to Congress just days before, Trump had called the law "a horrible, horrible thing"—because it hands out billions to rich companies—and urged lawmakers to get rid of it.

"Aren't you better positioned by being here?" Trump asked his guests. "No tariffs, less risk?"

One of the CEOs pointed out it took time to "shift ecosystems."

Another cautioned that scaling up would be a slow process. TSMC has all its customers helping them stay in front, he explained.

Musk chimed in: "We know; we're one of them!"

"What do we need to do to get you to commit to building new factories in the United States of America?" Lutnick asked the CEOs.

"Those who won't build here are going to have massive tariffs to pay . . . not 20 percent, like 100 percent," said Trump. "We're treated so unfairly, China tariffs us over 150 to 200 percent, India 175 percent."

"We have to have the components here," responded one CEO. "We need the full ecosystem."

"How are you doing with the European Union?" Trump asked. "Are they among the most difficult?"

"We don't build in the EU," said the CEO. "We make in Asia and import."

"They kind of leave us alone," said another CEO. "No one in Europe makes what we make."

"We lost ninety thousand factories with NAFTA," said Trump. "Maybe we can get them back. Autos are building in the U.S. They just stopped building three plants in Mexico. Canada tariffs our dairy at three hundred percent."

"April 2!" said Lutnick, referring to Trump's planned Liberation Day tariffs.

The room, overstuffed with dealmakers, crackled with possibility. After the President left, the others lingered, still consumed by the semiconductor problem.

Lutnick had something to ask of the CEOs, a mission to enlist them in—could they help him stop the President from doing something rash? Lutnick had been trying to persuade Trump against acting so hastily to impose steep tariffs on semiconductors. It was unrealistic to expect American tech companies to immediately end their reliance on foreign suppliers. Moving manufacturing to the U.S. would require a transitional period and Lutnick did not want to see U.S. companies at a competitive disadvantage. He encouraged the CEOs to take their message directly to Trump to reinforce what he was telling the President behind the scenes. "I need more voices calling in, texting, in his ear," he said.

"How do we avoid getting screwed on AI chips by China?" Musk asked the group.

"We need to force foreign countries to align with the U.S.," added one of the CEOs.

"Someplace unlikely to be bombed," Musk replied.

13

Natalie, give me the real numbers," the President called out. "Do your Google, do your computer thing, and give me the real numbers."

Sitting on a wooden chair with her back against a wall in the Oval Office, Natalie Harp frantically googled on her laptop. Harp's devotion to the President had remained undimmed through the hectic early months of the second term. Trump had taken to telling his staff that Natalie (or "Nathalie," as he would call her, using a French pronunciation) was the only one who loved him as much as his wife and kids. "All of you will go off and make money," he would say. "She'll never leave me."

Now, in the middle of a very tense meeting on March 26 with the President's economic team on the tariff strategy, Harp was trying to hunt down better information for the President than his staff had provided him.

"Nobody has fucking given me any numbers," Trump fumed. "Hard facts of how much China tariffs us, how much India tariffs us. You give me bullshit numbers."

Commerce Secretary Howard Lutnick pulled out a folder, saying, "Here are the numbers. Here are the numbers on how much each country is tariffing us."

But Trump was convinced that the real numbers for India and China were much higher than Lutnick's printouts. "No, these are bullshit numbers," he said, giving Lutnick a hard look. "These are fucking bullshit."

Harp, despite her best efforts, was not finding the numbers that didn't exist.

"No, these *are* the real numbers!" Lutnick insisted. "They come from USTR [the Office of the United States Trade Representative]." Turning to the President's trade representative, Jamieson Greer, Lutnick pleaded, "Right, Jamieson? Jamieson, say these numbers are real. Jamieson, speak up."

Greer, a trade lawyer who was not inclined to get into a spat with the President, just looked at Lutnick and said nothing.

The President's global tariff program, set to launch on "Liberation Day," was just a week away, but the rates were still undecided. Trump wanted to set the rates using a formula he had been devising in his mind. No one was sure precisely how it was being calculated, and it would vary by the day, sometimes by the hour. But how could he make his calculations with these bullshit numbers from Lutnick?

Adding to Trump's aggravation, Lutnick kept pressing for carve-outs. The commerce secretary was particularly concerned about the steep automobile tariffs that had been the subject of so much earlier discussion with auto executives, and leaders in Canada and Mexico. USMCA needs an exemption, Lutnick argued, referring to the trade alliance between the three countries.

"I told you, Howard, these tariffs are going to happen, and it's going to be fair," Trump said. "Across the board, it's going to be fair. No one gets exceptions. And look, maybe when we do it, then they'll come to the table and they'll be more fair to us. But it's across the board, no one gets exceptions."

Lutnick turned to Peter Navarro, Trump's trade counselor, and among the longest-serving and most loyal of MAGA stalwarts. "Peter, you agree with me," he said. "Tell him. *Tell him.*"

"Don't talk to me like that," Navarro retorted.

Lutnick bristled. "Tell him you agree with me!" he demanded again.

Navarro had a long history of opposing exemptions for tariffs, agreeing with Trump that too many carve-outs had caused problems in term one.

"That's not what you told me outside before this meeting!" Lutnick said. "That's not what you said."

"I don't know what you're talking about," Navarro snapped back. "Howard, you have to drop it!"

An exasperated Lutnick dismissed Navarro. "Why am I talking to you?" he said with a flash of temper.

As the scene unfolded, Stephen Miller and Scott Bessent sat impassively, saying nothing. Just then, Mike Johnson walked into the Oval.

"Hello," Johnson said to the room. "What's going on in here?"

"Good. The Speaker is here," the President said. "Mike, what do you think about a twenty-five percent tariff on foreign car imports?"

Lutnick saw an opening. "Tell him, Mr. Speaker," he said. "This would be a terrible decision because that number is too high! Think of what it will mean to consumers and your voters. . . ."

Everyone turned to Johnson.

"Honestly, sir," Johnson said, "the first thing that comes to my mind is a good friend of mine back home in Louisiana, who is a huge supporter of yours. He also happens to be one of the largest Toyota dealers in my region. I wonder how he is going to react when he hears this news, and what it is going to do to the business he's been in for decades. . . ."

"Yeah, he's gonna get killed," Lutnick said, seizing the opening. "And you're gonna have a hard time explaining this."

"So what do you think we should do?" Trump asked Johnson.

"I think Howard is making a very good point here, sir . . ." Johnson said.

Navarro then counterattacked, and he and Lutnick went at it again.

Cutting them off, Trump said, "All right, we're gonna do a presser. Get the press in here." Turning back to Johnson, he asked, "Why don't you stand right next to me while we talk about this new tariff?"

Johnson, clearly uncomfortable, replied, "Well, I don't know if I should do that. Sir, remember, I will have to be the one to help our House Republicans navigate through this and any fallout, so I shouldn't give any implication that it was my idea."

"Okay, whatever," Trump said. "Do whatever you want to do."

"The markets are going to tank if we don't do the exemptions," said Lutnick. "And you're going to own the market cratering."

"Okay, fine, I'll own it. So what?" Trump said.

The President was intransigent; it appeared to those in the room that he was beyond argument, beyond consequence.

Lutnick, fearing the tariff fallout could spill over into the broader economy, had argued the point as forcefully as he could, but in that moment had failed. Now that Trump had an audience, Lutnick understood there was no upside in continuing the debate. "Look, I understand the boss has made a decision," he told others after the meeting. "Now we just need to execute."

II

Nothing like Liberation Day had ever happened before.

The President had first referred to November 5, 2024, Election Day, as "Liberation Day." After the election, he took to calling January 20, 2025—Inauguration Day—Liberation Day. In mid-March, he began to hint without details or formal announcement, that April 2, 2025, would be the real Liberation Day. That day, the President declared, would "forever be remembered as the day that American industry was reborn, the day America's destiny was reclaimed, and the day that we began to make America wealthy again."

On April 2, claiming a national emergency, Trump imposed a baseline tariff of 10 percent on imports from every country, with an added "reciprocal" tariff on top of that, which had been calculated for each country through a formula that several top administration officials would privately describe as ill-conceived.

The closest precedent to the scale of Trump's tariffs—the Smoot-Hawley Tariff Act of 1930—had taken eighteen months of fierce congressional debate, drawn a public warning from over a thousand economists, and still proved catastrophic, triggering retaliatory tariffs that deepened the Depression. Trump had long cited Herbert Hoover's fate as a cautionary tale. And yet on April 2, 2025, he would announce a tariff regime that would dwarf Smoot-Hawley—born not from hearings or expert consultation but from a handful of Oval Office meetings and his own instincts.

In the days leading up to April 2, Lutnick and Bessent had shared the duty of calling their counterparts around the world to warn them. These warnings were vague, though, as they still didn't know what Trump would do. Trump didn't know, either; he hadn't decided. So they simply urged other countries not to retaliate, assuring them the tariff rates Trump would announce could be negotiated down.

Trump wanted to apply maximum pressure and keep his true intentions hidden, whatever they may have been. "He wants you to be uncomfortable," Lutnick would tell an associate. "If he [sets the number] high, and you're like, 'We can't do that.' Then he's like, 'Well, what *can* you do?'"

Bessent's greatest concern was that the markets hated what he called "uncapped risk." If Trump made clear that the numbers were just starting positions for further negotiations, then the policy might make sense to Wall Street. Bessent would attempt to explain it all in media appearances. Two days before the announcement, he laid it out on *Hannity*, which Trump unsurprisingly had watched. Afterward, he called Bessent and admonished, "Don't tell people they can negotiate down." Trump wanted to maintain maximum leverage and wield it to get the best deals.

A senior administration official likened the approach to a captor torturing a prisoner and then showing a measure of mercy. "In North Korea," the official said, "in the prisons or the camps, when you go in for the first two years they blindfold you and put you on your knees, but you can hear the guard's voice. Then in the second year, he stands you up and he takes your blindfold off, and you're in love with him. So he was conditioning people for that."

But these were not prisoners in North Korea; they were America's key trading partners, and they had leverage, too. The goal of the tariff strategy, meanwhile, wasn't entirely clear to anyone except for perhaps the President and Peter Navarro, who believed in tariffs as an article of faith. It was Navarro primarily—with some assistance from the Council of Economic Advisers—who had helped craft the rudimentary tariff formula, which Trump had settled on only the night before the announcement. The tariff rate for each country was calculated by taking the 2024 U.S. trade deficit with the specific country, dividing it by the total value of goods the U.S. imported from the country, and then halving the result.

Lutnick didn't like Navarro's formula at all, "because I graduated ninth grade," he would tell associates. Trump's team had also discussed a color-coded three-tiered tariff scheme—low/medium/high, green/yellow/red, 10 percent/15 percent/25 percent. The vice president thought it was elegant, but Trump thought it was too complicated, because no one could figure out which countries belonged in what category, and where to draw the line.

One Republican senator said later that he could not believe "how poorly thought through the tariff strategy was. It's not clear what their objective is, let alone their strategy. And it seemed to change from day to day. Sometimes the stated goal was to raise revenue. Sometimes it was to eliminate the trade deficit with every country. Sometimes it was a negotiating tool."

When a friend wished Scott Bessent a "Happy Liberation Day," he answered, "More like Happy Libation Day."

The next day, as the tariff plan was getting thrashed in the press, Trump would begin blaming Navarro to others, privately complaining about "Peter's stupid fucking numbers."

III

As expected, the markets plummeted in the days following April 2. The S&P 500 would lose more than $2 trillion on a single day. On April 3 and 4, the Dow Jones Industrial Average would decline by almost 10 percent, and the volatility in the days thereafter made the Dow look like the EKG of a heart attack patient. Worse still, the typical inverse relationship between the stock market and the bond market, where the bond market became a safe haven in times of stock market convulsion, was not holding. Both were plunging, with the bond market experiencing a historic sell-off, a frightful sign that investors were seeking their safe havens away from the U.S.

Scott Bessent reached out to the chairman of the Federal Reserve, Jerome Powell, urging him to make a statement that would reassure the markets. But, guarding the Fed's independence, Powell declined. He was determined to avoid the impression that the Federal Reserve might step in to rescue Trump from this self-inflicted crisis. If Trump wanted to stabilize the markets, Powell would tell associates, the President could simply reverse his policy.

By the evening of Sunday, April 6, Bessent and Lutnick were more concerned than ever. On an Air Force One flight from Palm Beach back to Washington, Trump was on the phone with his son Don Jr., while Bessent and Lutnick were pressing him. "We're in the middle of a trade war," Trump told his son. "I don't have time to talk."

Bessent tried to persuade Trump that he had gotten the world's attention and had maximum leverage, but that now was a good time to start negotiating. "The market's going to open in a minute," Bessent told the President. "And if you change your mind—or when you lower the rates—it will look like the market forced you to do it. You've got to pivot to talking about launching trade negotiations. Because you're a great dealmaker. You've got to show the markets that you have an endgame, because they're melting."

"It's short term, it's short term," Trump replied. "Scott, it's temporary. The Fed will cut rates."

Bessent walked the President through what he thought "short term" meant for the markets. If things went too far, and they waited too long to act, it might be too late to pull back from the brink.

Where was the edge of the cliff? No one knew. And neither Bessent nor Lutnick wanted to find out. But Trump would hold out with the unreasonably high tariff rates longer than most of his advisors could stomach. The President believed that if he folded too early the world would doubt his seriousness, and he had a much higher tolerance for risk than either Lutnick or Bessent or Wall Street. Bessent would privately marvel at this aspect of Trump's character, which he felt was a key ingredient in his success in politics. He would tell associates that Trump reminded him in this respect of his old boss, the legendary investor and major Democratic donor George Soros.

"They are the same animal," Bessent would say to others. "But George is in the market. President Trump is political. Incredible propensity to take risks, and incredible survival skills. And they oscillate between pushing the risk, cutting the loss."

Lutnick and Bessent had sharply clashed, but the edge of a financial crisis had forced them together with a shared purpose: to coax the President into a de-escalation.

Lutnick continued to impress upon the President that tariffs weren't one-size-fits-all, and that he must not put the major U.S. automakers at a disadvantage.

"Jesus, Howard, you keep bringing me all this shit from all these people," Trump said. "You used to be tough, and then you come to Washington and you're weak."

This had been a frequent line of attack Trump deployed against Lutnick during this tense period—one that recalled their long history in New York.

"You used to be a killer, Howard," the President would say. "I remember when you were thirty-five, you were a killer. And now, you've got your beautiful wife, and your big house, and you're just soft. And you're a pussy. You know what you are? You're a pussy."

Months later, when the tariff revenue really began rolling in and fears of a financial crisis had receded, Lutnick started responding to Trump with a quip of his own. He was, he would tell the President, "your twenty-five-billion-dollar-a-month pussy."

But on that fretful flight to Washington on April 6—with the world's investors holding their collective breath, uncertain of whether Trump would plunge the world into another Great Depression—Lutnick had no choice but to sit there and take it.

IV

Two days after Liberation Day, China retaliated, matching the 34 percent "reciprocal" tariff Trump had announced. Trump threatened that unless Xi Jinping stood down, he would impose an additional 50 percent tariff on goods from China.

Even ardent supporters of the President began to grouse.

In a not-so-subtle admonition against trade wars, Elon Musk posted a video on X of the Nobel Prize–winning conservative economist Milton Friedman rhapsodizing about the virtues of free trade and its capacity to "foster harmony and peace among the peoples of the world." Trump-supporting billionaire investor Bill Ackman also took to X to warn of a "self-induced, economic nuclear winter," and called for the administration to declare a "90-day timeout" on the tariff regime.

Bessent trusted that the President would eventually come down from the obstinately high tariff rates, but he feared the situation could run out of control before that happened.

"You lose leverage if this spills out into the real economy," Bessent told Trump, offering his advice. Bessent used a phrase from his Wall Street days to describe the risk: it was called the "screen going to the street." If that were to happen here it would be perilous, he thought, and hard to reverse, especially if a reactive panic set in.

The signals from the investor class were also becoming apocalyptic. JPMorgan Chase CEO Jamie Dimon told investors that recession was the "likely outcome" of the roiling markets. Legendary hedge fund manager Ray Dalio began warning that investors should focus less on tariffs and more on a "once-in-a-lifetime" breakdown in the political, geopolitical, and monetary systems.

Warner Bros. Discovery canceled all nonessential travel. Delta abruptly scaled back its annual projections. Airlines reduced their flights, assuming less money from travelers to book them. The economy seemed poised for a sharp contraction.

As the investor class prepared for doomsday, Trump posted another astonishing message to Truth Social. He announced that he was pausing the tariffs for ninety days, with one big exception. "Based on the lack of respect that China has shown to the World's Markets, I am hereby raising the Tariff charged to China by the United States of America to 125%, effective immediately," the President wrote in a wild communiqué to the world.

The trade war with China would intensify. But for the rest of the world, a temporary truce had arrived.

That afternoon, the markets surged nearly 10 percent on the news, and Trump surrogates rushed to the cameras to clean up the mess, claiming that pausing the tariffs was the plan all along. This was, they said, a genius negotiating strategy from the dealmaker of dealmakers, despite Lutnick telling CBS News three days earlier that "the tariffs are coming," without delay. The world had just witnessed a master class in economic brinkmanship, they would all say.

But in fact, Trump had blinked. The collapsing bond markets left him no choice. Investors were losing faith that the United States would be able to make good on its debt.

Trump himself would soon go before the cameras and undercut his team's talking points that this had been the plan all along. He made clear that his decision to pause the tariffs had been entirely ad hoc.

"Was this idea of doing a pause—did that just come about this morning?" a reporter asked. "Can you tell us exactly what came into consideration for you and your advisors?"

"For a period of time, I would say this morning, over the last few days, I've been thinking about it," the President said. "I've been dealing with Scott, with Howard, with some other people that are very professional. And I think it probably came together early this morning, fairly early this morning. Just wrote it up. We didn't have the use of, we didn't have access to lawyers. We wrote it up from our hearts, right? . . . It was written from the heart, and I think it was well written, too, but it was written from the heart."

For some in the White House, the whole episode was terrifying. Across the administration, officials were shaken at just how close to financial disaster Trump had willingly brought the United States, and the world.

V

Having weathered the tariff brinkmanship, Bessent was becoming increasingly assertive, feisty even. A week after the tariff pause, there would be a confrontation in the Oval Office that would also serve as a bizarre coda to Elon Musk's tenure.

Musk had taken it upon himself to fire the interim head of the IRS, installing his own interim director, with the goal of cutting the agency in half. Bessent, who by law oversaw the agency, didn't take kindly to this, and he finally had had enough. An argument between the two quickly escalated.

"Fuck you!" the treasury secretary had said to the billionaire.

Musk leaned into Bessent. "Say it louder, I can't hear you!" he taunted.

Fuck you! Bessent repeated.

Again, from Musk: *I can't hear you, say it louder!*

Taking a different tack, Bessent hit Musk where it hurt most—the emerging sense that he had vastly overpromised on what he could accomplish with DOGE.

"Elon, are the savings two trillion?" Bessent sneered. "One trillion? A hundred billion?"

At that, Musk lost it. "Fuck you!" he said. "What have you ever done?"

As Musk and Bessent walked out of the Oval Office, they continued to snap at each other. Then the situation got physical. Musk lowered his shoulder into Bessent, and there was a shove.

Bessent would later tell others that he had developed an "entente cordiale" with both Musk and Lutnick, but at the time, soon after the Musk fight, the treasury secretary told associates that had he not had another meeting to get to, he "would've knocked the shit out of" Musk.

When the President heard about the rumble he had one pressing question: "Who won?" he asked an advisor.

Part II

RETRIBUTION

14

"I am your retribution."

It was a single line in a speech, delivered at the Conservative Political Action Conference at a hotel in National Harbor, Maryland, in March 2023. Donald Trump was months into his third presidential campaign. Just over three weeks later, he would be indicted for the first time.

He would speak so openly about retribution in the months that followed that his campaign advisors worried he was damaging himself politically. "Tone it down," became the whispered note of caution. And so on January 10, 2024, just as Republican primary voters were about to make their preferences known, Trump told Fox News host Bret Baier, "I'm not going to have time for retribution." He added: "Our ultimate retribution is success."

But the reality was that retribution—against critics, prosecutors, investigators, journalists, and even late-night talk show hosts—was always at the top of Trump's second-term agenda.

During his four years out of power, Trump had faced an avalanche of legal troubles, and he would not forget it any time soon. In 2023, he became the first former President in American history to be criminally arraigned. It was a humiliating experience, and Trump, who prized control of his environment at all times, brooded throughout his new life as a full-time defendant. In short order during the spring and summer of that year, he would be criminally indicted four times in state and federal courts on dozens of charges: In March, he was indicted in New York state court on charges he falsified business records to conceal a preelection hush-money payment in 2016 to the porn actress Stormy Daniels to cover up an alleged affair. In June, a federal grand jury in Florida indicted him on charges related to his handling of classified documents after leaving office and for obstructing efforts to recover them. In August, he would be indicted twice, first in a federal court in Washington, D.C., on charges related to his efforts to overturn the 2020 election, and again in Georgia state court on racketeering charges also related to 2020.

But there was one upside to this cascade of indictments. It was all happening at the same time that Trump's presidential campaign was heating up, and the legal onslaught gave his political message an added charge. It delivered nonstop media coverage and the appearance of constant motion as Trump went from one arraignment to another, galvanizing his supporters, torquing his fundraising, and transforming what was already a movement into a force field.

It was also giving the candidate and his staff the sense they were fighting not just for an election, but for their lives. "If I lose, I'm fucked," Trump told an aide as the election grew nearer. "He *has* to win," one senior advisor said after Trump's second indictment landed, a sentiment shared by most in Trump's orbit. Privately, several aides said that they expected to be prosecuted should Kamala Harris win. The stakes were not, in the main, about tax reform or immigration or other policy priorities. This was about staying out of prison. To them, these actions against Trump and his intimates were all illegitimate—an act of legal war via subpoenas, investigations, and indictments. The same senior advisor would say, "I wouldn't want to be the people who did this to him" should Trump make his way back.

And indeed, despite his own complaints about the weaponization of government, Trump immediately sought revenge upon assuming office. Within hours of taking the presidential oath, the Pentagon removed the official portrait of the former chairman of the Joint Chiefs of Staff, General Mark Milley, for whom Trump had particular enmity. In the following days he stripped protective details from Milley and others he had viewed as disloyal, including former National Security Advisor John Bolton, former Secretary of State Mike Pompeo, and former Defense Secretary Mark Esper. All had been targeted for years by Iran, following the U.S. drone strike Trump had ordered that killed General Qassim Suleimani in his first term.

On the same April day that Trump announced his tariff pause, he went even further in his revenge mission. The White House issued a presidential memorandum ordering the Department of Justice to investigate an aide from Trump's first term—Chris Krebs, who had run Homeland Security's Cybersecurity and Infrastructure Security Agency. He also ordered the suspension of the security clearance of former senior Department of Homeland Security official Miles Taylor, who in 2018, writing as "Anonymous," had written a *New York Times* op-ed followed by a book about the "quiet resistance" within the government to counter Trump. Trump directed DHS to "review Miles Taylor's activities as a Government employee." Of Taylor, Trump would say, "I think he's guilty of treason."

Like so much of the policymaking of the administration that came after the pre-staged executive orders queued for day one, the orders issued on that April afternoon were improvised. Trump hadn't even been able to remember Chris Krebs's name. Days earlier, the President had been meeting with a few staff, including his personal counsel Boris Epshteyn and Stephen Miller, when he began to muse about past grievances, saying, "I remember, there was this lawyer who was in the administration who said the election was fair and there's no fraud. Who was he?"

"Oh, the DHS—I think you're talking about the DHS guy," Miller replied. "I forget his name."

Epshteyn pulled out his phone and did a quick search—"Chris Krebs," he said.

"Yeah, Chris Krebs," Trump said. "Whatever happened to him? He was a bad one. Take a look at him."

Miller, who was known as the keeper of grievances, then proceeded to have a presidential memo drawn up, unleashing the resources of the federal government on a man whose sole offense against Trump had been to attest to the security and validity of the 2020 election.

In the first term, Trump had wanted—and had even ordered—Justice Department investigations of his enemies. But those orders, some of which were delivered in private and through intermediaries, had not yielded the results he was looking for. Now, though, he no longer felt the need for middlemen—his targets would be written up in executive actions by his staff secretary and then endorsed by the White House counsel. Retribution was no longer a relatively furtive mission. It was now a very public, driving force of the Trump presidency, and it wouldn't stop with just individuals. The President and his team were determined to also neuter the institutions that had defied him.

II

On February 25, during a routine signing ceremony in the Oval Office, the President paused when he was handed one particular directive to sign. It ordered the suspension of security clearances for staff at Covington & Burling who had lent legal assistance, free of charge, to the investigations led by Jack Smith, the special prosecutor who had indicted Trump twice. Staff Secretary Will Scharf handed Trump the leather-bound order. The President looked almost giddy.

"This is a good one. Is everybody listening? Deranged Jack Smith," Trump said. When a reporter tried to change the subject as he was signing the memo, he cut her off. "I just want to savor this one, please," he said. Howard Lutnick, standing to Trump's left, laughed loudly.

"Who would like this pen?" Trump asked, brandishing the black Sharpie he had used to sign the document. "Here, why don't you send it to Jack Smith? He's a deranged person."

Asked moments later about such a targeted use of presidential power, Trump's giddiness vanished. "Excuse me, I've been targeted for four years," he said. "Longer than that. So you don't tell me about targeting."

More law firms would be targeted. Next up was Perkins Coie, a famous Democratic firm that had employed another Trump enemy, Marc Elias. And then, on March 14, came Executive Order 14237, titled: "Addressing Risks from Paul Weiss."

Paul, Weiss, Rifkind, Wharton & Garrison didn't actually pose a risk to the country. But it had once employed one of Trump's nemeses: Mark Pomerantz, who in 2021 became special assistant district attorney in the office of then-Manhattan District Attorney Cyrus Vance Jr. Pomerantz had been hired for one reason—to investigate the business and personal finances of Donald Trump, who was suspected of bank, insurance, and tax fraud. In late 2022, the new district attorney, Alvin Bragg, won a criminal conviction on tax fraud and falsified business records against the Trump Organization itself; its chief financial officer, Allen Weisselberg, pleaded guilty months earlier to a fraudulent tax scheme. But Weisselberg, who had started with the Trump family working for the President's father, was compensated handsomely by the Trump Organization and refused to cooperate with prosecutors against the President. Trump was not charged, and Pomerantz would resign in frustration. In his resignation letter, Pomerantz wrote that the office's investigation had yielded "evidence sufficient to establish Mr. Trump's guilt beyond a reasonable doubt" and that "the public interest warrants the criminal prosecution of Mr. Trump."

The executive order attacked Pomerantz by name, and threatened Paul Weiss's business by restricting its attorneys' access to federal buildings, including courthouses. But that wasn't the worst part of the order from the Paul Weiss perspective. The executive order threatened any client of Paul Weiss's that their business with the federal government could be terminated if they continued to work with the firm. The firm's clients included some of the most storied brands in America, which had billions of dollars' worth of business with the federal government. The executive order would be one of seven signed by Trump targeting law firms, and one of twelve orders or presidential memos naming specific lawyers. The use of executive orders for such a retributive purpose was both unprecedented and legally dubious.

In the real world, of course, public vilification by a President of the United States was impossible to ignore.

Days after Executive Order 14237 was signed, Brad Karp, the managing partner of Paul Weiss, made his way to the Oval Office. A mutual friend, New England Patriots owner Robert Kraft, had called the President on Karp's behalf two days after the order was signed—vouching for him, and asking whether Karp could come in to see Trump.

Karp's firm would be the first to raise the white flag in the face of such an unprovoked attack from the White House, but not the last. Karp would explain to confidants that Paul Weiss clients were calling in and telling him that "as much as we love you, if you don't resolve this with the Trump administration we will have no choice but to cut off business with the firm." Making matters worse, rival firms were targeting Paul Weiss's most valuable partners for recruitment as the Trump order threatened their business. So although Paul Weiss could have fought the President in court and likely won, Karp was convinced the 150-year-old firm would not have survived the battle.

Paul Weiss was one of the top white-shoe practices in the United States, with $2.63 billion in gross revenue the previous year. It also had a sterling history of pro bono civil rights work; Paul Weiss attorneys had assisted Thurgood Marshall in *Brown v. Board of Education* and took on Edie Windsor's landmark gay marriage case. But now its managing partner had judged the firm defenseless in the face of an all-out attack from the President.

Brad Karp entered the Oval Office on March 19, hoping to negotiate a deal to save his firm. The President walked in, joined by several aides, including Boris Epshteyn, and they all took a seat.

The original idea to target Covington had come from Stephen Miller's operation, but Epshteyn had picked up the broader concept and run with it. He was now in the driver's seat on the Paul Weiss deal. Those with a connection to anything judged "politicized" and injurious to Trump would have to be "held accountable," Epshteyn told others. This meeting marked a vindication.

Epshteyn had a long and sometimes fraught history with the Trumps—highly valued by the President as an enforcer, but viewed by many in his circle as a liability. He had known the family since meeting Eric Trump at Georgetown. But even Eric had privately complained to confidants over the years about Epshteyn's approach. His determination to stay as close as possible to Donald Trump and aggressively deliver perceived wins had led to his own indictment in Arizona the previous April, for his alleged role in a conspiracy to certify a slate of fake electors, though the case would suffer a blow in 2025 and it was unclear whether it would continue. In congressional testimony that year, the special counsel, Jack Smith, named Epshteyn as one of the unindicted co-conspirators in the 2020 election case against Trump.

Trump would joke about how Epshteyn could spin any development—good or bad—as a positive. But he liked Epshteyn and credited him with assembling a legal defense team that helped Trump stay out of prison. Where Epshteyn's money came from once the new administration began was less clear. He insisted to associates that he was never paid for pardons, never lobbied the President on anyone's behalf to receive them, and never sought retainer agreements from corporate officials—though some of those officials said privately that he had.

During the transition, Epshteyn had been accused of approaching prospective second-term appointees with a proposal that they pay him a retainer. For what, exactly, it was sometimes unclear. According to an internal review conducted shortly after the election, Epshteyn had allegedly lunched with Scott Bessent—who had spent more than a year seeking to become treasury secretary—in February 2024 and requested a "stipend" of $30,000 or $40,000 a month to promote Bessent at Mar-a-Lago. Bessent told others he had refused and called his own media consultant to complain. "I can't believe this asshole just shook me down," he said, according to the review.

That summer, according to the same review, after Bessent's name surfaced as a potential treasury secretary, Epshteyn allegedly pressed him again, this time suggesting a $10 million "investment" in a three-on-three basketball league he was promoting. Bessent told others he had refused, and the relationship soured. A week after the election, Bessent claimed to have heard through the grapevine that Epshteyn was "knifing him" at Mar-a-Lago, trying to torpedo his cabinet prospects. In Bessent's telling, Epshteyn told him over the phone: "You should have done what I told you.... I'm Boris fucking Epshteyn."

Epshteyn denied trying to shake down Bessent or anyone else. The conversations described in the review were either confected or misconstrued, he told associates; he had discussed a public relations contract with

Bessent, and the phone call was simply Epshteyn saying it was too late to help.

Trump had directed his incoming White House counsel, David Warrington, to investigate complaints about Epshteyn. Warrington issued a strong warning in a summary of his findings: "Epshteyn's conduct must be stopped and his employment and proximity to President Trump should be terminated. Otherwise, his conduct will likely lead to, at best a scandal involving the incoming Trump Administration, and at worst could lead to criminal indictments."

But Bessent did not make the allegations under oath. Ron Wyden, the ranking Democrat on the Senate Finance Committee, would release a letter saying that before Bessent's confirmation hearing, the nominee told the senator that Epshteyn had talked to him about a "public relations" retainer. After the hearing, according to Wyden, Bessent said in a written answer that no one had ever asked him for money in connection with his appointment.

And so here was Boris Epshteyn, back in the Oval Office. One advisor said that Trump simply liked him, describing Epshteyn as "my psychiatrist." "He's highly neurotic, but it's controlled," Trump would say approvingly. Other aides called him the "good news guy," but one said that Trump admitted that sometimes it was just nice to have someone tell him everything was going to be okay.

Another close advisor explained that Trump liked to keep people like Epshteyn close at hand. He valued lawyers he thought would do anything for him. Trump had also learned through bitter experience that it was unwise to make enemies of former aides—especially those privy to his secrets. In his first term, he had followed the advice of his lawyers and kept a safe distance from those caught up in scandals, among them Roger Stone, Paul Manafort, and Michael Cohen. Now, with a Congress that would not check him and presidential immunity afforded by the landmark 2024 *Trump v. United States* ruling, Trump had little reason to heed Warrington's warning.

"The people who think they killed Boris, they didn't," a senior aide would say. "They only made him stronger."

Back in the Oval, Epshteyn watched as the President flexed his power over the chairman of Paul Weiss.

Confounding some members of Trump's team, Brad Karp had come to the White House alone. Trump opened with a mini tour of the Oval Office, guiding him around the room, pointing out the oil paintings and a framed copy of the Declaration of Independence. During the show-and-tell, Karp mentioned that he'd had a heart attack two months earlier.

As they sat down, Trump asked the group if they were okay with him dialing in one of his attorneys. "Get Giuffra on the phone," he called out to an aide. Robert Giuffra—co-chair of Sullivan & Cromwell, another top Manhattan white-shoe firm, and Trump's lawyer—would listen to the entire meeting on speakerphone. He was expected to help Epshteyn hammer out the Paul Weiss deal. Trump was looking for a massive dollar figure to tout to the public.

Karp took a seat in the middle of a row of chairs facing the President's desk. Epshteyn and Steve Witkoff flanked him on the left, Susie Wiles on the right. What followed was a very long discussion of golf; Trump regaled the group with his recent tournament victory. Then he launched into a litany of grievances about his opponents—remarkably calm even as he excoriated them in the most brutal terms. He let loose on E. Jean Carroll, who had won a sexual-abuse judgment against him and had been represented by Karp's former law partner Roberta Kaplan. He complained about his two impeachments and took a swipe at Mark Pomerantz.

Through all of it, Karp mostly listened. Trump was genial, often flashing a broad smile, and spent very little time on the specifics of the Paul Weiss matter. Both men appeared to understand the endgame: Trump wanted a symbolic victory over the firm, and Karp was prepared to give him one.

Karp had offered an initial settlement of $25 million in pro bono legal services, mutually agreed upon by both sides. Epshteyn later told others he thought they could have gotten $100 million if they'd just asked. But as Karp was leaving the Oval Office, Trump turned to him and said, "So you'll give us forty million?"

Karp said he thought the deal was for $25 million. Trump smiled and repeated that he wanted forty. So $40 million it would be. The President directed Karp, Epshteyn, and Giuffra to work out the particulars.

Over the next twenty-four hours, Epshteyn negotiated aggressively, pushing Paul Weiss to commit to pro bono work on "weaponization" for the administration. Karp refused. With Giuffra playing mediator, they landed on three uncontroversial areas: combating antisemitism, promoting fairness in the criminal justice system, and assisting veterans. Paul Weiss would pledge $40 million in legal work across those causes over the next four years.

In substantive terms, the deal was almost meaningless—a short written agreement describing pro bono work the firm already did. Paul Weiss would easily surpass $40 million in those three areas just by continuing to operate as normal. But the headline number, with its appearance of a staggering concession, would add to Trump's power and the fear he could wield to bring more firms to heel.

When a senior Trump aide was told that Paul Weiss's capitulation had made everyone afraid of the President, the aide replied: "Good. They should be afraid."

Epshteyn gloated to friends about the deal and bragged about his new leverage over Karp. As one recalled: "Boris says, 'I'm in a pretty good place now. I'm the chairman of Paul Weiss.'"

But he had much larger plans. Within days, Skadden, Arps, Slate, Meagher & Flom had agreed to do pro bono work for initiatives favored by the President. Trump hadn't targeted Skadden in an executive order, but the firm said it was acting "proactively" to avoid any prospect of one. Trump's advisors treated each settlement as the new precedent. This time, the baseline figure would be $100 million.

III

By publicly marking individuals or entities for retribution by decree, and having his targets crumble in anticipation of such attacks, Trump had effectively opened up a new front for the second term, terrorizing his foes. And it would not stop with Paul Weiss.

Ever since Covington & Burling was targeted, the leadership of Harvard University had been on high alert. By the second week of April, lawyers for Harvard had been in talks for weeks with the administration's new antisemitism task force, hoping to agree on measures to ensure the safety of Jewish students on campus. This was in the wake of the previous year's demonstrations against the war in Gaza, when some students had been subjected to verbal abuse and physical assault.

Harvard was intent on avoiding the treatment that Columbia University had received just the month before, when administrators there had been informed that unless the school gave in to a list of demands that went far beyond concerns over antisemitism, more than $400 million in federal grants would be withheld, on orders from the White House.

When the broadside against Columbia came, members of the Harvard Corporation suspected they would be next. Lawyers for the university were already engaged in what they had seen as productive talks with Trump administration attorneys. And then, on the night of Friday, April 11, Harvard lawyers received an emailed letter that was so severe in its demands that it amounted to something close to a federal seizure of the university and the takeover of its prerogatives.

Harvard, in Cambridge, Massachusetts, was the oldest, richest, and most prestigious institution of higher learning in the country, with an illustrious history dating back to 1636. It had long relied on federal grants to fund vital research across a wide variety of disciplines, from public health studies to medical research to scientific discoveries in genetics and neuroscience, technology and engineering.

But concerns about the progressive bent of higher education had been a long-standing Republican focus going back decades. And the anti-Israel protests on campuses all over the country in 2024—and what Trump and many on the Right saw as university administrators' feckless indulgence of leftist students—had further fueled that anger among conservatives. Now Trump saw an opportunity to leverage federal dollars to crack down on these institutions, which he and many of his supporters saw as hotbeds of anti-Americanism and "woke" ideology. The very real menace of resurgent antisemitism on college campuses would provide the opening and the pretext.

Trump had more leverage than he had initially realized. All told, that spring the federal government had existing commitments to Harvard totaling nearly $9 billion in grants. When an aide informed him of this fact, on April 1, over lunch in his private dining room, Trump had wondered out loud, "What if we never pay them? Wouldn't that be cool?"

The April 11 letter, which was signed by the General Services Administration, the Department of Education, and the Department of Health and Human Services, essentially demanded government control over hiring and admissions at the university, subject to oversight and an annual audit through 2028. It proposed to police "viewpoint diversity" in both hiring and admissions. It demanded that the university overhaul its governance to the Trump administration's specifications. It insisted that the university immediately "shutter" any DEI programs, offices, committees, positions, and initiatives, and that Harvard "demonstrate that it has done so to the satisfaction of the federal government." The letter also mandated that Harvard, working in conjunction with the government, would audit "programs and departments that most fuel antisemitic harassment or reflect ideological capture" and punish any associated faculty found culpable.

Whether the Antisemitism Task Force or the White House had actually intended to go that far would soon be lost in the war of words that followed. As it turned out, the letter had been in draft form when it was mistakenly emailed to Harvard's lawyers just before midnight on April 11. The email had been intended only for internal circulation inside the Trump administration, and not for the president of Harvard just yet. But once it was made public, the White House didn't retreat from its demands. Harvard's president, Alan Garber, and the rest of the Harvard Corporation had been readying themselves for just such an assault, but did not expect anything of this magnitude. In a Zoom call over the weekend, members of the Harvard leadership team were in total agreement that the university must file suit immediately.

The stand on principle would not be a painless act. Garber's defiance provoked a quick response from the White House, with the Antisemitism Task Force immediately announcing that it would freeze $2.6 billion in federal grants to the university. Then the White House proceeded to pound Harvard over the next several months, using every lever in reach. The university's leadership watched as Stephen Miller's top policy hand, May

Mailman, herself a Harvard-trained lawyer, became more resourceful by the day in devising new ways to hurt the institution.

The administration moved to cut Harvard off from federal funding entirely—from the National Institutes of Health to the Department of Defense. Trump called for Harvard to lose its tax-exempt status. The Department of Homeland Security demanded records on foreign student visas, and when it deemed Harvard's response insufficient, the administration moved to revoke the university's ability to enroll foreign students at all. Trump then issued a proclamation barring international students and scholars from entering the country to attend Harvard. In a final blow, the Education Department reported Harvard to its accreditor, threatening the university's very standing as an institution.

In Cambridge, an awareness dawned: *They're not going to stop.* The Trump administration's onslaught was so intense, so relentless, that the leaders of the premier university in the country worried at the time that this battle could severely damage Harvard and perhaps profoundly change the university.

But they joined the fight nonetheless. And over the course of a punishing year, Harvard would go on to sue the administration twice and would notch up victories in lower courts over research funding and international student visas. The government would be forced to release more than $2 billion in frozen funds to Harvard, but by the end of 2025 the university's fate would still be hanging in limbo in the appeals court.

IV

The retribution campaign that yielded the quickest results for Trump was the crusade against the news media. As would become the pattern across industries, the default response would be capitulation.

The shot across the bow had been Trump's lawsuit against George Stephanopoulos and ABC News, filed months before Election Day. Trump claimed that the anchor of the network's flagship Sunday news show had defamed him when saying on air in 2024 that Trump had been found liable in a civil case for raping the writer E. Jean Carroll. The jury had found Trump liable for sexual abuse and defamation of Carroll, but had rejected the specific count of rape. Even though the judge in the case later said his own interpretation of the verdict was that Trump "raped" Carroll in the common parlance, and Stephanopoulos had displayed a news story describing the judge's view, the Trump team had been proud of the jury's verdict on that count.

Proving that actual malice was involved on Stephanopoulos's part would have been a very tall order, but shortly after Election Day, ABC News' parent company, Disney, looked to settle the suit. They did not want a multiyear court battle that had been filed in a district in Florida, where judges tended to be more favorable toward Trump. The legal challenge could also have been used to contest the landmark press freedom ruling by the Supreme Court in *New York Times Co. v. Sullivan*. The cost to the company may have been steep, especially with a vindictive President, whose government oversaw the licensing of local affiliates of broadcast networks. As a settlement, initially, Disney offered $500,000. The Trump team made clear at the outset it wanted much more.

In early December 2024, the President-elect's advisors and Disney had agreed on the framework of a settlement: $3 million to a charity for military veterans that the two sides would have to agree on. Trump also wanted a personal apology from the anchor. Stephanopoulos did not apologize, but he soon had what was deemed a "cordial" meeting with the President-elect at Trump Tower, and the situation seemed to have been resolved. But days later, the Trump team began trying to change the terms. Boris Epshteyn had told associates the President could get a vastly higher sum from Disney—$60 million, if not more. Suddenly Trump was no longer interested in the deal he had previously agreed to. Now that he had been told he could get more money, he wanted to try. After the Trump team discarded the initial framework, the only option Disney would agree to was to donate to the future Trump presidential library, where the public could track the donation. The sum of $15 million was discussed by the two sides; Trump agreed and then changed his mind again, while the lawyers prepared for a court-ordered mediation session to take place on December 13. The judge had scheduled depositions for Trump and Stephanopoulos to take place a few weeks later. Disney executives balked at efforts to keep raising the price;

they were concerned, too, about maneuvers by some on the Trump team to steer the money to an advocacy group aligned with the incoming President, and were moving forward with the court case.

By the end of the mediation session, Trump appeared to accept he had hit his limit, and the deal was entered with the court. It would be $15 million, put in escrow for an eventual Trump presidential library account, plus $1 million for Trump's legal fees, which had been covered for years by donors to his political action committee.

From there, the Trump team turned to CBS News. Trump had grown infuriated with the network's probing and critical coverage of his first presidency and the legal avalanche that followed him out of office, and he was determined to now shape and punish the network.

Kamala Harris had sat down for a preelection interview with the CBS flagship news program *60 Minutes*, which aired on October 7, 2024. (Trump, who had a contentious history with the program, demanded a number of preconditions for an interview himself that CBS refused to meet.) CBS first aired an extended version of a rambling and somewhat incoherent answer Harris gave to a question about Middle East policy. The next day, *60 Minutes* aired a much shorter edit from her response. The minor discrepancy—the product of editing, which was any broadcaster's prerogative—was suddenly fresh fodder for Trump's team. They began a weeks-long campaign against CBS to release the full transcript of the interview, insisting Harris's answers had been edited deceptively to portray her in a more flattering light. CBS believed it would have been unfair to Harris to simply release the entire transcript, something they hadn't discussed before setting up the interview, and which would set a precedent for the future. Their answer was no.

Trump's subsequent lawsuit, filed in Texas, a place where neither he nor CBS were located, accused the program and the network of "partisan and unlawful acts of election and voter interference," with the goal of pushing the election Harris's way. Trump's legal action alleged he had suffered "mental anguish" as a result. It was a preposterous claim, but to the shock of network executives, the judge in the case declined to dismiss the suit.

Now, back as President, Trump could inflict his payback. And there was added leverage. CBS was owned by Paramount Global, the entertainment conglomerate mired in debt and run by media scion Shari Redstone. In July 2024, she had announced a merger with Skydance Media, a production company owned by David Ellison, son of the multibillionaire tech executive Larry Ellison. While Trump liked Larry, who was one of his own political donors, he would grouse about the son, who had donated nearly $1 million to support Joe Biden's reelection. Paramount's own parent company needed the FCC to approve its merger with Skydance, a deal that would bring Redstone more than $500 million. This was a concern that floated in the background; no federal approval meant no deal.

In the meantime, Trump advisors had made it clear to Paramount that an apology and some money were going to be required to settle the *60 Minutes* suit. For veteran CBS News executives, an apology when they hadn't actually erred was unfathomable.

Boris Epshteyn oversaw the negotiations for the Trump team. Someone in the President's orbit initially floated $100 million for a settlement. But Paramount executives insisted that they would not pay any more than the $16 million Disney had coughed up.

Eventually, CBS News president Wendy McMahon and Bill Owens, the long-serving *60 Minutes* executive producer, agreed to release the full Harris transcript. But with no apology. It almost didn't matter; the list of grievances from the new administration was now down at the microscopic level. The administration had begun scrutinizing individual *60 Minutes* segments that had displeased the President. In April 2025, Owens resigned, later saying he had been encouraged to soften coverage of Trump. McMahon resigned a month later, saying she and the company did not agree "on the path forward."

Near midnight on July 1, Paramount said it had reached a $16 million settlement with Trump. The money would go to the Trump presidential library. Unlike the Disney deal, Trump advisors claimed privately that there was some flexibility in deciding the precise amount the library would receive from Paramount. *60 Minutes* agreed, too, that it would release full transcripts of future presidential candidate interviews, a change in network policy. Redstone, on advice of her lawyers, had recused herself from the Paramount board vote on the settlement.

For such a mighty news organization—once known as the "the Tiffany Network," as a mark of its prestige—this was a devastating moment in a history that was part and parcel of modern America. CBS had started out almost one hundred years before in 1927 as a radio network, United Independent Broadcasters; it became the Columbia Broadcasting System in 1928, and went into television thirteen years later in 1941. It had delivered the news from every front across the American experience. It had withstood—and indeed stood up to—the vicious and censorious era of the red-baiter Joe McCarthy. CBS had helped to shape the protocols, along with scores of other media companies from newspapers to radio and TV, of what courageous journalism meant. And now it had been brought to its knees. Trump had sued CBS over an edited interview—a nuisance suit that no President before him would have dared file, let alone win. But Trump didn't need to win in court. He had something better: the power to block Paramount's merger.

As with the ABC News lawsuit, the settlement with Paramount and CBS did not include an apology. But the broad perception across the news industry was that instead of fighting on principle for their journalists, CBS's owners had paid to make it all go away.

Around three weeks after the settlement with Trump, the FCC approved Skydance's purchase of Paramount, a deal valued at $8 billion, which gave the Ellisons a premier news media holding. Separately, Trump would claim on Truth Social that "we also anticipate" an additional $20 million in in-kind advertising or "similar Programming" from CBS as part of the settlement. Paramount officials said they had no idea what he was referring to.

Roughly a week before the FCC signed off on the merger, the network announced it would be canceling the comedian Stephen Colbert's late-night show—a platform from which he had frequently ridiculed Trump and excoriated the network for the legal settlement he called a "big fat bribe." Colbert said he felt freed to speak out.

When he learned that Colbert's show was being canceled, Trump celebrated the decision as a victory.

15

On election night 2024, New York's attorney general, Letitia James, attended a Democratic watch party at the Garden City Hotel, hosted by the chairman of the state party, Jay Jacobs.

Senior Democrats gathered in a separate war room to monitor the results, as attendees mingled in the main party area in a ballroom, where there was a cash bar and cookies served. As the results rolled in, with a Trump victory looking increasingly likely, the mood in both rooms darkened. Jacobs seemed eager to finish a television interview with Spectrum News, whose camera captured the largely empty room behind him. In the war room, James, seated at the far end of a long table, was at a loss for words. Like many Democrats, she had believed Kamala Harris would win. Shortly before 11 p.m., someone asked her if she wanted to speak to the ballroom crowd. James declined.

"No," she said. "I'm going home." There was, she would later tell an associate, just one thing going through her mind: "I'm going to be fucked."

She was not wrong: Letitia James had long been at the very top of Donald Trump's target list for retribution. In September 2022, she had brought a civil suit accusing Trump and his company of a decade-long pattern of fraud, inflating the value of his properties to secure more favorable mortgage and insurance terms. The lawsuit—which James's team won in February 2024—had endangered not just Trump's image and reputation, it had struck at the very heart of his business and wealth.

By the time Trump was first elected in 2016, James had built a career as a public defender and city official in New York, and had won citywide office as public advocate—a relatively powerless role she used, as others had, to position herself for higher office. In James's case, that meant channeling the deep anger that New York Democrats felt toward the real estate developer who had risen to the presidency from their own city.

Nearly two years later, in November 2018, James won a vacant seat for New York attorney general. She had campaigned openly on targeting President Trump. "I will never be afraid to challenge this illegitimate president," James had said in a campaign video. "I believe that this president is incompetent. I believe that this president is ill-equipped to serve in the highest office of this land. And I believe that he is an embarrassment to all that we stand for." Trump, she said, likely had "illegality" in his businesses. She promised to shine a light on his real estate days.

By March 2019, James had opened an investigation into the Trump Organization. The attorney general claimed the fraud her investigation had discovered was so extensive that her office would try to block the Trump family from doing business in New York State for five years and permanently bar them from running their eponymous company.

Trump and James came face-to-face on August 10, 2022, at the attorney general's offices at 28 Liberty Street. Trump would sit for roughly four hours for a deposition.

It was an extraordinary moment in a vicious battle of wills. But it started out, as such Trump contests often did, with a charm offensive.

In spite of his bitterness over the entire proceedings, Trump handed James a piece of paper with his cell phone number on it and told her to call him if she liked. James passed it to a member of her security detail. Since the case began, she had needed more or less constant security; such were the perils of taking on Trump. He then took a black Sharpie out of his suit pocket, signed a glass Coke bottle for James, and handed that to her as well. A memento bearing his signature could be worth something, he said. James looked at the bottle and laughed. A souvenir.

Aides told James she couldn't accept it. "It's a thing of value," they said.

She would hand the bottle off to one of Trump's Secret Service agents. "She asked me to sign it," Trump would later claim. "She brought it in."

The long windows of the conference room were covered, a request by the Secret Service as a measure of protection for Trump. But one of Trump's properties, the landmarked 40 Wall Street, was just a few blocks away; showing off, Trump approached the windows to see if he could catch a glimpse of it.

But there were no pleasantries when Trump and James were seated across the table for the on-the-record deposition. Trump, arms folded tightly in his familiar defensive posture, would refuse to answer James's questions. Trump had previously mocked people who invoked their Fifth Amendment rights against self-incrimination as obviously guilty. Now he would do exactly the same, except in his case, he suggested this was proof of his innocence.

"Anyone in my position not taking the Fifth Amendment would be a fool, an absolute fool," Trump declared in an opening preamble. And Trump would do just that, more than four hundred times during his four hours at the table.

With the trial set to begin in early October 2023, the presiding judge, Arthur Engoron, tried repeatedly to head off what would be a second Trump-related civil trial in New York that year. In a series of meetings with Trump, James, and their attorneys, Engoron would ask, "How can we settle this?" A figure of $150 million had been floated at one point. At another, $100 million.

Appalled at the sums being proposed, Trump spewed a string of invective at Letitia James. I am very rich, he jeered. My businesses are very successful. But James, he said, was not successful; she was a hack. You're dishonest, he said. Incompetent and awful.

Trump had taken to calling James "Peekaboo," and while she was unsure what it meant, she and most others assumed it was racist. Trump said it was innocuous, just an old nickname of someone he'd recalled from high school. "Didn't mean anything," he said. "It was just a nickname. But"—a pause—"I've called her much worse than that."

Trump blamed Engoron for failing to head off the trial with a deal. There would be no settlement.

James attended the trial herself, especially on the days that Trump was present in the courtroom. It was not typical for an attorney general to sit in on a trial, but given Trump's outsized presence in the room, she felt she should be there. Trump took copious notes as his former lawyer and now hostile witness, Michael Cohen, testified; Trump sometimes closed his eyes, appearing to sleep. His son Eric, who often came for the trial, exchanged pleasantries with James. The trial itself soon became something of a circus, as Engoron grinned broadly for a camera and got into a heated back-and-forth with Trump on the day he testified.

In February 2024, Engoron finally issued a penalty—Trump owed the State of New York roughly $355 million, plus interest. James and her aides were shocked. She would later tell an associate she was "aghast" as the judge's ruling was read. In bringing the suit, she had sought $250 million in damages, anticipating that the court would award the state somewhere around $200 million as a ceiling. She knew such a high figure was a ripe target for an appeals court to knock down when Trump inevitably challenged the decision.

And sure enough, the appeals court would eventually throw out the financial penalty, although it left the finding of fraud intact. But that would come later. In the moment, Trump had thirty days to pay more than $400 million in penalties and interest, and no bank would give him a bond to cover it because he lacked the cash assets for collateral. His allies approached some of their wealthy friends, asking if they would be willing to make personal loans to cover the bond for Trump. Most said no, a few said they would. It ultimately was not necessary, but the weeks of searching for financing were nerve-racking.

During this time, Trump's mind repeatedly cast back to what his father would think of his predicament. Fred Trump was a successful businessman whose brutality toward his sons was family legend. He had faced his own legal threats, including an arrest in 1976 for ignoring code-violation citations on a building he owned in Maryland; Donald was already working for his father's company at the time.

Donald Trump, seventy-seven years old and facing corporate Armageddon, had said months earlier to a confidant, "What would my dad think if he saw them coming after me like this?" The financial penalty was "a big number," Trump told the associate. "I don't know if my dad would be proud of me," he continued. "After them coming after me for half a billion dollars. I don't know if he'd be proud of me, but all I can do is fight."

II

During the time of his first criminal arraignment in April 2023, Trump was already plotting revenge. The intensity of his rage was clear to all, as he repeatedly complained that the Biden administration "Gestapo" was after him.

Trump's outrage and sense of persecution was genuine, even as his advisors looked for ways to play it up to his campaign's advantage. This had been especially true with the case brought against him by Manhattan District Attorney Alvin Bragg for falsifying business documents in the Stormy Daniels hush-money case. It was a different and distinct case from the one Pomerantz had denounced Bragg for refusing to bring in 2022, and with this one, the district attorney's office believed the documents and witness testimony would result in a conviction.

Even before that indictment was handed down, Trump's team began strategizing ways to tether any Bragg case to Joe Biden. Trump's supporters, one advisor said at the time, would not "tolerate" such a move and would see it as election interference. To his aides, Trump savaged Bragg, calling him a "fat pig," a "racist," and a "partisan." He and Letitia James, two Black prosecutors, were both "equal opportunity hires." It helped his cause that even some mainstream voices had criticized both cases; some argued that Bragg's novel legal theory and the long-ago events made it hard for the public to understand why the charges were worth bringing.

The Bragg trial would be a degrading experience for Trump; among other things, he was forced to listen to humiliating testimony as Stormy Daniels recounted in detail their sexual encounter. Trump refused to acknowledge an affair with Daniels, leaving his lawyers to hope jurors would find that credible. Neither Melania nor his daughter Ivanka showed up in court, and his advisors tiptoed around what they later privately acknowledged was the strain the trial caused for the family.

On the fourth day, a mentally ill man consumed by conspiracy theories set himself on fire in the park across the street from the courthouse. "Do you think he did it for me?" Trump queried an advisor. The answer didn't matter. "Let's tell people that he did it for me," Trump said.

On May 30, 2024, three months after the huge penalty in the Letitia James case had lacerated Trump, a criminal conviction in the Bragg case came thumping down. But by now his presidential campaign was fully harnessing the potent theme of Trump-as-martyr, persecuted for going after the Washington establishment. The former President happily embraced this as a reelection message; it was his default setting anyway. The compounding effect of his legal woes was giving Donald Trump the rationale for his return, and would help make him unstoppable as a political force.

Less than two months later, on July 15, 2024, the Republican Party would officially nominate Trump as its candidate for president. He knew that if he returned to power, he could have his payback.

But Bragg did not prove to be the target of much of Trump's ire—Trump and his circle of advisors blamed the judge and Biden more than they did the prosecutor. Rather, Trump reserved his special venom for Letitia James, who had gone after his money, and had gone first.

Trump wanted the New York attorney general, in the words of one close ally, taken out: "Six feet under isn't far enough."

Enter Bill Pulte. An heir to a homebuilding fortune, Pulte had come to Trump's notice in 2019 with some favorable tweets; he was also a Trump donor, and he had later connected with Roger Stone, who squired Pulte around Mar-a-Lago during the 2024 transition. Pulte had his eye on the position of secretary of housing and urban development, but he would ultimately accept the directorship of the Federal Housing Finance Agency (FHFA), a low-profile office he would turn into a howitzer for Trump's retribution agenda.

Pulte became for months an irritant to many of Trump's top aides. He had quickly grasped how to push the President's buttons, and he would fuel Trump's paranoia and encourage his perception that his other advisors were failing him somehow. Pulte would show up at the Oval Office or at the President's golf club in Sterling, Virginia, hoping to catch Trump at the buffet table. He would lug foam boards under his arm with photos to illustrate his case about various targets who should be prosecuted and the prosecutors who were doing nothing about it.

At one Oval Office meeting, Pulte's boards featured photos of the two U.S. senators from Virginia, both Democrats. Because these senators had supported one of Trump's choices for U.S. attorney, Pulte argued, that nominee should be viewed with suspicion and replaced. Then there was Pulte's insistence that Letitia James and Senator Adam Schiff of California, who had championed the 2016 Russia investigation, should be indicted.

Allegations of mortgage fraud became a hobbyhorse for Pulte. He would use his social media account on X to accuse people of crimes. His allies said he realized how powerful a tool his office could be, and maintained that he used only publicly available mortgage documents to make his allegations. Inside the White House, even those who wanted to see Schiff and James indicted were not so sure of that. Regardless, in short order, he made a criminal referral to the Department of Justice recommending that James be prosecuted for having listed both a property in Brooklyn and another in Virginia as her primary residences, which he said had given her more favorable mortgage terms for each property. Pulte accused Schiff of similar violations. Roger Stone had been softening the ground in public—posting on X in February the claim that James had committed mortgage fraud and that she had accused others of the same kind of crime. Stone then taunted her online in April: "Look for the FBI on your doorstep one morning soon."

III

Pulte was not the only one with a knack for egging the President on against his perceived enemies. In the days before Liberation Day, Laura Loomer had been raising hell on social media about a "vetting crisis" in the Trump administration, posting on X that various members of Trump's national security staff and intelligence community were disloyal. Loomer told associates Trump had seen her posts, called to tell her he was impressed by her research, and asked her to come to the White House. An Oval Office meeting was scheduled.

Like Pulte, Loomer was once a disciple of Roger Stone. A far-right activist who described herself as an "investigative journalist," she had become known principally as a purveyor of conspiracy theories and anti-Muslim tropes. Loomer and Stone got credit with Trump and his team for taking the lead in attacking Ron DeSantis when he challenged Trump in the 2024 Republican primaries. Her extreme advocacy for the President surpassed even Trump's most devoted sycophants. Trump called her "a fantastic woman, a true patriot," and Loomer made it her mission to search out and destroy any perceived disloyalty in the MAGA ranks and among Trump's staff. She made lists and lobbed a mix of true and unsubstantiated accusations.

In preparation for her meeting with Trump, Loomer got her nails and hair done and bought a new outfit—a red pantsuit.

In the midst of a frantic day of preparations for the Liberation Day address, Trump's assistant Margo Martin entered the Oval Office to announce that Loomer was waiting in the lobby.

"Bring her in," Trump said.

Martin escorted Loomer into the room, and Trump asked her to wait while he finished marking up a passage of his speech. JD Vance walked in to check on the progress of the address and took a seat. Howard Lutnick joined, along with Susie Wiles. Representative Scott Perry of Pennsylvania, who had been a significant behind-the-scenes player in Trump's efforts to overturn the 2020 election, was also present. The director of White House personnel, Sergio Gor—previously a Trump political advisor and the publisher of the President's books, now in charge of staffing the federal government—sat with his back to the wall.

After a few minutes, Trump looked up from his desk, turned to Loomer, and said, "What's up? What have you got?"

"I want to talk to you about some of the people in your administration who are undermining you and working against your agenda and your administration while serving in key intel and national security positions," Loomer said, opening the folder she had brought. "This is a great risk to you and your legacy—knowing that these individuals that I'm going to brief you on are Obama and Biden loyalists. Some of these people are Never Trumpers. Some of these people are Democrats."

Knowing the President liked absorbing information on paper, Loomer had gone to a FedEx before the meeting to get her list of names professionally printed and bound—organized, official-looking, and impossible for anyone to later claim they hadn't seen. It was her way of bypassing gatekeepers. She had printed five copies and gave handouts to the President and other members of his staff. Vance quipped, "Why do we need the CIA when we have Laura Loomer?"

Loomer asked the President, "Why would you want to have anybody who is affiliated with Obama and [former CIA Director John] Brennan and [former director of National Intelligence James] Clapper and Comey working in your administration knowing that they weaponized the intel agencies against you and your family?"

Trump turned to Wiles and Gor. "She's got a good point," he said.

The list contained the names of several members of the President's national security staff who Loomer asserted were disloyal—not to their missions, the country, or the Constitution, but to Trump. Her evidence was scant or, in several instances, specious. But scant and specious was the new standard, and the President listened attentively.

Her list included a four-star general, Timothy Haugh, who was both the director of the National Security Agency and head of U.S. Cyber Command. Loomer told Trump that Haugh had been "handpicked" for these positions by his great enemy, General Mark Milley. By association, Loomer targeted Haugh's deputy, Wendy Noble, as well as several National Security Council staff members.

Loomer also called for the dismissal of Alex Wong, the principal deputy national security advisor, on the grounds that his wife had worked for Joe Biden and that his late father-in-law was compromised by the Chinese Communist Party. These claims were especially galling to friends of Wong, whose family had escaped Communist China and who himself held hawkish views on China.

If Wong's wife had worked for Biden, she had also worked for Donald Trump. She had served as an assistant U.S. attorney in the District of Columbia from 2015 to 2024. But details mattered little now. That prosecutors were independent of politics was an increasingly alien view in the White House, and any service in the Department of Justice during the Biden presidency was highly suspect—it suddenly took on the air of allegation. The irony was that Candice Wong was a recognized Republican lawyer who had clerked for Brett Kavanaugh and had assisted his confirmation as a senior official in the Trump DOJ during the first term. The charge against Wong's father-in-law was even more infuriating to those who knew the family. A native Taiwanese who had become an American citizen, Wong's father-in-law had worked for a Hong Kong–based satellite company, AsiaSat, whose ownership structure included a British telecommunications company and a Chinese state firm. Major American investors would later join. But this was all Loomer needed to accuse the Wong family of being compromised by the CCP. She also posted photos from Alex Wong's wedding on social media—perhaps hoping that Asian faces in the wedding pictures would bolster her case that the Wongs were CCP subversives.

As Loomer reeled off her list, Trump's anger grew. He turned to Sergio Gor. "What the fuck, Sergio?" he said. "Why aren't we catching this stuff?"

Gor's personnel team did not officially handle NSC staffing, but he had the ability to stop hires if he wanted to. Gor had even taken heat for being too heavy-handed with the background-check procedures. But the dynamic in the room was not conducive to such an explanation.

"We'll take care of it," he said nervously. "We'll take care of it."

"Well, why were they hired in the first place?" Loomer demanded.

"We'll take care of it," Gor said again.

Loomer continued down her list, detailing the sins of each individual, until finally Trump snapped. "Fire them," he said. "Fire them. Just get rid of them. I want these people fucking fired now!"

Loomer pressed on with her case. But by now, Trump's attention was waning. He had to get back to speech prep, and to the seismic announcement that he was about to make in the Rose Garden.

Mike Waltz entered the room. His standing was already shaky. Just the week before, it had come to light that he had somehow included a journalist—*The Atlantic* magazine's editor in chief, Jeffrey Goldberg—on a Signal chat group among top administration officials that was initially intended to coordinate a meeting about an upcoming bombing campaign against the Iran-backed rebel group the Houthis. Hegseth would soon use the Signal channel to share sensitive information about the strikes, and after the leak the incident became known as Signalgate.

Waltz entered the room unaware of the ambush that awaited him. Trump handed him Loomer's list of names.

"Why aren't they fired?" Trump asked Waltz.

Stunned, Waltz stood in the dock, trying to formulate a response as he looked over the list. He protested that one of the staffers Loomer was aiming to get fired had been Marco Rubio's staff director on the Senate Intelligence Committee. "He's a pro," Waltz said. He added more: "And Alex Wong was recommended by [Arkansas Senator] Tom Cotton, and was vetted. The stuff about his father-in-law being a CCP agent is ridiculous. His family was persecuted by the Chinese government."

"I don't know what you're doing," Trump said. "But just get rid of them."

Waltz was in no position to argue further.

"Fuck, I've got a big speech today and I've got to deal with this shit," Trump said. "Just get it done. When in doubt, you've just got to let them go. Just fucking fire them."

"Alright, everybody out now," the President said, in a foul mood.

He gave Loomer a hug goodbye and said, "I have to go give this speech. We've got to get you in here more often. Come and see me soon."

Then, in front of Loomer, he turned to Gor. "Sergio, make sure you're working with Laura on this stuff. We have to get her in more often."

Wong would stay on in his job until Waltz's departure. But without any inquiry, and solely on the word of an internet provocateur, six of the officials on Loomer's list would be fired in short order. The National Security Council would be thinned out, and the agency that handled critical foreign signals intelligence and cybersecurity, the National Security Agency, would lose its leader. Loomer had been the judge and jury. Trump, the executioner.

IV

The showdown between Loomer and Waltz had played into Trump's long-standing paranoia about the NSC.

"Why do I need a whole State Department with Marco and whatever this whole National Security Council thing is, too?" he would muse occasionally in meetings with advisors. "Do we just need to DOGE one of these things? You tell me, why do I need this?"

In response, Waltz explained at one point that Trump needed an "air traffic controller."

"You need someone who, when you say this is what you want, someone that's pushing all agencies in the same direction," Waltz told the President. "And if you're asking what you want, then someone who is bringing you all those options."

Trump cut him off. "I'll just call everybody," he said.

The role of national security advisor to the President of the United States had, for decades, been a vital function of the White House—at its best serving as an honest broker to mediate between the many agencies and departments of the vast federal government. But Trump saw no need for a broker.

From as early as February, people close to Trump were intimating that Waltz was not long for that world. JD Vance had been at odds with Waltz. And Sergio Gor—who was fighting against others including Elon Musk—was actively undermining him, telling colleagues Waltz was trying to fill the NSC with people who hated Trump. Gor never mentioned that his office had given an approving nod to some of the hires targeted by Loomer. Susie Wiles was frustrated with Waltz as well and would later tell associates that the first Green Beret ever to be elected to Congress could never adjust to being a staffer. "He always acted like the principal," Wiles would tell others. While Waltz was a member of the cabinet he may not have seen himself as a West Wing staffer.

Concerning the Middle East especially, Wiles and Vance both felt that Waltz's instincts were too hawkish, that he was too sympathetic to the Israeli line. Defenders of Waltz countered that he was doing his best to implement the President's agenda, and they would soon have good reason to feel vindicated by Trump's actions. The unavoidable, if uncomfortable, reality for the anti-interventionist wing of the GOP was that Trump was, and had always been, far more comfortable projecting U.S. power abroad. He was far more attached to the Jewish state, and far more hawkish in his foreign policy instincts than JD Vance or Tucker Carlson. Trump had campaigned as the anti-war candidate, but both his presidencies revealed a willingness to use military force, especially against Iran. The pro-Israel hawks—or "neocons," as Carlson and others would deride them, even though most of them had no interest in the neoconservative project of promoting democracy abroad—would soon get from Trump the muscular U.S. actions, in Iran and elsewhere, that they had yearned for, for decades.

But rather than just fire Waltz, Trump proposed a reassignment—something he had not afforded top officials he fired in term one. Trump saw Waltz as a loyal soldier. And he did not want Waltz, who had given up a career in the House of Representatives, to spend just one hundred days in the administration and leave on a sour note.

In an Oval Office meeting on Thursday, May 1, Trump offered Waltz the high-profile role of ambassador to the United Nations, a post he had once considered fit for his daughter Ivanka.

"Mike, this is much more glamorous," the President assured Waltz. "Congratulations. This is a promotion. You're not a staff guy. And this isn't a staff thing. This is much better, much more prestigious."

"But don't be a Haley," Trump warned Waltz, referring to his first-term UN ambassador, Nikki Haley, who Trump believed had used the role to advance her own political ambitions.

"And don't be a Bolton," he added, referring to his first-term national security advisor, John Bolton, who had gone on to write a scathing book about his time in the Trump White House. "*No books*," he stressed.

"Absolutely not, Mr. President," Waltz replied. "You deserve to get unvarnished advice without somebody writing it down."

"That guy was always writing," Trump said of Bolton, a prolific notetaker. "I don't think he ever looked at me because he was just writing everything."

In the wake of all this, Trump gave Marco Rubio—who had already been given the jobs of secretary of state, acting administrator of USAID, and head of the National Archives—a fourth title: He would now also be the national security advisor.

V

Voices like those of Loomer and Pulte encouraging Trump's darkest instincts reflected the growing influence of Roger Stone on Trump's second term—though Stone and Loomer would later turn against each other.

The dream of a Donald Trump presidency had been nurtured longest by Stone, a political operative whose once thriving lobbying career had been tarnished by scandal years before, forcing him to the fringe of U.S. politics. Both Trump and Stone had been mentored by the infamous Roy Cohn and Stone understood well the politics of white grievance; he played to Trump's natural impulses. Most of Trump's first-term aides despised him, and he was held at an even greater distance in term one amid the Russia conspiracy investigation. Trump would give Stone—who used the phrase "Stop the Steal" in 2016 and maintained that 2020 was "rigged"—a last-minute pardon in January 2021. But Stone never visited the White House in that term.

Stone's access changed during the 2024 campaign. Susie Wiles and other top Trump campaign advisors had their own long-standing relationships with Stone. They believed he was smart and saw him as a victim of the same DOJ "weaponization" that Trump had complained about. Others on the team had an additional incentive to bring Stone back into the fold: They recognized it was safer to hold him close than to alienate him. Stone had a reputation as a dirty trickster, a label he claimed to dislike, but that captured the air of cloak-and-dagger menace he cultivated for decades. He was prone to publicly attacking those who refused to hire him; during his years on the fringes of politics, some candidates had hired him through third parties to keep him from becoming a headache. The fights and rapprochements between Trump and Stone over forty years were almost impossible to track. But at the end of the day, Trump always came back to Roger Stone. In his second term, he stopped pretending otherwise.

16

The memo from White House Staff Secretary Will Scharf was dated April 29, 2025. The subject line read "THE WRIT OF HABEAS CORPUS." Addressed to Susie Wiles and stamped "confidential," it was a blinking red warning light—a signal that the second Trump White House, back in power for just over three months, was approaching a very dangerous line.

Scharf was no resistance figure. A conservative who had bemoaned John McCain as too moderate for the 2008 Republican nomination, he believed Trump had been vindictively prosecuted. "We contest elections at the ballot box, not in the courts in this country," he said on ABC's *This Week*. After Boris Epshteyn tapped him for Trump's legal team, Scharf helped craft the arguments behind the dismissal of the Mar-a-Lago documents indictment and the case for broad presidential immunity before the Supreme Court. He had eagerly embraced some of the most controversial elements of the President's agenda.

As staff secretary, he was the final stop for paperwork flowing through the White House before it reached the President's desk. He was a low-key presence in the West Wing and a stickler for process. Colleagues had noted his concern when others broke the chain of command.

Among other duties, Scharf's office processed the executive actions and presidential memoranda behind what became known as the "retribution" agenda. As extreme as some of Trump's retributive actions turned out to be, they were often less extreme than he desired. A small group inside the administration worked quietly to steer the President away from moves that would inevitably be tied up or overturned by the courts. Their efforts grew more difficult as the year wore on.

Miller, according to West Wing officials, had targeted Scharf after an episodic charm offensive—quickly coming to issue sharp directives to the staff secretary on how that office should function. But Scharf was not alone in his concern. White House counsel David Warrington had told colleagues he was skeptical of some of Stephen Miller's more radical views of executive authority.

Earlier in April, the Supreme Court had handed down a ruling that dashed the administration's hopes for a free hand to expel illegal immigrants without a right to individual hearings. The ruling was complicated but turned in part on the idea that the detainees could go to court and file so-called habeas corpus lawsuits challenging the legal basis for their removal. But here was an opening: What if Trump simply claimed the power to suspend habeas corpus? Then the detainees would be blocked from receiving hearings or seeking court orders to prevent their removal. It was an opportunity for Trump to claim broader powers than he had asserted at any other point in his two presidencies.

The right that Miller and Trump had discussed suspending was among the most fundamental in the Anglo-American legal tradition, enshrined in the Constitution in the nation's earliest days. It guaranteed anyone held by the government the ability to challenge their detention before a judge. The Supreme Court had long held that anyone on U.S. soil and in the custody of the government—even people government officials said were non-citizens—was entitled to its protections. Only Congress could suspend habeas corpus—and only in the most extreme circumstances.

But despite having spent his first term filling as many federal benches as possible with conservative appointees, Trump was finding that judges—including those he thought of as his own judges—were still stymieing his agenda. His critics had often found courts that were friendly to their arguments to halt his policies with temporary orders. Now, Miller was encouraging something Trump had long dreamed of: to bypass the judges entirely.

It was not the first time the issue had come up. Miller had for a while been enthusiastic about suspending habeas corpus for migrants, raising it with the President and in larger meetings with other advisors. The President asked his aides about Lincoln's suspension of habeas corpus during the Civil War. Miller tasked the Justice Department with studying the issue.

Other officials who learned about the discussions were deeply alarmed. And Will Scharf put his concerns down in writing.

"The history of habeas corpus dates back to the very dawn of English common law," he wrote in his confidential memo to the White House chief of staff. "Denial of habeas corpus rights was a key grievance underlying the American Revolution, and the right to apply to the federal courts for habeas review dates to the beginning of the Republic."

The writ of habeas corpus, he wrote, prevented government actors from detaining, imprisoning, or executing individuals arbitrarily. The Latin phrase translated to "you should have the body," and the principle it encompassed was older than the Constitution, older than the Republic, older even than the Magna Carta.

Scharf laid out the United States law in unsparing detail. The Constitution provided that habeas corpus could only be suspended in times of rebellion or invasion, and courts had almost uniformly held that suspension required congressional action. Even where Congress had explicitly done so, the Supreme Court had insisted on alternative procedural safeguards—and had almost never permitted those alternatives where civilian courts were open and functioning. The sole exception was the military trial of captured German saboteurs during World War II.

Throughout American history, Scharf wrote, all three branches of government had been loath to interfere with habeas corpus, "doing so only in the direst of circumstances, and typically with respect to very limited categories of individuals."

Only one President had ever claimed he had the power to suspend the writ without congressional authorization: Abraham Lincoln, at the start of the Civil War, when Congress was out of session for a lengthy period.

In the entire history of the Republic, habeas corpus had been formally suspended by a leader only four times. Lincoln's unilateral action was the first; after a court ruled it illegal, Congress authorized the suspension in 1863. The second came during Reconstruction, when Congress passed the Ku Klux Klan Act of 1871 and President Ulysses S. Grant used it to crush white supremacist terror in nine counties of South Carolina, deploying the Seventh Cavalry alongside federal marshals. The third was in the Philippines in 1905, when the governor suspended the writ during an armed insurrection against American colonial rule. The fourth was in Hawaii after the bombing of Pearl Harbor, when the territorial governor declared martial law (and Franklin Roosevelt later approved). Even that suspension, which lasted nearly three years, was later rebuked by the Supreme Court.

Scharf's memo also cited George W. Bush, whose expansive claims of executive power helped lay the groundwork for Trump's second presidency. Among other things, Bush had claimed he could indefinitely imprison terrorism suspects at the U.S. base at Guantánamo Bay, Cuba, and that courts had no jurisdiction to hear habeas corpus lawsuits challenging the basis for their detention. After the Supreme Court ruled otherwise, in 2006 Congress passed a law purporting to strip the judiciary of jurisdiction to hear such lawsuits. But in a landmark 2008 case, the Supreme Court ruled that the detainees still had a constitutional right to file such lawsuits.

In every one of these instances, the country was at war or confronting armed rebellion, and in every instance but Lincoln's, the executive had acted with explicit congressional authorization.

"The upshot of these cases is that for all persons held in de facto U.S. territory habeas rights apply, or in the limited circumstance of military detainees an adequate alternative to habeas must be provided," Scharf concluded.

Scharf did not explicitly say in the memo what the President should or should not do, instead providing a dry recitation of the history of suspending habeas rights. But the implication was plain: A President had tried to do what Miller and Trump were pursuing only once in American history, under the most extreme circumstances the nation had ever faced, and even then it was found to be unlawful. And there was another implication the memo did not spell out: It would be the President, not Miller, who bore the consequences.

Suspending habeas corpus was not the only radical idea that Miller would endorse. He had pressed repeatedly for the President to invoke the Insurrection Act to deploy active-duty troops to American cities. Most West Wing staff agreed there had been moments during the George Floyd protests of 2020 when that might have been more defensible, but what was happening on the ground now bore no resemblance to the upheaval of that summer. Scharf privately told colleagues that, under the current circumstances, habeas corpus and the Insurrection Act were two lines the White House should not cross.

Many inside and outside the White House agreed, with some calling the push to suspend habeas corpus "insane"—believing it would roil the country and cripple the Trump presidency. But the President was interested. The warnings to the senior staff discussing the idea had to be as direct and forceful as possible.

II

Miller's vision of presidential power freed from judicial restraint was not merely theoretical. Trump's team had prepared an executive action for the President to sign on Inauguration Day—and later another action for DHS—to arm the White House with sweeping legal justifications, and tools, for mass deportation. The first described the influx of illegal immigrants as an "invasion"—language that could later serve as the pretext for invoking the Insurrection Act or the Alien Enemies Act. The second activated, for the first time, a 1996 law empowering federal officials to deputize local law enforcement for immigration crackdowns. The Trump administration would lean on local law enforcement in the first year until the ranks of ICE officers grew, but that power would remain a loaded weapon on the shelf. Federal judges would repeatedly rule that the surge of migrants into the United States did not constitute an invasion, but the administration kept pushing anyway.

Six weeks after Marco Rubio negotiated a deal with El Salvador's President, Nayib Bukele, to accept criminal deportees and imprison them in his notorious CECOT—the Terrorism Confinement Center—the United States dispatched its first planeloads of migrants. The administration would say later that CECOT was reserved for "the worst of the worst."

In the days leading up to Saturday, March 15, dozens of detained migrants were tagged to be transported. No one explained why. Many of them had not seen a judge.

The reason for the roundups would soon become clear: These men had been selected for three deportation flights bound for El Salvador. The federal government would later declare them members of dangerous gangs such as Tren de Aragua and MS-13, insisting their affiliations had been confirmed through rigorous screening.

Most astonishing was the legal mechanism the administration used to remove them. Trump had quietly signed an order invoking the Alien Enemies Act of 1798. The rarely used wartime deportation statute had been a key legal authority behind the internment of Japanese, German, and Italian nationals during World War II, and only twice before that in the country's history. Invoking the act to declare the men part of a broader "invasion" against the United States would allow for summary removals without hearings.

The three flights had staggered departures, ultimately taking off between 5 p.m. and 7:40 p.m.

Word of the plan leaked hours earlier. The American Civil Liberties Union and Democracy Forward rushed to federal court in Washington to seek emergency intervention. The case was assigned at random to Judge James Boasberg, who was known and disliked by the Trump legal team; he had overseen the grand jury proceedings that led to Trump's indictment for his efforts to overturn the 2020 election results.

Boasberg held an immediate virtual hearing and directed the planes to stay grounded, or be turned around if they were already in the air. "Whether turning around a plane or not embarking anyone on the plane, or those people covered by this on the plane, I leave to you," Boasberg told the administration's lawyers around 6:50 p.m. "But this is something that you need to make sure is complied with immediately."

Two of the planes had already taken off. Boasberg issued a written order roughly thirty minutes after his verbal directives, temporarily barring the administration from using the Alien Enemies Act to deport migrants. But the third flight—still on the ground in Texas at the time of the order—departed anyway. Stephen Miller had wanted the planes to keep going; David Warrington, Todd Blanche, Susie Wiles, and other top officials conferred quickly. As the planes were already over international waters, they decided they were on safe legal ground. The flights would continue to El Salvador. And the Justice Department would claim in court three days after the hearing that the third plane was filled only with people who had final deportation orders.

Miller liked the administration's chances with the Supreme Court's conservative supermajority, believing a favorable ruling on the use of the Alien Enemies Act could give Trump new tools to boost the numbers of those it deported.

But there was a significant problem, one that would highlight the reason that people being detained or deported by the government had a right to court hearings—the possibility of a mistake. There was a man aboard the third plane to El Salvador whose deportation was wrongful for a different reason, and his case would rouse intense outrage and public sympathy.

Kilmar Abrego Garcia was a Salvadoran national who had lived in Maryland for more than a decade after entering the United States illegally in 2012. He had a family and was picked up by police for loitering in 2019; federal officials would later claim he was a member of MS-13. An immigration judge said the government provided reliable evidence to support that claim about gang membership. But Abrego Garcia was also granted a non-removal order preventing him from being sent back to El Salvador; a court had established that he had a "well-founded fear" of persecution if he was sent home. He was eventually given a work permit and had regular check-ins with immigration authorities. His lawyer said he had no criminal record; two domestic violence allegations by his wife were dropped.

With Trump back in office, Abrego Garcia was detained by ICE agents on March 12, 2025, while bringing his son home. A Justice Department lawyer would acknowledge in a court filing that his presence on the flight to CECOT had been an "administrative error."

The federal government had mistakenly deported people before. But when mistakes were made, administrations had usually made good faith efforts to correct the error and bring those deported back to the United States. The Trump team had no interest in doing that now; the administration's hardest-line restrictionists believed the U.S. faced an existential threat from unchecked migration. This was no time to give in to the Left.

On April 10, the Supreme Court directed the Trump administration to "facilitate" Abrego Garcia's return, though the justices sent the case back to a lower-court judge to clarify how. The vagueness of the court's order gave them all the room they needed. Miller and Trump simply behaved as if the directive hadn't been issued at all.

Abrego Garcia had been in the Salvadoran prison for terrorists for a month by the time Bukele visited the Oval Office to finalize the deportation deal, four days after the Supreme Court ruling. The two Presidents were loose and proud, effusive in their mutual praise, and the room echoed with a chorus of agreeing cabinet members, in the manner typical of Trump officials.

"We know that you have a crime problem, a terrorism problem," Bukele told Trump. "We are eager to help." From there, the conversation proceeded with the words "crime" and "terrorism" used interchangeably.

When CNN's Kaitlan Collins, standing in the press scrum, asked Trump whether the U.S. would secure Abrego Garcia's return, he attacked the question and savaged her network. Then he turned to his cabinet and invited them to weigh in.

Their collective answer was a hash of self-justification and unreality.

Collins then asked Bukele whether he intended to return Abrego Garcia to the U.S.

Reading the room, Bukele sneered at Collins. "The question is preposterous," he said. "How can I smuggle a terrorist into the United States?"

Before the press was let in, as the two Presidents conferred quietly, Trump had been caught on a hot mic. "Homegrowns are next. The homegrowns," he told Bukele, adding: "You gotta build about five more places."

The Supreme Court justices would weigh in again five days later. The court's initial order stopped the administration from using the Alien Enemies Act to deport migrants.

III

Miller reveled in the media attention on the Abrego Garcia case. If controversy put a spotlight on the President's mass deportation efforts just as his first hundred days in office approached, all the better as far as Miller was concerned. To him, the case was an opportunity to shame the press and Democrats. The only obvious thing to do was more.

The administration mounted a sweeping effort to portray Abrego Garcia as a dangerous gang member. But the deep vetting that immigration officials claimed they were conducting more broadly turned out, in some cases, to be no more than a search of social media feeds and a scan of the men's tattoos. One deportee said his tattoo was in honor of his autistic daughter. In Abrego Garcia's case, the White House said the tattoos on his knuckles—a marijuana leaf, a smiley face, a cross, and a skull—were meant to signify the letters and numbers MS-13. His family maintained he had never been a gang member.

The dispute over Abrego Garcia's supposed gang history served as the backdrop for Trump's interview with Terry Moran of ABC News on April 29—the same date as Will Scharf's habeas corpus memo for Susie Wiles.

Days earlier, Trump had posted an image of himself holding a photo of Abrego Garcia's fist. "MS-13" had been digitally superimposed on the more ambiguous, but real, imagery on his fingers. "This is the gang that is, perhaps, the worst of them all. What is wrong with our Country?" Trump had written.

When Moran challenged him about the doctored photo, Trump insisted it was real, and continued to do so privately with aides long after Moran had left. None were eager to tell the President the letters were photoshopped.

The next day, prodded by a reporter, Trump alluded to the habeas corpus discussions for the first time publicly.

"There's one way that's been used by three very highly respected Presidents. But we hope we don't have to go that route," Trump said during a cabinet meeting, and then repeated himself. "But there is one way that has been used very successfully by three Presidents, all highly respected."

The White House, meanwhile, was lacing into anyone who called Abrego Garcia a "Maryland man." "Nothing will change the fact that Abrego Garcia will never be a 'Maryland father,'" Karoline Leavitt said. "He will never live in the United States of America again."

Kaitlan Collins and her colleagues would report on May 9 that Trump's cabinet meeting comments were a reference to suspending habeas corpus, and that the President was directly involved in discussions about whether to attempt it. Instead of recoiling from the report, Stephen Miller spoke to reporters outside the West Wing about the conversations.

"The Constitution is clear, and that of course is the supreme law of the land, that the privilege of the writ of habeas corpus can be suspended in a time of invasion," Miller said. "So it's an option we are actively looking at.

"Look, a lot of it depends on whether the courts do the right thing or not," he added.

When asked about it later, Trump denied he had ever seriously contemplated suspending habeas corpus.

When the President was pressed, he did not exactly hold the line. "If you're going to do that, that's a big one," he said. "You wouldn't do it for that particular person," he added, referring to Abrego Garcia.

The administration's defiance of court orders would quickly become a pattern in the second term—and threatened to escalate further. For weeks, Miller and Elon Musk had been pressuring the House to impeach federal judges who blocked executive action, another extreme measure, another point of leverage against the judiciary. It didn't go very far.

And by June, neither had the administration's efforts to resist the order to return Abrego Garcia. He was brought back from El Salvador—but only after the Justice Department secured the first criminal indictment he had ever faced in the United States, charging him in a conspiracy to smuggle migrants into the country. The charges stemmed from a three-year-old traffic stop.

Boasberg would later rule that dozens of migrants sent to CECOT on the deportation flights had also been denied their rights. They had been transferred from the Salvadoran prison to Venezuela and were still petitioning for hearings back in the United States.

The formal suspension of habeas corpus that Scharf had warned against never came to fruition in the first year of Trump's second term. But in July 2025, ICE issued a memo that would reinterpret existing laws to slow down those rights for thousands of immigrants inside the United States.

For nearly thirty years, immigration laws had been interpreted with a clear distinction between people stopped at the border and people arrested in the interior of the country. Many apprehended at the border could be held in mandatory detention without a hearing. But those arrested inside the United States—people who had been living in the country, some for years or decades—often faced an easier path to appear before an immigration judge and request release on bond.

The July memo eliminated that distinction. Under the new guidance for ICE, detainees were to be treated as if they were still standing at the border, no matter how long they had lived in the United States. And because of the severity with which the administration restricted asylum claims for people crossing the border, the vast majority would not qualify for a bond hearing.

The vast majority of federal judges ruled against the administration's interpretation of immigration law. Those judges ordered the government to change its practices, but the Trump administration frequently ignored them and kept going.

By November, the number of people with no criminal record held in ICE detention had increased by more than 2,500 percent. Nearly 70 percent of the people in ICE custody had never been convicted of a crime; they sat in detention facilities across the country, month after month, filing petitions for habeas corpus hearings that judges said needed to be allowed. Thousands were still waiting by the end of 2025. At least thirty-one people died in ICE detention centers that year.

The upshot of all this legal maneuvering was that Miller's team had found a way to gum up the works for migrants, for months on end. Among them was, still, Kilmar Abrego Garcia. He had been detained again by ICE after he was arraigned on criminal charges. He was kept in custody until a judge—exasperated with the Justice Department's tactics—ordered his release in December.

17

By midway through the year, a picture was emerging of how the Oval Office operated in Trump's second term. It was of a President spending his days at the Resolute Desk in a series of rolling bull sessions, accompanied by a core group of intimates; these were supplemented by a rotating cast of extras, and on any given day they could be Republican lawmakers, titans of industry, former pro wrestlers, country musicians, Gulf royals, crypto bros, or friends of felons seeking pardons. They would enter and exit the frame, with some invited to stay for meetings they had no business attending. The conversations ran fast, often straying far from the point, or from anything visitors imagined when they arrived at the White House. The President's sentences often began on one topic and ended far away.

The ever-present Natalie Harp was generally on a chair off to the side, her laptop open, head cocked, listening but never contributing unless ordered to by Trump. She fulfilled, in a flash, any request, whether a "Trump 2028" hat needed to be fetched from the merchandise room, a quick Google search, or producing the latest story from right-wing websites like Breitbart or Gateway Pundit. Once Dan Scavino became the head of the Presidential Personnel Office in late 2025, he mostly handed over Trump's Truth Social account to Harp.

Most presidents had adhered to the mantra that their most valuable commodity was time. George W. Bush and Barack Obama scheduled their days down to blocks of ten or fifteen minutes. The ideal "gatekeeper" function of a White House chief of staff was to guard those blocks of time against needless interruptions. But Susie Wiles had little interest in micromanaging her boss's time, perhaps correctly calculating it was futile. She could try to control access to who got into the Oval Office, and what their agenda might be, but otherwise she would let the President set his own pace.

In Donald Trump's White House, time was a flexible concept. To outsiders, the administration appeared a hive of activity, but those brought into the Oval Office would often remark that Trump seemed to have all the time in the world. Unless the meeting concerned an imminent military operation, Trump was usually relaxed, gossipy, unhurried. Many visitors to the Oval were charmed. Even those who didn't like him would often describe the President as solicitous and flattering, offering Diet Cokes and candy as if he were a greeter at one of his clubs. He would tell bawdy jokes and compliment his guests on how good they looked. He signed MAGA hats and extra ones for their kids and would urge them to come to Mar-a-Lago that weekend or to one of his golf clubs. He would spend hours examining the minute details of Oval Office decorations and plans for the ballroom he was plotting on the grounds of the East Wing. He loved showing off the quality of the speakers that piped his music—Pavarotti and Sinéad O'Connor and James Brown—into the Rose Garden patio. And he would regale visitors—especially foreign leaders—with the details of his 2024 election victory, subject them to his familiar litany of complaints about "Sleepy Joe," and pepper them with questions about the dangerous animals in their countries with the fascination of a child.

"I still can't fully describe what the Oval Office is like with him," said one visitor. "You'd have two people on two different speakerphones. Another person on a cell phone. I'll never forget talking about a highly classified program, and this guy—looked like just a salt-of-the-earth, country guy—walks in and he's got samples for the Rose Garden paving. Pops them on the desk. And the President stops what we're talking about, gets up there, and walks out there with him and I see a lot of hands moving. And he comes back and then looks over our shoulders, and the curator is there with somebody to drill the cherubs into the wall that he had brought up from Mar-a-Lago. And then he goes back to the people on the phone, gives them guidance. And then he tries to come back to us, but we're out of time."

This pattern would repeat all day long. The President's last three meetings of the day would often blur into one contiguous meeting. Trade, national security, a visiting CEO. All would be mashed together into one borderless conversation. Trump had run his days this way—unstructured and improvisational—since the years he spent working from his corner office in Trump Tower. But in his second term, Trump had made the White House more fully his home—not just fixing it in accordance with his aesthetic, but fundamentally changing the rhythms and structures and operations of the place.

In the first term, Trump usually came down from the residence to the Oval Office by 10:30 or 11 a.m., accompanied by valets carrying great piles of paper. An inveterate hoarder, Trump had previously stashed paperwork inside the White House residence in his *Beautiful Mind* boxes. Returning to the White House in 2025, Trump had brought his unique organizational style right into the West Wing—converting Jared Kushner's old office, adjacent to the President's private dining room, into an all-purpose hoarder space packed with papers, paintings, tchotchkes, MAGA paraphernalia, and various gifts he couldn't bear to throw away. The *Beautiful Mind* boxes, which became a symbol of one of Trump's two federal indictments, were no longer used to cart his papers around; instead, advisors just carried the documents loose.

Some mornings Trump would be up early making phone calls and posting on social media while watching TV. But occasionally, aides couldn't reach him during the hours between eight and ten, which they soon came to realize meant he had stayed up all night, on the phone or watching television or both, only to finally catch some sleep around four or five in the morning. One late morning, when no one had heard from the President and staff had been unable to reach him, an aide checked on the President only to find that he was still asleep in the residence.

Trump had every comfort close at hand. His longtime aide and personal valet, Walt Nauta (who bore the title director of Oval Office operations), would carry around not just the usual personal items—makeup, hairspray,

Tic Tacs—but also scissors so that Trump could snip his hair when he found that it was getting too long in the back, poking over his collar. Nauta would also have a steamer nearby to iron out the creases in the President's suit as Trump stood before him. The President had once offered Nauta's steaming services to British Prime Minister Keir Starmer.

Trump remained a night owl. He had never been a big sleeper, but now it seemed to his staff that he was sleeping even less, keeping stranger hours than he had in his first term. And while Trump had always been a homebody, during his first term he often got out on the road, appearing at dozens of political rallies. In the first year of his second term, he became almost entirely housebound, shuttling mainly between his comfort zones—the White House or one of his clubs. Following the 2024 election, Trump had told aides that he was done with rallies, done with campaigning. This was barely a surprise to those around him, given the two assassination attempts. He had worried about his personal safety traveling outside the White House during his first term but was now far more cautious than ever before.

There was another factor, one that Trump was even less willing to discuss. He had spent four years of the Biden presidency mocking his successor's age and clearly diminished stamina. But the fact that Trump had followed Biden by becoming the oldest man ever sworn into the office of the President did not mean he felt compelled to provide frequent health updates of his own. That he had aged since he last lived in the White House was obvious. There were the repeated bouts of drowsiness during mid-afternoon public events. And there were the near-constant bruises on his hands, which his aides first attributed to marks from frequent handshaking. Trump, who usually tried to conceal the bruising with makeup, later said they were caused primarily by the unusually large aspirin regimen he took as a blood thinner.

Trump had had cataract surgery not long after leaving office; one of his eyes would often catch the light in photographs, a telltale sign of the procedure. His new White House doctor issued a lengthy note in April 2025 after the President's physical exam, attesting to his fitness to serve.

The doctor provided another note a few months later, when photographers noticed a thickness around Trump's ankles as his pant legs hitched up while he sat at formal events. This time, the President was found to be suffering from chronic venous insufficiency, meaning his legs were not properly pumping blood back to his heart. Trump was upset about all the coverage of his swollen ankles, and he insisted that Karoline Leavitt address it at the podium. Others in the West Wing thought formally addressing his "cankles" was a peculiar choice, but it reflected the President's intense concern about his appearance.

He was also having trouble hearing, asking people to repeat questions they had just asked. Joint press conferences with world leaders were more often held in the Oval Office than in the East Room, in part because the acoustics were better, and he didn't have to stand for an hour.

Whatever thin verbal filter he had had in the past was gone. He was saying whatever he wanted, when he wanted.

Another note from the White House doctor came in October, after Trump made a visit to Walter Reed National Military Medical Center ahead of a trip to Asia, a long flight in a constricted space for a nearly eighty-year-old who had developed ankle swelling. The doctor said Trump had medical imaging, cardiac workups, and blood tests performed. The specific results or even types of imaging done weren't disclosed, but the doctor deemed the President's all-around health "exceptional."

Nonetheless, some of Trump's aides began to say privately that for the first time he was beginning to seem old to them. Those who spent time with him could see the signs—the moments of fatigue, the cupped hand behind the ear—but Trump's personal dominance in any room often papered over what his body could no longer fully conceal.

While it was true that Trump's days were loosely structured and his meetings were almost entirely unstructured, it was also true that information was guarded much more closely and far fewer officials were in the loop than ever before. He relied on a small core group, overseen by Wiles, that was more aligned than any configuration of his staff in his first administration. They kept information to themselves, mostly away from the media and from their own government. Senior officials at key agencies or on the National Security Council were often in the dark about major policies being hammered out in meetings.

When a meeting was convened to discuss the most sensitive matters—regardless of subject—a familiar coterie was usually in the room: Wiles, JD Vance, Marco Rubio, Steve Witkoff, Stephen Miller; on economic matters, Scott Bessent and Howard Lutnick would join. Supplementing that nucleus for military matters, Trump would often defer more to his chairman of the Joint Chiefs, Dan Caine, rather than his secretary of defense, Pete Hegseth; White House officials observed that Hegseth found navigating the President easier with Caine around. For serious intelligence matters, Trump relied on CIA Director John Ratcliffe. For using intelligence in personal-revenge missions, he could count on his director of national intelligence, Tulsi Gabbard. For the press, it was Communications Director Steven Cheung and Press Secretary Karoline Leavitt. For political affairs and personnel, it was James Blair and Sergio Gor, and later, Dan Scavino.

Trump made decisions so rapidly, and with so little process, that to be absent from the West Wing was not just to lose your chance to shape a policy—it was to lose your chance to know about it before the rest of the world did. Rubio was a case study of this dynamic. As secretary of state, he was America's chief diplomat, but he would spend less time abroad than any secretary of state in recent memory. After he added the role of national security advisor, he spent almost all his time in the White House. Rubio confided to colleagues he did not mind forgoing the foreign travel, but he did apologize to officials at State for spending so little time at Foggy Bottom. The Oval Office was now his de facto workspace, he would explain to them. The reason State was in the loop on what was happening, he would tell associates, was because he was in constant proximity to Trump and his decision-making rather than locked away on the seventh floor of the State Department.

If you were not by Trump's side every day, you might as well not have existed.

II

Despite his supreme self-confidence, Trump was starting to realize there were obvious limits to his ability to shape events globally. Xi Jinping,

Vladimir Putin, and Benjamin Netanyahu all understood that Trump was a force to be managed, and each had at times tapped him along and sought to manipulate his key advisors.

For Netanyahu, the principal objective was getting Trump on board his campaign to destroy the nuclear capacity of the Iranian regime. Anti-interventionists in the MAGA camp had been telling anyone who would listen that Trump was down on Netanyahu and dead against joining his war with Iran. Trump had played into this at times, saying different things to different people, depending on what they wanted to hear. In the early months of the administration, he had told an Israel skeptic on his team that he didn't "want any part of" a Netanyahu war against Iran. He told another advisor that Netanyahu was "a con man," one of the worst insults in Trump's lexicon (and contrasting unfavorably with "a hustler," a term of admiration from Trump). Several administration officials believed early on that Trump's presidency would be over if they allowed themselves to be drawn into a conflict with Tehran. Were that to happen, at least one of those officials vowed to others that they would resign. Accordingly, all the administration's diplomatic energies were being poured into trying to strike a deal with Tehran, and negotiations were well along, led by the eternal optimist Steve Witkoff.

But all this noise obscured a stubborn fact about Trump. The President already agreed with Netanyahu on the most important matter: that Iran could never be allowed to get a nuclear weapon. The main difference between the two leaders was that Trump was much more optimistic about the prospect of a deal with Iran. But Trump's patience was very short.

Many in the MAGA movement had forgotten—or had chosen to forget—that during his first term, Trump went against the advice of his national security advisor and secretaries of defense and state and tore up Barack Obama's nuclear deal with Iran. And later, against the advice of some of his advisors, he had ordered the assassination of Iran's most famous military officer in January 2020.

Trump's anger at Iran had only grown since then. Iran had plotted to kill him during the campaign, and while some of Trump's aides wanted to pretend otherwise, his feelings about the regime were more intense and less transactional than his views about nearly any other topic.

When Netanyahu's top aide, Ron Dermer, left a two-hour meeting with Trump, days after the 2024 election, he reported back to Netanyahu that he thought there was an 80 percent chance that Trump would agree to join Israel in a military campaign against Iran. Dermer was so optimistic that he convinced his wife to let him stay in government for an extra six months beyond his planned departure, to help ensure that the two countries worked together to destroy a military nuclear program that Dermer viewed as an existential threat.

Putin was proving to be a much bigger headache than Trump had anticipated. As for the unending war in Ukraine, in February the United States had voted against a UN resolution condemning Russia's invasion of Ukraine and demanding a troop withdrawal, a shocking move that had for the moment firmly aligned Washington with Moscow. Three months later, Rubio was skeptical that Putin actually wanted a deal, and Trump had reluctantly come around to the same view, having decided that the Russian President was a "bullshit artist" who was just stringing him along. There was no sin greater than making Donald Trump look foolish, and even as the ubiquitous Witkoff was still trying to strike a deal to end the war, many of the staff knew there was a good chance that Trump would simply lose interest and walk away.

Putin had sought to persuade Witkoff of his sincere desire to end the war, while at the same time relentlessly bombarding and terrorizing Ukraine and killing its citizens. Witkoff was highly amenable to this charm offensive. At one point, Trump's special envoy told the Russian President, "You guys are good at a lot of things, but you're really bad at PR."

Witkoff would persist in his efforts to find a breakthrough with Putin, based on a personal chemistry.

Putin seemed to play into this, while giving up absolutely nothing on the battlefield. Later in the year, while sitting with Witkoff at the Kremlin, Putin was doodling on his personal stationery—cream-colored, with the Russian presidential seal embossed in the corner.

"What are you drawing, sir?" Witkoff asked.

Putin held up the piece of paper; in thick, looping pen strokes it said

"3 + 2"—shorthand for the territorial framework that Witkoff had discussed with him, three oblasts Russia would keep outright and two where the fighting would freeze in place.

"Can you sign that for me and can I take it home?" Witkoff asked.

Putin signed the drawing, and Witkoff brought it home, where he had it framed in black with a taupe mat.

But as troublesome as those two problems were, no international dilemma vexed Trump more than China. As with the war in Ukraine, the President's tendency to promise easy solutions to complex problems and to effect them "very quickly" had also failed with Xi. He expected the crushing tariffs would bring the Chinese to heel, but not only had those failed to do the trick, the intensity of Xi's retaliation and the steadfastness of his resolve had the White House scrambling to de-escalate the situation while saving face.

One official described Trump as "schizophrenic" on the China issue, aware that the 145 percent tariffs he had imposed were unsustainably high and that he had effectively imposed a trade embargo against a major world economy. It turned out that Xi Jinping had far more leverage than Trump realized. Unlike Trump's first term, Xi was now well prepared for him. In addition to levying retaliatory tariffs, China moved to restrict the export of rare earth metals and magnets to the United States—materials essential to electric cars, drones, robots, and missile systems. U.S. imports of magnets dropped to a fraction of their prior volume within weeks, and global automakers and aerospace manufacturers faced factory shutdowns.

Although Trump had insisted that his tariff regime would not result in higher prices for American consumers, he soon took to saying, "Well, maybe the children will have two dolls instead of thirty dolls. And maybe the two dolls will cost a couple bucks more than they would normally."

Trump's staff bridled at this seeming indifference to the impact of his policies, especially since there was no promise more central to his 2024 campaign than the vow to provide immediate relief from inflation. "Trump's line about the dolls being more expensive is not a good one," said a senior official. "He's got to stop saying that. It's very much a 'let them eat cake' line."

Faced with the prospect of empty store shelves for the holiday season and significantly higher inflation, the President charged Scott Bessent with the job of de-escalating the trade war with Beijing. The tit for tat that had led to 145 percent tariffs had been, Bessent would tell associates, "unintentional." China was the only country to aggressively retaliate against Trump's tariffs, and neither side was eager to back down. At one point during the tumult, the President asked where the U.S. tariff level on China stood. When he was told it was 145 percent, he had responded, "Holy shit."

By the middle of May, after meetings in Geneva, both sides agreed to a ninety-day truce—the Americans lowering tariffs to 30 percent, the Chinese to 10 percent. The White House, in an absurd stretch, announced what it called a "historic deal." Privately, Trump would tell aides, "I knew they would fold." Market instability persisted, and something else had also happened: Several American weaknesses had been exposed—chiefly, that the United States was alarmingly dependent on China for many of the raw materials vital to its economy.

Also exposed was a basic truth of Trump's rather mercenary approach to Beijing: For all of his bellicosity regarding China—using the term "China virus" to describe Covid, and his campaign riffs on how China was "raping" America and stealing its jobs—Trump was actually not much of a China hawk at all. He had always viewed the relationship transactionally. He had little interest in human rights issues, was unmoved by the traditional approach to Taiwan, and cared about the island only insofar as he wanted a steady supply of semiconductors. In a rhetorical flourish meant to demonstrate his disregard, Trump, in private, would pick up a small object, such as a spoon, and say, "This is Taiwan."

While he maintained America's traditional stance of strategic ambiguity—refusing to say what he would do if China invaded Taiwan—those close to him said his private views were much clearer. They essentially boiled down to this: Why would I send American troops to fight a war over a tiny island that most Americans couldn't locate on a map?

Nor did he seem to care about Beijing's horrendous treatment of the Uyghurs or about its crackdown on activists in Hong Kong. During his first term, when pressed as to why he hadn't imposed sanctions on Beijing in response to human rights atrocities in Xinjiang, Trump answered, "Well, we were in the middle of a major trade deal."

To the extent that Trump had ever been stirred to respond to the human rights record of the Chinese government, it had been with admiration. During his first term, he had praised Xi Jinping for the swift and brutal way he dealt with suspected drug dealers—by summarily executing them.

The one area where Trump *was* hawkish was trade—but as time had worn on in his first term, it became clear that he really just wanted a big deal with Xi that he could tout as the greatest deal ever. The actual China hawks in that administration—Mike Pompeo, Peter Navarro, and others—had continually pushed him to confront China more aggressively, but Trump had held them off. At least until Covid descended—which he considered a personal betrayal on Xi's part—at which point he unleashed the hawks. Now the China hawks were almost all gone.

Xi Jinping operated with a certain sagacity and, even when reactive, seemed to follow a discernible, coherent strategy. He saw the United States as a declining power, progressively ungovernable, and dangerous on the way down in terms of Chinese interests.

In the jousting between the countries that had played out after Liberation Day, China had more than held its own, exercising crucial leverage, and for the ensuing months Trump would continue to de-escalate, ordering his staff to do nothing that would upset his hopes of a grand bargain with Xi. He would later demand that tough-on-China language be removed from his administration's national defense strategy.

Trump also wanted to get a deal to preserve TikTok in the U.S., having realized how popular he was on the platform and seeing this as a boon to his political movement. This gave Xi still more leverage to use against Trump.

At Treasury, Bessent would describe the administration's emergent China strategy as "de-risk but don't decouple," and would list the areas where the United States needed to become self-sufficient: pharmaceuticals, rare earths, semiconductors, steel, shipbuilding.

But Bessent believed the U.S. would lose any leverage it had if it were to completely disengage from China. "We don't want to create a North Korea of 1.4 billion people," he would tell others. "Would not be good for the world."

Trump shared Bessent's view. He was often suspicious of China's policies but made clear to his team he did not want to go as far as some China hawks wanted in cutting off trade with Beijing. Instead, he wanted deals he could tout to the American public. He continued to insist that his "great relationship" with Xi Jinping would always carry the day.

III

As the President prepared to embark on the first major foreign trip of the second term, to Saudi Arabia, Qatar, and the United Arab Emirates, Karoline Leavitt fielded questions in the briefing room about the purpose of the trip and about Trump's itinerary.

The twenty-seven-year-old had worked as a junior staffer in Trump's first term, then ran a failed campaign for a New Hampshire congressional seat before joining Trump's 2024 campaign. She would become a celebrity in MAGA circles and attract nearly 3 million followers to her Instagram account. She blended posts of herself on TV defending her boss with more personal content—videos with her toddler, reading him books, taking him to the Museum of the Bible. She would become the youngest White House press secretary in history. The only political era she knew was the age of Trump, and the President delighted in her rapid-fire beatdowns of the "fake news media."

"Oh boy, those lips. Ba, ba, ba, ba, ba. That beautiful little face. Ba, ba, ba. Right?" Trump said in an interview.

And on this Friday, May 9, the "fake news media" had questions, lots of them, about the possibility of Trump conducting personal business abroad, or visiting the sites of his company's real estate deals in the Middle East. Leavitt bristled at the questions, retorting that the President had sacrificed dearly for the sake of public service.

"I think it's frankly ridiculous that anyone in this room would even suggest that President Trump is doing anything for his own benefit," Leavitt admonished the press. "He left a life of luxury and a life of running a very successful real estate empire for public service, not just once but twice. And again, the American public reelected him back to this White House because they trust he acts in the best interests of our country and putting the American public first. This is a President who has actually lost money for being President."

Leavitt's umbrage was forceful, theatrical, and divorced from reality.

Just one week earlier, the government of the United Arab Emirates had announced that its sovereign wealth fund was investing $2 billion in USD1, the crypto stablecoin issued by the Trump and Witkoff families' World Liberty Financial. Eric and Don Jr. were senior executives, and the company's daily operations were run by Witkoff's son, Zach. In that single transaction, the Emirati investment transformed USD1 into one of the largest stablecoins in the world. Token sales alone brought in hundreds of millions of dollars.

Two days after Leavitt's indignant protestations, news broke that the President would be accepting a luxury 747 gifted to him by the nation of Qatar. The $400 million plane, which was being described as a "flying palace," had once been used by a member of the Qatari royal family, former Prime Minister Hamad bin Jassim bin Jaber Al Thani, and would, once refurbished to national security specifications, be used as Air Force One.

Trump had long complained about the condition of the two decades-old Air Force One jets and how embarrassing it was for the U.S. President to be traveling around on such shabby planes. He had made the decision that he wanted the Qatari plane immediately after touring it at the Palm Beach airport in February 2025, taking in its bedroom suite, luxury lounges, and expanse of wood paneling, gold-toned furniture, and white leather.

Initially, the Air Force had proposed paying for the plane, as it wanted to keep it for use in the Air Force One fleet for years to come. The Qataris were asking for $150 to $200 million for the plane, which was deemed a reasonable price given its age. But then it was announced that the aircraft would be a gift, an idea that a senior official would say was "generated at the POTUS level."

It was then further clarified that the plane would eventually be turned over to the Trump presidential library in his post-presidency, although some advisors expected that Trump would use the plane for his personal travel once he was out of office. White House counsel David Warrington and

Attorney General Pam Bondi, who had once been a registered lobbyist for Qatar on anti–human trafficking efforts, announced that in the legal opinions of both of their offices, nothing in the law would prevent the Defense Department from accepting the aircraft and then later donating it to the Trump library.

Confusion reigned as to how the plane, tracked as a sale, suddenly became a gift. In any case, on the same day that the news first broke, the President posted on Truth Social that the 747 was a "GIFT, FREE OF CHARGE."

Were the gift personal, it would have been unambiguously prohibited under the Foreign Emoluments Clause of the Constitution, which barred any officeholder from accepting presents from a foreign state without the consent of Congress. Before the Trump administrations, it had been the long-standing norm for Presidents to divest from potential conflicts of interest or to seek official guidance as to whether an offered gift was permissible. No President had ever tested the clause quite like this.

But Trump insisted it was a gift to the U.S. government, not to himself, and he went on the attack against anyone who questioned the legality or the ethics.

"I think it's a great gesture from Qatar. I appreciate it very much," he would say. "I would never be one to turn down that kind of an offer. I mean, I could be a stupid person and say, 'No, we don't want a free, very expensive airplane.' But it was—I thought it was a great gesture."

It soon became clear that the "free" plane would ultimately cost American taxpayers several hundred millions of dollars to upgrade for the President to safely travel on it by the target date of mid-2026. Criticism of the "gift" was resounding and occasionally even bipartisan. Laura Loomer, not long from her victory in thinning out the National Security Council, called the President's decision "a stain," and supported her point with a cartoon of the 747 modeled on the Trojan horse, only this time filled with armed jihadis.

18

For Trump, the highlight of his Middle East swing was the visit to Saudi Arabia. Aides all noted the way he lapped up the red-carpet treatment. Of the Saudis, Trump would say: "They really know how to receive someone." On one leg of the trip, he raced excitedly back to the press cabin on Air Force One to announce that soon fighter jets would pull alongside the plane to escort them to the next stop. He would be greeted at palace after palace with sword dances and horsemen accompanying his limousine. Everywhere he went, Trump's staff observed, he wore an expression of genuine, deep satisfaction. The smile never left his face as he marveled at the Saudi royal architecture—ballroom after ballroom, each more opulent than the last. As he beheld perhaps the most rarefied displays of state wealth on earth, he was in the planning stages for his own ballroom, the crown jewel in his plan to remake the comparatively demure White House into something like an American palace.

But when it came to the Middle East, the most pressing issue remained Iran, and Trump was finding himself wedged uncomfortably between an inscrutable Supreme Leader in Tehran, the Ayatollah Ali Khamenei—with whom his administration was vigorously pursuing nuclear diplomacy—and Benjamin Netanyahu, who thought the only way to deal with the Iranians was through the military.

Since the previous December, Netanyahu had been preparing to strike several targets in Iran, and he wanted Washington to join the effort, as only the United States possessed the thirty-thousand-pound "bunker buster" bombs that might penetrate the three hundred feet of granite and reinforced concrete that protected the Fordo enrichment facility. Fordo had been built in a mountain fortification to withstand a conventional bombardment.

Trump still hoped to force the Iranians into a diplomatic solution. But from the outset of the administration, the President had authorized U.S. Central Command, the branch of the military responsible for the Middle East, to coordinate with the Israelis on options, should a military strike become necessary. Four military options had been drawn up by CENTCOM Commander General Michael Kurilla by mid-February. Under the most limited option, America's role would be confined to a support function—handling refueling and passing along intelligence. A second option called for joint American-Israeli strikes, while a third placed the U.S. in the lead with Israel providing support, drawing on B-1 and B-2 bombers, aircraft from carriers, and submarine-launched cruise missiles. The fourth option—swiftly tossed aside—envisioned massive American airstrikes paired with an Israeli commando operation, backed from above by V-22 Ospreys or similar aircraft.

Netanyahu and Trump were in accord on the most important point: Iran must not be allowed to develop a nuclear weapon. Beyond that, Netanyahu believed that a confluence of factors in the region presented him with a historic opportunity: Trump was back in office, and all elements of Iran's "Axis of Resistance"—Hezbollah, Hamas, and its other proxy forces—had been severely degraded. For years, Netanyahu had avoided a major strike against Iran, fearing retaliation, but the risks of hitting now were far lower than they had ever been.

According to Netanyahu, the moment wasn't just an opportunity—it was an emergency. Citing intelligence that some in the White House found dubious, he claimed the Iranians were very close to producing enough highly enriched uranium for a bomb. But the nuclear clock was only one of several that Netanyahu said were working against Israel. Iran was racing to rebuild the air defenses that Israeli strikes had seriously degraded the previous fall. Tehran had sought replacement S-300 systems from Russia, but Moscow refused, saying all assets were committed to Ukraine. So Iran was attempting to produce domestic copies while also approaching the Chinese. At the same time, Iran was rapidly reconstituting its ballistic missile manufacturing capability. Netanyahu's argument was that Israel could not afford to wait until Iran had rebuilt enough missile capacity to overwhelm Israeli interceptors—at which point the cost of any strike on Iran's nuclear facilities would become prohibitive. Every week of inaction, in his telling, narrowed the window.

As spring unfolded, it became gradually clear to the White House that Israel would only be constrained for so long.

The President's team—particularly Steve Witkoff and JD Vance—had been holding off Netanyahu's increasingly urgent appeals. They had managed to thwart his plans once, in early April, a moment which coincided with relentless lobbying from Tucker Carlson, joined in the effort by Steve Bannon and the Turning Point USA founder Charlie Kirk, whose appeal to Trump was canny and nonconfrontational.

Always praising and never criticizing, Kirk harnessed the persuasive power of flattery: "The base has war fatigue," Kirk said publicly. "That's all young Americans have ever known—blood and death and sand. We want to focus on fixing America's problems first. This is an incredibly complex situation in Israel, but thank God we have a president who is working every day, and sometimes in the middle of the night, fighting to keep America out of yet another Middle East quagmire."

Privately, Kirk would tell associates that he was far more worried about what Trump might do than he was letting on in public, but recognized that airing those concerns could only backfire, reducing his ability to influence the President. As the leader of the nation's preeminent organization for young conservatives, Kirk was constantly in touch with college-aged Republicans and he could see that many of them were turning against Israel. A rift was opening up inside MAGA. While older Republicans still overwhelmingly supported Israel, a sizable cohort of younger MAGA adherents were asking questions at Turning Point events that sounded remarkably similar to the types of questions floating at gatherings of young leftists. These young right-wingers wanted to know why America was supporting Israel's "genocide" in Gaza, why the U.S. President was seemingly acting at the behest of a tiny client state. In darker corners of the movement—corners that were becoming more visible by the day—many of Trump's supporters were becoming more brazenly antisemitic and conspiratorial about the role of Netanyahu and "world Jewry." It wasn't just the well-known white supremacist internet personality Nick Fuentes but enough other voices to cause rising panic among traditional pro-Israel lawmakers and donors in the Republican Party.

Trump, however, was largely oblivious to this war within MAGA. He lived in a bubble, shuttling between his private clubs and the White House, and he was rarely shown anything but good news. He rarely browsed Twitter (now X), as he had in term one. His main inputs were Fox News, which was far more pro-Israel than the MAGA conversation on social media, and whatever snippets of information Natalie Harp printed out and brought him. Trump found Netanyahu exasperating, but the President was, some of his younger aides would say, a "Boomer" whose heart was with Israel. They speculated about whether he even cared so much anymore, knowing he would never have to again face the voters. He had the luxury now of thinking about his legacy.

Few in the administration were more worried about the divide over Israel than Kirk's close ally JD Vance. But as skeptical as the vice president was about Netanyahu, and as anxious as Vance was about a potential crack-up inside the MAGA coalition that could hurt him in 2028, the vice president had to be careful not to alienate Trump by pushing too hard against his instincts. Vance was worried about the U.S. getting pulled into an Israeli regime-change war in Iran—and his allies worked hard to make an anti-interventionist case to the President to counter Iran hawks like the right-wing commentator Mark Levin—but the vice president himself trod lightly. In a Situation Room meeting, he laid down a marker: "If we bomb their nuclear facilities, great. If we get sucked into a longer-term war, this will go down as a massive mistake." But he became more reticent in front of Trump once it became clear that the President was moving closer to Netanyahu's view.

Vance had enjoyed what could only be called a storied leap into politics, successfully campaigning in Ohio for the Senate in 2022, becoming Trump's running mate in 2024, and being sworn in as vice president in 2025. He was a populist, socially conservative, full-throated opponent of the Left, and he was a staunch opponent, too, of U.S. involvement in foreign wars. His network was a mix of the top rung of younger MAGA influencers, and some of the billionaire venture capitalism set in Silicon Valley.

Like Rubio, Vance had a young and photogenic family. And like Rubio's, the early Vance story was far from the cookie-cutter model.

Vance recounted in his 2016 memoir, *Hillbilly Elegy*, an upbringing in the shadow of an Appalachian culture, his mother's broken relationships, and a world riddled with drug use and alcoholism. Ultimately, his grandmother pulled him in close for survival and pushed him toward education. The book was regarded by many as a moving portrait of redemption through love and hard work but by others as a linear account of poverty with a narrow reliance on myths of welfare dependency to chart white working-class disaffection.

Vance had enlisted in the U.S. Marines as an eighteen-year-old and spent four years as a military journalist; he went on to Ohio State University and then Yale Law School—where he started writing *Hillbilly Elegy* on the side—and then into corporate law before he found his footing in the world of finance and venture capitalism, at Peter Thiel's Mithril Capital. He became a harsh critic of Donald Trump, identifying as a Never Trumper, a position from which he would commence a retreat when his eyes turned to a Republican senate seat in Ohio. A month after Trump left the White House in January 2021, Vance began a courtship, starting with an apology to the former President for describing him as "cultural heroin." Over the next year, Trump watched as Vance took on debates and public fights. Trump, who loved nothing more than a convert, was impressed by Vance's intellect and good looks. But some on the White House staff would observe that Trump had more personal chemistry with Rubio.

II

Until late May, Trump had held out hope for a deal with Iran.

After an unscheduled trip to Washington on April 7—Netanyahu again pressing his case for imminent military action, together with a special appeal for the bunker busters—the Trump team mounted a full-court press to rebuke him and impress upon the Israelis that they must not strike Iran alone, and certainly not without advance warning to the United States. Those who delivered that message included the President himself, along with Waltz and Rubio. The conversations were tense. As one senior administration official later put it, the President was absolutely serious about wanting a deal and this was no deception, as some would subsequently claim. Trump had seemed bullish that he was capable of reaching an agreement.

Trump had already told his team he wanted to send a letter directly to the Ayatollah Ali Khamenei. Witkoff and Waltz worked up a first draft. Its demands were blunt: direct negotiations on the nuclear program, with a deadline to reach a deal. No enrichment. No weaponization. No long-range missiles. Full access to inspections. Trump hoped they could resolve this peacefully—or, as the letter made clear, very bad things could happen.

Trump took the draft and added his own flourishes to make it "beautiful." He boasted about the letter to his cabinet and staff and would read it aloud to select visitors in the Oval Office. When he was satisfied it was just right, Trump had Witkoff fly to Abu Dhabi and hand-deliver it to the President of the United Arab Emirates, who would ensure it reached the Ayatollah. But the mullahs weren't much for beautiful letters, and there would be no diplomacy of personality—no affectionate back-and-forth between Trump and a rogue head of state, as there had been in his first term with North Korea's Kim Jong Un.

Instead, there would be something more conventional: several rounds of talks between Witkoff and his Iranian counterpart, Foreign Minister Abbas Araghchi, stretching through April and May, mediated by the Omanis. The sessions alternated between the Diplomatic Club in Muscat—described by one American official as "a social club for the Omani deep state"—and the Omani ambassador's residence in Rome. The talks were indirect. The

Omani foreign minister passed messages between the American and Iranian delegations, which spent their days sequestered in separate ornate rooms within each diplomatic compound, never meeting face-to-face.

If the terms had been solely Witkoff's and Araghchi's to decide, the United States and Iran might well have struck a compromise. Over two months of negotiations the men developed a warm rapport; both were congenitally optimistic and, at least in Witkoff's case, unencumbered by the weight of history. He tended to be light on specifics. When it came to something as complex as uranium enrichment, the devil was in the details—but this did not deter the indefatigable Witkoff from hoping to pull something off.

In his first meeting with Araghchi, on April 14, Witkoff suggested that Iran be allowed to maintain a civilian program at the levels negotiated under the 2015 Joint Comprehensive Plan of Action—the "Iran Nuclear Deal" signed by the Obama administration. This was the very deal Trump had withdrawn from in 2018, calling it a "horrible, one-sided deal that should have never, ever been made."

Hyperbole aside, Trump's more substantive critique had always concerned the JCPOA's ancillary terms. He was sharply critical of the deal's sunset clauses, including one that would see the agreement's restrictions on uranium enrichment levels expire in 2030. He also condemned the decision by the deal's cosignatories—the United States, United Kingdom, France, Russia, China, and Germany—to unfreeze approximately $50 billion in Iranian assets.

Trump would rant at length about the "pallets of cash" that Obama had delivered to the Iranians, insisting the billions were financing terrorism. Even if there was no concrete proof to support that specific claim, the unfrozen assets were certainly propping up the regime in Tehran.

But before Trump abandoned the deal, the terms of the JCPOA—enforced by a strict international monitoring regime that included intrusive inspections and the threat of renewed sanctions—had kept Iran out of the nuclear club.

Witkoff's schedule was totally overloaded. He was laboring to reach deals to end wars in Ukraine and Gaza, and at the same time struggling with complex nuclear diplomacy with Tehran.

He was sending mixed messages, in public and private. When he seemed to be endorsing the Obama-era standards for Iran's nuclear program, pro-Israel hawks turned against him. Rupert Murdoch's *New York Post* published withering attacks against Witkoff, which White House officials scrambled to defend.

Under pressure, and after consulting with the President, Witkoff changed tack. He insisted that Iran must scrap its nuclear facilities and enrichment program altogether. No enrichment of any kind, for any purpose, would be tolerated on Iranian soil.

The sudden change took some in the administration by surprise and frustrated the Iranians. A senior administration official vented privately that U.S. policy on any given issue amounted to "whatever Donald Trump said last on that subject.

"And then it will change in twenty-four hours, or in two hours, or in one hour, or in one minute," the official said. "So in a way the people who say, 'Well, process is bullshit,' they're right. It's not the easiest thing in the world to generate sympathy for the Iranians, but they were fucking pissed. They were frustrated by it."

The revised terms were unacceptable to Tehran. For the Iranians, enrichment capacity was a point of national pride. No enrichment had been the international demand for years prior to the Obama deal, but now it was a non-negotiable red line.

Through May, Witkoff and Araghchi continued to talk. At the same time, the White House picked up information that the Israelis were losing patience and preparing to launch a bombing campaign without any help from Washington. In a sign of the occasional opacity between even the tightest of partners, the intelligence came not from the Israelis but from the CIA. Some of Trump's advisors were worried that Netanyahu would launch an attack as soon as Trump left the region after his trip in May.

Inside the administration, there was a growing exasperation with the Israelis, a sense that they were unwilling to entertain any option other than a military campaign against Iran, and that they were steadily working to dislodge the White House from its diplomatic solution.

The Israelis' main worry was that Trump was so eager to get a deal that he would sign on to something that they couldn't live with. And the Iranians had grown increasingly frustrated by Witkoff's reluctance to commit anything to paper. In their final meeting, Araghchi's delegation insisted on a written draft to take to the Supreme Leader. When Witkoff finally submitted a one-and-a-half-page summary on the last day of May, it was a testament to vagueness and left out specifics about the White House position on enrichment.

Once the Iranians had Witkoff's draft in hand, they sat with it for more than a week. At the most crucial point in the negotiations, the proposal seemed to drop into a void. To Witkoff's team, it was as if the mullahs in charge of Iran existed in a time before instant communication, and had chosen an inopportune moment to deliberate in opaque silence.

This period when the negotiating parties fell out of touch would prove fatal to any prospect for the peaceful resolution of the Iran nuclear issue. During that time, Netanyahu would seize his moment, and strike.

In a call on Monday, June 9, the prime minister told Trump he was going to attack Iran. At that point, Trump could have tried at least three things to restrain Netanyahu: He could have cut off intelligence sharing; he could have stopped resupplying Israel with military hardware; or he could have taken the drastic step of publicly denouncing Netanyahu and his proposed war. But Trump chose to exercise none of his leverage over Netanyahu.

III

On the morning of June 12, the day the Israeli assault began, JD Vance, Marco Rubio, and Susie Wiles gathered in the vice president's office for a Catholic Mass with Communion. Vance's priest conducted the service. "To pray for the people," Wiles would later tell others.

The President would tell different people different things. His hawkish allies were often given the impression that he was determined to support Israel to the hilt and do whatever it took to prevent Iran from building nuclear weapons. But Charlie Kirk, who spoke to Trump over the weekend before the strikes, told others that Trump did not support Netanyahu taking military action against Iran while the U.S. was still trying to make a deal.

Even on the day of the attack, Trump seemed to be preserving his options. He had told Vance and Witkoff to reach out once more to the Iranians to see if they would accept an offer. And he told some associates that he had counseled Netanyahu against attacking Iran.

"I don't know about this," Trump told one aide just hours before the strikes. "I told Bibi don't do it." And for the first couple of hours after Israel commenced bombing, Trump resisted commenting on the attacks, leaving it to other Republicans, like Senate Majority Leader John Thune, to issue statements in support of Israel. If the campaign went badly, Trump wanted no part of it.

The first official statement from the administration on Thursday night came from Rubio. In a break from the tradition of administrations of both parties standing with Israel in wartime, the statement was muted and went out of its way to distance the U.S. from the attack.

The careful tone was not an accident, nor was it a genuine rebuke of Israel. U.S. intelligence had identified a prebaked Iranian contingency plan—standing orders, already delegated to field commanders—to strike American and Israeli targets simultaneously the moment Iran came under attack. Among those targets were U.S. military bases in the region. If those bases were hit, the United States would have had little choice but to enter the war directly—the very outcome Trump wanted to avoid. The studied neutrality of that first statement was a signal aimed squarely at Tehran: This was Israel's operation, not America's. The Trump administration needed to buy time before it could be drawn in on its own terms.

But by Friday morning, as it became clear that the first wave of strikes was stunningly successful, Trump, who had been watching the triumphal coverage on Fox News, began claiming credit for himself. In a series of phone calls with reporters, Trump praised the attacks, asserting that he had played a central role in coordination with the Israelis, and he warned Iran that more were coming.

On Truth Social, he posted: "Iran must make a deal, before there is nothing left. . . . JUST DO IT, BEFORE IT IS TOO LATE."

One witness to the whole episode, an official who served in Trump's first administration, was reminded that "nothing gets Trump's attention like success." He had seen the same dynamic with the Abraham Accords—Trump only became fully invested after the first agreement generated ecstatic press coverage. "Suddenly he was fully bought in because it was such a big diplomatic success."

Watching the nonstop adulation for Israel's bombing on Fox News, Trump could not abide being a bystander to history. He needed to get involved in a bigger, more dramatic way. He immediately began talking privately about dropping what he called "the big one"—the thirty-thousand-pound bunker-busting bomb Netanyahu had been craving. Only the U.S. had this bomb and it was the sort of dramatic intervention—a display of overwhelming force that did not involve American boots on the ground—that appealed to Trump.

The anti-interventionists in Trump's coalition went into overdrive to try to cool him down. Carlson again warned Trump that his enemies were trying to manipulate him into war, but Trump, annoyed by Carlson's criticisms, got into a testy back-and-forth with him on the afternoon of Friday, June 13, one day after Israel launched its first strikes.

Carlson was attending his daughter's engagement party when his cell phone rang around five o'clock. Trump started off gently, insisting everything would be fine with Israel and Iran. But Carlson, angry about the bombing campaign, was uncharacteristically sharp with the President.

"I just think you should know that everyone thinks you're being led around by the nose by Israel," Carlson told Trump. "And you run this big country. They're a tiny country with no resources and no actual strategic value, really—and so you dictate terms, you do not receive terms. That's just not the way it works."

"No, no, no, it's going to be great," Trump said. "I think you'll be surprised. We're going to take them out. It's going to be good. You have to use strength to get to peace."

Trump was giving Carlson his usual talking points. But the anger in his voice suggested that Carlson's criticisms had gotten under his skin.

"You're going to destroy your presidency. You won't do anything after this," Carlson told Trump. "If you get into a regime-change war with Iran, it's over. This is a trap laid by your enemies and the people telling you to do this hate you."

When the journalist Michael Scherer from *The Atlantic* asked Trump the next day about the concerns of people like Tucker Carlson—and how helping Israel fight Iran squared with "America First"—Trump made it clear that "America First" would mean whatever he said it meant. "Well, considering that I'm the one that developed 'America First,' and considering that the term wasn't used until I came along, I think I'm the one that decides that," Trump said of a term that had been used by American isolationists during World War II.

"For those people who say they want peace," Trump added, "you can't have peace if Iran has a nuclear weapon. So for all of those wonderful people who don't want to do anything about Iran having a nuclear weapon—that's not peace."

IV

Four days into the Israeli campaign, Trump nearly blew up the message that the United States was not a combatant. At six thirty in the evening of June 16, he took to Truth Social to declare: "Everyone should immediately evacuate Tehran!"

American forces were not flying combat missions over Iran. But Trump's post made it sound as if they were. Within the hour, Israeli journalists were falsely reporting that the United States was attacking Iran. Top Pentagon officials were alarmed, worried that Iran would seize on the reports as justification to strike American bases in Qatar or Iraq. The department scrambled to contain the damage. At 8:20 p.m., chief Pentagon spokesman Sean Parnell issued a carefully worded statement clarifying that U.S. forces were not participating in offensive operations in Iranian airspace. "American Forces are maintaining their defensive posture & that has not changed," Parnell wrote on X. "We will protect American troops & our interests."

When Trump learned of the Pentagon's clarification, he erupted. He demanded to know what the hell his people were doing. He didn't want clarifications—he wanted the Iranians frightened and disoriented, unsure of what was coming next. When it came to military operations, Trump preferred vagueness and menace.

He doubled down the next morning, posting on Truth Social that the United States had "complete and total control of the skies over Iran." Then he issued a demand that stunned even hawkish members of his own administration: "UNCONDITIONAL SURRENDER!"

His posts were confusing enough to keep the general panic level high. And from that moment on, the White House and Defense Department communications teams essentially downed tools for the remainder of the twelve-day war. No one wanted to get out in front of the President. When reporters called seeking clarity on American operations, they were directed to Trump's Truth Social feed. There was no strategic communication around the conflict, because there couldn't be. Trump was the communicator in chief—and everyone else had learned, once again, to get out of his way.

The "defensive" posture Parnell had described would last only five more days.

Nine days after the bombing began, the United States would enter the fighting directly for one day, launching "Operation Midnight Hammer," a high-precision military operation targeting Iran's most critical nuclear facilities. The strikes represented the most forceful direct U.S. attack against Iran in decades. The fortified nuclear site at Fordo was hit with twelve of the bunker busters, resulting in the site being "obliterated," Trump proclaimed.

By this point, most of the senior administration figures had buried their doubts and supported Trump's action, knowing they had no capacity to convince him otherwise. But some appeared better at making peace with the decision than others. On the Saturday night of the U.S. strikes, JD Vance seemed anxious, which some attributed to his fears that the war could spiral out of control. In the Blue Room of the White House that evening, after the bombing, Trump was putting the final touches on his address to the nation when the vice president suggested he soften some of the language. "I know what I'm doing," Trump shot back with an edge in his voice.

Seemingly irritated by Vance's second-guessing, Trump turned his back on the vice president without saying anything more.

The next morning, Sunday, June 22, Trump grew still more annoyed at Vance. After watching the vice president on the ABC News program *This Week*, Trump vented to others that Vance hadn't repeated his own new phrase that Iran's nuclear program had been "totally obliterated." Trump told one associate, "Everyone needs to say fucking 'obliterated.' . . . That's the word. Everyone just needs to copy what I say. Obliterated. Obliterated."

At this early stage, the precise damage to the nuclear facilities was not yet clear, and an initial intelligence report—reported by CNN and *The New York Times*—suggested the damage may have been more limited than Trump was claiming. Vance had been appropriately careful in his language on *This Week*, but Trump wanted to hear the word "obliterated."

As Rubio and Hegseth had done in their television appearances, Vance had emphasized on ABC News that the U.S. had no intention of pursuing regime change in Iran—this was a limited operation to take out the Iranian nuclear threat. Trump had said as much privately on many occasions. But just hours after Vance and the others made that assertion, Trump would say the opposite.

Exuberant in the moment, the President seemed to forget his own trepidation at being drawn into a regime-change war in the Middle East. He had reserved special scorn for President George W. Bush for doing just that in Iraq, with profound consequences still rippling out from that disaster. But flush with a success that seemed to carry no consequences at all, Donald Trump couldn't help himself, and he took to Truth Social on Sunday with an idea. "It's not politically correct to use the term, 'Regime Change,'" he wrote. "But if the current Iranian Regime is unable to MAKE IRAN GREAT AGAIN, why wouldn't there be a Regime change??? MIGA!!!"

Trump would soon drop that idea. The next night, Monday, June 23, Vance would appear on Bret Baier's *Special Report* on Fox News, where he would have to respond in real time to Trump's social media post announcing a ceasefire. Vance made sure to use the word "obliterated" several times to describe the destruction of the Iranian nuclear facilities.

The twelve-day war was now over, it seemed, and while Trump was exaggerating with his claim that Iran's nuclear program was finished, it had certainly been set back. Just as fortunate, the fallout seemed minimal. No American lives were lost, and a humiliated Iran's response consisted of tepid strikes at a U.S. base in Qatar. Perhaps a bit chastened, or a bit opportunistic, or both, Vance would go on to use the short campaign as an object lesson of Trump's brilliance. As was his wont, he attempted to put an intellectual framework around the episode.

"We are seeing a foreign policy doctrine develop that will change the country (and the world) for the better: 1) clearly define an American interest; 2) negotiate aggressively to achieve that interest; 3) use overwhelming force if necessary," Vance posted on X, on June 24, over a post from Trump in which he declared, "IRAN WILL NEVER REBUILD THEIR NUCLEAR FACILITIES."

Vance's post didn't quite fit the facts; it could hardly be said that Trump had exhausted the diplomatic avenue with Iran. And the truth was that Trump was largely reacting to events—rather than being a strategic driver—and that Netanyahu had been in the driver's seat.

But the whole episode once again demonstrated the way Trump could confound those who wanted to put him in ideological boxes or fit his actions into a coherent worldview. For all his "America First" rhetoric, contempt for Bush-era interventionism, personal irritation with Netanyahu, and the considerable risks involved, he had decided to bomb Iran anyway, and he had gotten away with it. As always, those searching for geopolitical or strategic motivations came away empty-handed.

Some in the room while the decision was being made to back up the Israeli bombing campaign recalled later an overriding impression of a President marveling at the Israeli military prowess, jealous of the resultant good press, and eager to get in on the action himself. In term two, Donald Trump was doing what he pleased without meaningful resistance.

Notably, the worst predictions of the anti-interventionist Cassandras had not come to pass. And now that Trump had a successful military strike under his belt, it would only embolden him further.

19

Lonnie G. Bunch III, the secretary of the Smithsonian Institution, excused himself from the videoconference to take a phone call. He rejoined the meeting after a few minutes, only to excuse himself again to take another call. The sequence repeated itself several times during the emergency meeting of the Smithsonian's Board of Regents. The interruptions kept coming, despite the crisis the museum system had on its hands.

It was June 2, and Bunch and the Smithsonian regents—including Vice President JD Vance—had gathered in haste. Three days earlier, Trump had announced he was firing the director of the National Portrait Gallery, Kim Sajet, describing her as "highly partisan" and a "strong supporter of DEI." It was not at all clear that Trump had the authority he professed to have to summarily dismiss Sajet, who had held the position for twelve years, and whose role fell under the purview of the Smithsonian board. And it wasn't at all clear what came next.

As Bunch tried to conduct the virtual meeting, it was, as some attendees would later find out, Trump himself who kept calling. While Bunch took Trump's calls, the board continued its discussion, trying to figure out what it was that had so offended the President.

It soon became clear that Trump was irate about his own photograph hanging in the Portrait Gallery. It was awful, he would say. And he objected to the exhibition label that accompanied it, which noted that he had been impeached twice.

At a certain point, Bunch stopped picking up the President's phone calls. He had enough to deal with on the video call. Vance and the newest Smithsonian regent, Carlos Giménez, were incensed with their colleagues on the board and were echoing Trump's message that Sajet had to go. Eventually they wrapped up, agreeing to deal with the matter at the next in-person board meeting the following week.

When Trump returned to power in 2025, his campaign to crush institutional DEI programs had quickly mushroomed into a larger attempt to remake American culture itself. Just weeks into his new term, Trump had taken over the John F. Kennedy Center for the Performing Arts, replacing its long-serving board chairman, the investor and philanthropist David Rubenstein, with himself. Performing arts lovers watched in growing horror as Trump and the new interim executive director, Ric Grenell, dramatically changed programming, dismissed staff, forced out board members, and imposed their own preferences on the institution. Trump would also anoint himself host of the center's prestigious lifetime honors ceremony.

For the ideologues in Trump's West Wing, the cultural takeover was an important course correction to "wokeness." That worked for Trump, too, but there was also another purpose. It gave him the kind of theatrical opportunities stymied since he was a young man. At his first board meeting after gutting the staff, the President had surprised attendees by declaiming his "aptitude for music" as a boy, something that he said had rankled his father. He had wanted to attend film school, but Fred Trump disapproved. Later Trump had tried producing a Broadway show in 1970 that flopped. Now, with the Kennedy Center, he could be the star, handing out awards.

Next, he had the vast complex of the Smithsonian in his sights.

II

Allies of Lonnie Bunch long believed that Trump would target him for dismissal even though the President had no authority to do so directly.

Trump would months later make his feelings about the Smithsonian's focus on the country's history of slavery well known: "The Smithsonian is OUT OF CONTROL, where everything discussed is how horrible our Country is, how bad Slavery was, and how unaccomplished the downtrodden have been—Nothing about Success, nothing about Brightness, nothing about the Future," he had written on social media.

It was both an attack on efforts to tell the full story of slavery in America and a signal that Trump planned to use the executive power of the presidency to order a new historiography—sanitized of the blemishes that any legitimate history called for, but enhanced with the President's point of view.

Lonnie Bunch was an avatar of the kind of American success story Trump had little interest in. The seventy-two-year-old Bunch was the first Black secretary of the Smithsonian, a position he had assumed in 2019, during Trump's first term. He was the grandson of a sharecropper, raised in Belleville, New Jersey, and had built a career as a professor and educator, spending most of his career working for Smithsonian museums before becoming the founding director of the National Museum of African American History and Culture. It opened to an exuberant reception in 2016, with President Obama presiding over the ceremony.

In the second half of Trump's first term, Bunch had published a memoir about his tenure building the African American museum from scratch over the course of a decade. Entitled *A Fool's Errand*, the book included a scene in which Bunch had given Trump a tour of the museum in 2017. Trump came off as remarkably uninterested in the history of slavery in the country he was about to lead. When they stopped in front of an exhibit about the Dutch involvement in the slave trade, Trump paused a moment, before turning to the director to remark, "You know, they love me in the Netherlands."

"I was so disappointed in his response to one of the greatest crimes against humanity in history," Bunch had written.

On March 27, 2025, the White House website had announced a new executive order titled "Restoring Truth and Sanity to American History." In the order, Trump took aim at federally funded cultural institutions for being beholden to "a divisive race-centered ideology" that portrayed "American and Western values as inherently harmful and oppressive." Executive Order 14253 targeted several individual museums in the Smithsonian complex, as well as the Smithsonian Institution itself, as examples.

Lindsey Halligan, a former insurance lawyer who had served on Trump's legal team between his terms, had come to the President early in the second term after visiting some of the Smithsonian museums. Halligan had told Trump she was horrified by what she would describe as "wokeness." Trump would charge Halligan and Vice President Vance with enforcing the executive order to remove "improper ideology" from the Smithsonian. Programs that degraded "American values" or that "divided Americans based on race" would be prohibited. Vance and Halligan would further be responsible for appointing new citizen members to the top Smithsonian board who were committed to the President's view.

The term "improper ideology" was alien to many Americans' ears, and redolent of notions of state censorship. The government would attempt to impose a new standard of art and scholarship, though in reality this was an amorphous notion, dependent on the whims of one man. The scene was now set for an extraordinary pitched battle, both inside and outside the Castle (as the Smithsonian's main building was known), as a microscope hovered over all federally funded institutions, on the lookout for violations of the new aesthetic.

On April 6, the Board of Regents had gathered for its traditional dinner ahead of the full board meeting the next day. The dinners were held at different locations within the Smithsonian network; on this night, it was in a large open area at the National Postal Museum. The Smithsonian Board of Regents was made up of seventeen members; the chief justice of the Supreme Court, John Roberts, served as chancellor and presiding officer, and there were three senators, three members of the House of Representatives, and nine citizen members, as well as the vice president, together overseeing the vast Smithsonian maze of museums and research centers. The board structure had been designed to insulate the Smithsonian from partisan politics.

The dinners were usually social gatherings, belied by the formality of the cloth-covered tables, servers, and three courses plated for the guests. That night, the new regent from Florida, Carlos Giménez, was in attendance, making his first appearance, and he was not particularly interested in pleasantries with his new colleagues.

Seated two chairs to Bunch's left, Giménez, a former firefighter and mayor, listened as the regents, one by one, expressed support for Bunch in the face of the harsh criticism from the White House. We support you, one regent said. We think you've done a great job, said another. When it was Giménez's turn to speak, his principal message was: I don't know you, and so I cannot support you. His words were softer than his belittling tone, which shocked Bunch and the rest of the room. No one rose to defend Bunch, a painful point that he would make to some board members afterward. The evening ended on a tense note.

At the board meeting the next morning, Giménez was ready for a fight, and toward the end of the meeting, he asked a seemingly benign question: Was there a process for reviewing exhibits?

The answer was complicated. Potential exhibitions had traditionally been assessed through a committee system to ensure accuracy, that the subject matter was appropriate and the content unbiased. These committee reviews were driven by scholarly research and peer review from experts in relevant fields. Major decisions were finalized by the secretary of the Smithsonian and the Board of Regents rather than federal agencies. In recent years, as the process began to incorporate more data on visitor experience, the Smithsonian had developed additional reviews taking into account visitor preferences. But even as the system evolved to better engage audiences, there were still differences in how they were conducted.

The institutional sprawl of the Smithsonian—twenty-one museums, the National Zoo, and fourteen research and education centers—meant that there was no flowchart or standard process for reviewing exhibits, but rather a patchwork of different applications. One museum might take a completely different approach from another. If someone was searching for a crack in the system to rein in the Smithsonian, this was it.

As Giménez pressed the other board members for details of how exhibitions were assessed and what filters they went through, it was clear the White House had found its opening. The regents assembled around the board table would soon realize it, too. Bunch told the group he was already trying to refine the existing process. But some would leave the room that day with a deep sense of unease about what might come next from the President's allies.

III

Two months later, on Monday, June 9, the regents arrived in the morning for their seasonal meeting. It had been just a week since the emergency videoconference to discuss Trump's order to fire the Portrait Gallery director, and the regents had dined the night before at the Museum of Asian Art. There they had the opportunity to view the *Ruffled Feathers* exhibition, which explored James McNeill Whistler's famous Peacock Room, with his pointed, and at the time controversial, commentary on art and commerce.

The June 9 board meeting was held in a large room on the ground floor of the Museum of American History, with its showcases of historic items including early board games and toys. The tables were arranged in a U shape and at the closed end of the U configuration, Lonnie Bunch sat next to the chair of the Board of Regents, health policy expert Risa Lavizzo-Mourey, Vice President Vance, and Chief Justice Roberts. The other regents sat along the sides, with Congressman Giménez at one end.

Vance told the group that they needed to follow Trump's orders; the President, he said, had already made his wishes clear about what the board should do with the National Portrait Gallery. Vance went on for several minutes, warning, "You cannot refuse him." Trump was the President, he reminded them, and he had the power. "He signs the checks," Vance added bluntly.

"This should be an institution for everyone. I am not demanding we hire someone with right-wing political views," the vice president added. "I am merely asking that we not make the face of this institution a left-wing crazy person."

Giménez, who had been escalating in aggression since his first appearance in April, was more wound up and hostile than Vance. The congressman was adamant that Portrait Gallery director Kim Sajet must be fired immediately.

Several of the regents tried to slow down the discussion, arguing personnel decisions were for the board to decide, not the White House. The matter—and the passions of their powerful fellow regents—should be taken under review. Prior to the meeting, several of the alarmed regents had agreed among themselves to pass a resolution stipulating this was their business to deal with, and that the President had no standing to make personnel decisions. They wanted to make sure their resolution was put to a vote before Vance and Giménez could get up their separate resolution—which was to fire Sajet forthwith. Despite Trump's earlier announcement that he had terminated her, Sajet was still showing up for work.

She's got to go, Giménez jumped in again. She's got to go right now.

Vance indicated again that if Sajet was not fired, the White House would explore the option of defunding the Smithsonian. Vance's warning met strong resistance. The White House did not have the authority to do that, some regents shot back. John Fahey, the former head of Time Life Inc. and National Geographic, and Democratic Senator Gary Peters of Michigan, were especially emphatic.

Vance argued that the Smithsonian was politicizing the history of the country. Peters responded succinctly: You're coming here threatening to cut off funding to the Smithsonian if we don't paint the picture you want. That's politicizing it.

Vance disagreed.

But things were not going Vance's way. He abruptly left the room for another appointment, putting Ben Moss, his policy director, in his seat while he was gone. The thirty-one-year-old Moss promptly pulled up an image on an iPad of the Statue of Liberty depicted as a Black transgender woman holding aloft a lamp filled with flowers. It was a painting by the artist Amy Sherald and was set to be shown at the National Portrait Gallery in September as part of a major exhibition of her work. "This image," Moss declared, "is also a problem."

Sherald was one of America's foremost contemporary artists, whose iconic 2018 official portrait of former First Lady Michelle Obama had made her a household name. Her upcoming National Portrait Gallery exhibition was titled *American Sublime* and comprised dozens of paintings in her traditional oeuvre: everyday portraits of Black Americans. The show had already been on display at the San Francisco Museum of Modern Art and the Whitney Museum of American Art in New York. The D.C. art world was eagerly awaiting its transfer to Washington.

Moss held up the digital image of *Trans Forming Liberty*.

"This," he said, "is not what Americans want to see."

A stunned silence descended. Was this what the White House meant by "improper ideology"? John Roberts, who was known as "the Chief" to his fellow regents, seemed caught off guard by the sudden shift in the meeting's topic. But Bunch's team and Roberts's advisors had anticipated a moment like this, where the Trump administration would challenge artistic content.

The debate around Lonnie Bunch's board table was becoming a chess game as various regents tried to hold their own against Giménez. Finally, a resolution stating that the matter of Kim Sajet's job came under the authority of the board was put on the table. Giménez tried to counter it with his proposal to immediately fire her. John Roberts, with the clarity of a man accustomed to enforcing the rules of regular order, pointed out that there was already a resolution on the table. He advised Giménez that the first one must be voted on before the next one could be brought up.

The vote stipulating that the authority to manage Sajet's job belonged with the board was approved, rendering the Giménez proposal moot. Later that day, the Smithsonian regents released a public statement reflecting the vote taken earlier, pushing back against the overreach of Trump and Vance. "All personnel decisions are made by and subject to the direction of the secretary, with oversight by the board," the statement read.

But four days later it was all over, anyway. On June 13, Kim Sajet quit, explaining in a note to staff that her resignation was "the best way to serve the institution." On behalf of the Smithsonian, Bunch would thank her for putting the Smithsonian ahead of her own position.

On July 23, Amy Sherald abruptly canceled her upcoming show at the National Portrait Gallery. In a letter to Bunch, she made clear she believed there had been a breach of faith with the gallery. She wrote that Bunch had discussed with her the possibility of installing a video adjacent to her work *Trans Forming Liberty*, and the video would feature person-on-the-street chats by people who were for and against trans rights. This went too far for Sherald, who said that "the video would have opened up for debate the value of trans visibility" and she didn't want it attached to *American Sublime.* Outraged that the institution appeared to be caving to political pressure, Sherald struck first with her own cancellation, removing her show in its entirety and stunning the art world.

In a statement to the media, Lindsey Halligan claimed Sherald's painting had recast a national monument "through a divisive and ideological lens" and that the Statue of Liberty was not "an abstract canvas for political expression."

"It is a revered and solemn symbol of freedom, inspiration and national unity that defines the American spirit," Halligan declared.

Removing the artwork, she said, was a principled and necessary step; and the administration was committed to ensuring the Smithsonian was free from ideological overreach and political distortion.

IV

A few weeks later, the White House dramatically underlined its intentions with a letter to the Smithsonian.

"Dear Secretary Bunch" it opened, before outlining a sweeping review in line with the President's executive order on "restoring truth and sanity" to U.S. history. It demanded a top-to-bottom assessment of everything from wall texts on exhibitions to websites and social media content. The White House signees would oversee interviews with curators and staff to look inside the process of selecting and approving exhibitions, and they would review current and future exhibitions with particular focus on the 250th anniversary of the Declaration of Independence. The museums had a total of four months to comply with these official requests. After that, the administration would provide its own final report in time for review in early 2026. The letter was signed by Halligan; Vince Haley, assistant to the

President and director of the Domestic Policy Council; and Russell Vought. In essence, the letter was a warning to prepare for a massive overhaul at every level of the most powerful cultural institution in America.

Bunch had considered writing an opinion article for a newspaper about what was taking place at the Smithsonian; he ultimately decided against it. But with this latest shock wave, the Smithsonian Executive Committee scheduled an emergency meeting for the next day, with John Roberts, Bunch, the three-person executive committee, senior staff, and attorneys all in attendance. Running for fifty-two minutes, the meeting went straight into discussions about the White House letter.

Bunch raised the prospect of the organization issuing a public letter to the White House, pushing back firmly and making it clear any review of the Smithsonian was the responsibility of the institution alone. But executive committee members promptly voiced concern that making such a letter public would pit them all directly against the President and would almost certainly become a political fight with Trump, one that could damage the Smithsonian in the process. It would become clear after the others spoke that Roberts, who appeared mindful of taking a long-view approach of the Smithsonian's best interests, shared those views. In his case in particular, his colleagues at the meeting thought, such a letter could pit the chief justice directly against the President, and not on points of law, but rather on cultural interpretations of how a country should see itself. The members of the executive committee shared the same concern. The idea was put aside.

For Bunch, this was a moment to consider his own future. He was as much of an institutionalist as Roberts, trying to take a long view of preventing enduring harm to the Smithsonian and its funding. But he would tell allies that he felt disrespected by Vance and Giménez. And as he was absorbing the brunt of a full-on assault from the Trump administration, he was being pressured by some of his closest allies, prominent philanthropists and friends among them, who wanted him to either quit or be more outspoken at this break point in history. So what path should he take?

Soon Trump requested a personal meeting with Bunch. A small group of regents would help him prepare. Few could forget the scenes of Volodymyr Zelensky being subjected to Trump's rage in February.

On Thursday, August 28, Bunch joined Trump, Lindsey Halligan, and Sergio Gor, the head of presidential personnel, for lunch at the White House. Scheduled for an hour, the meeting went for two and a half. They sat for a while in the Oval Office before a meal of chicken as Trump showed scale models of the new White House ballroom. After lunch, Trump took Bunch and Halligan on a tour of the White House, with the President stopping at different rooms to offer his own appraisals. He regaled Bunch with examples of his expertise in framing, noting which artworks were correctly framed and which were not.

If Bunch made any misstep that could have rattled the President, it may have been the moment when he corrected Trump on the question of which President had first lived in the White House. Trump thought it was John Quincy Adams; the correct answer was John Quincy's father, John Adams, in 1800. Trump was unaccustomed to being told by his own staff that he had his facts wrong, but appeared to take it in stride. The President gave Bunch another quiz in a game where only Trump could win. Which was the best building in Washington? Bunch volunteered the Smithsonian's Castle. No, Trump replied, it was the Eisenhower Executive Office Building next to the White House. He planned, he said, to have it painted white.

Then Trump moved on to a favorite topic. What were the three kinds of light a chandelier could throw? "There's white, there's silver, and there's gold," offered the President helpfully. "Guess which is the greatest of the three."

"Gold," Bunch replied. Trump seemed pleased.

Trump was not especially interested in discussing the Smithsonian review during his afternoon with Bunch, briefly telling him he was doing a good job and instead asking about the organization's plans to honor America's 250th birthday the following year. For all of his raging on social media about the Smithsonian and slavery, Trump's aversion to one-on-one interpersonal conflict was still intact.

Bunch had told Halligan that he intended to send a letter to the White

House stating the Smithsonian's position against interference with its programming; Halligan told colleagues that he mentioned the letter in passing, without describing its contents. Regardless, Bunch was becoming convinced that he could weather the storm.

Trump's real intentions, as always, were hard to discern. The outgoing chair of the Smithsonian Executive Committee told Bunch in the fall that a White House official had relayed that the President said his lunch with Bunch was one of the best he'd had.

In fact, Trump had turned to his aides after their meeting and offered a grim assessment of Bunch. *He hasn't changed,* the President said.

20

A sharp red point glowed on the surface of the oil painting.

It was Independence Day, Friday, July 4, and B-2 bombers had been roaring over the White House. As he awaited the evening fireworks, President Trump had taken refuge from the festivities on the South Lawn to entertain Speaker Mike Johnson with his own indoor version of a light show. Seated behind his desk, the President held a laser pointer and trained its light onto the painting over the fireplace—a portrait of George Washington carrying a dress sword.

"See the laser? It goes dim," Trump said. "You know what that's called? Expensive oil paint. Good oil paint."

The President flashed the laser over to the portrait of Ronald Reagan. "Nope. They used cheap paint on that one. See? The pointer doesn't dim. It's not dim with Reagan. It's dim with Washington."

Trump was grinning like a proud host showing off a personal museum. Before his guests could quite grasp what he was saying about the paint, the red dot skipped along the molding. "Look here at the top," said Trump, aiming the laser at the edge of the ceiling. "Right here. Maybe just a trim line. What do you think? Because there's $2 million worth of gold here. But I want more. And there's Melania."

The First Lady had joined them. It was clear she was not a great fan of all the gold. Trump explained to Johnson about Melania: "She's a minimalist. But this is the Oval Office. It just looks better."

For Trump, the past several weeks had been one triumph after the next. Two weeks ago it had been his successful bombings of Iran's nuclear sites. And now, earlier that afternoon, he had signed into law his major domestic policy bill, the "One Big Beautiful Bill Act." He was already wanting to reminisce with Johnson about their victory, which had required a flurry of late-night phone calls from Trump to whip reluctant Republicans into voting for the bill.

"Mike, we got the Big Beautiful Bill, and I got to tell you, every one of these motherfuckers, I called them and I said—I didn't say a word. They just picked up and said, 'We're with you one hundred percent, sir,'" Trump said. "And I was like, 'Woah. You didn't even know what I was going to ask.' And then I figured, he's kind of smart. Because if I'm calling you at two thirty in the morning, you know what I'm calling about. I'm not just calling to shoot the shit. And he says, 'We're with you one hundred percent, sir.' And they were going to be with us. As I just said, Mike, this whipping votes is easy."

Passing the bill had not, in fact, been easy. It had taken a monumental display of raw power, and had succeeded only because Trump wielded near-total command over his party in Congress, command greater than any President before him.

The bill was a mixed bag. It contained plenty for Republicans to like. The legislation revoked Biden-era subsidies for solar energy, wind, and electric vehicles. And it fulfilled major Trump campaign promises on border security, with a massive $170 billion boost to the Homeland Security budget, and other popular measures such as "no tax on tips" and investment accounts for babies born during the Trump presidency.

But many Republicans who ultimately voted for the bill were gravely worried about several key features. The legislation would cut an astonishing $1 trillion from Medicaid, the health coverage for millions of the poorest and most vulnerable Americans, and imperil the funding of rural hospitals and food stamps. Many of Trump's most fervent supporters relied on these programs. And the bill would, at the same time, blow out the national debt. It would raise the debt limit by $5 trillion—a betrayal of principle for fiscal conservatives, who had repeatedly promised voters they would slash deficits. The excesses of the Big Beautiful Bill would dwarf any savings made by DOGE.

It didn't help that the most powerful donor in Republican politics, Elon Musk, had made it his mission to tank the bill, publicly threatening to fund primary challenges against any Republican voting for it.

"I'm sorry, but I just can't stand it anymore," Musk wrote about the bill in a post on X. "This massive, outrageous, pork-filled Congressional spending bill is a disgusting abomination," he added.

"Shame on those who voted for it: you know you did wrong. You know it." Musk left out the fact that privately he had been complaining that the bill would harm his electric car company, Tesla.

When the President saw Musk's post, he looked at it for several beats, an expression close to pensive crossing his face.

"They always leave me," he finally said. "They always do this. This is why I can't have friends."

The President then called out to Natalie Harp with his French pronunciation: "*Nathalie*, get me my phone."

Instead of firing back on social media, Trump tried calling Musk, whose phone went straight to voicemail.

He tried again, and again straight to voicemail.

Looking a bit distraught, Trump said, "He never doesn't take my calls."

Trump's concerns about Musk aside, Mike Johnson's judgment had been vindicated. He had felt certain that the only way to pass such a volatile mix was to group everything into one bill that would be too big to fail. Trump had agreed. And now they had passed it.

II

Never before had there been a working relationship between President and Speaker quite like the one that the fifty-three-year-old Louisianan Mike Johnson had formed with Donald Trump. Longtime congressional observers could not recall a Speaker who had ever deferred so much to a President. Over the past thirty years, power in Congress had been flowing away from individual members and their committees and concentrating in the hands of leadership. Now, in Trump's second term, there was a new twist: Power flowed out of the Speaker's office directly into the Oval Office. In a reflection of just how utterly subservient Johnson was to Trump, congressional reporters in Washington would begin to refer to President Donald Trump also as "Speaker Donald Trump," a pithy take on the rapidly dissolving separation of powers.

Trump's relationship with Congress would be nothing like the first term. Back then, especially in 2017, his first year in Washington, many Republicans regarded his victory as a fluke and his presidency as a passing episode of craziness. Members back then were often willing to criticize Trump publicly. To the party's leaders, Paul Ryan in the House and Mitch McConnell in the Senate, Trump seemed less a figure of idolatry than a boorish curiosity, whose behavior they often tried to ignore.

But whereas Ryan carried himself as Trump's intellectual superior, Johnson cheerfully embraced his role as Trump's junior partner. After all, Johnson owed his speakership entirely to Trump, who had endorsed him at a key moment in his bid for leadership—meaning that Trump now owned him in a way he could never own Ryan. And where Ryan had sought to direct policy, Johnson made it clear that his sole purpose was to translate Trump's desires into reality. He benefited from the fact that Trump had learned a lot, too. In term one, Trump had regularly dive-bombed into the middle of congressional business, making unreasonable and unrealistic demands just as leaders felt they were getting close to crafting legislation. This time, during the passage of the Big Beautiful Bill, Trump would be notably hands-off, trusting Johnson to do what was needed and only engaging when brute force was required to overcome a member's resistance.

The dynamic had changed in the Senate, too, though more subtly. Unlike Mitch McConnell, a giant of the upper chamber who eventually became his own power center in Washington, Senator John Thune of South Dakota had needed to repair his relationship with Trump after criticizing him following the January 6 attack on the Capitol. As the 2024 election drew nearer, Thune began paying social visits to Mar-a-Lago and holding friendly chats over the phone. Trump did not oppose Thune's bid for majority leader and Thune repaid Trump's confidence by clearing the way for cabinet confirmations, including those of Pete Hegseth and Bobby Kennedy, that could not have passed muster under the Republican Senate in Trump's first term.

A deeply religious man, Mike Johnson was known for his polite, calm demeanor and for constantly texting around Bible verses. He was easy to underestimate, but he had a keen grasp of the full dimensions of Trump's relationship with GOP members; he was, after all, one of them: a young congressman who came up in the age of Trump. Because of that experience, Johnson understood the fear Trump inspired—with both the power and willingness to end a contrary Republican's career. But it was not just about the threats. He knew also, as did his colleagues, that Trump had a more powerful connection with Republican voters than any of them. And he knew that his own members were seduced by Trump.

Trump exploited those emotions. He understood that many Republican lawmakers related to him like starry-eyed fans rather than as elected representatives of a coequal branch of government. He offered more access than any modern president. Since 2017, he had handed out his cell phone number freely—even to the most junior members of Congress, who would never have dreamed of texting or calling the President. He invited them to play golf with him at his clubs, for dinner at Mar-a-Lago, and for flights on his private jet. He signed MAGA hats for their wives, husbands, and children. He gave rides on the presidential helicopter, Marine One. "Do you know who sits in that seat? That's Melania's seat," Trump told lawmakers who flew with him on Marine One, *The New York Times* reported. "She's the only one who sits in that seat. Do you know how special you are to be in that seat?"

Most previous Presidents had their staff handle rank-and-file members and typically the Presidents dealt only with the most senior lawmakers and members of leadership. But little-known Republicans would now gush over their ability to speak to Trump directly. "He's been very kind—he calls me Tim," Representative Tim Burchett of Tennessee gushed to *The New York Times*'s Annie Karni after a phone call from Trump had changed his vote on the President's budget resolution in February 2025. "He knows my district is very conservative, and he shares my passion for fiscal sanity, and I kind of dig that," Burchett said of Trump. "It's cool that the President knows my first name. I dig that." Many members, Trump knew, similarly had come to feel emotionally indebted.

Trump had worked long and hard to accrue that loyalty—with years of behind-the-scenes relationship building, combined with implicit and overt threats if people challenged him. It would serve him well in his second term. It seemed hard now for those around him to contemplate that just four years earlier, on January 20, 2021, no elected Republican of any stature had shown up to Joint Base Andrews for the bleak farewell at the end of Trump's first term.

Trump's second impeachment that month had been supported by more members of his own party than any previous impeachment of an American President. House GOP leaders had told each other they were done with Trump and on conference calls they canvassed what a "post-Trump" Republican Party might look like.

But by the week before the Iowa caucuses, three years later in January 2024, every member of the House Republican leadership had endorsed Trump's reelection. By the time he returned to the White House, Trump was received as a godlike figure on Capitol Hill and members competed to see who could pay him the most lavish respect. Some of these craven overtures would shock students of history, but the tributes came in droves.

In 2025 alone: Representative Anna Paulina Luna of Florida had introduced legislation to commission the carving of Trump's face in granite at the Mount Rushmore National Memorial in South Dakota; Representative Claudia Tenney of New York proposed re-designating June 14 (Trump's birthday) from "Flag Day" to "Trump's Birthday and Flag Day"; Representative Addison McDowell of North Carolina proposed renaming Washington Dulles International Airport as "Donald J. Trump International Airport"; the "Make Autorail Great Again Act," put forward by Florida Representative Greg Steube, would cut off every federal dollar to the "Washington Metropolitan Area Transit Authority (WMATA)" unless the agency formally rebranded itself as the "Washington Metropolitan Authority for Greater Access (WMAGA)" and renamed the DC Metro the "Trump Train"; Representative Warren Davidson of Ohio introduced the "Trump Derangement Syndrome (TDS) Research Act of 2025," which would "direct the National Institutes of Health (NIH) to study the psychological and social roots of what is known as Trump Derangement Syndrome, a phenomenon marked by extreme negative reactions to President Donald J. Trump"; Representative Brandon Gill of Texas introduced legislation requiring that all $100 bills featured a picture of Trump "on the front face of the note"; and Representative Joe Wilson of South Carolina one-upped him, introducing legislation that would require the creation of a $250 bill bearing the image of Trump to mark the 250th anniversary of the United States. (The bills would require an exemption to a law banning living figures from appearing on currency.)

III

Trump's control over Congress was aided by the fact that for the first time in his career in national politics, he had allowed an advisor to build a unified political operation around him.

During Trump's first campaign for office and during his first term, his team was riven by infighting and factionalism. There was much less of that now. Starting in 2021, Susie Wiles had stitched together a tight-knit inner circle and Trump would keep them all in place for the duration. They included two veteran GOP operatives, Tony Fabrizio and Chris LaCivita, forming a triumvirate with Wiles at the head of the campaign. LaCivita was a decorated Marine with decades of experience in national politics and a reputation for hardball tactics, most famously for conceiving the "Swift Boat" campaign to attack John Kerry's war record in the 2004 presidential election. Fabrizio was one of the most highly regarded pollsters in American politics. His numbers became such articles of faith on the Trump campaign that in dire moments the staff would sometimes say among themselves, "In Tony We Trust."

Wiles also brought on younger, loyal aides, including James Blair, a Florida political operative she had worked with in the lead-up to the 2018 governor's race; most of the team credited Blair with such an accurate read of the electoral data that it was clear to them by 8 p.m. on election night that Trump had won decisively.

They were all ruthless and all more effective at enforcing party-wide discipline than any previous iteration of Trump's political operation. When members of the 2024 Republican platform committee arrived at the convention in Milwaukee expecting the usual collaborative process, they were ambushed: their phones confiscated, debate and amendments forbidden, and Trump's own draft of the GOP platform presented to them as the final text. They were not allowed to change a word. The delegates were nothing more than rubber stamps.

The morning after his election victory, on November 6, 2024, Trump phoned his fundraiser, Meredith O'Rourke, telling her to keep up the momentum. This was the peak of his political leverage and he intended to make the most of it.

By then, Trump was already receiving phone calls from Fortune 500 CEOs, many of whom had criticized him in the past. He would soon have the power to crush their businesses or reward them if he felt so inclined. The price to get into Trump's good graces would be high. In conversations with O'Rourke, Trump would dictate the number—the exact dollar figure—he wanted her to extract from each CEO. Within days, millions of dollars, and then tens and hundreds of millions, were pouring into Trump's various fundraising accounts. So much was coming in, and so fast, that the Trump outside groups would have more money in their accounts than the Republican National Committee, the House Republican campaign arm, and the Senate Republican campaign arm—combined.

No President had ever marshaled this much political money as a lame duck. So much money was flooding the Trump accounts that the inauguration events were soon overfunded and Trump had to think about what else to do with all the cash. There would be a ballroom to build, a presidential library, a large triumphal arch in Washington, D.C., near the Lincoln Memorial. And there would be his political machine.

The stated goals of Trump's outside political groups would be to hold on to the House and Senate in the 2026 midterm elections, and to avoid an onslaught of subpoenas and a near-certain third impeachment that would result from Democrats taking control.

But they also planned to use the outside groups as weapons to enforce compliance. With Republicans holding only slim majorities in the House and Senate, Trump would need to keep wobbly Republicans in line to have a hope of passing his agenda. Wiles, LaCivita, and Fabrizio were mindful of Trump's determination to avoid a repeat of 2017, when his first major legislative effort—to repeal Obamacare—had failed when John McCain gave his dramatic thumbs-down on the Senate floor. Trump had never forgotten the humiliation and his advisors vowed it would not happen on their watch.

LaCivita told associates he thought Trump could sometimes be too forgiving of members he liked, where he could unexpectedly go soft. Trump would say things like "Ah, cut him some slack." Other advisors felt Trump could sometimes be too understanding of lawmakers' points of view, too willing to let them off the hook if they explained how certain votes might hurt their constituents. LaCivita and Fabrizio saw their role as enforcers—to ensure the fear of political death was never far from Republicans' minds.

Notwithstanding laws prohibiting fundraising on federal property, Trump and his team soon went around them. They would host "goodwill dinners" for big donors in what Trump called "the Rose Garden Club"—a paved-over patio with striped umbrellas where the old White House Rose Garden had been. By the fall of 2025, the *Axios* news site reported that Trump "had raised about $1.9 billion from an array of corporate donors to help finance his political committees, White House construction projects and celebrations of the nation's upcoming 250th anniversary." Of the President's evening fundraisers at his private clubs, an aide told *Axios*, "$10 million used to seem like a lot of money. Now it's like a ho-hum night."

As Trump began to govern, the giant and growing political bank balance augmented what was already a formidable apparatus of intimidation. Regarding the outside groups, LaCivita would explain, "It's the reason why the members of the House—the leadership of the House and the leadership in the Senate—are so willing to accept and to make law a lot of the things the President ran on, so quickly, without dissension, without debate. And when you do oppose, you get your fucking head kicked in."

It helped that Republican senators had an early demonstration of what happened to colleagues who opposed Trump's cabinet nominees. After Matt Gaetz withdrew his nomination, Trump's team decided they would not give in again on a major cabinet pick. Under previous Presidents, a nominee like Pete Hegseth—who faced accusations of excessive drinking, financial mismanagement, and had made a secret settlement with a woman who accused him of rape (an allegation he denied)—would have been a nonstarter. A powerful senator would have gone down the street and told the President they simply couldn't support him.

But such conversations were risky business in Trump's second term. Trump himself barely had to lift a finger. The MAGA machine had evolved so much since the first term that it was now virtually a self-driving car. It wasn't just that Trump had his well-funded political operation and a deep, visceral bond with the GOP base. He now had a social media army—Donald Trump Jr., Charlie Kirk, Steve Bannon, the right-wing influencer Jack Posobiec, and so many others—who had massive audiences and threatened any Republican who would consider voting against Trump's nominees.

Senator Joni Ernst of Iowa became an early test case of the new dynamic. As a sexual assault survivor and the first female combat veteran to serve in the Senate, Ernst harbored serious concerns about Hegseth, who had also voiced his opinion that women should not be allowed to serve in combat. After she briefly aired her misgivings, Trump's social media army came down hard on her and a dark-money group associated with Elon Musk began running digital ads in Iowa encouraging people to press Ernst to vote for Hegseth. Trump allies deployed other strong-arm tactics, threatening a primary challenger. Nothing seemed to be off-limits for Trump world. The details of Ernst's messy divorce began showing up on social media. She ended up withdrawing her opposition and voting for Hegseth, but less than a year later, this senator who had been seen as a rising star in the party announced she would not run again.

When Representative Thomas Massie of Kentucky voted against Trump on the Big Beautiful Bill, the Trump political machine promptly set up a super PAC in Kentucky, funded with more than a million dollars and dedicated to defeating the congressman in his next primary.

Republican members of Congress watched in fear and awe. No one wanted to suffer the Massie treatment. In the end, dozens of Republicans would vote for the Big Beautiful Bill even though they worried about voter backlash. To defy Trump on his signature legislation risked political suicide.

That was the route taken by Thom Tillis, the Republican senator from North Carolina who knew the Medicaid cuts would greatly harm his state, with the loss of billions of dollars and rural hospitals bearing the brunt. After much agonizing, Tillis concluded he could not in good conscience vote for the bill.

"What do I tell 663,000 people in two years or three years, when President Trump breaks his promise by pushing them off of Medicaid because the funding's not there anymore, guys?" Tillis said on the Senate floor before the bill's passage.

But by this point, his fate was sealed. Trump unleashed a verbal barrage, threatening to run a primary challenger against Tillis. The day after Trump's onslaught, June 29, this two-term U.S. senator announced he was retiring. His colleagues were in a state of shock. The episode, combined with the Trump team's ruthlessness against Massie, "reestablished that Trump was not to be fucked around with," said one close observer. "It was a reminder that this guy has the means, the capability, the ability, and the willingness to drown people. And drown people that get in his way."

The Senate approved the One Big Beautiful Bill by a vote of 51–50, with Vice President Vance casting the tiebreaking vote.

21

Elon Musk and Donald Trump finally split up at the end of May 2025 with a shower of invective from one side and the shattered trust of a broken marriage. After a public meltdown about Trump's Big Beautiful Bill, Musk escalated with another vicious serve against the President on June 5.

Trump, Musk posted on X, was one of the villains he had been warning his base about for years. "Time to drop the really big bomb: @realDonaldTrump is in the Epstein files. That is the real reason they have not been made public. Have a nice day, DJT!"

In a follow-up, Musk wrote: "Mark this post for the future. The truth will come out."

A month later, on July 7, the Department of Justice and the FBI released an unsigned one-and-a-half-page memo stating that after an exhaustive search of "its databases, hard drives, and network drives as well as physical searches of squad areas, locked cabinets, desks, closets, and other areas where responsive material may have been stored" and a corresponding review of more than three hundred gigabytes of evidence, the DOJ had concluded there was no evidence the notorious sex offender Jeffrey Epstein had maintained a "client list."

The memo also reaffirmed the original official finding that Epstein's death in 2019 had been a suicide. And with that, the memo indicated, the

Trump administration would not be releasing further information regarding the Epstein case, and no further investigation of uncharged third parties was warranted. The memo was accompanied by the release of video footage from the federal prison in Manhattan where Epstein had died, footage that officials said supported the conclusion of suicide.

Less than five months after Attorney General Pam Bondi had referred to a secret "client list" of high-profile predators, the case was closed. Or so it seemed.

If the administration expected the memo would be the last word on the Epstein case, and that the President's most ardent supporters would accept the purported conclusions of the Department of Justice simply because the department and its investigative agencies were now controlled by Donald Trump, they were sorely mistaken. The memo was an earthquake, and it was received by a portion of the MAGA base as a betrayal. It amounted to an abrupt disavowal of the sinister conspiracy theories that some of Trump's closest confidants had hyped during the Biden presidency and that they had promised to expose once Trump was returned to power.

On the *Lex Fridman Podcast* in September 2024, when asked about the "client list," Trump had responded, "I'd certainly take a look at it. . . . I'd have no problem with it." The list "probably will be" made public, he said, but he sounded half-hearted.

Trump's campaign allies and surrogates were far less circumspect. Donald Trump Jr. and JD Vance had invoked the Epstein files as a broader campaign message to argue that "powerful people" in the government were hiding the truth from Americans. Just weeks before the election, Vance told the podcast host Theo Von, "Seriously, we need to release the Epstein list. That is an important thing."

In the engine room of the MAGA movement during the 2024 campaign, the Epstein files were potent fuel. An Epstein information ecosystem of right-wing "influencers" had manned the coal shovel. Elon Musk had used his social media platform to repeatedly question why a "client list" had not been released. His posts reached hundreds of millions of users. The far-right conspiracy theorist Alex Jones used his Infowars platform to aggressively promote theories about a global pedophile ring. Tucker Carlson and Charlie

Kirk had both insisted the government should release the documents and floated the idea that there was a massive cover-up in progress. Congresswoman Marjorie Taylor Greene, who had seemingly never met a conspiracy theory she did not embrace, spent much of her political capital lobbying for the release of the files. There were so many more. Laura Loomer, conservative activist Scott Presler, Chaya Raichik from Libs of TikTok. The Hodgetwins. But when it came to propagating the Epstein files as evidence of a "deep state" capable of evil, two podcasters were not to be outdone.

On his own show *Kash's Corner*, and in appearances on programs like Benny Johnson's *The Benny Show*, Kash Patel—a National Security Council director for counterterrorism and Pentagon chief of staff in the first Trump era—had repeatedly claimed that the government was hiding Epstein's "black book" or "client list" of pedophiles. In a 2023 interview, he challenged officials to "put on your big-boy pants and let us know who the pedophiles are," and he frequently asserted that the FBI was deliberately withholding names to protect the powerful. Patel promised a second Trump administration would release "everything" to restore public trust.

On *The Dan Bongino Show*, Bongino's background as a Secret Service agent had lent authority to his claims of a cover-up. "What the hell are they hiding with Jeffrey Epstein?" he'd asked his large audience. The release of the files would "rock the political world," he promised. The "Washington swamp" was "not telling you the truth."

Now he and Patel—whose appointments to run the FBI had been greeted with righteous enthusiasm by Epstein files obsessives—were tightly connected to a memo that stated, in black and white, that while information in the government's possession showed ample evidence of Epstein's own wrongdoing, there was no evidence of a wider conspiracy.

Both men had been raising alarms internally that the Epstein crisis was gathering momentum with the base. Bongino hated the memo. He told Patel it would in no way align with their promises of transparency after taking over the FBI, and he objected to putting the FBI seal on the letterhead. He was overruled.

Patel privately shared many of Bongino's concerns. But in an internal email on Wednesday, July 2, the FBI director gave his support.

"Thanks for the edits, and I still believe this is the correct vehicle forward," Patel wrote to a small group of colleagues, including Deputy Attorney General Todd Blanche. "I'm happy to add any additional sentences to compete [*sic*] the short fall. But I do think we addressed specifically why more can't be released as it relates to specific topics ie court order, csam [child sexual abuse material], victim protections etc."

Bondi rarely used her Justice Department email and was not on the chain where they workshopped the memo that set off the crisis. She was aware of both the planned memo and the prison video release, but was not involved in editing the document.

Inside the White House, Trump had no interest in releasing anything. And senior officials—including Susie Wiles and her deputy, James Blair—were initially skeptical about the reach of the Epstein crisis. They told colleagues that Republican voters didn't care, and they had Tony Fabrizio's polling to prove it. The Epstein brouhaha, in their view, was driven by fringe conspiracy theorists and amplified by noisy online influencers who didn't represent a meaningful bloc of voters.

Bongino told anyone who would listen that this was a grave mistake.

"It's not an online story. You don't understand," he told several White House advisors.

Wiles, Blair, and others thought at the time that engaging with the Epstein situation would only enlarge it—putting an official stamp on the matter. Besides, Trump had weathered every storm imaginable for years. Why would this be any different?

Nevertheless, Trump attempted to keep his angry supporters in line. On July 12, the President took to Truth Social to defend Pam Bondi against criticism and he urged his "boys" and "gals" to stop "wasting Time and Energy on Jeffrey Epstein, somebody that nobody cares about." Trump told aides he was very unhappy with some of his most influential supporters including Charlie Kirk, Tucker Carlson, and Megyn Kelly, all of whom were publicly urging the administration to come clean. Kirk had held a Turning Point USA event the previous day that had turned into a complete Epstein grievance fest, with one speaker after another taking shots at Bondi over her handling of the Epstein situation. Trump had called Kirk and scolded him.

As with the Israel issue, nobody in Trump's orbit had a better feel for the younger part of the MAGA base than Kirk, who saw that the Epstein "cover-up," as it was now viewed, was cutting through to an alarming extent. Donald Trump Jr. and JD Vance—both of whom spent a lot of time on X and were tapped into the same younger and hyper-online portion of the base—were also very worried. They urged the White House to change course and to force the DOJ to release more of the files. Vance feared losing some of the so-called "low-propensity voters," the young men who were not traditional Republicans but who had voted for the Trump-Vance ticket in 2024. This was an audience tuned in to the "manosphere" podcasters like Joe Rogan, and it was worrisome that the podcast hosts themselves were rebelling.

But there was one major obstacle in the path of a solution: The President himself still had no interest in transparency. In fact, he wanted the whole Epstein issue buried and he was snapping at anyone who mentioned it. His staff largely avoided the subject in their conversations with Trump over the coming days, forced to fret among themselves.

On July 8, with reporters still pushing on Epstein, Trump snapped, "Are people still talking about this guy, this creep? That is unbelievable. Do you want to waste the time?"

Finally, on July 16, in an exasperated Truth Social post, seemingly desperate to make his case in language that might be resonant with his base, Trump somewhat nonsensically called the Epstein case a "hoax" by Democrats, and then proceeded to heap abuse on members of his party and his base, disavowing their support, calling them "PAST supporters" and "weaklings" who had "bought into this 'bullshit,' hook, line, and sinker."

The President's anger and his defensive response made it look as though he had something to hide. The story that Trump seemed unable to escape was his old party-days friendship with Jeffrey Epstein, who would be unmasked, over many years, as one of the most abusive predators and pedophiles ever to have cultivated the powerful. Everything about the story was depraved; but for the women caught in his web, many of them underage, it was far worse.

If July 16 at the White House had been tough, the next day things would get even worse. The official line was that while Trump and Epstein had been friendly for years in New York and Palm Beach (something undeniable, given the documentary evidence of a close friendship was abundant online), Trump had broken with Epstein twenty years before, and that from then on Trump had assumed a very dim view of the sex offender. White House aides ascribed the break to Epstein's abhorrent behavior with young girls, while Trump himself would later say he broke with Epstein because Epstein "stole" young girls who worked at the spa at Mar-a-Lago. Some White House aides cringed at Trump's explanation.

Now the Trump team was having to deal with a new story on the way from *The Wall Street Journal* that would raise from the dead, yet again, the uncomfortably chummy relationship between Trump and Epstein.

The *Journal* story took readers back to 2003, when Epstein, already a notorious bachelor, was celebrating his fiftieth birthday. The paper planned to report that Donald Trump, and many others, had created birthday cards and letters to be assembled into a special birthday book. The year before, in a profile of Epstein in *New York* magazine, Trump had been quoted as saying of his friend: "I've known Jeff for fifteen years. Terrific guy. He's a lot of fun to be with. It is even said that he likes beautiful women as much as I do, and many of them are on the younger side."

The Trump birthday card for Epstein was bawdy and seemed in keeping with their shared attraction. It depicted a nude woman, hand-drawn, and inscribed with an imagined dialogue between the two men about a "wonderful secret." The card was signed with what appeared to be Trump's jagged Sharpie signature, in place of the woman's pubic hair. Trump advisors giggled privately about the description of the drawing, but most claimed it was a forgery.

Trump called the *Journal*'s editor in chief, Emma Tucker, in an effort to kill the story. Practically shouting, he told Tucker that she must "hate America." He told her he would file a lawsuit.

Trump also called Tucker's boss, News Corp CEO Robert Thomson, and News Corp's owner, Rupert Murdoch, directly.

The presidential tantrum staved off immediate publication, but not for long. "He doesn't like being threatened," said one close observer of Murdoch.

II

The Situation Room was the secure, twenty-four-hour intelligence and crisis-management center on the ground floor of the West Wing, the nerve center for national security decision-making for the President and senior staff. It provided secure communications, enabling the President to contemporaneously process intelligence coming in from the military, the intelligence community, and Homeland Security to handle crises and formulate policy. It was not a single room, but rather a complex of secure conference rooms, offices, and workstations designed to accommodate the most critical and classified discussions and operations necessary for the United States government to function. On May 1, 2011, the White House photographer Pete Souza had famously snapped President Barack Obama and his national security team including Vice President Joe Biden and Secretary of State Hillary Clinton receiving live updates as Navy SEALs raided the Pakistan hideout of Osama bin Laden, killing him in the process. The operation had ended the ten-year manhunt for the mastermind of one of the greatest atrocities ever committed on U.S. soil—the 9/11 attacks, resulting in the death of almost three thousand Americans.

The Situation Room was not typically used to deal with political issues like the Epstein files, but on July 17, 2025, at about six o'clock in the evening, it was the setting for a gathering of Trump's most senior advisors to figure out how to gain some measure of control over the crisis enveloping the administration.

Everyone needed to get on the same page about how to tamp down the Epstein media swarm. Ignoring it hadn't worked. They needed a gesture of transparency to appease an increasingly angry base, and to convey the idea that the President was sympathetic to their concerns. Which itself was a problem, because he clearly wasn't.

Vice President Vance was seated at the head of the table in the John F. Kennedy Conference Room with other senior administration officials arrayed around—Chief of Staff Susie Wiles, White House counsel David Warrington, Press Secretary Karoline Leavitt, Deputy Chief of Staff Taylor Budowich, Communications Director Steven Cheung, Deputy Attorney General Todd Blanche, Associate Attorney General Stanley Woodward, and Deputy Chief of Staff James Blair. Attorney General Pam Bondi and FBI Director Kash Patel joined on the speakerphone, which sat on the table in front of Vance.

The vice president could see more clearly than any of the White House officials in the room just how profoundly Epstein was dividing the MAGA coalition. He jumped in early, saying, "This is a huge problem." Another senior official said later that Vance had been pounding on the Epstein issue since the release of the memo and had been telling people in the administration that Bondi needed to do a full public mea culpa. He was pressing for the administration to release all the Epstein files and calling for a congressional investigation. Vance had floated internally an extraordinary PR gambit—that the White House enlist Tucker Carlson to interview Epstein's former girlfriend and co-conspirator, Ghislaine Maxwell, in prison. It might help the President to have Maxwell say he did nothing wrong with Epstein.

Vance said he wanted all the files released as soon as possible. Beyond the moral argument—that the public had a right to know—Vance made a pragmatic case that few in the room wanted to hear. Congress was going to force the release of the files eventually, he argued. It was already clear that a bipartisan coalition was forming on the Hill, and the momentum was only going in one direction. If the administration got out ahead of it and released everything voluntarily—including whatever material existed about the President—they would at least get the credit for transparency. The alternative was to let the story drag on for months as information dripped out, each new revelation renewing the cycle of suspicion and fury. Better to rip the bandage off and move on.

Even the unsubstantiated anecdotes about Trump should go out, Vance argued. They were going to surface regardless, and if the administration was the one publishing them, it would demonstrate good faith and take the oxygen out of the conspiracy theories. This was an argument no one else was willing to make.

There was a push by some to have DOJ officials call a press conference to explain the department's position on the Epstein affair, beyond the short statement that had precipitated the crisis. At this point in the meeting, James Blair spoke up. "With all due respect," he said, "the communications strategy of this group got us here. I don't know that it's going to get us out. And if you're going to go in front of the press, you've got a lot of work to do." He began to ask pointed questions, demonstrating how difficult a press conference might be.

The Justice Department had struggled with just how to dispose of the Epstein matter since the beginning of the second term. Because the issue was all-consuming for the President's political base, but also potentially compromising for the President himself in ways that officials in the new administration didn't fully understand, the way forward was fraught.

And the Trump Justice Department was subject to pressures that no other DOJ would typically face. Bondi herself had done some of that damage, committing what had been widely regarded as two egregious missteps early on.

First, in an interview with Fox News on February 21, Bondi had seemed to both confirm a client list existed and hint at its imminent release. When asked whether the DOJ may be releasing the list of Jeffrey Epstein's clients, she responded, "It's sitting on my desk right now to review."

On February 27, the White House Communications Office had scheduled a lineup of cabinet officials to brief popular right-wing influencers in the Roosevelt Room. The session began with the vice president, followed by the secretary of state, walking the influencers through the administration's agenda. In attendance was a who's who of online MAGA: Mike Cernovich, Liz Wheeler, Collin Rugg, and DC Draino. The President himself had brought them all to the Oval Office and given them custom-designed challenge coins as a token of his appreciation. Before everything went wrong, one of them would remark, "It was the best day of my life."

When it was time for the group to meet the attorney general, Bondi and her team walked into the Roosevelt Room carrying boxes. Bondi had brought binders as handouts for the influencers; her aides would later tell colleagues that the FBI had prepared them and assured her that they contained revelatory details. Someone on her staff said, "Watch this, this is cool. This is going to be epic." The White House staff had no idea what was in the handouts. As Bondi's staff started distributing the binders, the blood pressure of other staff in the room skyrocketed as they realized what was happening: The attorney general was handing out something she was calling "the Epstein files" that had not been vetted by anyone in the White House. One official, opening the binder, began flipping through pages to see if Trump's name was mentioned anywhere. A few pages in, right in the middle of the page, there it was.

Keir Starmer, the British prime minister, was in the White House that day. If news broke that the Epstein files had been released before the President was to meet the press with the prime minister—if even as some sort of confusing gimmick—that would be all the journalists would want to talk about. And Trump would be blindsided.

One of Trump's aides hastily steered the influencers out of the White House, telling them the content of the binders was embargoed until after the President's press conference with Starmer, but that the Communications Office would be more than happy to talk about the files after that. As the influencers left, they all snapped selfies in front of the White House holding their binders, quickly posting the pictures to social media. They had created a shock wave of anticipation for what might be in them—and it was followed immediately by the influencers getting thrashed online for not sharing the information.

How could something so important be embargoed? Was the Trump administration trifling with the influencers? Yes, as it turned out.

Bondi's binders contained information about Epstein and his activities that had long been publicly available. They contained almost nothing new. But they had set the hares running. When Bondi had met the influencers in the Roosevelt Room, she told them that this was just the first tranche of files. There would be more coming, she assured them. But that story would change, too. And by early July, the administration would send out a different message: *Never mind.*

Like some in the White House, Bondi had either grossly underestimated, or simply been blind to, the base's appetite for information about Epstein and those in his sphere of influence, and for justice to be finally done. She had somehow simultaneously oversold and trivialized the Epstein files.

Once the team at the DOJ began looking at some of the Epstein material, it was disturbing. Bondi was particularly rattled by Epstein's collection of pornography that investigators had shown her. She wanted other Trump officials to understand how much of it there was. And yet it would be months before the Justice Department grasped the full complexity and volume of what it possessed.

III

Several weeks before the release of the DOJ memo, Bondi and Todd Blanche had briefed the President on the status of the Epstein review.

"We've gone through the files," Blanche told Trump. "There's not a lot there. A lot of child pornography—obviously we can't put any of that out. There are some mentions of you, but nothing substantive."

The files contained a trove of 302 forms—records of FBI interviews with witnesses. Trump was mentioned numerous times, as were other prominent men. Releasing the 302s was a nonstarter.

But doing nothing had made everything worse. For weeks, Patel and Bongino had grown more infuriated as they realized the scale of the mess for which they had become the public face. They reassured allies—on social media, in private conversations—that they were taking the matter seriously. But the pressure was building. Bongino wanted to say something definitive to the MAGA base, and he and Patel pushed for the immediate release of the surveillance footage from the federal facility where Epstein had died. The video release turned out to be a disaster.

The Justice Department ended up releasing roughly eleven hours of prison video intended to show that nothing nefarious had occurred. But the footage contained a "missing minute"—a visible time stamp jump from

11:58:58 p.m. to midnight. The DOJ attributed this to a nightly system reset. To many of Trump's followers, it was yet more evidence of a cover-up. White House officials said they hadn't been told about the gap before the release. Social media lit up with blame—not just for Bondi, but for Patel and Bongino, too.

None of the three had ever experienced anger from the base at this volume. It was disorienting, especially for Patel and Bongino, whose power and influence had been built online. The movement that had treated them as heroes was now turning on them.

After the release of the memo, and the predictably furious reaction, Kash Patel was still trying to stay on good terms with the White House. But Dan Bongino had had enough.

On Monday, July 7—the day the memo was released broadly—the deputy FBI director showed up to a daily Justice Department meeting with the FBI staff and the attorney general. Bongino was in a volcanic mood. As soon as he entered the room, he erupted at Bondi, shouting at her.

"You fucked this thing up from the start," Bongino yelled. "The way you've been talking about this—that dumb fucking charade with the Epstein files, the *They're on my desk* nonsense, all the promises to the folks out there."

Patel and Bongino both told a White House official that Bondi needed to resign.

Two days later, on Wednesday, July 9, the two men were summoned to a meeting with Wiles and Bondi in the Situation Room complex. They were the last to enter the small, wood-paneled room. Seated around the table were Bondi, Wiles, Blanche, and Taylor Budowich. The moment Bongino sat down, Wiles told him she'd been informed he had leaked a sensitive story about Epstein and Trump to ABC News.

"I'll tell you what," Bongino replied. "I'll give you a hundred thousand dollars cash right now. I'm not kidding. Walk out to West Exec, put that reporter on speaker, and get him to admit I leaked it. A hundred thousand dollars."

Wiles snapped back, "Well, we all got ourselves into this—"

Bongino cut her off.

"No no no no no. *We* didn't get ourselves into anything. I warned you guys about this the whole time and you ignored me and exactly what I said was going to happen happened. And now you're pretending I was in on this. I was never in on this."

Bongino's aggressive response to Wiles startled the others; she was the White House chief of staff, essentially a stand-in for the President.

Wiles put Bongino on the spot. "Going forward," she said, "we're all in. We're all going to agree to move forward. Are you in or not?"

"No. I'm not," Bongino said. "This is not my plan. I'm not part of this going forward. Forget it. I'm out of here."

He stormed out of the Situation Room and onto West Executive Avenue, where he climbed into the back of Patel's armored SUV and directed the driver to take him to FBI headquarters.

Some of Bongino's friends hoped he would resign right then—an act of protest over the Epstein cover-up that would have made him a MAGA martyr and only grown his following. But White House advisors urged him to stay. If he quit over Epstein and went public, it would severely damage the President. Bongino told associates he would remain for Trump's sake, and keep pushing for more Epstein information to be released.

Privately, he seethed. In conversations with confidants he lamented what the job had cost him. He said he'd lost tens of millions in podcast revenue, family time, and his audience. He was getting his head kicked in over a strategy he had opposed from the start.

The relationships at the top of the DOJ were by now beyond dysfunctional. At another meeting in July, in Susie Wiles's office, Bongino and Patel told the chief of staff they suspected Bondi had leaked against them.

"Blondie fucked this whole thing up," Bongino later told a confidant, repeating Laura Loomer's derisive nickname for the attorney general. "She was the one on TV saying over and over they had all this stuff. There was never anything. We were always clear about that. But now everyone thinks we did something wrong. And I gave up everything. I had the number one show on the radio. I gave up forty-four million dollars. Living my best life. And now it's all disappeared, because people think we screwed something up with Epstein."

Bongino paused.

"This is going to be President Trump's Iran-Contra."

In the Situation Room meeting on July 17—ten days after the release of the memo that had put nothing to rest—Todd Blanche laid out what he saw as their best options.

Option one was to petition the court to unseal the grand jury testimonies, which were almost certain to contain no significant new information, and which everyone agreed was a good idea. Under the Federal Rules of Criminal Procedure, the secrecy of grand jury materials was regarded by most federal judges as almost always inviolate, and the bar for its release was exceptionally high. If the liberal judge refused to unseal them—as Blanche predicted—they could shift the blame for the Epstein cover-up away from the Trump administration and onto Democrats. Blanche's suggestion would make it appear that the White House wanted the materials released, when it was almost certainly impossible.

Option two was to have DOJ lawyers question Ghislaine Maxwell. Blanche was happy to interview Maxwell himself; he had been more deeply immersed in the Epstein material than any others among the DOJ leadership. The Justice Department had had a hostile relationship with parts of the Manhattan federal prosecutor's office since the first week of the second Trump term. And Maurene Comey, the daughter of the former FBI director whom Trump had fired in 2017, had been the main prosecutor on the Epstein case. She was fired with no explanation a day before the Situation Room meeting convened. She was well-liked by her colleagues, and Trump's team at the DOJ believed they wouldn't get much help from the Manhattan office.

"What if we got her to talk to Congress?" Vance proposed, referring to Ghislaine Maxwell.

Blanche raised the possibility that Maxwell's lawyer might expect something in return for her candor.

White House counsel David Warrington described the options available, without advocating for any of them. There is the option of giving her a pardon, he said, or she could also have her sentence reduced.

At that, several around the table spoke up to register their strong disapproval.

"Pardoning Maxwell, a trafficker of young girls, would create a huge PR problem," said Steven Cheung. He predicted that in the wake of a pardon, the Epstein accusers would be fanning out on TV, telling their stories and ripping the administration to shreds.

James Blair was also adamantly opposed to a pardon. "We can't offer Ghislaine Maxwell anything," he said. "A, I don't know why we would. And B, if we give Ghislaine Maxwell any sort of break whatsoever and then she turns around and says nice things about us, or says nice things about us and we give her a break, it will undermine the entire point of her saying good things. That will feed the conspiracy theory, period. If there's nothing for her to say that hurts us, we shouldn't have to offer her anything."

The consensus was that option one was the best course of action. Wiles told the group she would handle the matter with Trump, and ask if he would send a Truth Social post calling for the release of the grand jury testimony.

Just then, the *Wall Street Journal* story broke. A Situation Room staffer brought in printed copies, and as the group sat quietly and read the story, Wiles readied another denial for the President to post on social media.

IV

In late July, another Epstein crisis meeting convened in the Situation Room, with most of the same group: Wiles and Vance, Todd Blanche, David Warrington, Kash Patel, Pam Bondi, James Blair, Steven Cheung, Taylor Budowich, and Karoline Leavitt. This meeting would coincide with Trump aides being caught off guard by news that a subpoena would soon land from the House Oversight Committee, led by Republican James Comer, which caught the White House off guard. It had been pushed by committee Democrats, with the help of Republicans Thomas Massie and Marjorie Taylor Greene, and it compelled the release of voluminous material the Justice Department had on Epstein.

At the same time, in the face of DOJ stonewalling, Massie and Democratic Congressman Ro Khanna had filed H.R.4405, the Epstein Files Transparency Act, in the House, and although they did not yet have the votes for the bill, the push had begun in earnest. It would become the next battleground over the Epstein files as the President dug in against releasing information.

In the Situation Room, Blair told his colleagues they would try to make sure they were cooperating fully with the House subpoena, but the priority was to release information that demonstrated Trump was not involved in Epstein's crimes.

Todd Blanche gave an assessment of the Epstein material he had personally reviewed or been briefed on, including a volume of child pornography. The conversation turned to how these files should be released to the public. The idea in the works had been to put all Epstein-related material up on a public-facing website. That way, they could overwhelm the MAGA-sphere with far-greater volumes of real information—in the form of a huge database. The website had been easy to build and they were looking at potentially launching it within a week. They had already accumulated a mountain of material that Blanche had been scrolling through, and it included piles of documents from both civil and criminal cases. They planned to release it all. Under this plan, Blanche could then appear on the Joe Rogan podcast to tout the transparency from the White House.

But as it turned out, this searchable public website would not go live on their initial timetable of the next week. And the version of the website they had originally conceived would never be released to the public.

Two weeks later, on August 13, they held yet another Epstein meeting in the Situation Room, convening at 6 p.m. for two hours to refine the strategy. Again, the group included Wiles, Bondi, Blanche, Patel, Blair, Budowich, Cheung, Leavitt, and Vance phoning in from the UK, where he had been having meetings, including with the deputy prime minister, David Lammy.

Vance once again pushed aggressively to release as much of the Epstein files as possible. And with an eye on the public messaging, he proposed that he should be the one to appear on the influential Joe Rogan podcast. Vance had just gotten off the phone with Rogan, and he later told others that Rogan said he wouldn't have Blanche on his show, but he would take Vance.

Vance argued in the meeting that if he were the one to do the Rogan interview then only a portion of the conversation would be about Epstein. He said the rest of the interview could be about the President's recently passed legislation and what it would do for working families.

The bigger conversation was how to handle any public relations risks for the administration. The challenge would be any embarrassing or damaging allegations about the President, even if they were unsubstantiated. If everything publicly available was on a big website, it could include all kinds of potentially humiliating material.

One of the officials in the Situation Room raised the subject of a particularly vile, uncorroborated accusation against Trump that had come to light in unsealed filings from a 2015 defamation case brought by Virginia Giuffre against Ghislaine Maxwell, which was settled two years later. Giuffre, who met Epstein when she was a teenage spa attendant at Mar-a-Lago, became one of his most outspoken victims. She took her own life in April 2025. Giuffre had said in 2016 that, to her knowledge, Trump had done nothing improper.

In the Giuffre case file were emails sent to a journalist by another Epstein victim, Sarah Ransome, who later sued Epstein and Maxwell herself. Epstein settled that case. In the emails, Ransome claimed she knew a girl in Epstein's sex-trafficking ring named Jen, who said she had sex with Donald Trump, that he had a nipple fetish and had flicked and sucked her nipples. Ransome wrote that she had seen evidence when she shared a bathroom with Jen. "They looked incredibly painful as they were red and swollen and I remember wincing when I looked at them," she wrote.

Ransome's credibility was not uncomplicated; she made other claims that she later retracted, saying she had only done so because she feared for herself and her family. In December 2023, a federal judge ordered the unsealing of some Giuffre case files. The document that connected Trump to the claim about abused nipples became public the following month. It was just an allegation and had not been made publicly by "Jen," but the disclosure led to some embarrassing news stories.

Trump's advisors in the Situation Room who were even aware of the nipple claim seemed to have only a passing familiarity with it. Many in the room thought this was all just discredited nonsense. But some argued that none of the credibility issues would matter if a government database gave Ransome's claim a stamp of validity. There was a vast horde of Epstein fanatics in the MAGA base, and they wanted the names of rich and powerful men to tear apart.

An administration official had already searched for Trump-related materials on the still-private test version of the DOJ's Epstein website, and the nipple material was among the first things to show up. Others in the Situation Room understood quickly that the partial emails could get fresh life breathed into them if they were included in a "public-facing and searchable" Epstein library that carried the branding of the Justice Department.

"This is out there," one of the officials told the group in the Situation Room. "They're going to make a huge scene of this even though it's not true and everybody knows it."

Blanche argued that in context, the Ransome document—and her disavowal of some of her other claims—would make clear why the nipple allegations related to Trump hadn't been pursued for prosecution. Besides, these allegations had long been available online, so there was no reason to leave them off the public-facing DOJ website.

The vice president said he thought the President would be okay with releasing the files, saying Trump had been accused of worse. "I think we should put it out," he said. "It would cause people to say we're going further than we need to." Wiles quickly responded that the President would not, in fact, be okay with it. It was a point no one wanted to continue arguing. One of the officials would later describe it as a "surreal" experience to be discussing Donald Trump and abused nipples in the White House Situation Room.

Having chosen opacity over transparency, this was what the White House was left with. The nipple claim was, in miniature, the entire problem the White House had with the Epstein files: Piles of accusations were impossible to disprove, and equally impossible to make go away. Every door they opened led to another room, and in every room were more claims from more women. And now they were threatening to avalanche onto a President who wanted nothing to do with any of it.

The discussion illuminated something else that was relevant and pointed to the way forward. The subpoena from James Comer's committee had specifically requested DOJ files and criminal cases. They would simply comply with the subpoena. The House demand did not seek material from civil cases, like the nipple claim, that did not originate with the DOJ. Those were separate matters, and wholly outside the remit of the Justice Department. The subpoena was the only thing they had to adhere to.

Soon it would become clear that what had started that month would bring relentless scrutiny of Trump's lifestyle in earlier days. This self-inflicted crisis would paralyze the White House for the rest of the year every bit as much as the Russia investigation of eight years earlier. Vance had predicted exactly this trajectory—and as the months rolled on and the crisis only deepened, his early and insistent warnings that the administration was squandering whatever control it had over the story proved difficult to dispute.

V

As the Epstein crisis ground on, Trump received a welcome burst of good news from an unlikely source.

Director of National Intelligence Tulsi Gabbard had been in bad shape with the President. She had been cut out of meetings, sidelined from major national security decisions, and was treated as an afterthought and a subject of derision by Trump and his inner circle. Less than six weeks earlier, Trump had berated Gabbard in front of a room full of people over a video she had filmed of herself visiting Hiroshima, one of the two Japanese cities destroyed by American atomic bombs during World War II. In the video, she warned of a "nuclear holocaust" brought on by saber-rattling "warmongers."

Trump, on the verge of joining Israel in strikes against Iran, was enraged. Gabbard, he said, was using her perch in his administration to build her own brand. If you want to be President, he said sharply to her, you have to leave this job.

But Gabbard had now found a way to redeem herself. On July 23, six days after the Situation Room meeting where Blanche discussed the possibility of interviewing Ghislaine Maxwell, she stood at the White House briefing room podium with a dramatic announcement: President Obama and his most senior intelligence advisors had been part of a "yearslong coup and treasonous conspiracy" to harm Trump, she declared. She had referred the matter to the Justice Department for prosecution.

Trump was delighted. He had long wanted Democrats prosecuted over what he repeatedly called the "Russia hoax"—the special-counsel investigation that had produced indictments of Roger Stone, Paul Manafort, and Michael Cohen, and brought subpoenas down on his family and his business. He would never accept that Russia had meddled in the 2016 election to help him win it.

The criminal referral was flawed at best. Obama was shielded by the same presidential immunity ruling the Supreme Court had issued before Trump won the White House again, and the matter was now yet another hot potato landing in Pam Bondi's lap. But while Gabbard's effort would take several more months to start yielding results, it gave Trump something he badly needed: a distraction from the Epstein debacle. And it set in motion something he hoped would undo the stain of "Russiagate" on his legacy for good.

22

Almost immediately after Trump won the 2024 election, he began pondering what to do about Jerome Powell.

Of all the institutions in Washington, none vexed Trump more than the Federal Reserve. By law it was independent of a President's control—one of the few instruments of national power that lay beyond his reach. This was power of great attraction to Trump—power over the economy and power to create money out of thin air.

In his first term, Trump had wanted to direct the actions of the Fed and he had wanted to fire Powell. But he had been talked out of it and ended up doing relatively little aside from airing his grievances on Twitter. In his second term he was determined to enforce his will over the Fed. And standing in his way was the same stubborn man he had tangled with in term one.

During the 2024 transition, as Trump weighed whom to appoint as treasury secretary in his second term, he had met at Mar-a-Lago with Kevin Warsh, a former Federal Reserve governor he knew from his first term. In a case of sliding doors, he had interviewed Warsh in 2017 for the job that he later gave to Powell—a hiring decision Trump came to rue.

Trump told others he thought Warsh was handsome. Before settling on Scott Bessent for treasury secretary, Trump had considered giving Treasury to Warsh or even attempting to install him early to lead the Fed before

Powell's term expired. Two years later, in early 2026, Warsh could finally see his chance for the top of the Fed when he was nominated as Powell's successor. But not before a thunderstorm of Trump-style vilification had enveloped the central bank as Powell and the President battled over independence.

As he had in his first term, Trump canvassed advisors about firing Powell and about the likely consequences. During the transition his advisors repeated the warnings he received during term one: The case would likely go up to the Supreme Court and he might lose. In the meantime, advisors cautioned, the markets would probably have a meltdown. Trump reluctantly accepted their advice. But the problem of Powell continued to gnaw at him.

The President had not always regarded Powell as an enemy. Trump had elevated Powell from the Federal Reserve Board of Governors to chair the central bank in the fall of 2017, on the recommendation of his treasury secretary, Steven Mnuchin. Trump didn't know Powell, but at first glance (and that was about all he took before making the appointment) he was impressed by the former investment banker, who looked "straight out of central casting" with his trim suits and purple neckties.

"You're going to be great. I trust you," Trump had told Powell after informing him he was going to be the Fed chair. "I know you're going to be independent. I trust you to do the right thing." Trump soon regretted the decision, complaining that Powell was sabotaging his presidency by raising interest rates. He was still grumbling to aides eight years later, "Mnuchin fucked me."

In retrospect, the purple neckties Powell insisted on wearing should have been a warning sign. Powell, a model of rectitude, would tell associates he wanted to avoid wearing a color that could link him visually with one of the two political parties—Democratic blue or Republican red. "We are nonpolitical," Powell told a gathering of business journalists. "We don't do that and so purple is a good color for that."

Trump had no use for purple. He wanted a Fed chairman who would serve as his vassal and whose priorities would have little to do with the actual job description of chairing the central bank, which was to manage the long-term interests of the U.S. economy, balancing the twin goals of steady price levels and low unemployment. Instead, Trump wanted the Fed chair to juice the short-term economy to boost his popularity.

Back in the early summer of 2018, only five months after Powell was sworn in, Trump began a public campaign to pressure the bank into cutting rates. It had been a long time since a President had made such a concerted effort to interfere with the Fed, but the institution had always withstood political pressure from the White House, and since Richard Nixon, Presidents had mostly respected the Fed's independence.

But Trump would interfere more aggressively and more brazenly than any President before him. Powell would later tell others it was a "shocking experience" and "such an incredible violation of norms." The Fed raised interest rates four times in 2018, with Trump growing angrier at Powell each time; Trump's rage only deepened through 2019.

The attacks from Trump had bothered Powell at first, and he told associates he felt "bad" about it, but after a while he developed a thicker skin. He was a savvy political player himself, and he knew he enjoyed strong bipartisan support in Congress. In private, Republican senators encouraged an approach that Powell already instinctively believed was the right one: Just ignore Trump, don't engage. "He wants you to engage," Powell would later tell others. "If you engage, you're playing his game."

Trump's approach to the Fed could best be understood in the context of his view of the presidency as an instrument of unchecked power and dominance. His concept of the central bank's role was quite at odds with its mandate.

The framers had taken measures to avoid the danger of allowing a President the power to create money. Instead they gave Congress the authority to coin money and regulate its value in Article I, Section 8 of the Constitution. Congress then took its own steps to ensure monetary policy would serve America's long-term interests. Beginning with the Federal Reserve Act of 1913, Congress had constructed layers of insulation to give the Fed independent authority over monetary policy—structures specifically designed to prevent any one President from stacking the board. These were the walls Trump wanted to tear down.

In defending the Federal Reserve's independence, Powell had set himself on a collision course with the President. "My only question is, who is our bigger enemy," Trump tweeted in the summer of 2019, "Jay Powel [*sic*] or Chairman Xi?"

It didn't help that Powell exemplified the type of Washington establishment figure whose approval Trump craved even as he resented him: the policy wonk who would occasionally invoke higher principles. Trump would privately refer to such people as "Boy Scouts" and he didn't mean it as a compliment.

For his part, Powell had told associates he thought Trump "would be navigable" in a second term. In Powell's view, Trump was inheriting "a heck of an economy" with high growth, low inflation, and low unemployment. Powell figured that Trump was a "survivalist," with "an animal intelligence about him," and that he would just surf the wave of the economy. He did not anticipate Trump doing anything to disrupt a soft landing from the high inflation of the early Biden years.

II

Ironically, it was Trump himself who would make it more difficult for Powell to lower rates.

The tariffs Trump had imposed in the first several months of the second term injected great uncertainty into the economy and brought inevitable price increases and the potential for elevated inflation. Powell quickly had to manage both a sluggish labor market and inflation that was above the Fed's 2 percent target rate. Tariffs would not help with either factor, Powell thought.

On April 16, two weeks after Liberation Day, Powell declared at an event hosted by the Economic Club of Chicago that Trump's tariff regime constituted "very fundamental changes" and "there isn't a modern experience on how to think about this." He said "the level of the tariff increases announced so far is significantly larger than anticipated" and warned of challenges to both inflation and the labor market.

Trump erupted on Truth Social the next day: "Powell's termination cannot come fast enough!"

With financial markets still on edge so soon after Liberation Day, two of the President's closest aides urged him to reassure the world that he was not about to add a new massive disruption by firing the chairman of the central bank. Susie Wiles and Scott Bessent privately told Trump he should do more to project stability. Why, Wiles wanted to know, had Trump threatened to fire Powell? "You know it causes instability. And we need stability right now," she said to him. Bessent suggested to the President that he assure the markets he was not firing Powell. "You've told me you're not firing him," Bessent told Trump. "You need to say it because it's hurting us. So, if you're not going to fire him, then you need to say it."

On April 22, Trump finally did say it. He claimed he "never did" plan to fire Powell and he blamed the press for misinterpreting him. That he was finally willing to publicly rule out firing the head of the central bank—even though he so clearly still wanted to—was an indication of the pressure he was feeling just two weeks after pushing his tariff policy to the brink of a financial crisis.

Trump had not lost his determination to bend the Federal Reserve; he just needed a new angle. In May, he told advisors he planned to try a different tack with Powell.

Public pressure hadn't worked, so why not see if a private conversation might persuade Powell to push for lower rates? Trump mused about inviting Powell to the White House for lunch, but quickly thought better of it, telling an aide that if the conversation went badly he'd be "stuck" with Powell. He decided an Oval Office meeting would be preferable. An invitation was sent to the chairman. It was hardly welcome and Powell would later tell associates, "the perfectly appropriate number of meetings between a Fed chair and the President" is "zero."

But he did not want to further inflame the situation by turning Trump down. And he knew exactly what he wanted to say. Powell was known as an over-preparer, but he didn't feel the need to prepare for this meeting—he knew what Trump was going to say and his own response would be straightforward.

On May 29, Trump had just finished his intelligence briefing when he was informed that Powell was waiting in the West Wing lobby. Powell had come alone. He entered the Oval Office and took a seat opposite Trump. Vance and Bessent took chairs on either side of Powell and other advisors joined the meeting as well.

Trump opened with a monologue, a recitation of the case he had been making in public: Economic conditions were ideal to cut rates, and by refusing to do so, Powell was putting America at a disadvantage. *Everybody else is cutting. You need to be cutting. The Europeans are laughing at us. There is no inflation. Trillions of dollars are coming into the country.*

Powell sat there impassively, for what seemed like around six or seven minutes. When Trump finished there was a moment of silence. Then he said, "Well?"

"Oh, would you like me to respond, sir?" Powell asked.

"Please," Trump said.

Powell did not give the answer Trump was hoping for. "As long as the labor market is so solid—and at this point, it's in really good shape—we and all other forecasters are expecting that there will be a wave of price increases from the tariffs," he told the President.

"And it's because some of that is going to get passed along, and we have to manage the risk and make sure that that doesn't turn into an inflation problem. And it's in everyone's interest that we do that."

Powell added, "We don't want to be in a situation where we cut rates too much, too soon, and the inflation turns out to be more persistent than we think, and now it's next year and rates are too low and inflation's too high. You don't want that. We don't want that," he said. "Our job is to make sure that that doesn't happen."

"Oh, that's not going to happen," Trump replied. "And if that does happen, I'll be the first to ask you to raise rates."

"We're watching to see," Powell told the President. "And if it turns out that the inflation is very contained or lower than what we expect, then that would matter in our decisions."

The meeting was shorter than a typical Trump meeting, only around half an hour. Powell was polite, low-key, and he even cracked a minor joke. When Trump called him Jerome (instead of Jay, like everyone else), Powell said no one but his mother called him that. But as polite as he was he also made it clear he wasn't going to let Trump bully him, and he left the room without making a single concession.

Still, the meeting ended on a reassuring note. Referring obliquely to his public threats of firing Powell, the President said, "All those things I've been saying about you—don't worry about that. I'm not doing anything."

Despite his conciliatory demeanor, Trump was frustrated after the meeting, and it didn't take long for his anger to again rise to the surface.

On June 18, in an impromptu gathering on the South Lawn of the White House, where Trump had summoned reporters to show off his new eighty-eight-foot flagpoles, the President went off on a rant about Powell. Breaking the fourth wall, Trump narrated his inner thoughts about the playbook of manipulation and intimidation he had attempted against the Fed chairman.

"Now we have a man that just refuses to lower the Fed rate, just refuses to do it. . . . I think he hates me, but that's okay, you know. He should. He should. I call him every name in the book trying to get him to do something," Trump said. "I've been so nice to him, fellas, you wouldn't believe. . . . I do it every way in the book. I'm nasty, I'm nice. Nothing works. He's like, just a stupid person."

Trump had demonstrated a shocking appetite for risk so far in his second term, but firing Powell would pose too much risk even for him.

He's not going to fire him, said a close aide at the time, adding: He's just going to torture him.

III

Around two weeks after his outburst on the White House lawn, Trump was meeting in the Oval Office with top aides, including the director of the Office of Management and Budget, Russ Vought, and James Blair. Vought and Blair were there to brief the President on a topic that had nothing to do with the Federal Reserve, but Trump was distracted by a foam-board chart propped on an easel nearby. The chart, titled "World Central Bank Rates," compared U.S. interest rates to those of the rest of the world. It triggered a Trump monologue about how "it's so fucking ridiculous" that Powell was keeping interest rates high compared to other countries.

"I want to bust his fucking balls, honestly," Trump said of Powell. "What about that fucking building? Can we stop it? Can we stop construction? I just want to bust his fucking balls. Fuck him."

Unsurprisingly, Trump had taken an interest in the renovation underway at the Federal Reserve's headquarters complex in Washington. The project's scope was enormous, a full interior overhaul of the Marriner S. Eccles Building and the adjacent Martin Building (completed in 2020), both of which had been originally designed for a 1930s-era workforce. The renovation would have to preserve historic facades, stonework, and interior features, which added complexity and costs to a project already estimated at $2.5 billion. Powell had addressed the renovation during his testimony to the Senate Banking Committee on June 25, conceding the project had changed somewhat from the initial plans.

Here was Trump's opening. One advisor later observed, "He's a builder, so he just knows life is fucking hell when you can't build your shit."

Trump asked if they could stop construction. "I'll look into it," Vought said.

"No, don't look into it," Trump replied. "Bring me a plan."

It didn't take long for Vought's general counsel at OMB, Mark Paoletta, to find one. Vought informed Blair that there was an organization called the National Capital Planning Commission that controlled urban planning in the Washington area. Vought said the President was allowed three appointees on the commission, including the chair. He thought they could assert that Powell was out of compliance with the Fed project's original plans because he had testified to Congress about features of the renovation that had changed. It was the kind of petty bureaucratic sabotage that had hamstrung the Trump administration in term one; now it was Trump's turn to play the game.

Vought sent over to Blair a one-page summary of the research and scheduled a meeting with Trump, Susie Wiles, Mark Paoletta, and Blair for the morning of Wednesday, July 9.

"Oooh," Trump said after Vought and Paoletta told him about the Planning Commission. "And I can just appoint new people?"

The answer was yes. His appointees could take over the Planning Commission.

"Okay, well, why don't you just go on the board, James?" Trump said to Blair. "It's like a two-week campaign. You know what to do. I just put you on the board. You have fun, you be vicious, you do a job."

"Got it, sir," replied Blair, whose day job otherwise involved much weightier matters, including overseeing the White House political and legislative operations.

"Pick who you want" for the board "and come back to me," Trump ordered them.

The team hustled out of the Oval Office with a problem: None of them knew the first thing about the National Capital Planning Commission. Vought quickly determined there was a residency requirement and that board members were supposed to have some planning experience—a low bar that they immediately set about clearing. Blair, who lived in Virginia, could point to his time overseeing the Florida Department of Transportation in the governor's office. "That's planning," he reasoned. Vought found a member of his own staff, Stuart Levenbach, who could cover the Maryland requirement. That left the chairmanship.

Blair ducked into the office of Will Scharf, the President's staff secretary. Any planning experience?

As a matter of fact, Scharf replied, he had some from the Missouri state government. That was good enough. Within minutes, Scharf had been appointed chairman of a federal commission he knew nothing about—and told that his first board meeting was the next day.

Trump signed off on the appointments that afternoon and Scharf stayed up all night reading documents and preparing to chair the meeting.

The next day, July 10, the Trump officials took their seats around a curved table in the offices of the National Capital Planning Commission and Scharf informed the room that the President had named him the chair. Scharf and Blair said they were honored to be working with the professional staff of the NCPC and that their mission was simply to improve and beautify Washington, D.C., a mission dear to the President's heart. For the next two hours, they sat through a mind-numbing discussion of land-use plans, native planting concepts, and the endangered monarch butterfly—arcana that might have seemed an odd use of time for two of the most powerful officials in the Trump White House.

Then, around the two-hour mark, after they had trudged through the formal meeting agenda, Scharf turned over to Blair to address the room. The mood quickly shifted from sleepy to savage. Blair, who had been courteous and solicitous in his brief opening remarks two hours earlier, now launched into a harangue about one project in particular: the Federal Reserve complex.

"Some have started to refer to this as the Taj Mahal near the National Mall," Blair said as Scharf, seated beside him, cracked a smile. Reading from a sheet of paper, and his iPhone, Blair compared the building costs of the Fed renovation to historic costs, in today's dollars, for the Palace of Versailles, the U.S. Capitol Building, and the Qaṣr Al Waṭan, the presidential palace of the United Arab Emirates, which Blair and Scharf had recently visited during their trip with the President to the Middle East. The Fed building, he declared, cost more than this opulent palace.

It was immoral, he said.

As his fellow commissioners listened in silence, Blair announced he was requesting "a full review of plans of the Federal Reserve project," a detailed explanation of any deviations from the original plans, and a site visit. Scharf thanked the attendees for their participation and ended the session.

The meeting would set off a six-week onslaught that would show just how far Trump was willing to go to challenge the independence of the Federal Reserve.

Over at the Fed, Powell and his team had been trying to figure out what Trump was up to with his sudden fixation on the renovation costs. At first Powell thought, *What the hell is this?* But after Trump's aides had taken over the Planning Commission, Powell figured they were looking to fire him for cause, for being a bad construction manager.

Powell was determined to fight for his job, and for the principle of independence for the central bank. And he was wealthy enough, from his days as an investment banker, to personally sustain a long legal fight.

During the first term, Powell had hired high-level lawyers at his own expense to prepare to fight his potential firing. Regarding Trump's threats, Powell had told then–Treasury Secretary Steven Mnuchin that he was "highly confident of winning" if it ever came to a legal fight. The tensions would die down during Covid as Powell slashed interest rates to zero and began a massive bond-buying program. Trump would give Powell "the most improved player award." Powell would later tell others that he never had any doubt that if Trump did try to fire him, the President would lose at the Supreme Court. "You can tell the Supreme Court does not want to mess with the Fed," Powell would tell associates. "They've said it about as clearly as they can."

As so often happened in Trump's world, mischief-makers seeking to curry favor with the President soon came into the mix. Bill Pulte, the director of the Federal Housing Finance Agency who had pushed the legal pretext to go after Letitia James, had found a housing-related angle—interest rates—to justify his intrusion into discussions about the central bank.

A witness to one such discussion between Trump and Pulte said that Pulte, talking "100 miles a minute," had for weeks been whipping up Trump about the need to fire Powell. The aide recalled Pulte telling the President, "The Fed is making it impossible for people to own homes, we need to get rid of this fucking guy."

On July 14, Pulte walked into the Oval Office carrying his typical stack of foam boards highlighting enemies of Trump to be targeted. Among the stack was a blowup, on White House stationery, of a draft letter firing Powell. Trump loved it.

The next day, the President waved around a copy of the "fire Powell" letter in a meeting with House Republicans. Trump asked the lawmakers if he should send the letter, and then he told them he probably would. One of the members, Representative Anna Paulina Luna of Florida—who had pushed for Trump's image to be carved into Mount Rushmore—told him she wanted to post on social media that Powell was going to be fired soon. Trump told her to go ahead. She did, and four days later, she went even further, referring Powell to the DOJ for criminal investigation.

Trump, meanwhile, was musing privately about appointing Vice President Vance as the Fed chair, perhaps for an interim period. He told Pulte to keep up the good work, to keep kicking "the crap out of" Powell.

Five days after being referred to the Justice Department for criminal investigation, on July 24, Powell showed his mettle during a highly unusual visit Trump made to the Fed's construction site—a visit Blair had demanded at his first Planning Commission board meeting. Pulte lurked behind them on the tour, and Trump was also joined by Russell Vought, who wore hiking boots along with his suit.

Powell, in a hard hat and the familiar purple tie, corrected the President on live television, telling Trump the cost figure he was using for the Fed renovation—$3.1 billion rather than $2.5 billion—was wrong because it included an additional building that had already been completed. Trump was otherwise gracious during the site tour. After the tour he made a classic Trump pivot from what he had been egging Vought and Blair into behind the scenes. With media cameras running, he took on a more conciliatory tone.

"There's always Monday-morning quarterbacks. I don't want to be that," Trump said. "I want to help them get it finished."

Powell seized the moment, releasing a statement from the Fed thanking Trump for supporting the completion of the building. For a while, the whole renovation play seemed to have fallen apart right there, and at Trump's own hands.

Nevertheless, seven months later, the U.S. attorney for Washington, D.C., former Fox News host Jeanine Pirro, would send subpoenas to the Federal Reserve over the renovations, targeting Powell specifically. The attorney general and deputy attorney general would both tell associates they had been blindsided by the extraordinary move. Pirro would tell White House officials that she had authorization for everything she did, without specifically saying from Trump. Powell promptly revealed the investigation, publicly calling it an attack on the bank's independence.

IV

If he wasn't going to fire Powell, Trump was still searching for other ways to tilt the Fed his way. The President's team began looking for pressure points in the ranks below the chairman.

Bill Pulte had a foam board for that as well.

The face of the woman displayed on the board had been blown up, a way to make the image as unflattering as possible. Above it was the title "The Fraudster." Alongside were photos of two documents with signatures that Pulte said were evidence of fraud. The woman, Pulte said, was named Lisa Cook. Trump was intrigued.

Cook was the first Black woman to serve as a Federal Reserve Board governor, appointed by Biden in 2022 and reappointed with a term running to January 2038. She had grown up in a small town in Georgia, and she was among the first Black students to desegregate her local schools; her academic research focused on the economic toll of racial violence.

During her first three years on the Fed board, Cook had voted in lockstep with Powell and she had kept a relatively low profile. That was all about to change.

In keeping with his earlier campaigns against real or perceived Trump enemies, Pulte posted on social media a letter he had sent to the Justice Department, urging an investigation into Lisa Cook for mortgage fraud. Pulte claimed in the letter that Cook had "falsified bank documents and property records to acquire more favorable loan terms, potentially committing mortgage fraud under the criminal statute." Pulte said that two mortgage documents Cook had signed two weeks apart—one in Michigan, another in Georgia—listed both properties as a "primary residence." On the day Pulte first posted the accusations against Cook, Trump posted on Truth Social, too: "Cook must resign, now!!!"

Cook refused.

Trump then went further than any prior President had gone in his effort to wrest control over the Fed.

On August 25, Trump posted on Truth Social a letter addressed to Cook, saying, "you are hereby removed from your position on the Board of

Governors of the Federal Reserve, effective immediately." Trump cited in his letter Section 242 of the Federal Reserve Act of 1913, which stated that a Fed governor could be "removed for cause by the President."

But Trump's definition of "cause" was, at that point, merely an accusation. No fraud had been proven. There had been no trial. No case had even been brought. Trump was using an unproven claim to advance his long-running effort to seize control over the economic policy machinery of the United States.

Powell was appalled. He was personally close to Cook and he viewed her as a capable and hardworking Fed governor. When Trump moved to fire Cook, Powell immediately understood the stakes.

"Oh, honest to God, that's the end of it. If he can do that, that's the end of Fed independence," Powell would later tell others. He told associates, "We need help from the Supreme Court of the United States, and we need help from Republicans in the Senate. We're going to need help from both groups, because if they're just going to lie down, then you won't have an independent Fed.

"If he can fire Lisa in that way," he would add, "who among us?" To sum up the moment, Powell would invoke a line attributed to Lavrenti Beria, Stalin's notorious secret police chief: "Show me the man and I'll find you the crime."

It was a watershed moment in the history of the central bank—made all the more remarkable by the fact that the top players on Wall Street were largely silent. Congressional Republicans, too, were mostly silent and the financial markets barely reacted. Only the courts stood in the way of Trump's power grab.

Privately, Powell told Cook, "We have your back." But in the context of the Federal Reserve, that assurance meant something very specific. Many liberals were hoping Powell would issue a public statement excoriating the President for this abuse of power. But Powell was not about to do that. What Powell did do was keep Cook on salary. The Fed issued a statement saying it would abide by whatever the courts ruled, but in the meantime, even though she had been fired by the President, Cook was still getting paid, and she was still connected to her Federal Reserve email account.

As the battle between Cook and Trump began to play out in the courts—and as the courts allowed Cook to stay in her job while she fought—former chairs of the Federal Reserve made clear in a friend-of-the-court brief that they saw this as a break-glass moment for the institution.

Cook had not chosen this fight, but her role was clear: Her lawsuit would determine something much more important than her own future; it would help decide whether the Federal Reserve would maintain its independence, or whether the U.S. President would now have access to awesome new powers.

23

Donald Trump was tired after a long day of campaigning when he took a seat at the end of the long boardroom table in a windowless conference room at the Ahern hotel in Las Vegas.

It was early evening on June 8, 2024, and two senior executives from the artificial intelligence giant OpenAI, Greg Brockman and Brad Lightcap, had arrived to give the seventy-seven-year-old presidential candidate his first lesson in AI. This would be a demonstration of the company's breakthrough platform, ChatGPT—an offer they had also extended to President Biden, who had declined to take them up on it, and later to Kamala Harris's team after she replaced him as the nominee. The company's cofounder, Sam Altman, had planned to attend, too, but he was down with Covid.

Trump was not into AI. He was an extreme version of a late adopter when it came to tech. He did not use email and he had only begun sending text messages in 2022. He viewed the artificial intelligence revolution with a mixture of ignorance and wariness.

But when Brockman connected his laptop to the TV close to Trump's chair and brought up on screen the ChatGPT interface, the look on Trump's face went from exhaustion to a wide-eyed *Wait, what is this?*

To show off ChatGPT's capabilities, Brockman took the text of an executive order on AI policy from the first Trump administration and pasted the whole thing into the prompt field. He asked ChatGPT to summarize the order into a sentence where every word started with the same letter. The sentence appeared instantly. Brockman then asked it to turn the order into a poem and it did that, too.

Trump read over the lines of the poem, bowled over by its eloquence. "Those words it's using," he said. "They're beautiful."

Trump turned to one of his aides and said, "Maybe this will take your job." The aide replied that he already used ChatGPT and it had improved his work.

Trump was now very interested. "How do you actually build this thing?" he asked the two executives. What were the limits of what they could do?

Throwing in some industry jargon, Brockman and Lightcap explained to Trump that it really came down to the "supply of compute." And what *that* really came down to was energy—vast amounts of energy. Someone in the room chimed in to add, "Compute is like the new oil."

They discussed the difficulty of getting permits to build data centers, and Trump, with his background in construction, offered to help. He asked where the money came from. Was it public money? It was private money, they told him; they just wanted permission to build. It was an answer Trump liked.

But Trump did have a pressing concern that was typically self-reflective. "If someone were to make a sort of fake AI of my voice saying that—you know, something bad, like nukes are launching, and there's only like fifteen minutes for Russia to figure out if it's real or not, like how can you tell?" he asked, then added his own tech guru into the mix. "I was told by Elon that no one can tell."

Brockman told Trump that AI itself could be helpful for deepfake detection. "No human can tell the difference," he said, "but if you have a smart AI, it can actually help you."

"Oh, that's interesting," Trump said.

Brockman added that cryptographic signatures could help decipher whether an image or a video was real or not.

Trump asked how they thought about the risks and how they would make sure the benefits of AI would outweigh the risks. Brockman replied that they were trying to mitigate risk as well as innovate.

He showed Trump ChatGPT's "voice mode," where he could dictate commands into his phone. Trump seemed delighted as they asked ChatGPT questions about the history of his hotels. He asked if they could improve one of his Truth Social posts. He had a draft Truth post printed on a sheet of paper and Lightcap took a photo; they uploaded it onto ChatGPT and an "improved" version appeared.

Brockman explained to Trump how image generation worked, and then Doug Burgum, the governor of North Dakota, who had arranged the meeting and was also in the room, asked ChatGPT to create an image of a blond woman on a Friesian horse—a breed his blond wife preferred. Brockman was now sitting next to Trump at the end of the conference table and all of Trump's aides crowded around as he typed the commands into his laptop. It generated the image of the blonde on the specific breed of horse and Trump said, "Wow. That is, like, very, very detailed."

Brockman told Trump that ChatGPT users had been getting tons of views using the image generator and that Trump should give it a try.

"Oh, I will," said Trump, whose Truth Social feed would soon become a repository of AI slop.

Trump was hooked. The meeting was supposed to last only fifteen minutes, but it went on for an extra twenty with Trump enthralled by the technology. The conversation would culminate with a discussion about the need for an effort like Operation Warp Speed—the Trump administration's name for the race to deliver a Covid vaccine in 2020—but for data centers.

The meeting had taken only thirty-five minutes, but given what would come later, it would surely be one of the more significant half hours in the history of AI.

As President, Trump would cast aside his previous fears about the dangers of unchecked artificial intelligence and turn America sharply away from the Biden administration's cautious regulatory approach. He was captivated by the masters of this new universe—especially the billionaire internet investor David Sacks, a campaign donor and friend of Elon Musk, whom Trump appointed chair of the President's Council of Advisors on Science and Technology, and Jensen Huang, the founder of the chip developer Nvidia, now the world's most valuable company.

II

Trump had spent his first term obsessing over coal mines and steel plants, but it had become painfully clear that those industries would never return to their old strength. As he began his second term, AI-driven companies dominated the stock market, and if he wanted to run the economy hot he could do no better than fuel the fire. He thought he could piggyback on the AI revolution, and its insatiable demand for energy production and construction of data centers, to bring back the boom times of American manufacturing. And this goal made the CEOs of the cutting-edge AI companies the most valuable corporate leaders in his eyes.

None would be more valuable than Jensen Huang, a man not even on Trump's radar during his first term. Huang had no presence in Washington back then. He didn't lobby, he made no campaign donations. He was an engineering whiz with no interest in politics. When the Biden administration began imposing strict and complex regulations on chip sales, Huang was forced to dial into Washington, but he was still doing far less politicking than many of his rivals. He had not even attended Trump's second inauguration.

"Who the hell is he? What's his name?" Trump would later recall, describing the moment he first heard about Huang. "His name is Jensen Huang of Nvidia. I said, 'What the hell is Nvidia?'"

Jensen Huang had cofounded Nvidia in 1993 as a small graphics-chip startup that nearly went under in its first decade. With his leather jackets and shock of silver hair, he made a striking impression and he was ruthlessly intense even by Silicon Valley standards. He ran Nvidia for thirty years at an unforgiving pace, betting its future on an unproven idea: that its graphics processing units could become far more than gaming chips.

When AI researchers discovered they could train neural networks far faster on Nvidia's GPUs than on traditional chips, the architecture that had seemed like a fringe experiment became the backbone of modern AI. By 2025, Nvidia controlled more than 80 percent of the global market for the chips needed to train the most advanced AI models. Huang had built something close to a monopoly over the most powerful new technology on earth.

With the new regulations constricting his industry, avoiding Washington could no longer be an option.

Trump held the power to greatly help or damage Nvidia through export controls. Huang would need to persuade him that it would make sense to sell Nvidia chips to countries all over the world. Washington's national security hawks were warning against doing anything that might help America's enemies build their technological capabilities, and Huang knew he had to influence the administration's policy in the other direction. He could not do so unless he built a personal relationship with Trump.

On April 4, 2025, Jensen and his wife, Lori, arrived at Mar-a-Lago to attend a candlelight dinner with the President and a group of tech and crypto donors. Trump was intrigued by Huang and the more he learned about him, the more impressed he became. Trump was being told, constantly, that this brave new world of AI depended almost entirely on Huang's company. In Trump's parlance, Huang was "hot." "You're taking over the world, Jensen," Trump would later say.

Trump saw something else in Huang. As a President determined to make big deals for America, he was on the constant hunt for leverage, seeking out what America possessed that foreign leaders most desired.

China hawks on the MAGA right, like Steve Bannon, had argued for banning all chip sales to China, but Sacks and Huang told Trump that it was better to back Nvidia selling its chips to as many countries as possible, to preserve the company's place at the center of the world's AI ecosystem. Much better, they argued, for the world to rely on U.S. technology rather than China. Trump was dazzled by the numbers they threw around—not just billions but *trillions* in new investments—and he saw quickly how a boom in capital expenditures in the rush to build chip plants and data centers could set off a U.S.-manufacturing renaissance that could prop up an otherwise shaky economy.

He would not gut all of Biden's restrictions—Nvidia was still banned from selling its most advanced chips to China—but he otherwise gave free rein to the AI industry in one of the biggest bets of his presidency.

Everybody wanted Nvidia chips. Especially the energy-rich Gulf states that wanted to remake themselves as AI hubs. In May 2025, Huang joined Trump's traveling entourage for his trip to the Middle East, where Trump announced major deals with the United Arab Emirates and Saudi Arabia to buy from Nvidia. Huang gave Trump what he craved most: headlines to burnish his image as a dealmaker President.

"America's unique advantage that no country could possibly have is President Trump," Huang would say in July. He promised Nvidia would invest $500 billion in U.S. manufacturing—a headline-grabbing number to convey that here was a President bringing in money and jobs.

For a man who kept score as Trump did, Huang was the Tom Brady of the Fortune 500. It wasn't just that he was personally worth $150 billion; it was that he controlled the most valuable company in the world with a valuation seeming to grow by a trillion dollars each time Trump—himself a shareholder—checked in on it.

At the height of his trade war in April, Trump had initially tightened restrictions on sales to China. But he would later backtrack, allowing the sales of two different versions of older-generation Nvidia chips in a highly unusual arrangement wherein the U.S. government took a 15, and later 25, percent cut of all sales of these chips to China. The moves raised legal questions and worries that America's national security might be bought off for the right price. But Trump appeared not at all concerned.

Huang also seemed sanguine about the risks of China obtaining American technology. Officials in the U.S. intelligence community were concerned that he was, at best, naive and overly carefree in his interactions with the Chinese. Huang maintained close ties to executives and local leaders in China, and he outmaneuvered China hawks inside the Trump administration in his bid to sell more high-end chips to Beijing. He portrayed the AI revolution as a wholly positive development for mankind and rejected forecasts of mass unemployment as the prognostications of doomers who didn't know what they were talking about. He dismissed concerns about AI systems creating deadly bioweapons or uncontrollable autonomous drones.

The debate over chip sales to China became somewhat academic after the policy change, since the CCP would make it difficult for Chinese companies to buy Nvidia chips anyway. But Trump administration officials would quietly marvel at just how influential Huang appeared to be with the President.

Trump's mind meld with Huang would create an administration policy that largely sidelined the AI naysayers and charged ahead in a rush to unleash innovation and growth in AI development. Companies like Meta agreed to build massive data centers in the U.S., promising thousands of jobs and untold economic growth. Administration evangelists like the tech investor David Sacks portrayed this as the next great frontier for America, comparable to President John F. Kennedy's space program in the 1960s.

III

One group that refused to instantly buy all the happy talk was Trump's own MAGA movement.

It would not be quite as easy as he might have imagined to persuade MAGA that the lords of Big Tech—who until very recently were seen on the hard right as censorious liberals bent on destroying America—were actually patriots with America's best interests at heart. Among other things, the Big Tech CEOs favored high-skilled immigration, the H-1B visas loathed by many on the Right. Republican senators squashed an administration-backed effort to shove language into the Big Beautiful Bill that would have prevented states from regulating AI for a period of ten years. Senators like Josh Hawley of Missouri worried about the implications of stopping states from passing laws to protect children or to protect certain jobs from being taken by AI. At the state level, Republican governors, including Sarah Huckabee Sanders of Arkansas and Ron DeSantis of Florida, pushed back. Trump said he would do it anyway, by executive order.

MAGA luminaries warned about the potential for dangerous new weapons with minds of their own, and the risk of AI putting millions of Americans out of work. Tucker Carlson would release a nearly two-hour podcast that demonized AI, drawing parallels to occultism and exploring how artificial intelligence might connect to the "mark of the beast" mentioned in the Bible's book of Revelation. Steve Bannon declared on his *War Room* show that AI was "the most dangerous technology in the history of mankind." There were signs the AI revolution was adding a new fracture in Trump's base.

Trump had already released over the summer an AI "action plan" that amounted to a tech industry wish list. The President canceled a previous executive order from Biden that required AI developers to report models that might threaten public health, the economy, or national security. And he had already eliminated restrictions Biden had imposed on exporting high-end U.S. chips to data centers abroad, which had been justified on security grounds. Now Trump's AI action plan would order a whole-of-government effort to accelerate AI development, and the massive construction to support it.

Soon, the U.S. government would be sitting on not just a 25 percent cut of Nvidia chip sales to China; in August, Trump stood over the semiconductor giant Intel, demanding a 10 percent stake in the company, which would make the government its biggest shareholder. All it had taken was a flurry of attacks by the President on his own social media channel.

IV

The CEO of Intel, Lip-Bu Tan, took a seat in the Oval Office on August 11, beside Commerce Secretary Howard Lutnick, and opposite President Trump. Tan had requested the meeting at short notice because it was an emergency.

The previous Thursday, at 7:39 a.m., Trump had posted on Truth Social a message that had rattled both Tan and the entire leadership team at Intel.

"The CEO of INTEL is highly CONFLICTED and must resign, immediately," Trump had posted. "There is no other solution to this problem. Thank you for your attention to this problem!"

The post sent both Wall Street and Silicon Valley scrambling for answers. American Presidents did not normally reach so directly into the boardrooms of corporate America—especially not a Republican President, representing the party that had once treated free-market capitalism as a sacred principle. Compounding the shock, Trump's demand had come seemingly from nowhere; the President had not mentioned to his staff that he wanted to force a change at the top of Intel. There had been no meetings on the subject. And now Intel's stock price—already in the doldrums—had fallen by 3 percent after Trump's post.

Alarmed administration officials began pointing fingers. Some focused on Senator Tom Cotton of Arkansas, claiming he had phoned Trump to whip him up about Intel. It was a reasonable assumption, because two days before Trump's Truth Social post, Cotton had sent a letter to Intel's chairman, Frank Yeary, raising concerns about Lip-Bu Tan's ties to China.

But they were wrong. Cotton had simply sent off a letter to the Intel board asking questions, a routine action for a senator. He had not spoken to Trump about Intel before the President's Truth Social post, which had surprised Cotton as much as anyone else.

Cotton had concerns—media reports linked Tan to investments connected to the Chinese military, and the company Tan had most recently led, Cadence Design Systems, had pleaded guilty to illegally selling chip-design technology to a Chinese military university. But Cotton was still in fact-finding mode. He had not reached any conclusions or made demands beyond sending Yeary a list of questions.

Eventually, the backstory of Trump's demand for the CEO to quit was revealed. He had been watching TV, *Mornings with Maria* on Fox Business, that morning. Maria Bartiromo, the host and a friend of the President's, had run a segment discussing the letter Cotton had sent to Intel. Five minutes later, Trump had posted on Truth Social. Bartiromo's segment was all the evidence he needed.

Lip-Bu Tan's phone had started ringing before five o'clock that morning, as he was on the West Coast. By the time most of America was awake, the newly installed CEO of Intel was facing a presidential demand for his resignation.

He had been in the job for only five months, and he had not taken it because he needed it. Tan was a self-made billionaire—a venture capitalist with nearly two hundred successful IPO-backed investments and a celebrated turnaround at Cadence Design Systems behind him. Friends had warned him against the Intel job. "You have a heck of a record, you have a heck of a reputation," he recalled one telling him. "People only remember the last one, so don't do it." But Tan saw Intel as a national infrastructure asset—the only American company capable of leading-edge chip R&D and manufacturing on U.S. soil—and felt an obligation to try to save it before he retired.

He already faced a daunting-enough mission—rescuing a company that had fallen far behind other chipmakers at the worst possible time, the dawn of an AI revolution that would depend on an endless supply of microchips. And on top of that, Tan's own future was now in serious doubt.

Tan responded the way he later said he approached every crisis: as an engineering problem to solve. He maintained his daily routine—swimming, gym—and then set about figuring out a path forward. Knowing that Trump often bonded with CEOs, Tan reached out to Susie Wiles and to Howard Lutnick, asking to see the President. Trump agreed, and a meeting was set for the coming Monday.

Tan met first with Lutnick at the Commerce Department for a pregame huddle before they headed to the Oval Office. Lutnick had an unsentimental view of the situation. He saw Intel had badly lost its way, but he also thought it made no sense that under the CHIPS and Science Act, signed into law by President Biden in 2022, the U.S. government would simply hand over $11 billion in grants to a $100 billion company as an incentive to build semiconductors in the U.S.

Lutnick had been mulling for months what to do about Intel. He had talked privately with colleagues and top tech executives about whether they should split up the company or put together a rescue—what he described to associates as "a consortia of the great American companies." America needed a world-leading domestic chipmaker as a national security imperative, Lutnick believed. But whatever the government did for Intel, he told others he wanted American taxpayers to get something concrete in return.

Tan had prepared intensely over the weekend and arrived with a clear plan. He told Trump he had been born in Malaysia, grew up in Singapore, came to MIT forty-seven years ago, and had been a U.S. citizen ever since—an immigrant who had embraced the U.S. and risen to lead a major tech firm while fueling innovation through venture capital.

He told Trump how he had built up his former company, Cadence

Design Systems, into an extraordinary success, more than doubling its revenue. And now he was going to do the same with Intel; he just needed some time to implement his turnaround plan.

Tan's preparation paid off; he gave Trump the impression of a CEO who, far from being a Chinese spy, was a committed American patriot.

Trump asked some basic questions: *How did Nvidia get so far ahead of Intel? How do you plan to turn Intel around? What do you need to do it? How much time do you need to do it?*

Tan told Trump he thought he needed two years.

When the conversation turned to his China ties, Tan told Trump he had been shocked to learn that Cadence had illegally sold its chip-design software to the Chinese military. He had been CEO when it happened, but said he had no knowledge, describing the sales as relatively small and made through his Asian office. He appealed to Trump as a fellow boss who would understand the challenge of keeping up with every little thing that happened in his own organization.

Tan had convinced Trump that he was not a Chinese spy; but getting off the hook was not so straightforward.

"I can cure your problem," Trump told Tan. "I'll solve your problem, but you have to give ten percent of Intel to the country."

It was a stunning moment as the President of the United States told the CEO of Intel that he wanted a stake in his company. Even for Trump, this was an aggressive move. And it did not take much for Tan to realize that both he and Intel would face serious problems if he rebuffed the President.

"I could support that," Tan replied.

In the days that followed, Intel's leaders and administration officials hammered out the specific terms. And eleven days after the meeting, the Trump administration announced an arrangement that shocked corporate America and horrified free-market conservatives in equal measure: Under the deal, the U.S. government would receive a 10 percent ownership stake in Intel in exchange for approximately $8.9 billion in accelerated CHIPS Act funding—grants that Intel had been promised but whose delivery had become genuinely uncertain under the Trump administration, despite the company having already met key milestones and invested billions in U.S. manufacturing.

From Intel's perspective, the company had traded equity for certainty, converting a shaky promise into guaranteed capital. But the power dynamics were unmistakable: A sitting President had effectively forced a publicly traded company to hand over a large ownership stake as the price of receiving money it had arguably already earned.

Recalling the episode months later, Trump would say, "I should've asked for more. It was so easy."

The deal was stunning for another reason altogether. U.S. intelligence officials who were monitoring the situation experienced severe whiplash. Like Tom Cotton, many in the intelligence community had serious concerns about Tan serving in such a strategically sensitive role given his deep history with China. And in the space of less than a month they had witnessed the President demand the removal of Tan and then turn around and give him his full-throated endorsement—all without anything resembling a serious investigation or policy process.

But the deal was done. And by the fall of Trump's first year back in office, Big Tech was doing very well indeed.

Intel had lived to fight another day. After the government had acquired 10 percent of the company, others looked to invest in the new, Trump-backed Intel. A month after the deal, Nvidia said it would buy $5 billion of Intel's stock, acquiring about a 4 percent stake in its competitor. Nvidia and Intel then announced they would join forces to develop and manufacture new custom chips.

Jensen Huang, meanwhile, had trillions of reasons to be happy with the Trump presidency. In October, Nvidia would become the first company ever to reach a valuation of $5 trillion.

President Trump had "completely changed the game" for AI, Huang declared. And nobody could doubt that he had.

Part III

THE ENEMY WITHIN

24

On the morning of Tuesday, August 5, Donald Trump sat in the Oval Office behind a desk littered with stacks of papers. Stephen Miller, Pam Bondi, and Kash Patel were seated opposite. Other aides were spread around the room, including the ubiquitous Natalie Harp, laptop at the ready, near the door. They were gathered to discuss a suite of upcoming executive orders, many of which had originated with Miller's sweeping domestic policy projects. Suddenly, Miller swiveled, turning the discussion to something else on his mind, something that had happened in Washington early on Sunday morning.

"One of our people got jumped by a bunch of thugs and kids," Miller told Trump. The details were that a nineteen-year-old DOGE employee, Edward Coristine, had been badly beaten up in the early hours of the morning on August 3, near Dupont Circle. Police had described the incident as a thwarted carjacking involving Coristine and his girlfriend. Miller told Trump that Coristine was trying to protect her by pushing her into the car, leaving him to face the brunt of the assault.

Miller had photos from the attack on his cell phone, shared with him by his wife, Katie, who at the time was working for Elon Musk's xAI. Coristine was one of the hundreds of young techies Musk had recruited into DOGE. The pictures showed the young man looking dazed, his shirt stripped off and his torso and white pants bloodied. Miller referred to him as "Edward," but also mentioned the name by which Coristine was best-known on social media and in the administration: Big Balls. Trump instantly recognized it. Big Balls had become the most famous DOGE figure after Musk, a nickname that belied the physical reality of this rail-thin tech staffer.

Trump looked at Miller's photos. "Wow," he said. "He really got beat up. Who beat him up?"

"There's a lot of these young gang members going around threatening and assaulting random people on the street," Miller replied.

"Wow," Trump repeated. "This city's out of control."

The President quickly suggested Coristine appear on television to talk about the assault. "We could get him on TV, right?" Someone mentioned *Fox & Friends* as a possible venue. Miller said he would need to check with Big Balls and then he moved to pitch the President on something else.

Miller had a draft of an executive order ready to go, written months earlier at Trump's direction, for what would amount to a takeover of Washington, D.C., using National Guard troops to protect federal assets. The deployment would establish dominance over the capital, a move Trump had been pushing for since his first term. Bondi chimed in that the streets of Washington were quite perilous. The President approved the idea on the spot.

"Let's try to get it done quickly," Trump said, sending Miller off to finish the job. "We need to take care of this thing. It's too dangerous," he added, "especially for our people."

II

As Trump entered office for his second term, he had made it clear to his aides that he wanted to see troops patrolling the streets of Democratic-led cities, which for years he had described as crime dens. In 1990, in a throwaway line during an interview with *Playboy*, Trump had highlighted strength as a premium characteristic in all settings when he praised the Chinese government for its bloody suppression a year earlier of the human rights protests in Tiananmen Square. President George H. W. Bush's administration had harshly condemned the violence, which, according to the Chinese government, had killed 241 people, and, according to human rights watchers, had killed over 2,000. But Trump had admired the use of force.

He compared it favorably to the way Soviet President Mikhail Gorbachev had handled uprisings in the same period.

"Russia is out of control and the leadership knows it. That's my problem with Gorbachev. Not a firm enough hand," Trump had opined to *Playboy*. When he was asked if he meant a "firm hand, as in China," Trump replied, "When the students poured into Tiananmen Square, the Chinese government almost blew it. Then they were vicious, they were horrible, but they put it down with strength. That shows you the power of strength. Our country is right now perceived as weak."

When in 1993 the Washington, D.C., mayor, Sharon Pratt Kelly, had asked President Clinton for permission to call up the National Guard to fight crime, Clinton declined. Most big-city mayors thought such use of the National Guard was a staggeringly bad idea. One person, however, thought it was brilliant. "I, for one, love it," Trump told a forum of business executives and elected officials at the time.

Around thirty years later, and shortly before Trump announced his 2024 campaign, he said he wanted to use troops to crack down on crime across the country.

"In places where there is a true breakdown of the rule of law, such as the most dangerous neighborhoods in Chicago, the next President should use every power at his disposal to restore order—and, if necessary, that includes sending in the National Guard or the troops," Trump said in August 2022.

No one in Trump's circle was as forceful an advocate for troops in U.S. cities as Stephen Miller. During Trump's first term, Miller consistently and aggressively argued for their deployment, either to quash illegal migrant crossings at the southern border or during the nationwide unrest that followed the killing of George Floyd in Minneapolis in 2020.

From the start, Miller had an impulse for autocracy that matched Trump's, and he believed that everyone from judges to journalists to activists were incorrect when they challenged the President's authority. But in term one, Miller was still quite inexperienced and easily dismissed by Trump's military leaders.

The conflict over troop deployments came to a head during the George Floyd protests. On Sunday, May 31, 2020, protesters lit a fire in the basement of the historic St. John's Episcopal Church on the other side of Lafayette Square from the White House. It was known as the Church of the Presidents. The fire was quickly extinguished, but it became a symbol of an out-of-control center of the federal government.

The next day, Trump raged at his defense secretary, Mark Esper, and Attorney General William Barr when they opposed his demands for U.S. troops to quell the protests. Both watched as a red-faced Trump threw what Barr would later characterize as a "tantrum" about their inability to stop the demonstrations.

"We look weak," Trump bellowed, Esper would recall later. The country "looks weak." "You are losers!" he said, flinging one of his favored insults. "You are all fucking losers!" Going at full throttle, Trump asked his handpicked chairman of the Joint Chiefs of Staff, General Mark Milley, why violence couldn't be used to stop the demonstrators. "Can't you just shoot them. Just shoot them in the legs or something," Trump said. Those in the room were aghast.

Trump's desire to use the military never abated as protests continued throughout that summer and he repeatedly pushed Barr to deal with the situation more aggressively. Trump was enamored of the idea of military deterrence and determined to break down resistance to using troops against protesters.

He would return to office well-prepared to make good on this threat. At the Center for Renewing America, led by Russ Vought, a staffer had sent an email in early 2023 laying out policy topics for the group to draft. One batch was described as "day one" ideas. Included on that list was "Insurrection—stop riots **—Day 1, easy." It was a reference to the Insurrection Act, and carve-outs in the law that would let a President elide the prohibition against using troops for domestic law enforcement.

From the start of the second Trump term, Stephen Miller was devising ways to put these ideas into action. Within weeks, he had come up with a proposal for an all-volunteer use of the National Guard to support ICE in all fifty states as part of the administration's efforts for the largest mass deportation ever. When the question inevitably came up about who would pay for it, Miller said the money would come from the Defense Department's coffers.

Miller was also intent on reviving another idea from the first term: a federal takeover of Washington, D.C. Some groundwork had already been done. Trump's advisors had drafted an executive order invoking the Insurrection Act during the 2020 protests. It would have gone into effect had the city's mayor, Muriel Bowser, not managed to contain the violence. Ultimately, the executive order remained on the shelf.

In term two, Susie Wiles and other aides had been doing their best to work with Bowser instead of constantly escalating. Wiles had helped connect Bowser with Trump at Mar-a-Lago after the mayor sought a meeting during the transition. And so began a back-and-forth between the Democratic mayor and Donald Trump's chief of staff.

But Stephen Miller was not interested in détente. He was biding his time for the right moment to strike. And the attack on Big Balls would provide him with the perfect justification for a long-held dream.

III

The path toward the aggressive use of the military in U.S. cities was greatly helped along by the new and unusually pliant duo of the attorney general and the defense secretary, or as Trump would soon rename him, the secretary of war.

Pam Bondi had served eight years as Florida's attorney general and knew her way around law enforcement, but she was seen as every bit as opportunistic as Trump himself. Hegseth, a former Fox News host and combat veteran whom many Republican senators privately regarded as unqualified to run the Pentagon, had no experience managing a large organization, let alone the world's most powerful military. What they shared was an almost unquestioning deference to the President's instincts—and neither was inclined to resist Stephen Miller.

The opening battle in the conflict between the Trump administration and the nation's major cities would not come in Washington, D.C., however, but in Los Angeles.

Early on Friday, June 6, federal officials launched a series of raids to hunt for illegal immigrants in Los Angeles. Masked agents swarmed Home Depot parking lots, car washes, and a clothing company in the downtown Los Angeles Fashion District, among other worksites. The effort would soon be taken over by Border Patrol commander Greg Bovino. Short in stature, Bovino was inspired to do his job by the 1982 Jack Nicholson crime thriller *The Border*. He had carefully honed an aggressive image, taunting his critics on social media and holding an assault rifle in an online profile picture. His swagger was on full display during the L.A. mission. "We're not going to hit one location, we're going to hit as many as we can," Bovino told the Associated Press. "All over—all over—the Los Angeles region, we're going to turn and burn to that next target and the next and the next and the next, and we're not going to stop. We're not going to stop until there's not a problem here." Television personality Dr. Phil McGraw had embedded with one of the ICE units, underscoring the premium the administration put on the public spectacle of enforcement.

Street protests began to form. They were confined to a small area of the city at first, but grew increasingly violent. ICE agents in riot gear clashed with some of the protesters. A police squad car was smashed by chunks of cement hurled from a bridge overhead. Stores were looted, and fires were set in dumpsters. The images played out on cable news channels, offering the nation a reminder in miniature of the riots of 2020.

It was under the shadow of that memory that Trump announced the next day that he would call in the National Guard, without California Governor Gavin Newsom's agreement. Sending in the Guard without a governor's consent had been extremely rare in U.S. history; the most recent instances in the twentieth century involved Presidents protecting newly granted civil rights in the segregated South. Stephen Miller had agitated for going even further and using the Insurrection Act, which would allow the President to deploy troops for broad law enforcement purposes to crush civil unrest, but other officials pushed back. Still, few if any of Trump's aides disagreed with the idea of sending in the Guard; most of Trump's current team thought his first-term government had waited too long and let the violence play out excessively in liberal cities around the country after the death of George Floyd.

The evening before the Guard call-up, Susie Wiles messaged Newsom—with whom Trump had a peculiar hot-and-cold relationship—to say that federal agents needed help from the Los Angeles police. Newsom told Wiles that the risk of a dangerous confrontation was emerging, but he stressed he had the situation under control heading into the weekend. Their exchange did little to change the trajectory of events.

It was just after 1 a.m. on Saturday, June 7, when Trump spoke with Newsom, just before giving the Guard the go-ahead. But Trump was not interested in talking about immigration enforcement. His first question was whether Newsom was running for President in 2028 and whether Kamala Harris would run as well. Trump wanted to pat himself on the back for the nickname "Newscum." He boasted to the governor that he had done better than Harris in their 2024 debate. It was a sentiment that few, including his own campaign advisors, would agree with.

Eventually, Newsom forced Trump to the point. "You're going to defund California?" he asked. Trump said he wasn't, but he liked the term.

An initial two thousand Guard troops arrived in Los Angeles the next day, a development that seemed destined to stoke greater conflict between soldiers who were not trained as anti-immigration or anti-crime forces and the rioters and protesters in the city. They would later be followed by an additional 2,000 Guard troops and 700 active-duty Marines. In Paramount, California, earlier that weekend, Bovino had directed a group of agents to "arrest as many people that touch you as you want to. Those are the general orders all the way to the top. Everybody fucking gets it if they touch you." California sued the Trump administration, and a judge would ultimately find that the deployments had violated the 1878 Posse Comitatus Act forbidding federal troops from being used for domestic law enforcement. The armed forces began to leave in July, with only a few hundred troops remaining in the city.

In Illinois, advisors to Governor JB Pritzker watched what was happening in Los Angeles with alarm. Illinois officials were already spending 75 percent of their time battling with the Trump administration in court, and they had been preparing for Trump to try to send in the National Guard to their state once he was in office. They were certain they would be next.

But it was Washington, D.C., a federal enclave where Presidents had more flexibility to call up the National Guard, that was Trump's next focus, with Stephen Miller leading the charge. The district's Home Rule Act allowed for only a thirty-day federal takeover of the city's police without approval by Congress. Still, even a monthlong deployment was a victory to Miller.

He worked closely with Homeland Security Secretary Kristi Noem, and they coordinated with the army secretary to install a new emergency police chief for Washington.

Trump maintained that this whole experiment was necessary. "Our capital city has been overtaken by violent gangs and bloodthirsty criminals, roving mobs of wild youth, drugged-out maniacs, and homeless people," he declared, even though violent crime had been diminishing in the city for some time. "And we're not going to let it happen anymore."

Trump also said he wanted to use the opportunity to clear out homeless encampments that had increased around Washington since the pandemic, suggesting the deployment was as much about aesthetics as a criminal crackdown. Trump was likely hoping to channel Mayor Rudy Giuliani's sweeps in the late 1990s to remove the homeless from the streets of New York City. It was a period in New York that Trump often spoke of wistfully.

To maximize attention on their efforts, Stephen Miller, Pete Hegseth, and JD Vance decided to visit D.C.'s Union Station, where the homeless population had soared and troops had been deployed. Vance, offering to buy lunch at Shake Shack for the Guard troops, found himself shouted down by protesters in a city dominated by Democratic voters. Miller mocked them as "elderly white hippies," while Vance called them "crazy."

Mocking their critics had been the goal, but it did little to impress Trump, who made clear to aides he was unhappy that Vance had put himself in a situation where he could be booed.

"Why would they do it over there, when there's all this shouting and protests? It's so stupid," Trump had vented to advisors before getting to his real point, which was that he should have been involved in any public showmanship around the D.C. deployment. The next day, Trump met up with cops on the beat in Anacostia, in the southeastern section of Washington, D.C., to hand out pizza.

Trump called the city "out of control," despite data showing otherwise. He insisted Washington officials had fabricated crime data. But the optics were striking, which seemed more pertinent and useful to the White House. These theatrics were not incidental to the policy; they *were* the policy. But a formula was now emerging for clashes with cities run by Democrats. And after what had happened in Los Angeles, administration officials were thinking hard about what they would do if governors refused to call up the Guard.

While every U.S. President was also the commander in chief of the military, no President since Richard Nixon, defending himself during Watergate, had declared himself the chief law enforcement officer. Trump would be the only President in modern history to interpret the title to mean that he was the nation's top cop.

IV

Amid all the heavy-handedness of the administration's quasi-war effort around major cities, a sudden news flash from a news organization in Minnesota shed light on tensions about calling up the troops in one very particular corner of the government. And it suggested things were not as clear-cut for at least one of Trump's hard-liners who was now tasked with sending in the troops.

On October 3, *The Minnesota Star Tribune* published a startling story online. Stephen Miller's deputy at the Homeland Security Council, Anthony Salisbury, had been messaging over the Signal app while traveling in Minnesota. These messages, observed in a public place and "in clear view of others," according to the newspaper, resulted in a set of images that the *Star Tribune* had obtained and published.

The Signal messages were between Salisbury and Patrick Weaver, a senior advisor to Pete Hegseth. Weaver was conveying Hegseth's concerns that the President had not provided him with sufficiently clear instructions on whether or not to deploy troops into Portland, Oregon, a city that Miller and Trump had been preoccupied with since the first term.

"Between you and I, I think Pete just wants the top cover from the boss if anything goes sideways with the troops there," Weaver messaged to Salisbury. They were discussing not a National Guard deployment, but active-duty members of the 82nd Airborne. Weaver said that Hegseth favored the National Guard being sent instead.

The conversation was another dangerously loose discussion for an administration obsessed with leaks, and particularly given Hegseth's own blunder of sharing highly sensitive military plans during the Signalgate scandal back in March. But it also indicated that Hegseth was eager to get a clear directive from the commander in chief.

A few days earlier, in the last week of September, Hegseth had sent around two hundred Guard troops to Portland; ahead of those orders, it had been primarily Miller directly pressing the secretary to deploy active-duty troops. But Hegseth wanted more information and much more clarity to come directly from Trump.

So on Saturday, September 27, the President posted his own somewhat confusing message on Truth Social.

"I am directing Secretary of War, Pete Hegseth, to provide all necessary Troops to protect War ravaged Portland, and any of our ICE Facilities under siege from attack by Antifa, and other domestic terrorists," Trump blasted. "I am also authorizing Full Force, if necessary."

It still wasn't exactly clear what he meant—which specific troops, and to do what? Trump continued to describe Portland, a city dominated by white liberal voters who prided themselves on protest activity, as "burning" to the ground. There were indeed protests in Portland, and some at ICE facilities became violent, but they were nothing like the chaos in the summer of 2020, when the federal courthouse was besieged. A federal judge would later permanently block Trump from deploying National Guard troops there.

By the time of the Portland deployment, Trump had repeatedly threatened to send National Guard troops into major Democratic cities. The administration made little pretense of allowing civilian forces to contain protests before activating the Guard, which undercut any claim that these were emergency responses. Democratic governors were emphatic: They did not want Trump calling up troops in their states.

But troops were only one part of the equation. Throughout the summer and fall, the tactics of ICE agents and Border Patrol officers deployed to Los Angeles and Chicago grew so militarized that the line between law enforcement and armed occupation all but vanished. In Chicago, a "sanctuary city" that prohibited local officials from assisting federal immigration enforcement, Bovino resurfaced. Immigration officials deployed a chemical agent near a school.

Bovino was completely unleashed during "Operation Midway Blitz," which started on September 8 and targeted what the administration called "criminal illegal aliens" allowed into Illinois. In one raid that he led in the final hours of September, Border Patrol agents targeted what they claimed were hundreds of dangerous Venezuelan gang members in Chicago. The agents rappelled from a Black Hawk helicopter into a residential building the Tren de Aragua members had supposedly taken over. They went door-to-door, zip-tying residents as they moved through, including U.S. citizens and children. DHS claimed that two out of the thirty-seven people arrested were Tren de Aragua members but never gave evidence. Nobody was charged with a crime, according to reports.

The use of force against protesters escalated in tandem. An ICE agent struck a pastor in the face with a pepper ball at one demonstration. At another, Bovino threw tear gas into a crowd, with DHS later saying in a statement that he had been hit with a rock before doing so—a claim he would subsequently admit under oath was false.

Questions about the mounting use of excessive force were routinely waved off by Bovino, ICE, and Homeland Security officials alike. Stephen Miller would declare that all ICE officers "have federal immunity in the conduct of your duties," another sweeping statement of authority that exaggerated the protections ICE officers had. The administration had slashed ICE training from roughly five months to six or eight weeks in its rush to expand the ranks, but rather than acknowledge the raids were spiraling, Homeland Security and the White House doubled down, releasing slickly produced propaganda videos portraying Chicago as a war zone. One video used footage from raids that had not even taken place in the city.

Trump's relationship with Pritzker ran mostly on animosity. Pritzker had mocked Trump as a fake rich guy at the 2024 Democratic National

Convention, and after winning the election, Trump had dismissed the governor on a phone call with an associate as "that fat shit in Illinois." Still, Trump was fixated on the far-fetched idea of getting Pritzker to call him up to invite the troops in himself—a call Pritzker had no intention of making.

Prior to the Black Hawk raid, Pritzker and his advisors caught wind that Trump was about to ask his ally Governor Greg Abbott to send Texas National Guard troops into Illinois. Pritzker went public with the rumors—an attempt to blow up the element of surprise that Miller depended on and Trump relished.

Shortly before Pritzker's press conference, Trump again announced he wanted the governor to call and request the troops. Then he said he would send them in regardless, without specifying a date.

"No, I will not call the President asking him to send troops to Chicago," Pritzker fired back. He called it an "unhinged" request from an administration that had refused to collaborate. "I refuse to play a reality game show with Donald Trump again."

Pritzker urged the protesters to stay disciplined. "We know, before anything has happened here, that the Trump plan is to use any excuse to deploy armed military personnel in Chicago," he said. "If someone flings a sandwich at an ICE agent, Trump will try and go on TV and declare an emergency in Chicago. I am imploring everyone—if and when that happens—do not take the bait."

Despite his plans being exposed, Trump forged ahead. Within weeks, a small Texas deployment arrived in Chicago, prompting an immediate legal challenge. A federal judge halted the deployment until the Supreme Court could weigh in. The highest court would ultimately say that Trump couldn't use the statute he had relied on to call up the National Guard for conditions like those in Chicago. It was a dramatic pushback by the Supreme Court against Trump's efforts to expand his power, and it would soon lead Trump to roll back his blue-state Guard deployments.

But Trump had already raised the stakes. Two months earlier—in a rage over judges trying to check his power—the President responded with a threat of his own: He could simply invoke the Insurrection Act.

"Everybody agrees you're allowed to use that and then there is no more court cases, there is no more anything," he said. "We're trying to do it in a nicer manner, but we can always use the Insurrection Act."

Miller had been urging Trump to do exactly that for months. And so Will Scharf, the staff secretary, composed another confidential memo for Susie Wiles, one that laid bare how seriously the White House was weighing what would amount to the most dramatic domestic use of presidential power in recent American history. The memo was dated October 29, 2025.

"The Insurrection Act serves as a break-the-glass exception to the traditional, general prohibition on the use of the military in the domestic setting," Scharf wrote, methodically tracing the history of its invocation.

He noted that Lincoln had used the act to prosecute the Civil War, that Grant had invoked it to crush the first Ku Klux Klan, and that it had been deployed during labor strife in the late 1800s. "And perhaps most notably in recent history," Scharf wrote, "three Presidents invoked the Insurrection Act to deal with the nonenforcement of federal civil rights law and court orders by state and local governments in the South."

What Scharf's lawyerly summary left out was the magnitude of those moments. Between 1957 and 1968, Eisenhower, Kennedy, and Johnson had used the act seven times—to send federal troops to escort Black students past segregationist governors into schools in Little Rock and at the University of Alabama; to put down the violent siege over integration at the University of Mississippi; to protect marchers on the road from Selma to Montgomery; and to quell devastating riots in Detroit and across the country after the assassination of Martin Luther King Jr. In the decades since, it had been invoked only thrice more—by Reagan during a federal prison riot in Atlanta, and by the first President Bush to stop looting in the Virgin Islands after Hurricane Hugo. Bush had invoked it again during the 1992 Los Angeles riots, when the acquittal of four police officers in the beating of Rodney King triggered six days of destruction that left sixty-three people dead, nearly 2,400 injured, and whole blocks of the city in flames. And as Scharf himself pointed out, even then it had come only after a request from the governor of California. What Miller was pushing had no precedent in any of it.

Scharf's memo pointed out that the Insurrection Act gave the President enormous latitude. But it was not a green light.

"While most legal analysts agree that the Insurrection Act does provide the President with exceptionally broad powers and authority, essentially unreviewable by the other branches of government," Scharf cautioned that it would almost certainly be challenged in court the moment it was invoked, slowing the process and "potentially obviating any advantage to be gained in terms of the flexibility that it would provide to the President."

Privately, Scharf stressed to colleagues repeatedly that suspending habeas corpus for immigrants and invoking the Insurrection Act without genuine need were two steps the White House could not afford to take.

But the gravitational pull of the idea remained strong for the men at its center. The fact that the troop campaign was Stephen Miller's consuming mission—amplified at every turn by Trump—was hardly a secret. "To me, a town, it looks better when you have military people," Trump would say.

Even as public opinion was tilting away from him on his signature issue of immigration, Trump, and Miller, dug in deeper, operating on grievances and instincts cemented in the first term. And when, the day before Thanksgiving, two young Guard members were shot at close range in Washington just blocks from the White House, it became a near-certainty that uniformed troops would patrol America's streets for some time to come.

25

Jane, respectfully, shut the fuck up," the White House Communications Director Steven Cheung posted on X.

Coming as it did from the most senior communications official in the entire Trump administration, Cheung's volley carried the weight of an official government response to the *New Yorker* writer Jane Mayer, who had said that the shooting of two National Guard members was "so tragic, so unnecessary," because the Guard had been deployed for "political show."

As shocking as Trump's immigration program was, no less shocking was its marketing.

Previous administrations had generally adhered to time-honored standards dictating the correct form and language for government communications. And as norm-breaking as Trump himself was in his first term, his administration's official social media channels had been anodyne, consisting of standard press releases, photos, and scheduling updates.

In term two, everything changed.

Late in the Epstein fiasco, as one Trump associate after another was tarred with a broad brush for appearing in the document dump, Cheung would state that two prominent lawmakers who had pushed for the release of the Epstein files, Democrat Ro Khanna and Republican Thomas Massie, were "some of the dumbest retards ever to be in Congress."

No White House communications director had ever communicated like this. The tone—abusive, offensive, trolling—had been set from the top and set from the start.

On February 14, 2025, the White House posted a "Happy Valentine's Day" message with a red heart emoji on its social media channels. Under that message was a pink card of President Trump's face beside his border czar, Tom Homan, with a new take on the traditional love poem: "Roses are red, violets are blue, come here illegally, and we'll deport you."

Four days later, the White House posted a video of migrants in shackles being marched onto planes. The only sounds heard in the video were the harsh metallic clatter of chains skittering across the tarmac, the snapping of handcuffs onto migrants, the clanging sounds of shackled feet shuffling up stairs to the aircraft, and the background roar of jet engines. The White House captioned the post: "ASMR: Illegal Alien Deportation Flight." It was a reference to the popular ASMR (autonomous sensory meridian response) videos of people making noises—whispering, scratching, crinkling noises—to induce pleasurable tingling feelings. The clip provoked outrage for presenting the deportation of shackled immigrants as a relaxing experience for viewers.

In late March, the White House used ChatGPT to turn a photograph of a Dominican woman—a convicted fentanyl dealer—into a popular meme format, converting the chained and weeping woman into an animation character with cartoonlike references to Japan's Studio Ghibli. And in April, the administration displayed mug shots of immigrants arrested by ICE as lawn signs on the White House grounds.

The New York Times's television critic James Poniewozik observed that the second-term Trump administration understood that "governing and power require potent images that end-around analysis and go for the primal." He wrote that Kristi Noem's social media content deployed the "tropes and techniques of various TV and social-media genres in miniature" borrowing from "terrorism dramas, crime dramas—the kinds of stories, like '24,' that have in the past suggested that personal liberties and due process can get in the way of safety." The same was true across the administration.

Some of the output from the Communications Office for the fight over immigration seemed cruel, even juvenile, but the way the Trump team saw it, they had cracked a strategy with a dual purpose: sending a message of harsh deterrence to illegal immigrants, and goading the Left into defending the honor of criminals.

After the Ghibli-style image provoked exactly the sort of reaction from liberals that the White House had wanted, the head of the digital team, Kaelan Dorr, posted that it was "disappointing that folks are more upset about this meme than they are about the fentanyl crisis.

"The arrests will continue," he added. "The memes will continue."

II

Overseeing the communications operation was the staffer who channeled Trump's id more exactly than any other. Steven Cheung was an astonishing sight roaming through the West Wing: physically enormous, with a low brow, a shaved head, great slablike hands, and an omnipresent sneer. His friends called him "Panda." No less an authority than the actor Mel Gibson had taken note of the comms chief's attributes. Approaching Cheung at an Ultimate Fighting Championship event in 2023, the star of *Mad Max* and *Lethal Weapon* had told him, "God, you have a great look. You look like you could be a villain in a movie."

Trump was often fixated on male beauty; his appraisal of a job seeker's handsomeness could be a prerequisite for the most highly visible administration posts—but he liked his enforcers to look like enforcers. It was the case with Roy Cohn, the reptilian lawyer and fixer whose sunken eyes and waxen skin were never a problem for Trump. Cohn, Trump once told the journalist Tim O'Brien, "was brutal, but he was a very loyal guy. He brutalized for you." Similarly, he would say Cheung was his Luca Brasi—a reference to Don Vito Corleone's ruthless hit man in the Mafia classic *The Godfather*. He would privately describe Cheung as "like the more violent version of Kim Jong Un," and in conversations with aides Trump would say that Cheung reminded him of Xi Jinping: "No games."

Cheung's ethnicity was of great fascination to Trump. On a plane trip during the 2024 campaign—an episode that would become campaign lore—Trump had put the question directly to Cheung. "Do you have any white in you? Are you pure-blood Chinese or do you have any white in you?" the candidate asked. "Nope, just full Chinese," Cheung replied.

Trump told Cheung that "most Chinese people aren't aggressive like you are." Cheung laughed along with the other staff on the plane who overheard the exchange.

Trump and Cheung were both sports fanatics and enthralled by violence. Cheung was obsessed with pro wrestling and attracted to its flamboyant personalities—wrestlers like Hulk Hogan, the Undertaker, Roddy Piper, and Dusty Rhodes. Like Trump, he was an early fan of the Ultimate Fighting Championship. In between his political jobs Cheung had run communications for the UFC; like Trump, he was less interested in policy or ideology than in spectacle and dominance. For both, elections were a means to those ends.

Throughout the 2024 campaign, Trump had encouraged Cheung's aggression—which, in the primary season, had been channeled against his main rival, Ron DeSantis. Trump was delighted when Cheung called DeSantis a "cuck" and he roared with laughter over short clips on cable news of Cheung mocking DeSantis over the height of his boots. "High heels," Cheung crowed. When they transitioned from campaigning to governing, there was never a thought that Cheung would flick the switch to propriety. Trump told him "never change."

The White House messaging style was pure Cheung and it was unadulterated Trump: deliberately inflammatory; obsessed with the use of force; mocking and dehumanizing Trump's enemies, all with an eye toward the visual effects. Trump's advisors also knew they now had far more leverage over the social media companies. In term one, Twitter and Facebook were controlled by executives skeptical of the President; but entering the second term, the media team saw no risk of being deplatformed or shadow banned; X, Facebook, Apple, TikTok, and Google had all bent the knee.

III

Cheung brought into the White House his friend Kaelan Dorr to run the digital operation. Tall, bearded, and bespectacled, Dorr was an army brat whose family had moved around twenty or more times as he was growing up. Like Cheung, he was an original from the Trump 2016 campaign and the first Trump administration. To build the digital team he wanted, he deliberately avoided hiring people with experience in government. Instead he recruited right-wing culture warriors in their twenties who had made viral content for groups like Charlie Kirk's Turning Point USA and for college sports teams. At thirty-three, Dorr was the graybeard of the digital team. He instructed his videographers in the objectives; they wanted to force the Left to "defend the indefensible." Their content would be designed to provoke more than to persuade, and engineered for the maximum chance to go viral and fire up the Trump base. On those metrics, they did not disappoint.

The ASMR video racked up 104 million views. The Valentine's Day card was viewed by 37 million people. The Japanese-style cartoon of the weeping shackled fentanyl dealer received 76 million views. And that was just on X; these posts racked up tens of millions more views on TikTok, Instagram, and Facebook.

Dorr was obsessed with music, with finding the perfect catchy tune to dramatize the clips. In all this, the White House coordinated closely with the Departments of Homeland Security, Justice, and Defense, and they turned the government into an in-house film studio, shooting and producing spectacles of Trump administration actions.

Stephen Miller would push them to collect reams of footage of immigration raids and arrests from all over the country to share on social media. The White House would post highlight reels of ICE arrests and deportation videos set to "Ice Ice Baby" by Vanilla Ice and "Closing Time" by Semisonic. To intensify the provocation, the administration's digital creators set the raids to the backing tracks of liberal artists who protested the Trump administration's mass deportation agenda. The pop singer Sabrina Carpenter would describe the White House as "evil and disgusting" after one of her songs was used in a video of ICE agents chasing down immigrants; another artist, Olivia Rodrigo, complained about her song "All-American Bitch" being used as the soundtrack for a video encouraging illegal immigrants to self-deport.

Previous governments would have been mortified at the first hint of denunciation by these pop stars, but the Trump administration courted such reactions, knowing that more conflict meant more online engagement. The White House lampooned the artists' complaints. When the country singer Zach Bryan appeared to criticize ICE, the Department of Homeland Security released a video of immigration raids set to the backing track of Bryan's hit song "Revival."

The over-the-top posting would become one of the most striking features of the Trump administration. It was also unceasing. When somebody on X mentioned that JD Vance could do "the funniest thing ever" by deporting a writer who had criticized his fashion choices, the vice president responded with a GIF of the actor Jack Nicholson nodding and smiling.

Defense Secretary Pete Hegseth filled his X feed with macho videos of his workouts; later in the year, when he was accused of war crimes in the boat-bombing campaign, Hegseth made fun of his critics by posting an AI-generated image of a book cover of the popular children's character Franklin the Turtle. It was titled *A Classic Franklin Story: Franklin Targets Narco Terrorists.* The cover showed the turtle in combat gear, firing a missile from a helicopter at drug traffickers in speedboats.

FBI Director Kash Patel posted a highly produced video of himself dressed in camouflage and stomping about as rock music played and FBI agents blew open doors with explosives.

Gregory Bovino—who would become famous for marching in a double-breasted olive overcoat with brass buttons that one senior White House official privately described as his "SS coat"—would release a video of National Guard troops and horse-mounted Border Patrol agents marching through a park in downtown Los Angeles to the song "DNA" by the rapper Kendrick Lamar.

These were previously unimaginable uses of a White House communications department, to taunt adversaries and mock everyone else.

The administration made powerful use of left-wing protests against ICE; all the better when they spiraled into riots. Press Secretary Karoline Leavitt dramatized such images in June: standing at the White House podium, flanked by a picture of a masked protester riding a motorcycle, waving a "Viva Mexico" flag, with a backdrop of fire and smoke. "Let this be an unequivocal message to left-wing radicals in other parts of the country who are thinking of copy-catting the violence in an effort to stop this administration's mass deportation efforts: You will not succeed," Leavitt admonished.

The totally unfiltered content would even carry over to the Justice Department—and not only by the hand of Pam Bondi or Todd Blanche. The assistant attorney general for civil rights, Harmeet Dhillon, would complain on X about online influencer "retards"; she solicited ideas for how to grow her social media following and lamented that it had stalled since she entered the federal government.

From the President on down, it would be a government of, by, and for the "posters." And, concerning to those who yearned for a return to some level of civility and basic decency, it did not take long for some high-profile Democrats to copy the tactics. Over the summer, a reporter had asked Gavin Newsom how he differentiated himself from Trump given that his own official press office had recently called Stephen Miller a "cuck."

"Well," said Newsom, "it's a response to Steven Cheung and the White House and his use of that word. I don't think they understand any other kind of language."

Cheung later told White House colleagues he was glad to have successfully dragged Newsom into the gutter because, in his mind, it would make Newsom "unelectable" in 2028.

But to what end was all the trolling? Nobody could doubt that this White House had produced more viral content—more views—than any previous administration. And it was arguably having some of its intended deterrent effect on migrants. Many were leaving the country—self-deporting in Miller-speak—and very few were trying to cross the southern border in the first place.

But it was also proving a double-edged sword. As the first year wore on, pollsters consistently found that Trump's harsh deportation program was turning off many of the swing voters who had delivered him the 2024 election. These were voters who cared much less about internet posting than the cost of living; and Republicans would badly need their votes in the 2026 midterms.

26

Around 2:30 p.m. in Washington, on Wednesday, September 10, a group chat on Signal buzzed with some vague but unsettling news. Andy Surabian, a close friend and advisor to both the vice president and the President's oldest son, shared a link about a shooting at a Turning Point USA event in Utah where Charlie Kirk was speaking. Charlie was their friend. The replies came in fast.

Hey Charlie, is this true? Charlie, are you OK?

The group included not only Kirk and Surabian, JD Vance and Donald Trump Jr., but several senior White House and administration officials and other influential operatives. Kirk was normally a chatty participant. Now he was silent, and his friends felt a knot in their stomachs.

Around three thousand people had shown up to see Kirk at Utah Valley University. He had been holding events at universities for years; they were the staple of his brand as he built Turning Point from scratch into the most formidable youth organization on the American Right. At colleges, he would sit under a tent in a central location and, in a format he called "Prove Me Wrong," take questions from all comers in open debate. His questioners were often liberal students who disagreed passionately with Kirk's positions on civil rights, Islam, feminism, gun control, transgender rights, and abortion. He would spend weeks training for these debates and he always came well-prepared. His team would edit the clips for TikTok and they would often go viral.

In recent years Kirk's friends and family had grown worried about his campus appearances. Their concerns intensified after two assassination attempts against Donald Trump in 2024 and as left-wing campus protests spread against Israel's war in Gaza. Trump himself had warned Kirk that these "radical Left lunatics," as he called the protesters, were "vicious," and Kirk had privately conceded to a friend that he was a sitting duck, with lax campus security. He traveled with security guards, but unless he spoke behind bulletproof glass like the President—a step he was unwilling to take—the reality was that he was defenseless against a skilled marksman at an open-air event.

Within minutes of the gunshot, cell phone videos were popping up on X. Students in the crowd were running and screaming. Someone shared in the Signal group a video filmed from a distance. Kirk had clearly been wounded, perhaps fatally. They could see his head snapping to the side and his body slumping from the chair. Surabian immediately called Don Jr., who was traveling in Europe on a different time zone and might not be seeing the messages. It was Don Jr., during the 2016 campaign, who had first welcomed Kirk into the Trump family orbit. Don had become like an older brother.

Before Surabian could get a word in, Don Jr., accustomed to fielding calls about news stories, said, "All right, what hit piece are they doing on me now?"

"Charlie's been shot," Surabian said. "And it's not good."

"Oh my God, are you kidding me right now?"

Don reminded Surabian this was the third time in the last eighteen months he had called him to say somebody close had been shot. Surabian had been the friend who first reached Don about both attempts on his father's life. Don said he would call someone on Kirk's team straightaway.

Also on the Signal group was White House Deputy Chief of Staff Taylor Budowich. Seeking more reliable information, he sent his assistant down to the Situation Room. He asked his team to hold off on telling the President anything until they knew more. Trump was in the Oval Office meeting with an Indian steel tycoon and Howard Lutnick.

The staff in the Situation Room knew nothing. A frustrated Budowich began cold-calling local Utah hospitals. He finally reached somebody who said Kirk was at Timpanogos Regional Hospital, in Orem, Utah. He was in the operating room, he had lost a lot of blood, and the doctors were doing everything they could. From there, Budowich joined JD Vance, and together they went to brief Susie Wiles in her office.

But it was too late, by then, to manage the flow of information to the President. A colleague told Budowich that Trump's youngest son, Barron, had already called to tell his father that Kirk had been shot.

The nineteen-year-old Barron was a big fan of Kirk's and he had phoned in a state of distress. He had been worried about an assassin taking another shot at his father. "This is what happens when you go out there," Barron said. "This is what *happened*."

Trump tried to settle his son. "Calm down, honey, calm down," he said. But he was clearly unnerved himself.

Budowich, Leavitt, and Steven Cheung had joined the President in the Oval. They briefed Trump on what they knew, which was still very little.

"Where was he shot?" Trump asked.

One of them said it looked as though Kirk had been shot in the neck.

"In the neck?" Trump said. "That's not good. That's not good."

Budowich told Trump they were gathering more information, and he shared what little he knew from the hospital. "We have our people on it," Budowich said. "We'll give you updates when we know more."

"Man. Charlie," Trump said. "He's such a good guy. He really helped me out in 2024. He got the youth vote."

At around the same time, others in the Signal group heard some encouraging news, relayed by a person close to Utah Governor Spencer Cox. Kirk was in a "stable condition," they were told, but in emergency surgery. The messages in the group stayed hopeful.

Charlie, we're praying for you, dude. Keep fighting.

For around twenty minutes they allowed themselves to believe Kirk might survive. One member of the group chat would later describe this as a "horrible window of false hope." The information was wrong. Kirk had died almost instantly.

Don Jr. called Surabian to tell him. Surabian shared the awful news in the Signal group: "Guys, he didn't make it." Budowich received a call from one of Kirk's close aides, who asked if the vice president was with him.

Everyone knew how much Charlie meant to JD. It was Kirk who had first encouraged Vance, despite his history as a Never Trumper, to run for the Senate in 2022 as a Republican. Kirk had been the first to convince Surabian that Vance could be trusted—a relationship that ultimately led to the Trump family's support. Vance would tell others that Kirk was more responsible than anyone else for his rapid ascent to the vice presidency.

Budowich rushed upstairs to Stephen Miller's West Wing office, where Vance had gathered with Miller and Marco Rubio. Kirk's aide, on speakerphone, confirmed his death. Budowich and Vance decided first to go downstairs and alert Susie Wiles before going in to tell the President.

Trump was finishing up his meeting when Vance, Rubio, and Budowich arrived in the Oval Office. When they told him Kirk was dead, Trump leaned back in his chair and said, "Wow. Wow." It was quiet for a moment. Then: "Whatever we need to do to help Charlie and his family, we need to do it. I want to give him a Medal of Freedom."

Rubio told Trump they were looking into whether this was a lone shooter or part of something bigger. Vance said he was in touch with Kirk's people. Someone suggested Trump should film a video, an address to the nation.

"Yeah, yeah," Trump said. "Just get it written up and set up for me."

Nobody knew anything about the gunman at that stage, but Trump was already describing the assassination as a group effort, using the pronoun *they*. "We need to be looking at these people," he told his aides. "They're killing our people. They tried to kill me."

Trump would later tell an aide that Kirk "got shot because of me." The aide understood him to be saying that "they"—whoever "they" were—had killed Kirk because they could not get to Trump. The President asked to see video of the shooting and when Natalie Harp produced it on her laptop, he quickly looked away. "It's horrible," he said. "Poor Charlie."

Budowich and others in the White House who had served on Trump's 2024 campaign initially suspected Iran was behind the murder. During the campaign, they had been briefed on Iranian plots to kill Trump. His aides had been told that if Iran's assassins couldn't get to Trump, their next best option could be the soft targets around him—his children and close allies. These briefings had spread intense fear and paranoia on the campaign, paranoia that carried over into the government. It occurred to Budowich that Kirk was a very visible, very soft target.

In Trump's address to the nation from the Oval Office that afternoon, he blamed the rise of political violence exclusively on the Left and hinted of a coming crackdown. "For years, those on the radical Left have compared wonderful Americans like Charlie to Nazis and the world's worst mass murderers and criminals," he said. "This kind of rhetoric is directly responsible for the terrorism that we're seeing in our country today. And it must stop right now."

At 6:21 p.m. there was a moment of relief when FBI Director Kash Patel, en route to New York, announced on X that officials had the suspected assassin in custody. An hour and a half later, he had to send out an embarrassing correction: The suspect had been released after interrogation. It was the wrong man. Pam Bondi, who had clashed repeatedly with Patel and held a low opinion of him, sent word to the White House: Kash must be fired.

II

In the age of smartphones and fragmented media it was rare for Americans to experience an event together. Kirk's death was an exception. His murder would be the biggest news story of the year, online data would show later. Many on both the Left and Right grieved, even those who had disagreed with Kirk's views. But many others had ghoulish reactions. Some on the Left celebrated his murder, sharing their joy on social media. And some on the Right spread wild rumors and theories about "the Jews" being somehow involved.

The chilling clips of Kirk's shooting were suddenly everywhere. Such gruesome violence would never have made it to air in the era of broadcast news and heavily regulated public airwaves. Now any American with access to TikTok or X could watch what they wanted. Thanks to social media algorithms, tens of millions more were exposed to the assassination involuntarily.

Consumed by grief, the White House, and nearly the entire cabinet, stopped functioning for a time. Nearly all the senior staff had a personal connection with Kirk. After the 2024 election he had moved his family from Scottsdale, Arizona, to Palm Beach, Florida, to help the Trump team staff up the government. Inside the transition headquarters, Kirk had grilled job seekers on their MAGA bona fides and on their loyalty, which included asking some about their views of January 6.

A visitor to the West Wing that day described it as "like a zombie movie." People were moving around as if in a trance. "It was just like this wet blanket of doom." People were crying all over the West Wing. Will Scharf, the staff secretary, stood grimly near the West Wing entrance, looking on as the flag that the President had installed on the North Lawn was lowered.

Wiles gave a speech to her traumatized staff, around thirty people crowded into her office, the only senior official in the West Wing who would give that type of group speech that day. Standing near the fireplace, she told people to take care, to hug their families, but keep using their voices. "Everybody needs to be careful," she said. There wasn't the luxury of security for everyone, and many of the most high-profile staff remained unprotected. "But we shouldn't be afraid, because that's what they want us to be," she said.

Few took it harder than Vance. He quickly decided he would go to Utah to offer the vice presidential plane, Air Force Two, to Kirk's widow, Erika, to return his body to Arizona. Vance, his wife, Usha, and three of Kirk's closest friends—Taylor Budowich and the GOP strategists Arthur Schwartz and Cliff Sims—flew west on September 11 to collect the casket.

During the flight, the group's conversation veered from grief, to memories, to more practical conversations about the impact of Kirk's death on the conservative movement. The question was not abstract. Beyond Trump himself, arguably no one was more significant than Kirk for gluing together the modern Right. He was a tough operator, a MAGA enforcer with a huge following. The Trump team relied on Kirk to defend the President online, to crush anyone in his way. Kirk was a key agent in purging Congress of any remnants of the traditional Republican Party still skeptical of Trump. He was a trusted advisor to both the President and vice president, the most prolific political fundraiser of his generation and, many believed, a future President himself.

And yet, despite all this, Kirk had managed to stay friendly with nearly all factions that made up Trump's ideologically diverse coalition. This was no small feat. Those who truly understood the MAGA movement grasped the reality that Trump's coalition was bound together less by shared values or policy views than by shared enemies and collective devotion to a President of mythic status.

The 2024 Republican presidential primaries had resolved none of the burning disputes between the party's various factions. The only thing anybody seemed able to agree on—besides immigration restriction—was that they were for Trump. People who hated each other and held diametrically opposing views on matters as fundamental as America's role in world affairs—people like Tucker Carlson and Senator Lindsey Graham—all laid claim to MAGA. Through the sheer force of his personality, Trump papered over these disagreements, stripping the Republican Party platform in 2024 down to a series of platitudes. He would make America great again, bring peace to the world, bring about a new golden age where everything was affordable and life would be magnificent. It was a party united by the red hat and common hatreds—of Democrats and the mainstream media.

But the sharper minds in Trump's inner circle recognized that when their charismatic leader left the stage—and that moment was coming fast—there was a serious risk that MAGA could descend into anarchy and fratricide. There had been early signs: MAGA infighting over H-1B visas, the Jeffrey Epstein scandal, the wisdom of bombing Iran, and the debate over America's Israel policy, which was already veering into deranged antisemitic conspiracy theories promoted by figures such as the podcaster Candace Owens. The response to Kirk's death revealed a widening schism. Instead of the Right unifying in its grief, parts of the coalition began warring with each other as some on the far right insisted Israel was behind the killing.

Kirk had been determined to elect JD Vance President in 2028, but now it would be up to Vance to hold together this fractious coalition without his indispensable friend.

On the Air Force Two flight back to Washington, after leaving the Kirk family behind in Arizona, Vance received updates from Kash Patel on the investigation. Later that night, Patel told Vance he was confident they had their suspect.

Tyler Robinson was a twenty-two-year-old gamer from Utah. He had grown up in a conservative Mormon family, but his mother reported he had recently shifted toward left-leaning political views, especially concerning gay and transgender rights. Robinson was in a romantic relationship with his roommate, who was transitioning from male to female. He had allegedly explained his motive in text messages, writing that he'd "had enough of [Kirk's] hatred" and that "some hate can't be negotiated out." His bullet casings were etched with an overlapping mix of anti-fascist slogans, video game references, and internet memes.

There was no evidence that Robinson was connected to any network or organization, and certainly not to Iran, but the anti-fascist slogans were enough for Trump to connect the suspect to "antifa"—a decentralized, leaderless movement of activists who opposed far-right ideologies, white supremacy, and what they characterized as fascist or authoritarian governments.

As he was wont to do, Trump had been putting out contradictory messages. In one breath, he said he would "like to see people respond" with "nonviolence." In another, the day after the murder, he told reporters, "We just have to beat the hell" out of "radical Left lunatics."

For Vance, the news of Robinson's arrest did little to ease his racing mind. Over the next few nights, the vice president stayed up late watching videos of the shooting on his phone, finding clips from different angles and studying the footage for clues to a broader conspiracy. His instincts told him there was a larger plot behind the murder. He went down countless online rabbit holes, becoming so consumed by the videos and the theories that his wife, Usha, told him she was worried about him.

III

Stephen Miller was a friend of Kirk's, too, but more than anyone on the President's staff, he saw in the tragedy an opportunity to expand power and advance his agenda.

For months before the assassination, activists in the North Arlington community where Miller and his family resided had been protesting Miller himself and his immigration crackdown with growing intensity. They had stuck posters on utility poles and at parks, displaying Miller's photo and the address of the home where he lived with his wife and three small children. Other posters around the neighborhood called Miller a Nazi. A group that called itself Arlington Neighbors United for Humanity—its acronym, ANUFH, pronounced "enough"—declared to the Millers on social media: "Your efforts to dismantle our democracy and destroy our social safety net will not be tolerated here."

While the behavior felt menacing to the Millers and alarmed them, it was not clear that it rose to the level of a crime. Nevertheless, they instigated investigations, which went up to the FBI. Miller had earlier demanded a 24/7 security detail, as well as sought, through official channels, protection outside his home from Governor Glenn Youngkin's office. He would soon put his home on the market and instead seek housing on a military base.

Miller's wife, Katie, would say on Fox News that the day after Kirk was murdered, a woman had confronted her outside her home, telling her, "I'm watching you." According to court documents and Secret Service footage, the woman—one of those who had organized the anti-Miller protests—had been near the Millers' home, motioned to her own eyes, and pointed at Katie. On Fox News, Katie discussed chalk messages that the protesters had scrawled on the sidewalk outside her home, saying, "Stephen Miller is destroying democracy."

Katie described the collective protest activity as "terroristic threats." "If we don't step up and start putting people in cuffs for these actions, what comes next?" she said.

Officials would obtain messages from the activist's group chat, in which the woman pledged to make Stephen Miller's "life hell." Soon there was an FBI search warrant for the woman's phone.

Stephen Miller had long been thinking about strategies to dismantle the institutional Left, especially the network of nonprofits that funded demonstrations around the country. He portrayed nearly all liberal protest activity as the work of paid agitators. He had a particular enmity for the efforts to thwart ICE agents, including in some cases doxing them. Miller fiercely defended the growing practice of federal immigration agents wearing masks, unusual in U.S. law enforcement because it helped to shield officers from public accountability.

Kirk had shared Miller's view. He would often tell associates he wanted to see racketeering laws used against left-wing groups like Black Lives Matter. He wanted to see investigations of major Democratic donors like the LinkedIn founder Reid Hoffman—an enemy of Vance's major donor Peter Thiel. Kirk wanted to see a money-laundering investigation into ActBlue, the online platform for Democratic Party fundraising.

"The last message that Charlie sent me was, I think it was just the day before we lost him, which is that we need to have an organized strategy to go after the left-wing organizations that are promoting violence in this country," Miller said in an appearance on Kirk's podcast five days after his death. "I will write those words onto my heart and I will carry them out."

No evidence had emerged that Tyler Robinson was working on behalf of any organization, left-wing or otherwise, but Miller had already been conditioning the public for a broader crackdown. Two weeks before the murder, on August 26, he had declared in an interview with Fox's Sean Hannity that "the Democrat Party is not a political party. It is a domestic extremist organization." Now he could utilize this rhetoric to widen the investigative focus from a single disturbed gunman to a left-wing omni-threat comprising a vast network of progressive nonprofit groups and organizations affiliated with Trump's political opposition.

The conspiracy Miller described was so vast that it evoked the anticommunist "Red Scare" of the mid-twentieth century. He was not basing his crackdown entirely on a hallucination; data showed there had been a recent uptick in left-wing violence, including an elevenfold increase in physical violence against ICE officers in 2025 compared with 2024, according to the Department of Homeland Security. But to argue, as Miller did, that terrorism and political violence were exclusively left-wing problems was to ignore not only recent data but decades of studies. After Kirk's death, the Trump administration removed from the Justice Department's website one representative study: The DOJ's National Institute of Justice had published a paper showing that since 1990, far-right domestic terrorists had committed more ideologically motivated murders than the far left—more than 520 compared with 78.

"We are going to channel all of the anger that we have over the organized campaign that led to this assassination, to uproot and dismantle these terrorist networks," Miller said on the podcast. "The organized doxing campaigns, the organized riots, the organized street violence, the organized campaigns of dehumanization, vilification, posting people's addresses, combining that with messaging that's designed to trigger and incite violence. And the actual organized cells that carry out and facilitate the violence. It is a vast domestic terror movement. And with God as my witness, we are going to use every resource we have at the Department of Justice, Homeland Security, and throughout this government to identify, disrupt, dismantle, and destroy these networks and make America safe again for the American people. It will happen and we will do it in Charlie's name."

IV

Trump privately told Vance and Miller to "go wild" in their efforts to crack down on left-wing "terrorism."

Vance declared they would "go after the NGO network that foments, facilitates and engages in violence," but said they would not be targeting constitutionally protected speech. And yet, when he hosted Kirk's radio show on the Monday after the assassination, Vance suggested the administration would be looking at the Ford Foundation as well as the Open Society Foundations, the nonprofit run by the Democratic donor George Soros. Vance said those two organizations received "generous tax treatment" and had helped to support the left-wing magazine *The Nation*, which he claimed had twisted Kirk's words to smear him after his death. Vance encouraged listeners to call out those celebrating Kirk's murder. "Hell, call their employer," he said.

In the days and weeks that followed, the Trump administration took this advice to heart. The State Department announced it would review the legal status of immigrants "praising, rationalizing, or making light" of the Kirk assassination. The Defense Department began investigating members of the military who had made inappropriate comments, ultimately expanding to nearly three hundred investigations covering service members, civilian staff, and contractors. More than a dozen service members were suspended or relieved of duty in the next two weeks.

After the late-night host Jimmy Kimmel was accused of implying that the assassin was a MAGA adherent, FCC Chairman Brendan Carr joined a right-wing podcast to warn, "We can do this the easy way or the hard way." Hours later, ABC suspended *Jimmy Kimmel Live!* Two major ABC affiliates, Nexstar and Sinclair, also suspended Kimmel's show; Nexstar's case was especially notable given that at the time of the suspension, it was seeking FCC approval for a $6.2 billion acquisition of the media company Tegna. Kimmel would return quickly to air, but the message was clear.

The Trump team was now threatening to deploy the powers of the federal government to crack down on what Attorney General Pam Bondi described as "hate speech"—a concept more often invoked by the Left and that some conservatives pointed out was at odds with the First Amendment. "It's not free speech when you come out and you say, 'It's okay what happened to Charlie,'" Bondi warned. In another shot across the bows on September 16, she said, "And employers, you have an obligation to get rid of people. You need to look at people who are saying horrible things. And they shouldn't be working with you."

Next came the presidential orders.

On September 25, Trump signed National Security Presidential Memorandum/NSPM-7, "Countering Domestic Terrorism and Organized Political Violence." This directed the attorney general and the secretary of homeland security to "designate domestic terrorism a national priority area" and coordinate with the National Joint Terrorism Task Force to "disrupt entities and individuals engaged in acts of political violence and intimidation designed to suppress lawful political activity or obstruct the rule of law."

The National Joint Terrorism Task Force had been established in June 2002 to coordinate the growing network of agents and investigators that had spread across the country after Al-Qaeda's September 11 attacks. Under George W. Bush, the "war on terror" focused on foreign extremists. But a few weeks before winning reelection in 2024, Trump had told Fox News he believed the country faced a more pernicious threat. "We have the outside enemy, and then we have the enemy from within," he said, referring to Democrats he accused of undermining him. "The enemy from within, in my opinion, is more dangerous than China, Russia, and all these countries."

Trump's new memorandum homed in on the very same tactics that Miller's family had encountered in North Arlington. NSPM-7 was also highly selective about the groups and ideologies investigators should focus on. There was no mention of any right-wing ideology, no mention of white supremacist violence, or the attempt by pro-Trump groups such as the Proud Boys to prevent the peaceful transfer of power after the 2020 election. No mention of the 2022 attack on Nancy Pelosi's husband, the threats to mosques and synagogues, or the 2025 assassination of Melissa Hortman, the leader of Minnesota's House Democratic caucus, who was killed alongside her husband. NSPM-7 focused exclusively on the Left.

On the same day, the Department of Justice instructed U.S. attorneys' offices to investigate George Soros's group. Orders were given to the Treasury and the Internal Revenue Service to target the funding streams of left-wing "terrorist" groups. In an interview on *The Charlie Kirk Show* on October 14, Scott Bessent compared Kirk's murder to the national tragedy of 9/11 and said he was following a money trail, though to where, exactly, it was not yet clear.

NSPM-7 designated Homeland Security advisor Stephen Miller as the person the National Joint Terrorism Task Force would provide regular updates to. And the attorney general would make recommendations about which groups should be designated as a "domestic terrorist organization."

Eight months into Trump's second term, Miller had become one of the most powerful White House officials in modern history. "We will do it in Charlie's name," he had promised. Now he had the tools and the permission structure to try.

27

Time was running out on James Comey, and the President knew it. By late September, Trump was lashing out at his advisors over the slow progress of his retribution campaign. The statute of limitations for the only crime they thought they could pin on Comey—the FBI director Trump had fired months into his first term—was about to expire. If the Justice Department didn't move fast, Comey would walk away. Making matters worse, Letitia James had also still not been indicted.

Trump had been complaining about Pam Bondi for months. For those in his closest circle, this rant about the attorney general was becoming a recurring theme. "She doesn't know what she's doing," he railed. "Nobody trusts her." This was in stark contrast to what he said publicly—that Bondi was fabulous and that he had total faith in her talents.

"I don't know why I picked her," he told an advisor in one of his typical venting sessions about Bondi. "She comes to all these events to play around but doesn't want to do the job."

"The job," in Trump's mind, was to bring cases against his targets. He was especially focused on those responsible for the years-ago investigation into whether his 2016 campaign had conspired with the Russians. He also wanted prosecutions of nearly anyone who had investigated him after leaving office. Instead, he complained, Bondi and the deputy attorney general, Todd Blanche, were letting everyone off scot-free.

Kash Patel was also in the crosshairs. For years, MAGA loyalists had been promised that once Trump returned to power, Democrats would be frog-marched out of their homes and offices in handcuffs. Patel himself had stoked those expectations in his book *Government Gangsters*, naming Trump's enemies and laying out the case for going after them. But six months into the administration not one of those targets had been charged. The online right, which had lionized Patel during his bruising confirmation fight, was turning on him—and so was the President. Trump had taken to calling him "Flashy Kash" to other advisors, mocking Patel's conspicuous use of Justice Department jets and demanding to know why the FBI director hadn't delivered on the promises of payback. There were senior FBI officials Trump wanted fired, too, and he insisted Patel had moved too slowly. In mid-August, Trump abruptly brought on Missouri Attorney General Andrew Bailey as a "co–deputy director" of the FBI, alongside Bongino. Bailey was a Stephen Miller ally who had vied for Bondi's job during the transition, but Trump had been bored by him during their meeting. The co–deputy director role was created specifically to bring aboard Bailey, who Trump advisors privately predicted would eventually take over from Patel.

Patel, conscious of the dark clouds, told associates he was aware of Trump's disappointment. But what Trump either did not grasp or did not care about was that whatever Patel's shortcomings, the FBI director could not simply indict people. That power belonged to prosecutors—the same ones Trump was simultaneously berating for doing nothing.

Trump had stopped focusing on Comey as a target until May, when Comey posted on social media a shot of shells on a beach forming the numbers, "86 47." Trump officials interpreted the slang for "getting rid of" something or someone as a threat against the forty-seventh President. The former FBI director took the post down and said he didn't condone violence, but the Secret Service investigated him anyway. Comey was now firmly back on Trump's radar.

Prosecutors would probe whether Comey perjured himself during a 2020 Senate hearing when he answered questions about the Russia investigation. The statute of limitations on that incident was set to expire on September 30,

2025, and Trump had been pressuring Bondi and Blanche for weeks to act. The prosecutor who would need to bring the indictment was Erik Siebert, the U.S. attorney for the Eastern District of Virginia and one of Trump's appointees. For a time, Trump advisors liked Siebert. A police officer before he was a prosecutor, Siebert had generally done what the DOJ asked of him, embracing the administration's crackdowns on violent illegal immigrants and exploring whether there were ways to indict Comey. But Siebert had also been warning Blanche's office for weeks that there wasn't enough evidence to bring the Comey case to trial. At the same time, Bill Pulte had been in Trump's ear, telling him that Siebert was weak and should be held in suspicion because Democratic senators had supported his appointment.

As September 30 drew closer, word spread around the White House that charges against Comey were imminent. But instead, Siebert's team produced a memo for top brass at the Justice Department, laying out why a case would be nearly impossible to win. Their two-month investigation into whether Comey had lied before Congress in 2020 was a dead end. With no Comey indictment coming, Siebert knew his job would not last much longer. Facing the inevitable, he resigned.

With a volt of anger, Trump tried sending Pam Bondi an intemperate direct message over Truth Social on September 20. But somehow his message was posted publicly.

It was a rambling screed about the lack of prosecutions against Comey, Letitia James, and Senator Adam Schiff and it was addressed to "Pam" with the warning "We can't delay any longer." In an odd Trumpian detour buried in this missive, the President also praised his West Wing aide and former personal attorney, Lindsey Halligan, telling Bondi, she "likes you, a lot."

When panicked advisors alerted Trump that his post was public, the President backtracked, privately professed regret, and then posted a follow-on message, this time praising Bondi. But everyone had seen Trump's plea for action, which bordered on orders. A president publicly directing an attorney general to press charges against named individuals was the latest, and most blatant, violation of the post-Watergate boundaries between the White House and the DOJ.

Like Bondi, Todd Blanche was caught between his own legal judgment and the demands of a volatile President. Blanche had represented Paul Manafort in the offshoot of the Russia investigation, and thought Comey's behavior surrounding the conspiracy probe into Trump had been disgraceful. He also loathed Letitia James. But, among other things, Blanche doubted Bill Pulte had the goods against James, who had said she made an honest mistake on her forms. Blanche warned West Wing officials that such cases required evidence of underlying intent. He also argued directly with Trump about it, saying he would be delighted to bring charges against James, and that no one wanted to do it more than he did, but the mortgage documents case was flimsy. Blanche's resistance further wound up the ambitious Pulte and Pulte's allies inside and outside the administration.

By September, Trump told associates that Pulte had insisted to him that Blanche wouldn't pursue the James case because Blanche had made erroneous statements on his own mortgage documents. An aggravated Blanche told colleagues that the claims were not true, and he reminded White House officials that he had gone through a Senate confirmation process where his financial information was scrutinized.

Trump remained irate over the lack of progress against James. He told one advisor that Blanche needed to grasp that he didn't really care whether she was ultimately convicted. The President's true goal was to drag into court the New York attorney general who had won a nearly half-billion-dollar civil fraud judgment against him.

"I want to make her life miserable," Trump told the advisor.

When asked about the remark, Trump did not deny it so much as hedge. "I don't think so," he said. Then he added: "But I would have said it." He went on to call James "a dirty cop" and "a very corrupt person. Highly political. Not smart."

II

Soon after his errant Truth Social post, Trump announced he would nominate Lindsey Halligan to replace Siebert as the U.S. attorney for the Eastern District of Virginia. Up until then, Halligan had been working as the senior associate staff secretary to Will Scharf in the West Wing. Boris Epshteyn,

Trump's personal counsel, advocated for Halligan to replace Siebert, and Trump, who had often remarked on her beauty, liked the idea. She was almost certain to do as Trump asked.

But Halligan's legal experience was in insurance law, not criminal law, and her targets—a former FBI director and the current attorney general of New York—were going to be seriously lawyered up. There was also a significant question about whether her appointment was even legal; Presidents were permitted only one "acting" U.S. attorney appointment per district, and Trump had already used his.

Todd Blanche confided to colleagues that he was concerned about appointing someone a judge might regard as an illegitimate appointee to bring these high-profile cases. After the sugar high of "indicted" headlines wore off, he explained, they would be left with cases that were almost certainly going to be dismissed, and they would spend the next six months "getting skullfucked" by judges—Blanche's colorful shorthand for long and detailed judicial objections.

But Trump was losing patience. On the morning of September 24, when the President arrived in the Oval Office, he declared to an aide that he thought he needed to fire both Bondi and Blanche. "They don't do anything," he said angrily, pointing out yet again that prosecutors from the other side had never seemed to have any trouble going after *him*.

MAGA influencers had spent the summer targeting Bondi and Blanche as insufficiently loyal, with particular vitriol after the Epstein files debacle. Soon, there were complaints from corners of Trump's base that more wasn't being done by the government to help people arrested in connection with the January 6 Capitol riot; the blanket pardons weren't seen as enough. In mid-September, Trump advisors asked online influencers to boost Bondi and Blanche on social media, creating a parade of digital positivity that could, if needed, be printed out and shown to Trump. Even Laura Loomer, who had been one of Bondi's chief antagonists, had recently forged a peace with her over a lunch in the West Wing.

Susie Wiles told associates she was mindful of how much tumult could be tolerated. If the President fired both his attorney general and deputy attorney general right now, it could trigger an all-consuming crisis for the White House. This was especially the case after Trump's post telling Pam Bondi whom to indict, and to hurry up. Wiles summoned Blanche and Bondi to a meeting to discuss the path forward. The President had made his desires clear, she reminded them.

And he had a running list of people he wanted charged, a list his advisors had been keeping track of. In addition to those already named on Truth Social, it included Judge Juan Merchan and his daughter; Judge Arthur Engoron; and the group at Citizens for Responsibility and Ethics in Washington (CREW).

Mostly absent was Alvin Bragg, the prosecutor who had actually secured a criminal conviction against Trump, but who Trump advisors felt certain had been strong-armed into bringing the case by President Biden's allies.

Absent entirely was Michael Cohen, whose congressional testimony helped trigger the Letitia James case and who had served as Bragg's star witness. A possible reason for that absence would surface about four months after Trump's Truth Social post chastising Bondi for lagging on prosecuting his enemies. Cohen would declare publicly that he had "felt pressured and coerced" by Letitia James and Bragg over what testimony he should provide at the trials.

III

On the afternoon of September 25, James Comey was finally indicted. It was an unusual process, and there was confusion about what had actually happened and what evidence had been presented. Eventually, charges on two of three counts were brought against Comey, one for false statements to Congress, the other for obstructing a congressional investigation.

Trump was in the Oval Office when the indictment was announced. Kash Patel called the President to celebrate the news. Trump seemed both elated and fatigued, with weeks of travel and the shock of Charlie Kirk's murder catching up. Lindsey Halligan also called Trump about her victory, but she had some complaints, too. I'm so tired, she said, her voice coming over speakerphone. The speakerphone was a regular, and decades-long habit for Trump, and disconcerting for callers who only realized later that they had been on an open line with no idea who else was in the room.

I've been doing this all myself, Halligan went on, adding that she had received no help from senior Justice Department officials. FBI officials supported her claim, while others at DOJ denied it and said that senior lawyers in Blanche's office had helped her to prepare.

Halligan's complaint matched Trump's own suspicions. Regardless, the White House now believed it was well on the way to a series of prosecutions. Officials could tick off a list of who they expected to be indicted in the coming weeks: Letitia James, John Bolton, and former CIA Director John Brennan, plus the conspiracy case that Tulsi Gabbard had referred to the Justice Department. And grand juries in Florida would begin considering evidence against a slew of Obama-era officials in connection with the Russia investigation.

James would be indicted on October 9. This time, Pam Bondi and Todd Blanche learned about it from news reports. And Trump's advisors were not prepared. Trump was alerted by Wiles, who told others she had learned of the indictment on TV. Trump officials assured their MAGA allies that even more charges would soon be brought against James.

John Bolton's indictment came a week later from a different prosecutor's office. This followed an investigation that had been underway during the Biden era and, on its face, was more substantive. It related to classified material prosecutors said Bolton had illegally shared with his wife and daughter while he was Trump's national security advisor in the first term—while preparing to write a damning tell-all about Trump.

But Blanche had been right about what would come next. The gratification for Trump was instant but fleeting. Contested by defense lawyers, the James and Comey indictments were dismissed days before Thanksgiving. A judge said Halligan had misrepresented the law to the grand jury in the Comey case, and that Halligan's invalid appointment rendered both indictments moot.

Trump waved away the collapse. "He got out on a technicality," he said of Comey. "They didn't appoint Lindsey Halligan" properly, in the court's view, but "I think she was appointed perfectly." The case, he noted, was on appeal. It was exactly what Blanche had predicted—not a technicality but a foreseeable crash.

The judge added that the Justice Department could revive the charges against both Letitia James and James Comey if it used a legitimately appointed prosecutor. The statute of limitations in the Comey case would make that difficult. Prosecutors tried at least two additional times to indict James in the following weeks, but grand juries rejected both attempts. And so the year would come to a close with Trump's revenge agenda failing to come to full flower.

Part IV

PLUNDER

28

Donald Trump, in sharp contrast to his predecessor, liked to produce a great spectacle of transparency. He invited the media in to watch his cabinet meetings; he posted screenshots on social media of groveling private text messages from European leaders; and he said things on a daily basis that no other President would say, giving Americans the impression they were receiving an unfiltered stream of consciousness from their leader. But as poor as his impulse control could sometimes be, Trump kept many secrets. Most of his government—including most of the White House staff—often had no idea whatsoever about what was being hashed out inside Trump's tight inner circle.

In the late spring of 2025, a tiny group of Trump's most trusted advisors had begun planning a secret military campaign that—in the most generous reading—would test the extreme edges of legality. Many lawyers, including those who specialized in armed conflict, would later use much blunter language to describe what they were seeing: phrases like "extrajudicial killing" and "murder."

Stephen Miller was, as ever, at the center of it all. Mistrustful of the "deep state" and of many of his own colleagues, Miller was a master of concealment. He avoided putting his requests in writing, favoring phone calls and quiet talks. When he needed to discuss sensitive matters, he preferred one-on-one conversations to limit leaks. He built his own systems of secrecy, which allowed him to make plans away from the prying eyes of much of the rest of the administration, including, in some cases, out of sight of the White House office that tracked the flow of paper to the President.

As deputy chief of staff for policy, Miller had his hands on all domestic matters. But he also wore a second hat: homeland security advisor, a role that only enlarged his immense influence. Miller ran a staff of around thirty at the Homeland Security Council, a post-9/11 creation that coordinated homeland security activities across federal agencies. Control over the HSC gave Miller a say in national security and foreign policy, especially in the Western Hemisphere. Miller would now be included in the President's top secret intelligence briefings and in meetings with foreign leaders. He had fought hard for his seat at the table, to be in the room for calls with heads of state—even when the subject matter seemed unrelated to his responsibilities.

Miller's obsessive and highly public focus on immigration had led some to overlook that he had also developed strong views on U.S. foreign policy. For years, Miller had told associates that he thought the State Department, Defense, and CIA had their priorities upside down. He told them he thought it was crazy that the most sought-after roles at these agencies were those focused on Europe, Russia, and the Middle East—distant countries that, in his view, were far less relevant to U.S. security. Instead, Miller thought America's foreign policy should focus on the Americas. What could be more "America First" than that? He wanted to know—and he asked the question repeatedly and with great intensity—why couldn't they bring home America's troops from far-flung places and deploy them to the southern border and in American cities to guard against suspected Marxist subversives and Third World criminals?

"What's a better use of our Navy?" Miller would say to colleagues rhetorically. "Sitting around in the Middle East or right here protecting our shores?"

Miller's bitter memories of term one rivaled Trump's. Back then, both Miller and Trump had wanted to use the U.S. military closer to home, but they had been stymied by senior officials at the Defense Department. Trump had wanted to know why they couldn't simply drop bombs on the drug labs in Mexico that were producing the fentanyl killing tens of thousands of Americans every year.

Trump had some role models in mind. He told his first-term advisors there were no drug problems in China or the Philippines because those countries' leaders simply executed drug traffickers. Presidents Xi Jinping and Rodrigo Duterte didn't worry about whiny lawyers hand-wringing over concepts like "international law" or "due process"; they just killed the drug dealers, Trump would say.

In his second term, Trump was determined to handle traffickers Duterte-style. The former Philippines President, as it happened, had been surrendered to the International Criminal Court two months into Trump's second term, to face allegations of crimes against humanity in his "war on drugs." But the U.S. was not a party to the treaty that established the ICC, and Trump was not worried about any other legal constraints. He was commander in chief of the world's most powerful military and he had broad presidential immunity.

And now Trump and Stephen Miller had the perfect operative: Secretary of State Marco Rubio. As a senator, Rubio had criticized U.S. policymakers, and not without cause, for ignoring the Western Hemisphere. He had long wanted to force regime change in Cuba, and he had unfinished business in Venezuela with Nicolás Maduro. In 2017, when Rubio was a senator, the Maduro regime had threatened his life. The threat was taken seriously enough for Rubio to receive a security detail. Now, as secretary of state and national security advisor, he had even more security—and much greater power. Susie Wiles would later tell associates that the pressure campaign against Maduro was, at least in part, "Marco's revenge."

But it was a very different Rubio who was now working for Donald Trump. Long gone was Rubio the idealist, later the "neocon," who as a senator gave heart-stirring speeches about the need to secure democracy and freedom for the Venezuelan people. Trump himself professed to be allergic to all that, and as secretary of state, Rubio presented himself as a hardcore realist, careful to avoid discussion of lofty principles. While he publicly praised Venezuela's opposition leader, Maria Corina Machado, as 2025 wore on he would privately dismiss her as a replacement for Maduro. Instead, he argued to Trump that Venezuela would be more stable, and American interests in Venezuela would be better served in the short term, by replacing Maduro with a malleable apparatchik and otherwise maintaining his corrupt regime.

In explaining his profound shift to associates, Rubio would say that when he was a U.S. senator he was "an independent contractor on behalf of the people of Florida. When you become secretary of state or national security advisor or both, I am no longer an independent contractor." He would say of Trump: "The people of the United States elected him President. They elected him to be the commander in chief and head of foreign policy making, and our job is to implement it."

As for Venezuela, Rubio would tell others that a democratic transition there could not happen overnight and that the country was not, at this moment, capable of conducting free and fair elections. The entire system had been so corrupted by the regime that to try to force major change in a short space of time would result in chaos and mass migration that would harm the United States. He saw the Maduro regime as an organized crime syndicate, but he worried about who would fill the vacuum if they uprooted the entire regime. He feared a civil war and shoot-outs in the streets. So in his view, the U.S. national interest would be better served by sticking with a corrupt but pliable figurehead than by pursuing the ideals of freedom and democracy.

The changes from Trump 1 to Trump 2 were even more pronounced at the Pentagon. In term one, the Pentagon's leaders were unnerved by Trump and contemptuous of the young Miller, with his inexperience and his aggression. But now they had installed a Trump devotee atop the newly named Department of War.

During transition meetings after the 2024 election, Miller had lobbied for a like-minded defense secretary whose thoughts about the American military and contempt for by-the-book lawyers were much more in line with the aggressive mindset he shared with Trump. Pete Hegseth—an Iraq War veteran and author of the book *The War on Warriors: Behind the Betrayal of the Men Who Keep Us Free*—had a long history of complaining about the U.S.

military rules of engagement that, in his view, foolishly shackled America's "warriors," reducing their "lethality." Hegseth thought the new class of generals had gone "woke" and soft. He had defended military officers charged with war crimes; and he referred to military lawyers—judge advocates general, or JAGs—as "jagoffs." Soon after taking over the Defense Department, Hegseth would remove the "jagoffs" by simply replacing the military's top legal officers.

Over at the Justice Department, Trump and Miller had installed a new breed of lawyers who hunted for edgy justifications to green-light Trump's most aggressive requests. Much of the media's attention had naturally focused on the radical overhaul of DOJ leadership, which was dominated by Trump's own personal lawyers. But equally as significant as those appointments—arguably even more so in the context of a legally dubious military campaign—were the changes Trump had made inside the Office of Legal Counsel, which served as general counsel to the whole government and was vital to Miller's operations. In typical administrations, the OLC had been led by seasoned attorneys. But in late July, Trump's second-term OLC was taken over by thirty-five-year-old T. Elliot Gaiser, who was widely regarded as talented but relatively light on experience on account of his age. But he came with a valuable résumé: Gaiser had worked on the team of attorneys who had tried to help Trump overturn the 2020 election.

Trump had promised during the campaign to use the military to destroy Mexican drug cartels producing the fentanyl killing so many Americans. In the early months of the administration, inside the White House Homeland Security Council, Miller had been workshopping the means to fulfill that pledge. But it was complicated.

Mexico's President, Claudia Sheinbaum, was cooperative with the Trump team, doing almost anything asked of her to stem the flow of migrants and drugs across the southern border. But Sheinbaum drew one red line: She could not allow U.S. military strikes inside her country. This was a deeply sensitive issue in Mexico and it brought to the surface a painful history of U.S. subjugation and conquest. The mere discussion of this idea would inflame intense Mexican nationalism and it could put

Sheinbaum's leadership and cooperation in peril. The Trump team held off for the moment.

But in May, when Trump told his closest aides that he wanted to get tougher on Maduro, Miller got to work on a lateral idea. Together with Rubio, Hegseth, chairman of the Joint Chiefs of Staff Dan Caine, and CIA Director John Ratcliffe, they began planning a military operation that would shock the world.

II

On the campaign trail in 2024, Donald Trump had talked a lot about drugs—the scourge of opioids that had become an epidemic in America over the previous decade. Fentanyl had been killing more than 100,000 Americans a year; the annual death toll had fallen under President Biden, but it was still a shockingly high 80,000 in 2024. The chemicals to make fentanyl were shipped from countries in Asia, including from China, to Mexico, and the fentanyl produced in Mexican labs was trafficked across the border into the United States.

At no time during the 2024 campaign did Trump say anything about Venezuelan speedboats. They were not on the radar of anyone on the front lines of the opioid crisis. This was not to say the Venezuelan government was innocent of any kind of drug trafficking. The first Trump administration had indicted Maduro as a drug trafficker in 2020. But the drug being trafficked out of Venezuela was cocaine, not fentanyl. Cocaine, popular with Americans for decades, had long been treated as a criminal problem. The U.S. Coast Guard regularly interdicted boats suspected of carrying cocaine in the Caribbean and Eastern Pacific; if drugs were found on board, the Coast Guard would seize the cargo and arrest the traffickers.

But Trump wanted to take the Duterte approach: to just kill them.

Rubio agreed. He thought the old approach hadn't worked, that it had been a mistake to treat drug smugglers as criminals. He argued that Latin American drug gangs had priced the Coast Guard interdictions into their business models—they expected to lose a certain tonnage of drugs on the high seas every year. But if the U.S. military were to start using Reaper drones and Hellfire missiles to blow up the drug boats, that would send a very different message to would-be smugglers. Rubio was convinced that "fear of the reaper" was a powerful deterrent.

Hegseth loved the idea; he thought it made perfect sense to treat the drug cartels the same way he'd treated the Al-Qaeda elements he had fought in Iraq.

But to justify blowing up speedboats in the Caribbean as self-defense—boats that were by no plausible definition "armed combatants" threatening the United States—the Trump team would need to redefine words and phrases like "terrorist" and "weapons of mass destruction."

Until Trump's second term, a "terrorist" was understood to be somebody using violence to sow fear, in order to advance political, religious, or ideological goals. Drug smugglers, by contrast, were motivated by profit; it was better for their bottom line if their American customers stayed alive and kept buying cocaine.

The U.S. military had a history of supporting Latin American governments who were trying to dismantle drug cartels—with an especially well-funded campaign in Colombia in the 2000s. But it had been a support role.

Trump wanted direct combat. He described Latin American drug smugglers as "terrorists" carrying "weapons of mass destruction" intended to cause mass-casualty events inside the United States, similar to the September 11 attacks. The administration produced no evidence that Latin American gangs had committed or planned terrorist attacks inside the U.S.; they simply asserted that these gangs and cartels were terrorists.

The Constitution posed another problem. Only Congress had the power to declare war. In 2001, after Al-Qaeda terrorists had flown planes into the World Trade Center and the Pentagon, Congress had authorized war against the terrorist group and its confederates. Congress had authorized no such war against cocaine smugglers.

This was not an obstacle for Trump. Early in the second term, he had laid the groundwork by designating cartels and gangs, like Venezuela's Tren de Aragua, as foreign terrorist organizations. The statute allowing such designations did not authorize military force; instead, it banned Americans and banks from financially supporting or transacting with the designated organizations. Such details did not slow down the Trump administration.

In late July, Trump signed a secret directive for the U.S. military to commence using lethal force against designated drug cartels and gangs.

III

There were two parallel conversations about the emerging campaign—one public and one private.

In public, the world was watching a week-by-week escalation by the Trump administration against the Maduro regime. On July 25, the Treasury Department's Office of Foreign Assets Control (OFAC) identified the Cartel de los Soles (Cartel of the Suns) as a Specially Designated Global Terrorist organization for its involvement in narcotics trafficking and corruption. The Cartel of the Suns was a figure of speech in Venezuela, referring to corrupt elements of the military involved in drug trafficking, but the Trump administration treated it as a literal organization.

On August 7, the administration increased the bounty on Maduro to $50 million—doubling it from the $25 million set under Biden. And throughout August, as the administration ratcheted up its rhetoric against Maduro, calling him an illegitimate leader and a drug kingpin, a gigantic amount of naval firepower moved into the South Caribbean Sea, near the coast of Venezuela.

Senior administration officials briefed the press that they were focused entirely on a counterdrug mission. But in private, Trump was talking about a lot more than that. He was obsessed with seizing Venezuela's vast oil fields. And he wanted Maduro gone. In August, CIA operatives quietly entered Venezuela; their mission was to find out everything they could about Nicolás Maduro—where he went, what he ate, whom he spoke to, and where he slept.

A vision of an even bolder mission was coming into focus for Trump.

From the earliest days of the administration, Pete Hegseth couldn't get enough of the videos of American missiles blowing apart suspected terrorists in Africa and the Middle East. And he wasn't the only one.

Hegseth would walk down the hallway from his spacious office at the

Pentagon to the cramped quarters of his junior military aide. Ricky Buria, who would later become Hegseth's chief of staff, would be waiting for Hegseth at his standing desk, with a video queued up on the desktop computer. The videos Buria would play for Hegseth had come over the Defense Department's classified communications system from the commanders at United States Central Command, covering the Middle East, and Africa Command. They showed drone strikes on suspected Islamist militants in Somalia, Syria, and Yemen. Hegseth would stand there, next to Buria, watching closely.

If Hegseth especially liked a video he would say to Buria, "We should get this to the President." The footage would then be sent to the White House, edited for length and, in some cases, for gore. Some videos could be particularly gruesome; after the strikes, body parts could be seen scattered everywhere, and those were often cut. A U.S. official familiar with the videos described them as "Hegseth's snuff films." Others with knowledge of the practice said the secretary was simply keeping the commander in chief informed of operational successes.

Trump, who had publicly celebrated such strikes as awesome displays of American military power, loved the videos and sometimes posted them on social media. But there was one category of footage that Hegseth showed no interest in sending over to the President: Perhaps sensing that Trump would not want to see videos of the U.S.-backed Ukrainian military blowing up Russian soldiers, the defense secretary did not publicize strike footage from that conflict.

The boat-bombing campaign in the Caribbean and Eastern Pacific would be tailor-made for videos on social media. On September 2, Trump was talking to a group of reporters in the Oval Office when he casually announced, "We just, over the last few minutes, literally shot out a boat, a drug-carrying boat, a lot of drugs in that boat."

Soon after, Trump described the strike in more detail on Truth Social. He said he had killed eleven people on a boat smuggling drugs on behalf of Tren de Aragua. And he posted a grainy aerial surveillance video of a boat exploding over water.

Trump's statements, and the video, raised immediate questions. On what legal authority had he blown up the boat? Who was on it? Would the administration be releasing any evidence to support its claims? After the 9/11 experience, with the Bush administration touting supposedly ironclad intelligence about Saddam Hussein's weapons of mass destruction—intelligence that turned out to be false—journalists covering national security were reflexively skeptical. And they had other questions, too. If this was a drug boat, why were there eleven passengers? Typically these small boats carrying drugs used as few people as possible; the more people on board, the less room for drugs.

The administration refused to release its detailed legal rationale for the strikes and said little beyond broad assertions that these were "narco-traffickers" trying to harm the United States.

It soon emerged that the administration was hiding something else. The video Trump released on social media from the first boat bombing was not the full story—and far from it. It was an edited snippet, showing only the first strike. Reporters would learn that the unedited surveillance video showed there had been additional strikes against the speedboat, and the additional strikes raised more alarming questions. The first strike had not killed everyone on board, as *The Intercept* first reported. After the first missile hit, *The New York Times* would report that two men climbed onto the overturned hull and waved for help, a signal that they were not a threat. Then Frank M. Bradley, the three-star commander of the Joint Special Operations Command running the mission, had ordered additional strikes, which killed them.

In the weeks and months that followed, the strikes expanded to include other groups, including Colombians suspected of ferrying cocaine in the Eastern Pacific Ocean. As a clearer picture emerged of Trump's boat-bombing campaign, concerns rang out from across the ideological spectrum. Democrats were unsurprisingly outraged. But so were some Republicans, such as the anti-interventionist Senator Rand Paul of Kentucky, who told Fox Business, "You cannot have a policy where you just allege that someone is guilty of something and then kill them."

The boat-bombing campaign was so audacious that it disturbed even the Bush administration official most associated with extravagant claims of sweeping executive power in the 9/11 era. As a lawyer in George W. Bush's Office of Legal Counsel, John Yoo had written secret memos claiming Bush had the power to authorize interrogators to abuse terrorism suspects, including by waterboarding, to force them to talk against their will—notwithstanding the anti-torture laws. But Yoo told *Politico*'s Ankush Khardori he thought the Trump administration was unjustified in comparing Venezuelan drug smugglers to Al-Qaeda terrorists. "They're not attacking us because of our foreign policy and our political system," Yoo said of the drug smugglers. "They're just selling us something that people in America want. We're just trying to stop them from selling it. That's traditionally, to me, crime."

The uniformed military was bound to silence, but signs of deep concern within its ranks were seeping out. Admiral Alvin Holsey, the commander of U.S. Southern Command, responsible for military operations in the region, abruptly left his post the month after the first strikes. Holsey made no mention of his reasons in his public statements, but many news outlets reported that he had privately clashed with Hegseth and that he harbored serious concerns about the boat strikes.

The administration was undeterred. Trump was excited about the publicity the campaign was generating. He was asserting dominance over America's backyard, a Trumpian twist on the nineteenth-century "Monroe Doctrine" of keeping European powers out of the Western Hemisphere. The *New York Post* would dub it "the Donroe Doctrine," to Trump's delight. In his vision, the Donroe Doctrine would involve a breathtaking display of military might that would show China, Russia, and Iran who was really in charge of the Americas.

On September 15, the Trump administration blew up a second boat in the Caribbean. Then a third on September 19; a fourth on October 3; a fifth on October 14; a sixth on October 16; a seventh on October 17; an eighth and ninth on October 21 and 22; and a tenth on October 24. On October 27, the military hit four boats and killed fifteen people in the Pacific.

Trump would inform Congress in early October he had "determined" that the United States was in a formal armed conflict with unspecified drug cartels he had deemed terrorists. The reality of this was widely contested. But Trump knew Republicans in Congress would sooner or later fall in line. And he didn't seem particularly interested in trying to make a public case, to sell his escalating conflict to the American people. When reporters pressed Trump aides for answers, they would often be directed to Trump's Truth Social feed.

"I don't think we're going to necessarily ask for a declaration of war," Trump told reporters on October 23. "I think we are just going to kill people that are bringing drugs into our country, okay? We are going to kill them, you know? They are going to be, like, dead," said the President.

The Pentagon moved warships into the region, along with an attack submarine, P-8 Poseidon surveillance planes, and F-35 fighter jets. Elite special operations forces were training near the Venezuelan coastline. By early November, the U.S. had a larger military deployment in the Caribbean than at any time since the Cuban Missile Crisis of 1962.

It became obvious that this was about a lot more than speedboats and coke.

29

Of all the glittering prizes Donald Trump coveted, few had seized his imagination as much as the Nobel Peace Prize. As October loomed, he seemed ever-more fixated on the imminent announcement of an honor he was convinced he deserved. Some advisors assumed he was jealous of Barack Obama, who had received the Nobel in just the first year of his presidency. Trump would complain that Obama got the prize "for doing nothing." Republicans and foreign leaders like Benjamin Netanyahu had quickly identified this obsession as an easy way to maneuver into Trump's good graces, and they soon began nominating him.

Trump was desperate for a major peace deal to burnish his reputation. Until now, he had been forced to dress up and exaggerate lesser deals, and minor conflicts, to cast himself as a historic peacemaker. He was getting nowhere with the Russia-Ukraine war. But with a weakened Iran, and the dynamics in the Middle East upended, there was a rare window to push for a ceasefire between Israel and Hamas. If he pulled off a deal of such international consequence—a deal that had eluded Biden—this could be his best shot at the Nobel.

Steve Witkoff had been a tireless driver toward a grand Middle East deal of almost any stripe through the first half of the year. But an initial ceasefire he had helped Biden's negotiators push through just before Trump was sworn in had crumbled after two months. Witkoff relied on few if any staff, and he shared little with anyone outside the President's inner circle. It would often be difficult to evaluate whether his sunny accounts of his dealmaking squared with reality.

Within days of the inauguration, Bill Clinton had traveled to the Middle East, where the ceasefire was still holding, to meet with Mohammed bin Salman, as well as the crown prince of Abu Dhabi and some senior ministers in the Emirates. At the time, MBS was pushing forward on an agenda called Vision 2030, to diversify the Saudi economy, and he suggested to Clinton that the new Gaza ceasefire would be key to its success. Aware that this information might be useful to the new President, Clinton reached out first to Jared Kushner. Trump then called Clinton, turning on the charm, and connected him with Witkoff. Clinton was struck by the next conversation. Witkoff dominated the call, and it was clear to the former President that Trump's envoy viewed the conflict essentially as a real estate dispute rather than a regional struggle shaped by centuries of grievance and history.

Trump himself would grumble privately about his special envoy. "He's the big dealmaker," Trump said to an associate in July, venting about the lack of progress in Ukraine. "But it's time for him to get some deals."

Even Witkoff's fans inside the White House thought that he needed some help.

II

Jared Kushner had had a fraught and controversial history in the first Trump administration, dogged by conflicts-of-interest questions and internal knife-fighting with other advisors. One of the beats he had been assigned was Middle East diplomacy, a high-stakes, combustible role for which he had no experience.

But in Arab nations with royal hierarchies, Kushner, an Orthodox Jew, was treated as a crown prince in his own right, a more reliable Trump emissary than any other, because he was family. Kushner made a positive early impression on the Gulf leaders by spending a lot of time asking questions and listening—building trust with them. By the end of Trump's first term, Kushner had durable achievements, pushing through Trump's most significant foreign policy initiative, the Abraham Accords, which normalized relations between Israel and Bahrain, Morocco, and the United Arab Emirates. And in the weeks before Trump left office, Kushner had helped negotiate an end to the more than three-year regional blockade against Qatar, led by the Saudis.

After the 2020 election loss and the calamitous final weeks of the first Trump term, Kushner and Ivanka Trump had decamped to Florida, where Kushner launched the investment firm Affinity Partners. The relationships Kushner had developed in the Middle East in his official role would pay off. In time, the Saudi Crown Prince Mohammed bin Salman directed his country's Public Investment Fund to send $2 billion to Kushner's boutique firm, over the objections of some of the fund's own board members. *The Wall Street Journal* reported that MBS said he felt Kushner's work on the Abraham Accords showed "considerable business acumen," though the *Journal* also noted that some advisors to the crown prince said the kingdom's commitment to Kushner was seen "as a political investment more than a financial one." Kushner also became close with Sheikh Mohammed bin Abdulrahman bin Jassim Al Thani, the Qatar prime minister, who oversaw the Qatar Investment Authority. It, too, directed money to Kushner's fund, as did wealth entities from the UAE. These deals would spark accusations of conflicts of interest and inside dealing, which Kushner, back to being a private citizen, shrugged off. His standard response to critics was to say that nobody could point to any decisions he had made that weren't in the best interests of the United States.

Kushner had helped Steve Witkoff during the transition, initially with negotiating staff appointments, and then, once Trump was in office, connecting him with key Middle East figures. He remained largely a hidden hand with Witkoff until later in 2025. But he had been working behind the scenes for months, too, as an informal advisor to a group of senior administration officials who sought his counsel or welcomed his advice. They were among the most influential members of Trump's team, including Susie Wiles, Scott Bessent, Marco Rubio, and Mike Waltz. Kushner referred to some as his "repeat customers," whom he wanted to see succeed. Battered by the public shellacking he took in term one, and wanting to spend more time with his young family, Kushner told associates he would much prefer to remain an informal advisor living in Miami than to join Trump's full-time staff again in Washington. Kushner was more attuned to the risk of stories about business conflicts than his two brothers-in-law Eric and Don Jr. He stayed mostly out of view, but he would eventually reemerge publicly, when the moment was right.

The Israel-Hamas conflict seemed intractable. And Netanyahu operated in public and behind the scenes on the basis that Trump would ultimately back whatever he wanted—a position that the U.S. bombing of Iran's nuclear sites in June only seemed to have affirmed.

If negotiating the Abraham Accords had been a complicated diplomatic achievement, pulling on the relationships and a new scale of diplomacy to tie in all the major players of the region behind an Israel-Hamas deal would be a different order of magnitude altogether.

Unlike much of Trump's second cabinet and his West Wing aides, Kushner knew his way around Washington. And like Trump, he had contempt for standard processes and protocols, regarding bureaucracy as a needless roadblock to progress. Deals could only be accomplished if there was a willingness to forgo traditional American postures on refusing to negotiate with terrorists, or by rejecting the premise that perceived conflicts of interest were a problem as opposed to a negotiating asset. That posture, so discomfiting and even infuriating to Kushner's colleagues in Trump's first term, was not only accepted but broadly admired in the new Trump world.

III

Kushner, in fact, had already been at work on a postwar rebuilding plan for Gaza with the former British Prime Minister Tony Blair, who had consulted with Kushner in term one and reached out again quietly during the 2024 transition. Kushner had subsequently met with Netanyahu during a trip to Israel in July 2025, and again in August. He had kept Witkoff and Rubio apprised of his work, and he and Blair had jointly presented their ideas to

Trump on how to handle Gaza, with its millions of Palestinian refugees, in a meeting at the White House.

When Trump looked over the plan, he offered a predictable comment about the prospects for building a Trump-branded hotel in Gaza—a remark an advisor quickly insisted was made in jest. With Kushner now more visibly involved, Blair, too, would remain a part of the next steps.

Kushner and Steve Witkoff lived just a short distance from one another in wealthy South Florida enclaves. They would take long walks together, sometimes lasting several hours, to discuss the Gaza dealmaking. For a time, the two went back and forth between each other's homes as they tried to build a feasible concept for the next phase of winding down the conflict. One of those meetings in Witkoff's living room, on September 8, was with Netanyahu's longtime advisor Ron Dermer. At Witkoff's Miami home, they hammered out, over three hours, what a hostage deal and ceasefire for Gaza might look like. Dermer had been hard at work on a day-after plan for Gaza, but he understood that any concept that seemed to have originated with Israel would be dead on arrival. He needed the Trump administration's buy-in. After modifying the proposal, their intention was to first present it to Qatari intermediaries representing the Hamas leadership.

The Americans' optimism ended dramatically about twelve hours later when Israel fired missiles at a site in Doha, Qatar, targeting a meeting of Hamas negotiators focused on a possible end to the war. Much of the "abroad" leadership of Hamas had lived under the protection of Qatar for years, including one of the organization's most senior figures, Khaled Mashal.

This was a stunning airborne attack on the capital of a U.S. ally whose leaders could help broker the very deals Trump was hoping for.

Kushner and Witkoff were enraged. *Dermer lied to us*, they told White House officials. Dermer had been sitting in Witkoff's living room only the day before and uttered not a word, not even a hint, about what was coming—an attack on the same people the U.S. was counting on to help them. They considered it a breach of trust at the highest level. Dermer insisted to them that there was no bad faith and that the reason he gave no warning about the Doha strike was because the discussion and decision to strike had only occurred the day after their meeting.

Trump had also been surprised by the strike. Witkoff had wanted to alert his contacts in Qatar, but by the time he learned of the strike, it was too late. The fighter jets were reaching their target.

The Qataris' first reaction to the attack was that they were done trying to help Israel. Kushner's initial reaction was the same. He later told an associate that he thought to himself, *I'm fucking out. The Israelis are crazy.* The Netanyahu government, he thought, *was out of fucking control.* And if the Israelis were willing to lie to himself and Witkoff, who were trying to help them, then *fuck them.*

Trump, at first, did not display the same level of fury. He quizzed people on the day of the attack about what they thought; he seemed unable to decide how aggressive a posture to strike until he learned how it was playing. Ultimately, he decided there was a level of humiliation involved that he wasn't willing to sustain. It couldn't stand.

Other wheels turned as well. Some of Trump's closest advisors, believing Netanyahu had manipulated the President into joining the strikes against Iran in June, also saw this as an opportunity to rein in Netanyahu. Tony Blair suggested Kushner could combine the broad postwar plan for Gaza they had been working on with a ceasefire plan, a type of grand bargain that only rare moments of history sometimes allowed.

Kushner, livid about the Israeli strike on Doha, tabled the discussion for a night. But by the next morning, he was ready to start work. He composed the first draft of what would become a roughly twenty-point plan for a ceasefire and an ultimate hostage deal that morning. He sent it to Witkoff, who made his own changes. Witkoff was pressing the Qataris to come back to the table, a difficult task given they were angrily rallying regional outrage against Israel.

At the White House, there were already discussions about convening a meeting with Middle East officials while Trump was in New York for the UN General Assembly later that month. Sheikh Mohammed, the Qatari prime minister, was among those who would travel to the U.S. for the event, and Kushner and Witkoff met with him for an hour in the lower level of the Fifth Avenue Hotel on West 28th Street, over tea and coffee. They heard out the furious sheikh about how violated he and the Qataris felt by Israel.

You have two options, Kushner and Witkoff argued. One was to use the attack to isolate Israel even further after the two years of devastation in Gaza had galvanized public opinion against Netanyahu. It would be their right to react that way, and understandable, they said. But the other option, they told the sheikh, was to use the moment for leverage—to get Israel back to the table.

With the sheikh sitting between Kushner and Witkoff in the hotel bar, Kushner whipped out his MacBook and showed him their draft of the plan. The sheikh, leaning in, made suggestions around the types of changes that would help to bring Arab countries on board, eventually taking control of the laptop keyboard and making edits himself.

Witkoff joined Trump on Rosh Hashanah, the Jewish New Year, for a meeting with eight Arab and Muslim leaders who had arrived in New York for the General Assembly. He brought a one-page document that encapsulated the key points in the revised peace plan. Among other things, it called for Hamas to put down its weapons, to disavow violence, and for Israel to withdraw some of its troops.

We're here for peace, Trump told the group, before inviting each leader to openly speak their mind. The meeting quickly turned into a bashing-Israel session, with the Arab and Muslim countries airing their anger at Netanyahu. Most thought the Israeli strike on Doha had darkened the prospects for a Gaza ceasefire. How could future negotiations be undertaken in good faith after such a breach?

For his part, Trump laid down some new constraints on Israel—specifically, that he would not allow Israel to annex the West Bank. But the conversation overall was not going well. Witkoff handed Trump a note asking him to call on him to add something to the discussion. When Trump handed the floor to Witkoff, the special envoy walked the group through a proposal for Gaza to be run by a technocratic committee that would form an efficient government. Schooling would be redesigned to cultivate more tolerance of Jews, he said.

But what was not an option, he added, was ignoring Hamas outright.

What Witkoff lacked in diplomatic background or historical knowledge he compensated for with a selling delivery and a calm, the-sun-is-always-shining presence. The Middle Eastern leaders reacted positively, and Trump fed on their enthusiasm. The key insight for Kushner and Witkoff was that demanding the immediate return of all hostages—both the living and the remains of those whose bodies were scattered throughout Hamas's underground tunnels—could mean waiting forever. They had to focus on first rescuing those who were still alive.

Trump continued to advocate for the plan in private meetings and calls with Arab leaders, betraying no sign of a willingness to bend for Netanyahu, cajoling them to stay the course. If anything, his accommodations ran toward the Arab nations this time. The emir of Qatar called the President to say he could not be certain Hamas would be willing to commit to everything, because they would want to include retaining at least some of their less powerful weapons for self-protection. I'm okay with that, Trump said.

IV

When he was finally brought into the bigger picture, Netanyahu—who was also in New York for the UN conference—was less than thrilled. It would take many hours of talks between Kushner and Witkoff on one side and Dermer on the other to alleviate his concerns. Netanyahu was also looking toward the United Nations event, where he would have to describe to skeptical world leaders the necessity of the two-year war between Israel and Gaza. At one point, Netanyahu found Witkoff and Kushner waiting outside a hotel room while he worked on a draft of his UN General Assembly speech. Kushner and Netanyahu had what the Israelis saw as a very productive meeting in those few days. Kushner and Witkoff would shuttle back and forth from Netanyahu's hotel, the Loews Regency, to Le Bilboquet on East 60th Street. It was a Witkoff-owned restaurant, complete with "the owner's own Cajun chicken recipe" on the menu, and it became their temporary cafeteria. Staying close to the Israelis at this critical juncture was vital.

Recognizing his leverage was weak, Netanyahu finally appeared poised to agree to the plan. In the wake of the Qatari strike, Israel was as isolated geopolitically as it had been in years. Netanyahu told associates he would agree to some kind of deal the Trump administration was seeking. But he was doubtful that Hamas would do the same, which made it easier for him to seem reasonable by going along with it. While the frontline fighters in Gaza might be eager for a ceasefire, some of the political leadership of Hamas in Doha could be far less invested. Netanyahu prepared to see Trump at the White House the following Monday.

Witkoff, meanwhile, was certain Netanyahu would try to upend any informal agreement before his meeting with the President, or at least find a way to change the terms.

He warned Kushner: "I'm telling you, Bibi is going to try to go around us at the last minute to get out of this, and he's going to call the President." Kushner disagreed, confident the deal would hold. But just to be on the safe side, they alerted Susie Wiles. The situation was precarious, with many moving parts; from the hostages, to the twenty-point plan, to the apology the Qataris were demanding from Israel. If Netanyahu thought he could once again successfully appeal to Trump directly, they had to be prepared.

Sure enough, on September 27, an unseasonably warm night in New York, Kushner and Witkoff were interrupted in their meetings by a call from Wiles. Netanyahu had just requested to speak with the President that evening, and he was moments from calling through the White House operator. Witkoff and Kushner rushed to alert Trump. They suspected—without knowing for sure—that Netanyahu was going to try to scuttle the deal. Trump cut through it all, saying, Why don't you guys just join me on the phone?

Trump was in a foul mood by the time Netanyahu was patched through after difficulties on the switchboard to connect the call. Trump immediately erupted with a cannon blast of anger that continued uninterrupted for what others later said seemed like twenty minutes. Netanyahu could barely get a word in.

Bellowing, Trump told Netanyahu he was sick of his antics. I've done everything to protect you. You better fucking go along with this. It's been going on for too fucking long. Everybody's sick of you, Bibi, Trump said. All the Jews are sick of you. Even the two Jews on this call are sick of you, Trump added, referring to Kushner and Witkoff. You can't back out of this. I'm the best friend Israel ever had. Everybody hates you, and I've stood by you, he continued to shout. I'm telling you, Trump yelled, this is a great deal for Israel.

Others later described the call as "epic." Trump ticked through the list of controversial decisions he had made supporting Israel through both of his presidencies.

He warned Netanyahu that if he backed out now, it would be the last straw. We will get a divorce, Trump said. We will break up. When the President finally stopped talking, there was a second of silence.

Then Netanyahu spoke. He insisted he was not calling to pull out of the deal. Who gave you the wrong impression I was calling to get out of the deal? Why would the President think that? I don't know why you're yelling at me, he complained, sounding injured.

Why are you calling me then? Trump asked. Well, there's a couple of issues, Netanyahu ventured. The prime minister later told associates that he had noticed that certain people had been stirring up trouble, trying to drive a wedge between himself and Trump, and that he was only calling to clear the air. But before he could elaborate, Trump cut him off again. You've got Jared and Steve on the phone, he said, just work it out with them. But we're getting this deal done. You're finishing it.

Their conversation ended with Netanyahu repeating that he was an honest broker and would do what was right. Trump, his head of steam released, told Netanyahu they were fine. He loved him, too, the President said. It was easy for Trump to be magnanimous once he had gotten what he wanted.

For the first time in his relationship with Netanyahu, he had used his leverage to prod the Israeli leader into a compromise. Netanyahu understood what a difficult position he was in, especially after the disastrous Doha strike. But only Trump could have pulled off this wrestling match between such complex players. When it came down to it, Netanyahu knew that Trump was hugely popular in Israel, and he had to manage that power in a way he had never had to do with Joe Biden.

What followed immediately afterward was a tense call between Kushner, Witkoff, and Ron Dermer, who sounded aggrieved, having heard Trump's fury. He asked who had misinformed the President that Netanyahu was going to reject the deal.

It's your fault, not ours, Witkoff said, pointing out that he and Kushner had been disrespected twice, first with no warning of the Doha strike and then by Netanyahu end-running them with a leader-to-leader call. Dermer had been short on sleep and acknowledged that he should have given them a heads-up about the reason Netanyahu wanted to speak to the President, which he maintained had nothing to do with the deal.

Dermer understood that the prime minister would need to make some kind of apology to Qatar, to ensure that the country with the most influence on Hamas would not undermine the U.S. proposal. Two weeks earlier, Dermer had discussed with Witkoff the idea of Netanyahu making a three-way apology call with the emir of Qatar and Trump. This would be more understandable to people back in Israel, given Trump's popularity there. And Netanyahu was due at the White House on Monday.

Some White House aides were surprised that Netanyahu hadn't canceled his official meeting with the President after the way Trump had spoken to him. But he showed up. Shortly after, Trump got the Qatari prime minister on the phone and handed the receiver to Netanyahu, who was sitting in a chair beside him in the Oval Office. Netanyahu, who had brought a carefully worded script for the apology, which he later posted online, began reading out his regrets over the phone. Trump, with a somber look on his face, kept the phone cradled in his lap, an image captured in an official photo and swiftly released on social media.

The picture didn't tell the full story, but it created an indelible image: Netanyahu in a submissive position, on a short tether pulled by Trump.

V

There was still skepticism about the deal in many quarters given the shock of the Israelis bombing Qatar. But when Netanyahu told Kushner that Israeli intelligence suggested Hamas would reject the deal, Kushner didn't agree. "I've lived through this with intelligence," he replied. "When it comes to finding terrorists with expensive weapons, the intelligence is great. When it comes to giving perspective on negotiations, it can be very misleading. The Arabs are telling us that they're going to be on board." Netanyahu got behind the plan and Kushner and Witkoff turned to the next step, dialing their Arab contacts, pushing for statements of support. They needed Hamas to agree quickly.

But the Hamas negotiators were not ready. Even so, Witkoff and Kushner would days later push Trump to announce Hamas had signed off on the deal—boxing them in.

The pair tag-teamed, living on cell phones to muscle through the plan. After briefing Trump, Vance, Hegseth, and Rubio in Washington, they flew to Egypt for secret meetings with top Hamas officials.

It would be a surreal moment in history, and yet it was rooted firmly in on-the-ground grievances that went back to the establishment of the State of Israel in 1948. Now two New York Jews, a son-in-law and a golfing friend of the President, were preparing to meet Hamas, a designated terrorist organization that for years had maintained a fully-armed choke hold in one of the most vexed enclaves in the world.

Witkoff and Kushner holed up at the Four Seasons Resort at Sharm El Sheikh on the Red Sea, opting to share a villa. When it finally came time to meet with Hamas, suddenly and late at night, an aide from Sheikh Mohammed arrived to fetch them. But the aide came with well-honed advice, warning Kushner he was going to take a lot of abuse for meeting with Hamas, and what did he need all this for? Kushner asked Witkoff what he thought. Witkoff told him, If you want me to tease you for the rest of your life for being a wimp, then you don't have to come. Kushner was soon dressed and ready to go. He joked later with Rubio that during the negotiations with Hamas over prisoner swaps, he felt as though he and Witkoff were "the general managers of a terrorist football club."

But the struggle to lock down the final deal, even then, was not over. The discussions, which had already been underway for days, included the Egyptians, Turks, Qataris, and four senior Hamas representatives.

The Hamas officials had concerns that were bluntly stated: Would the Israelis kill them if they agreed to the deal, which entailed laying down major weapons? So much hung in the breach. Kushner and Witkoff gave their word that if Hamas released the hostages and honored the deal, so, too, would the other side. Witkoff delivered a message that Trump would stand behind each guarantee in the plan. Time ticked away. The Qatari prime minister had a looming meeting in Paris and Kushner insisted he couldn't leave until the deal was sorted out. The prime minister eyed Kushner and replied archly, "Jared, unlike others, I don't leave until my business is done."

Once the terms with Hamas were finally agreed upon, Kushner and Witkoff headed next to Israel. They had believed everything was sealed, but even at the last minute, there was a problem. The list of hostage names that each side would be releasing did not match up. To resolve the standoff, they worked through the night again, a process Kushner later described to associates as "hand-to-hand combat" with each side as he and Witkoff tried to will the deal into existence. But finally the moment came.

Kushner was back in a familiar negotiating role for a Trump government, but without the baggage of last time. He was poised to accomplish something significant—building a new government in Gaza from scratch, he would say to Witkoff. It was a prospect so improbable and yet so enticing that Kushner would remain involved. And he would no longer stay behind the scenes; he was, he would tell an associate, "scared shitless" that the deal could still fall apart, and he felt he would need to shepherd it through to the end. On October 11, he made a rare speaking appearance at a rally in Tel Aviv in support of the Israeli hostages, alongside his wife, Ivanka, and Witkoff.

Witkoff, for his part, praised Trump, and the crowd cheered loudly and chanted "Thank you, Trump!" Earlier, when Witkoff had tried to acknowledge Netanyahu, the boos from the prime minister's own citizens at the rally were deafening.

Donald Trump, Witkoff, and Kushner had effectively parlayed their regional relationships to establish a ceasefire—fragile, tenuous, and episodically challenged as it may have been—in a war so devastating that it had shocked the conscience of the world. Trump, as was so often the case with any accomplishment, promptly oversold it to the public. His descriptions of what the deal would mean in terms of lasting peace in the region were typical of his bombast and unceasing demands for credit.

But with the hostages freed and the violence largely halted, it was a case where he had legitimately earned it.

VI

When a friend congratulated Kushner on the ceasefire and the hostages, Kushner replied, "This isn't the end—it's just the beginning."

The next step was to build a mechanism that could carry Gaza from its fragile ceasefire into something far more ambitious—transforming a hellscape of rubble into what Trump, with his usual hyperbole, envisioned as a showcase of luxury towers, marinas, and business parks. That mechanism came to be known as the Board of Peace.

But before anyone could contemplate waterfront developments, Gaza had immediate and desperate needs. Some type of international security force would have to provide a measure of order and, eventually, disarm Hamas. Basic services—water, power, sewage—had to be restored for a shattered population. And vast sums of money were required for clearing debris and unexploded ordnance, erecting temporary housing, and importing mountains of supplies for reconstruction.

The countries considering contributing troops and police—Indonesia, Kazakhstan, and Morocco among them—needed the imprimatur of international law before they would commit. That meant enshrining the concept in a resolution to be voted on in the UN Security Council.

Kushner assembled a tiger team of Abraham Accords veterans and private-sector deal guys, pairing them with the newly confirmed ambassador to the United Nations, Mike Waltz, and his staff. Waltz adopted the same playbook that had produced the twenty-point peace plan: pull in the key Arab nations first, then expand to majority-Muslim countries, before approaching the skeptical Europeans, Russians, and Chinese.

After weeks of breakneck negotiations and steady engagement with capitals around the world, the resistance began to crack. In a pivotal moment, Waltz worked with eight Arab and Muslim-majority nations to issue a joint public statement alongside the Palestinian Authority. The mantra deployed against hesitant Europeans was blunt and effective: *You can't be more Catholic than the pope.* If the Palestinians themselves supported this, how could anyone justify standing in the way?

When the vote came, the resolution passed with thirteen in favor.

Russia and China abstained. The Board of Peace was born. And in a flourish that surprised no one, Trump installed himself as its chairman, holding the only veto, while just over two dozen other countries signed on as members. Though nominally focused on rebuilding Gaza, the founding documents gave the board wide latitude to take on other projects. It was a conveniently open-ended mandate for a President still chasing the Nobel Peace Prize.

30

By mid-October, the President had lawsuits running against individuals and institutions throughout America. Some were part of his retribution binge, some were against his own government, some were against the media, and others slotted into his anti-woke war. In most instances, Trump had the upper hand, but one legal action presented an unusual risk. This was Trump's $10 billion libel lawsuit against Rupert Murdoch, his prestige flagship *The Wall Street Journal*, and the reporters who had investigated and written the story about Trump's signature on a fiftieth birthday card for Jeffrey Epstein.

Murdoch's empire had been entwined for decades with reporting on New York City and that included the combative real estate swamp, home to big personalities, slimy deals, and also to Donald Trump. It was Murdoch's tabloid, the *New York Post*, that had helped Trump become a fixture of celebrity gossip pages, and hone his habits for self-promotion. The source described in the paper as "a person close to Donald Trump" was often Trump himself. During Trump's savage and public split with his first wife, Ivana, in the early 1990s, she had used the rival *Daily News* as her preferred vehicle to air her side of the story, while the *Post*'s Cindy Adams, a former beauty queen, was Trump's. Before Trump won the 2016 election, Murdoch had long thought of him as something of a clown. But Trump was notable for his unbuttoned, freewheeling views and Murdoch would tell people his appearances on Fox News always delivered high ratings.

Rupert Murdoch had always wanted to be close to a U.S. President but neither of the Bushes nor Ronald Reagan had treated him as a confidant. With Trump in the White House, News Corp became a kind of home base, rooting for him and supporting him in distinctive ways through his first presidency. Trump had revered Murdoch for decades—in his first term, he was so attentive to the mogul that he had once yelled at an aide for the sin of putting Rupert on hold instead of barging into the Oval Office to interrupt the President and tell him "Rupert is on the line." Trump always hungered for any morsel of gossip about Murdoch and the inner workings of his empire. He grilled Murdoch about his succession plans during a memorable Oval Office visit in 2017, in the hope that News Corp would not one day be led by Rupert's far more liberal son, James.

Both Trump and Murdoch were strong-willed and they had sparred often over the years, especially after January 6, when Murdoch seemed desperate to move on from the outgoing President.

But suing Rupert Murdoch was something else altogether. Murdoch had a reputation as one of the toughest businessmen on the planet. In 1985, at a time when Australia barred dual citizenship, he had given up his Australian citizenship and become an American, enabling him to buy a string of TV stations that became Fox News, eventually spreading to every corner of the U.S. He was a controversial newsman, unpredictable, and with a history of hard political campaigning in a slew of countries. He loved nothing more than a great story. And he had so much money that few had an appetite to go up against him in court.

The frazzled and furious President instructed his lawyers to depose Murdoch about the chain of command that led to the story going to press. Privately, Trump had told an advisor that Murdoch's faculties were slipping and that he would never want to take the stand in court against him. But Trump wanted to humiliate Murdoch as payback—black eye to black eye.

Three months after Trump sued Murdoch and the *Journal*, a distinct change in sentiment hung in the air. On October 16, Murdoch arrived at the White House for dinner with the President, with some of his key staff from both Britain and the U.S. The dinner had been in the mix for several weeks and Murdoch's presence followed a phone call some weeks earlier from the editor in chief of the *New York Post*, Keith Poole. Poole, who talked often to Trump and was a favorite of the President's, had alerted the White House that his boss would like to join them for dinner, and to bring his wife.

Poole's guest list was interpreted at the White House as a smoke signal that Murdoch wanted to make nice with Trump and that he was perhaps interested in settling the *Wall Street Journal* lawsuit. After all, many parts of the Murdoch empire were still on friendly terms with the Trump team—and not only Fox and the *Post*. There were even discussions among some News Corp executives about the possibility of a book that would present Trump as the "President of Peace." They believed it would be a bestseller. But behind the scenes, many at News Corp remained adamantly opposed to settling the *Journal* suit. They did, however, want to take down the temperature with Trump.

Murdoch's evening with Trump would be startling in more ways than one. The hostilities between the President and the tycoon had suddenly cooled. Trump was in an avuncular mood, and there were no verbal fisticuffs or punishing riffs. Instead, an attentive host and his key people greeted an important guest. Aside from Rupert and his wife, Elena Zhukova, the News Corp contingent included Poole from New York; the CEO of News UK, Rebekah Brooks; two of her top staff; and several reporters and columnists from Murdoch's newspapers. The Trump side included JD Vance and his wife, Usha; Marco Rubio; Susie Wiles; Karoline Leavitt; and former Fox host Jeanine Pirro, now the U.S. attorney for the District of Columbia.

Before dinner, Murdoch, his wife, and the News Corp editors and journalists met Trump in the Oval Office for a tour of what the President had on show for visitors that week. The group posed for pictures. The President had with him mini-replicas of his proposed monument near the Lincoln Memorial, the "Arc de Trump," as well as the White House ballroom. A bunch of MAGA caps from a side office—now more like a gift shop—were tossed around.

They moved to a small room with eighteen-foot ceilings and a vista of the Washington Monument. An oval table was set with White House china and polished silver, accented by gold place cards inscribed in calligraphy, crisp white linen napkins, and printed menu cards at each seat. They were now in the Blue Room, an exquisite salon where Abraham Lincoln, in 1863, was said to have shaken hands for hours before ascending to his office to sign the Emancipation Proclamation. In the 1960s, the room had been revived by Jackie Kennedy, who set about reacquiring pieces of the original Pierre-Antoine Bellangé furniture ordered from Paris by President James Monroe in 1817 and auctioned off in 1859. A ten-year restoration of the Bellangé collection, overseen by White House curators and supplemented by good replicas, was unveiled by Melania Trump in 2018. Old chairs returned in sublime condition with newly gilded frames and plump turquoise and gold upholstery. Tiered sapphire drapes framed views through the South Portico.

When Murdoch was seated, beside Trump at the head of the table, the President became solicitous and the two talked back and forth. The fire-breathing of weeks earlier seemed a distant memory. Trump told old war stories and asked Murdoch's opinion on all kinds of subjects, from Iran to the war in Ukraine. What did Rupert think? Trump was strikingly deferential. Dinner was comfort food, nothing adventurous: a salad with a heavy creamy dressing, followed by a chicken dish and a cake dessert. Wine was served, but most of the staff were drinking Coca-Cola, with the President on Diet Coke refills every ten minutes or so.

At one point, Trump suddenly steered the conversation in a new direction. He engaged Murdoch in one of his favorite parlor games: Who did he like best between JD Vance and Marco Rubio? The unspoken subtext was the 2028 presidential campaign and who Trump might end up blessing as his successor.

With both Rubio and Vance sitting at the table, the President said to Murdoch, "They're both great."

Then he added, putting the question directly to Murdoch: "What do you think of JD?"

Trump spoke in a joking way, but some in the room detected an edge. Vance was sitting silently at the other end of the table from Trump and Murdoch.

Murdoch replied like a cautious diplomat.

"Well," he said, "I think JD has the potential to be great."

Vance—who knew full well that Murdoch had privately tried to talk Trump out of choosing him as his running mate in 2024—laughed it off, saying sarcastically, "Oh thanks, thanks Rupert, thanks a lot." But to some at the table, he seemed taken aback.

"And what do you think of Marco?" Trump asked, homing in.

This time, Murdoch was immediate and unequivocal.

"Marco is brilliant," he declared.

The other guests would talk privately about the moment for weeks after the dinner.

Age might have reduced Murdoch's energy—he walked with a cane—but his drive was legendary. He had steered which political parties his newspapers would support, through decades and across multiple countries. Sometimes his upscale newspaper would back one political party in an election, while his populist newspapers supported the other side. Betting on Murdoch's favor was a gamble that many politicians had taken and lost. Even at ninety-four, his every utterance was parsed for its deeper meaning.

Trump, noncommittal himself when asked by journalists or even confidants about the prospects for Vance succeeding him, often pivoted to say that Rubio was great, too, and the party had a "good bench" for 2028.

Now Trump moved the dinner conversation on, galloping through topics like a talk show host interviewing Murdoch on the news of the day.

At one point, as they discussed Venezuela and Trump's boat-bombing campaign, one of Trump's advisors showed a phone to some of the dinner guests. The screen revealed what was still non-public footage of a strike earlier that day on a semisubmersible vessel. Trump told Rubio they should release the video straightaway.

When Vance spoke to guests near his end of the table, Trump intervened several times, shepherding conversation back to the whole group, directing the flow. Trump remained on his best behavior, laying it on thick, asking more and more questions of Murdoch, seeking his opinions. There was none of the usual onslaught about how Fox News or the *Journal* were treating him "unfairly."

At one point, Murdoch, with striking subtlety in contrast to the thundering of his media outlets, tried to draw Trump toward the idea that the President needed to be more attentive to domestic economic issues—a reference that chimed with the hot topic of "affordability" on talk shows, podcasts, and the mainstream news. Murdoch's message was almost sotto voce: Things were going well internationally, but these were not the only issues people cared about.

II

The question of who Trump might endorse for 2028 had been rumbling in the background for some time. He was prone to chewing over ideas, floating thoughts with aides around him.

He had canvassed many of them about a JD-Marco ticket and whether it would be formidable. He asked others how they thought Vance would stand up against Gavin Newsom in a presidential battle. Gavin looked the part, Trump thought. But how would JD perform? Trump had asked one confidant whether Vance was too polarizing for a general election.

Donors were constantly in Trump's ear, talking up Rubio's talents; many of them felt comfortable with the more establishment-aligned Rubio, whose populism had a softer edge, who had a history of neoconservatism, and who seemed likelier than Vance to stand strongly behind Israel. Trump was confident that whomever he endorsed would win. He had a lot of skin in the game, having endorsed Vance for the Senate and selected him as vice president. But he was very impressed by Rubio, with his Cuban background and the rave reviews he was receiving in the press for his more subtle expression of the America First doctrine.

During Trump's redecorating spree in the Oval Office, when someone had asked him about the near-certainty that the next president would remove what he had done, the President had replied without missing a beat: "Cubans love gold."

Rubio seemed to be having the time of his life as a secretary of state who was constantly by Trump's side, at the seat of power inside the Oval Office.

But Rubio and Vance were good friends. During the 2024 campaign, when Vance was at a low point, getting pummeled in the media for a 2021 comment calling Democrats a party of "childless cat ladies," Rubio had texted him, offering to come out on the trail for moral support—he'd carry Vance's bags, do whatever he needed. Now in the administration, Rubio had assured Vance privately that he was not running for President in 2028 and that he would enthusiastically support Vance's bid. Rubio would repeat that statement publicly. It was understood inside the White House that Rubio would not run against Vance without the explicit blessing or direction of the President. In the first year of the administration that scenario still seemed far-fetched, though by early 2026 some of Trump's advisors had begun to change their minds, noting just how much Trump was going out of his way to pump up Rubio.

Trump enjoyed creating conflict where there was none and it was a hallmark of his management style. Behind their backs, White House officials would gossip about the Vance-Rubio dynamic, with some observing that Trump seemed to have a warmer personal chemistry with Rubio. But Trump thought Vance was brilliant, a great intellect, and he often remarked on how impressive it was that Vance had gotten into Yale without having a rich father. Trump thought he was handsome, too, and that nobody did better than Vance sparring on CNN against tough interviewers.

III

Vance was in many ways the polar opposite of Trump. Where Trump was a pure instinct player—unreflective, quick to make big decisions, and at ease with using the full force of American power—Vance was a worrier, and far more analytical, poring over the minutiae of policy and political strategy.

Where Trump would glance at the top-line numbers of polls and carp about his pollster "fucking Fabrizio," and his numbers, Vance would examine the cross-tabulations of Fabrizio's surveys—the data tables that broke down results by age, gender, race, and party identification.

As the year progressed, Vance's worries had accumulated. He had watched Trump run a hawkish foreign policy—bombing Iran, toying with regime change in various countries, continuing the supply of weapons to Ukraine—and act in a far more interventionist way than a President Vance would have done.

Some of Vance's allies worried that he had never quite found his footing in the administration. He remained a key part of Trump's inner circle, but his influence on the policy direction of the administration was often hard to trace. He was "very online," many White House aides would say—too closely following every beat of the conversation on X, too eager to get into fights with random trolls, too eager to be a troll himself.

Vance would often joke in private that he was a natural "doomer"—always latching on to the most negative possibilities. And there was plenty of doom around. Public polls were uniformly awful, and Trump's private polling was no better, with the President losing substantial support from independent voters. Worse still, Trump had lost ground on his strongest issue—immigration—with voters giving the administration little credit for sealing the border, and increasingly souring on the harsh deportation tactics.

Above all, the private polling showed that Americans felt the cost of living was still too high. And Vance was among those most concerned about the President's seeming disengagement from an issue that had helped to vault him back into the presidency. Vance would tell colleagues they needed to focus less on foreign policy and more on the home front. He was obsessed with the challenge of making it easier, more affordable, for younger Americans to own homes and raise families. Trump could be persuaded to talk about his affordability policies, but as he read the lines with boredom from the teleprompter it was evidently not where his heart was. Lately, it seemed his heart was mainly with his ballroom decoration.

Some of Vance's frustrations were typical for the often-thankless job of vice president. But he had it better than some. He was in the room for the key decisions—something that could not be said for many vice presidents through American history. By the end of the first year of the administration he was still in pole position to succeed Trump. Polls showed that Vance's popularity among Republican voters remained very high—and tracked Trump's approval almost exactly.

But Vance had a bigger problem. Many of Trump's advisors would privately observe that the President did not seem to care much what happened to the party or to its nominees once he was no longer on the ballot. In fact, he seemed to take some satisfaction in the unspeakable: Republicans losing when he wasn't running. The next month, when Republicans performed badly in the off-year elections, Trump would say he was "honored" that people were saying they couldn't win without him on the ballot.

Trump had already climbed his own mountain with his improbable comeback in 2024. If Republicans were wiped out in the 2026 midterm elections, or in 2028, he could simply boast that they couldn't win without him. Trump could barely be stirred to even think about the midterms.

Vance had been forced to come to terms with the fact that his fortunes would rise and fall with those of perhaps the most mercurial man ever to occupy the White House. The only thing Vance could be certain of was that Trump was not going to make it easy for him.

31

You buy a piece of land, you get a permit, you get the concrete, and you build a building," Trump would say to aides. "Then you sell the building. There's a building there."

For Trump, building a fortune had always been straightforward—something physical, something you could see and touch. Real estate and construction made intuitive sense to him. He had never been a master of high finance, and most Wall Street elites had always looked down on him. Now he seemed mystified by the vast riches coming his way from crypto. He did not know how crypto worked, he would admit, but his sons did. And it had his attention. In the early months of the administration, advisors came to meetings prepared for the President to ask them what was the latest value of his crypto tokens.

Throughout his life, Donald Trump had monetized everything he could. Fame, which he craved on a cellular level, was hard to buy outright. But wealth was the full measure of a person for Trump. He had spent years arousing suspicions that he inflated his personal net worth and level of liquidity to project the image of a financial heavy-hitter. He challenged—even sued—anyone who suggested he was worth less than he claimed. No product was too small to peddle with his name attached, provided it brought him income—from a line of steaks, to vodka, to a dubious vitamins enterprise.

Six months into his second term, Trump was wealthier than he had ever been, thanks largely to investments in the speculative business of cryptocurrency, an industry his new administration was responsible for regulating. It had notoriously malleable guardrails, it was rife with ethical red flags, and it had the potential to be exploited by malign foreign actors.

The most consequential deal was brought to Trump by his two older sons, Don Jr. and Eric, who in turn had been approached by Zach and Alex Witkoff, the sons of Steve Witkoff.

The company the two families formed, World Liberty Financial, was announced in September 2024, two months before the election. The idea had been brought to the Witkoff sons months earlier by Zachary Folkman and Chase Herro, two entrepreneurs whose reputations troubled some of Trump's advisors. Their previous crypto venture, Dough, had ended with millions stolen by hackers. Folkman's prior ventures included a dating-advice company called Date Hotter Girls.

Steve Witkoff envisioned World Liberty as a company that would include all five of his and Trump's sons, including Barron, who spent hours online as a gamer and who was fascinated by crypto. And by October 2025, *Forbes* estimated the college-aged Barron's wealth at $150 million.

The company's website listed Trump and Witkoff as "Co-Founders Emeritus," their glossy headshots alongside their sons, Herro (cap on backward), Folkman, and three operational staff. A tiny disclaimer stated that Trump and Witkoff had been "removed upon taking office." Witkoff would ultimately divest. But for a year after the inauguration, photos of Witkoff and Trump remained in prominent positions on the website.

There was also a huge investing partner in WLF—a fact that would remain a secret for over a year. In January 2026, *The Wall Street Journal* revealed that four days before Trump was sworn in, a 49 percent stake in World Liberty had been acquired by Aryam Investment 1. The company was run by associates of Sheikh Tahnoon bin Zayed Al Nahyan, who controlled $1.5 trillion of Emirati sovereign wealth funds. Sheikh Tahnoon was a major power player in the Middle East, and a close associate of both Jared Kushner and Steve Witkoff. A UAE fund backed by sovereign wealth had already invested more than $200 million in Kushner's investment fund.

The Aryam stake in the Trump-Witkoff crypto venture would be a $500 million investment, with half paid up front: $187 million to Trump entities, at least $31 million to entities affiliated with the Witkoffs, and another $31 million to entities associated with Herro and Folkman. The second payment—another $250 million—was due by July 15, 2025. Two executives from Tahnoon's company had joined WLF's board of directors, but that also remained a secret until the revelations in the *Journal*.

The overlap of business relationships and government work, once a source of consternation for first-term Trump officials, was now an accepted part of Trump's new administration. White House officials generally shrugged off news accounts of conflicts of interest. There was little risk of any real consequences in Trump's first year back in Washington; Republican lawmakers feared him and he held a tight grip on the Justice Department.

To the extent anyone in the White House thought about the overlapping public and private relationships in the first year of the term, they were seen as an asset. Witkoff had business relationships with Emirati officials through a New York hotel prior to Trump's second term; in 2023, Qatar's wealth fund would purchase the property. Now he was in business again with the Emiratis through World Liberty.

Howard Lutnick's old firm, Cantor Fitzgerald, bragged of record profits in 2025 as his two sons took over the company, entering into cryptocurrency partnerships and raising funds for AI data centers while their father aggressively pushed foreign firms to invest in such centers.

In the years between his presidencies, Trump had come to believe he had been too accommodating of long-established norms. He had stopped short of what most ethics watchdogs had demanded in his first term—putting his holdings into a blind trust—and instead agreed, reluctantly, to turn over control of the Trump Organization to his sons. He would, however, stop them from making any new foreign deals during his first term. But there were still conflicts of interest involving those who used Trump's private clubs either to access him directly or to spend in ways he would appreciate. He flouted anti-nepotism norms by appointing his daughter Ivanka and son-in-law Jared as senior White House staffers.

Trump made it clear that if he won again, things would be very different. His sons could do as they pleased. As could the sons of Steve Witkoff.

"I prohibited them from doing business in my first term, and I got absolutely no credit for it," Trump complained in a *New York Times* interview in early 2026, talking about his sons. "I didn't have to do that. And it's really unfair to them." He added, "I found out that nobody cared, and I'm allowed to."

That Donald Trump had once described cryptocurrency as a "scam" was not an issue, either for him or for anyone around him. In the years leading up to his second election, Trump had launched his own non-fungible tokens (NFTs) in the form of Trump Digital Trading Cards, ranging from images of Trump as a superhero with laser eyes to the $99 "SuperTrump" card depicting him in a comic-book hero costume. In mid-2024, he promised crypto fans he would fire the regulator Gary Gensler, chairman of the U.S. Securities and Exchange Commission. Gensler, viewed as a major enemy of the crypto industry, resigned the day Trump was sworn in.

As soon as Trump returned to office, he moved swiftly. He appointed the tech investor David Sacks as his special advisor for AI and crypto—a position otherwise known as the crypto czar. On Friday, January 17, 2025, rapt investors and at least two cabinet nominees, Scott Bessent and Howard Lutnick, had attended the crypto inaugural ball at the Mellon Auditorium. Snoop Dogg, in a gleaming black tuxedo, gold-rimmed shades, and long braids, performed a live set. Sacks told the ecstatic room, "The reign of terror against crypto is over." Early in the evening, word had gone round that Trump was even launching his own meme coin, $TRUMP. Before the night's end, the coin had already reached a market capitalization of $1 billion.

Six days later, Trump signed an executive order to promote advancement of cryptocurrencies and work toward a national digital currency stockpile. Supporters of various cryptocurrencies would jockey to have their preferred tokens in the stockpile.

There was also an entirely separate, but very lucrative, crypto endeavor, American Bitcoin, forged by Eric and Don Jr. Eric was the face for the new company, a bitcoin miner in Texas, which listed on the Nasdaq stock exchange. Cantor Fitzgerald, the Lutnick firm, was among the group of sales agents working on one of its programs.

The value of Bitcoin for ordinary investors sank precipitously in early 2026, but by then the Trumps had already made their gains. A *New York Times* tally estimated that the Trumps had made more than $1 billion in new cash and other assets in the first year of the second term.

II

There was one company that would play an outsized role in determining the Trump and Witkoff families' success. Binance was the largest cryptocurrency exchange in the world and its founder, Changpeng Zhao, had been rated by *Forbes* as the twenty-first-richest person on the planet; his estimated net worth was $86 billion. Zhao had also been indicted in the U.S. for his role in financial crimes that allowed terrorist groups and other bad actors to use Binance. He pleaded guilty in late 2023 and served four months in federal prison in California. He was released a few weeks before the 2024 election. Zhao had been banned from any leadership role in the company, but he remained a major shareholder.

During the transition, Binance began looking for lobbyists who might help Zhao obtain a presidential pardon—with prices being offered by private negotiators sometimes in the millions. Trump advisors waved away questions about what might happen with clemency for Zhao, when the subject was gingerly raised by people Binance had tried to hire to push for the pardon.

The people and entities involved in World Liberty Financial were opaque at first and it would take time and dogged reporting by the very news outlets Trump called "the enemy of the people" to untangle. In September 2025, *The New York Times* reported on a meeting earlier in the year between Steve Witkoff and Sheikh Tahnoon. The Emiratis had successfully sought access to critical computer chips made in the United States, with many going to a tech firm that Tahnoon controlled—a controversial request given the UAE's significant business relationships with the Chinese tech industry. A few months before that meeting, Witkoff's son Zach had told a crypto conference in Dubai that MGX—the Emirati state-owned investment firm chaired by Tahnoon—would complete a $2 billion investment in Binance using World Liberty's USD1 stablecoins. World Liberty was free to invest the $2 billion in money market funds or other financial vehicles, keeping the interest for itself. "We thank MGX and Binance for their trust in us," Zach Witkoff told the astonished audience in Dubai. An MGX spokeswoman would say later that MGX had selected USD1 for the transaction after evaluating several stablecoins; White House officials said there was no connection between the deals. As for Binance, Trump announced he was pardoning Changpeng Zhao on October 23.

The Wall Street Journal soon revealed that Binance, prior to the pardon, had quietly begun building technology to support World Liberty. A spokesperson for World Liberty would later say that Binance had provided its own previously used open-source contracts to spare World Liberty "the headache" of repurposing them, but not for any gain or exchange.

Binance also hired the lobbyist Ches McDowell, a hunting buddy of Donald Trump Jr., to advocate for the Zhao pardon. The *Journal* reported that McDowell had arrived at the White House with the younger Trump to make his pitch and that Don Jr. had left the room during the pardon talks.

Once the pardon was in place, Binance—still banned from operating in the U.S., but free to operate internationally—stepped up enticements it offered for stablecoins, to include World Liberty's offering.

Trump had told a close aide that the gratitude he received from people he had pardoned was like nothing he had ever experienced in his life. The presidential pardon power—pure, unobstructed, and enshrined in the Constitution—functioned in the way Trump believed all presidential authority should: quickly and unilaterally.

In the final weeks of his first term, and largely lost in coverage of the Capitol riot, Trump had doled out controversial clemency grants—to Roger Stone, Paul Manafort, Steve Bannon, Jared Kushner's father, and many more. And in the second term, such headline-grabbing clemency grants would begin immediately, and not only for those connected to January 6.

A formula soon developed: Pardon seekers would tell Trump they had been persecuted by a weaponized justice system—just as he had. This formula was successful not just for Zhao but for many other clemency seekers. White-collar criminals with long sentences were another category that Trump looked favorably upon.

David Warrington, the White House counsel, had attempted with Susie Wiles to instill some kind of process around clemencies. Wiles had put the brakes on some of these pardons over the summer, after a pardon for Paul Walczak, a wealthy tax cheat whose mother was a Mar-a-Lago member and Trump campaign donor, had attracted unwanted headlines. But the system broke down anyway. People seeking pardons went to Trump directly.

Early in the term, Warrington considered whether the Supreme Court's presidential immunity ruling, vague in some respects, would apply to senior officials as well. Most top Trump appointees were certain they would be targeted for prosecution once the President was out of power. But they likely wouldn't need the protection of the immunity ruling anyway; Trump repeatedly told aides in private that he planned to preemptively pardon "anyone who came within 250 feet of the Oval Office" before his term ended.

III

The world of crypto was far from the only enriching path for the Trumps as he reentered the presidency.

Eric Trump would forge new land deals in the Middle East heading into 2026. And Don Jr. had entered into a partnership with 1789 Capital, a conservative-leaning investment firm, whose valuation grew exponentially after Trump won. The firm invested in government-regulated companies, and one, the rare earths startup Vulcan Elements, signed $620 million in contracts from the Pentagon in December 2025. Don Jr.'s seat on the board of a widely used prescription drug website was announced the day after his father rolled out the administration's effort to provide cheaper access to prescription medicines. An aide to Don Jr. later contended that the President's son had five children to provide for and brushed off questions about conflicts of interest as "a laughable and ridiculous standard."

Eric Trump had taken command of the effort to build the Trump presidential library on a patch of land in Florida. The Florida attorney general, after consultations with Eric, had agreed to hand over to the Trump family, free of charge, the deed to a $67 million piece of property attached to a college in Miami. This would not be a normal presidential library; the family had plans afoot for a skyscraper on the site with a hotel, and Eric was eyeing funding from Middle East sovereign wealth funds. The fundraising effort would also be bolstered by firms with business before the federal government—and even by some cabinet secretaries.

Howard Lutnick would personally donate $25 million to the Trump library fund. Trump had been privately complaining about news stories focused on the moneymaking ventures of Lutnick's sons intersecting with administration policy. Lutnick's donation seemed to mollify the President. More than once, in front of Lutnick and several advisors, Trump ribbed his commerce secretary, saying the only reason he put up with his "bullshit" was because he "gave me" $25 million for the library. At other times, Trump would marvel at the donation. "Isn't Howard the best?" he said on one occasion. "I asked for twenty-five million for the library and he gave it in one second. Isn't that amazing?"

Jeff Bezos had been cultivating his own relationship with Trump. In mid-July, he had visited the President in the Oval Office for a meeting that included Stephen Miller. Musk had departed his government role roughly six weeks earlier, and Trump had simultaneously pulled the nomination of Jared Isaacman, a Musk ally, to run NASA.

Trump opened the meeting with pleasantries. Bezos had recently gotten married in Venice—a multiday, celebrity-studded extravaganza—and the President wanted to hear about it.

Everyone was at your wedding, Trump marveled. How was it?

It was great, Bezos replied. When the conversation turned to the guest list and Bezos mentioned that the actress Sydney Sweeney had attended, the President's interest deepened.

"Ooooh," Trump said.

Then they got down to business. Bezos had come to talk about space—specifically, about Space Launch Complex 37 at Cape Canaveral, and more broadly, about the dominance of Musk's SpaceX over America's launch infrastructure. SpaceX controlled the vast majority of U.S. launches and held a near-monopoly on low-earth-orbit satellite coverage through Starlink. Until Amazon's Kuiper satellite constellation came online, there was no serious American alternative for satellite broadband. Bezos's Blue Origin was the most plausible domestic competitor for launch services—but only if the government opened the door.

Bezos did not trash Musk. There was no need to; Trump was, in that moment, very receptive to any pitch from a major competitor to his former friend.

Bezos framed his argument around national security. The country could not afford to rely on a single provider for something so strategically important, he told Trump. It was a powerful argument, and not without recent precedent: During the war in Ukraine, Musk had unilaterally restricted Starlink's use near the front lines, a decision that had alarmed Pentagon officials and underscored the risks of dependence on one company, no matter how capable.

Bezos suggested that Trump could direct Steve Feinberg, the deputy secretary of defense, to advise officials in charge of space-related contracts that the President wanted "contractor diversity." That was the key phrase from Bezos.

"You don't want to be reliant on one company," Bezos said. "You need contractor diversity."

It didn't have to be Blue Origin, Bezos added—though of course he wanted it to be. The point for the country was that a single supplier in such a critical domain was a vulnerability. The Defense Department had always wanted multiple providers for national security payloads. This was simply sound strategy.

Trump told Bezos he would look into it. But in the months that followed, Musk found his way back. He and Trump reconciled in September at Charlie Kirk's memorial service in Arizona. David Sacks was the go-between, telling Trump, who was set to speak, that Musk wanted to come and say hello. By late fall, Musk had once again begun writing large checks to Republican campaign committees ahead of the 2026 midterms. In November, Trump renominated Isaacman to lead NASA. And on November 20, the Department of the Air Force signed off on SpaceX's plan to redevelop Space Launch Complex 37 for Starship operations—authorizing up to 76 launches and 152 landings per year from the very pad Bezos had hoped the President would keep out of Musk's hands.

The President was tickled when he read news reports of Joe Biden struggling to raise money for his own library; Trump immediately stepped up the pressure to outdo his predecessor. After the Saudi Crown Prince Mohammed bin Salman had visited the White House in October, Eric Trump told the team that he wanted to move quickly to seek library funding commitments from the Saudis.

No single gift was known to be as large as the first one Trump received in 2025: the luxury Boeing jet owned by the Qatari royal family, negotiated by Steve Witkoff as a present to be turned over to the Trump library. But it was far from the only offering from a foreign dignitary or player seeking Trump's favor.

Gianni Infantino, president of the global soccer federation FIFA, had cultivated Trump ever since their first meeting in 2018, when the U.S. was selected to host the 2026 World Cup along with Canada and Mexico. Infantino attended Trump's second inauguration and visited the White House repeatedly throughout 2025 as preparations for the competition accelerated. Trump would also attend the 2025 Club World Cup final in New Jersey that summer. During the trophy ceremony, Infantino handed Trump a winner's medal as an apparent gift. It was gold, but not nearly a match for the golden Club World Cup trophy, which Trump had also decided to keep after Infantino brought it to the Oval Office earlier in the year. FIFA would later tell BBC Sport that there were three versions of the trophy: the engraved original remained at FIFA headquarters; the second was with the winning team, Chelsea; and the final replica was with Trump.

On Super Bowl Sunday in February 2025, Trump and his three older children traveled to the Superdome in New Orleans to watch the game. In a private box, they mingled with NFL commissioner Roger Goodell. Infantino came in to say hello.

The following day, Trump signed an executive order pausing enforcement of the Foreign Corrupt Practices Act of 1977, the landmark American law against international bribery. Trump had long complained that the law put American businesses at a competitive disadvantage overseas. But the timing was notable for another reason.

FIFA had spent more than a decade mired in one of the largest corruption scandals in international sport. In 2015, American prosecutors charged fourteen people—seven arrested in a dramatic early-morning raid at a Zurich hotel—for systematic bribery at and around the organization stretching back years. The rolling plea deals and convictions went on for years, and the United States government held firm that the cases were a critical blow to international corruption.

Two of those convictions had been overturned by a Brooklyn federal judge in 2023, opening a broader debate about whether the government had overstepped. A higher court reinstated the convictions in July 2025, and the two defendants—both media executives who had dealt with FIFA—appealed to the Supreme Court. Some Justice Department officials warned that if the government failed to defend its own convictions, this could jeopardize related corruption cases and require the repayment of millions in penalties. Other prosecutors, dating back to the Biden administration, had believed it was not worth continuing to try to preserve the verdicts.

D. John Sauer, Trump's solicitor general and former personal lawyer, told associates he believed the case was almost certainly going to lose badly if the Supreme Court took it up.

Trump had been skeptical of corruption cases for many years. And besides, he told an advisor, speaking of the World Cup, "They're coming here."

Why do we care about some bribery charge involving Qatar? he asked the advisor. It was an argument he made frequently in private in the fall months of 2025, and his thoughts were well known in the senior ranks of the Justice Department.

Sauer directed the Brooklyn federal prosecutor, Joseph Nocella, to ask the court to withdraw the two convictions, *Bloomberg Law* reported. Nocella wanted to keep fighting, but Sauer did not want to debate it. On December 9, late in the process and as the Supreme Court was deciding whether to take up the case, Nocella sought to dismiss the charges.

Four days earlier, Infantino had arrived at the Kennedy Center for yet another event ahead of the 2026 World Cup. There, he presented the

President—who openly coveted the Nobel Peace Prize—with the inaugural "FIFA Peace Prize." Trump proudly hung the medal around his neck. The mockery was widespread, as was criticism of Infantino, who was accused of violating the organization's expectations of political neutrality.

Soon there were so many favors and so much money coursing through the Trump orbit that an unusually large number of administration staff were eyeing exits before the first year had even ended. Many officials, looking at how much others were making outside the government, were asking themselves: Why not me?

IV

For many who joined Trump's new administration, the old Trump from the 1980s—representing celebrity, glitz, and seemingly fabulous wealth—was the aspiration. They wanted that life. Part of his public pitch for decades had been that anyone could have it, if only they followed his lead. Several top officials soon began using their government roles to do exactly that.

They began living Instagram-worthy lives. Leading the way was Kristi Noem, the homeland security secretary, who used a Coast Guard jet for travel. Later in the year, she acquired two Gulfstream luxury jets for the Coast Guard and planned to add a third—this one outfitted with a bedroom. Despite only being built to accommodate eighteen people, the agency insisted it would be used to deport migrants.

Lori Chavez-DeRemer, the labor secretary, allegedly spent tens of thousands of dollars in government money on needless travel that bolstered her political brand, or allowed her to visit her home back in Oregon. A whistleblower complaint accused the secretary of using her perch—and the cover of her office—to pursue an affair with a subordinate.

Kash Patel, the FBI director, was not far behind. Even as he purged the Bureau's ranks of career officials who had investigated Trump, Patel reportedly used a Justice Department Gulfstream to fly to Pennsylvania to watch his musician girlfriend perform. Patel had previously criticized his predecessor, Christopher Wray, for using government jets for unnecessary travel.

Patel liked being part of the Trump traveling roadshow, with its atmosphere of an endless party. He attended a Miami UFC match with the President, Elon Musk, and several cabinet officials in April. He went to other fights on his own, traveling on government jets. In early 2026, he would drop into the U.S. men's hockey team locker room in Milan after they won Olympic gold against Canada. Video of Patel whooping and cheering and chugging a beer went viral on social media. All the while, the agency he led was in turmoil after a year of firings, forced retirements, races to the exit by demoralized agents, and embarrassing public missteps from Patel related to high-profile crimes.

It was all a far cry from 2017, when Trump's first health and human services secretary, Tom Price, was forced to resign for chartering private planes on the government's tab. Eight years later, that scandal seemed quaint. Government jet travel had become the norm for cabinet officials, and the President had no problem with it—at least until it attracted unwanted headlines.

Noem appeared to have other perks too. She had angered fellow Trump officials by reportedly moving into the Coast Guard commandant's residence at Joint Base Anacostia-Bolling. Her aides said it was because of threats against her, but for some Trump officials this use of military housing seemed unjustified and it raised red flags.

By year's end, a number of other senior Trump officials had moved onto military bases, citing security concerns. In some cases the threats were immediate; one senior White House official was relocated to military housing after a threat from Iran. Stephen and Katie Miller looked at a number of military-base options that could accommodate a family with three young children and another on the way. Senior DOJ officials would also end up moving onto bases. The various requests from Trump officials were straining the supply of military housing. With so many senior Trump officials living on bases—more than half a dozen by year's end—the result was a kind of self-reinforcing bubble: Senior aides were walled off from the city where they governed, seeing threats around every corner.

Trump had still grander ideas for what the government could do for him. He believed he was owed reparations for the way he was treated in his first term—and his four years out of office. Before the 2024 election, he had filed a $230 million claim against the Justice Department over the January 6 investigation and the Mar-a-Lago documents case. Instead of withdrawing it when he won the election, he had, with his personal lawyer Boris Epshteyn, discussed having the Justice Department settle with him.

In Trump's first term, the Republican National Committee had covered more than $400,000 in legal bills for the President and his family related to the Russia investigation. But the family, seeing itself and its businesses as under investigative siege, wanted still more. Eric had asked RNC chairwoman Ronna McDaniel, in front of the President in the Oval Office, to press the party apparatus to cover the Trump Organization's bills for the nascent Letitia James case. McDaniel had refused.

In early 2026, Trump and his sons filed a $10 billion lawsuit against the IRS and the Treasury Department over the leak of his tax returns in the first term. The President brought the lawsuit in his "private" capacity, but his aim was plain: to force a settlement while still in office.

"What I would do, tell them to pay me, but I'll give one hundred percent of the money to charity. I don't want any of the money," Trump told an NBC interviewer, who questioned why he would seek $10 billion from the U.S. Treasury given the country was trillions of dollars in debt.

Melania Trump had also found an opportunity for herself in the sudden swirl of money. The Jeff Bezos–owned Amazon had paid $40 million to license a documentary on Melania during the transition, with at least $28 million going straight to the First Lady.

Nearly all of this before Donald Trump had finished twelve months back in Washington. And yet it would not be enough—something Trump had forecast forty-five years earlier, when an interviewer asked at what point he would consider himself and his family financially secure for life.

It was October 1980. Trump replied that he thought about his business "literally twenty-four hours a day," and that he enjoyed it.

"If I didn't, I will stop," he said. "There's no question in my mind that I'll stop because I do understand it's all basically a game. We're all here to play the game, and we're all hopefully going to play it well."

32

Above the fireplace in what used to be the President's bedroom on the second floor of the White House, a plaque had once hung bearing a short but moving inscription: *In this room Abraham Lincoln slept during his occupancy of the White House as President of the United States, March 4, 1861–April 13, 1865.*

When she remodeled the room, Jacqueline Kennedy had the plaque removed. But as she prepared to move out of the White House following her husband's assassination, she had another plaque made, restoring the Lincoln inscription, and adding just below it: *In this room lived John Fitzgerald Kennedy with his wife, Jacqueline, during the 2 years, 10 months, and 2 days he was President of the United States, Jan. 20, 1961–Nov. 22, 1963.*

With this gesture by a brokenhearted First Lady, two murdered Presidents had become quietly joined in history in the room where they had spent the most personal moments of their presidencies. It was an intensely private memorial that only a few would ever see.

When the Nixons arrived at the White House, the mantelpiece itself was replaced, and Jacqueline Kennedy's plaque, immortalizing a moment in time, vanished into federal storage, to gather dust.

As a young man in New York, Donald Trump was determined to stamp his name onto physical structures. He was Fred Trump's son, he was on the make, and he wanted to leave his own indelible mark on Manhattan—the wealthiest borough in the city and one his father had never conquered. Putting his name on a gleaming Fifth Avenue tower was an exercise in branding into the American consciousness. For Donald Trump, to be famous was to exist.

Forty years later and at the pinnacle of American power, the by-now-seventy-nine-year-old Trump was obsessed with dreams of legacy and determined to use the scope of an imperial presidency to imprint his name on everything, including the low-rise cityscape of Washington, D.C.

By the norms of history, the naming rights for monuments belonged to subsequent generations, and those honors were conferred by Congress, by historians and commissions, and by public acclaim. It was the American way. But Donald Trump had long since demonstrated that he could adore himself far more, and in greater detail, than anyone else might. Why wait? He had watched in rage as his name was removed from buildings in New York City in protest during his first presidency and after its calamitous end. It was a mistake to assume others would praise you for your efforts, he told *The New York Times* in 1980. "If you let people treat you how they want, you'll be made a fool," he said, before adding, "I don't want to be made anybody's sucker."

John F. Kennedy had never named anything for himself. Nor had any other President in American history openly campaigned for a public structure to bear his name—though a few, like Washington and Hoover, had buildings or landmarks named for them by others while still in office. President Gerald Ford went so far as to refuse to sign a bill that would have renamed a courthouse and federal office building after him. Ford said he knew of no federal buildings that had been named for a President while still in office, and if he were to accept the honor it "might begin a precedent I believe it best not to establish."

One of Kennedy's legacies, together with the First Lady Jackie Kennedy, had been turning the White House into a showcase for American arts and high culture, inviting poets, musicians, actors, and dancers to perform at social events, special concerts, and state dinners. When Kennedy was slain it seemed natural that a nation searching for a way to celebrate his life would name a cultural center in his honor. On January 23, 1964, the National Cultural Center—created by an act of Congress at the end of the Eisenhower administration—was officially renamed the John F. Kennedy Center for the Performing Arts, to serve as the "sole national memorial" to the thirty-fifth President.

Since then, the Kennedy Center had served as the cultural center of the capital city, the longtime home of the National Symphony Orchestra and the Washington National Opera, and the host of the world-renowned Kennedy Center Honors.

In this most political city in the country, the Kennedy Center was for decades managed by a bipartisan board, maintaining a reputation for political neutrality, focused on artistic excellence rather than partisan favor. But Trump had refused to attend the Kennedy Center award ceremony during his first term because so many of the artists had made it clear they were anti-Trump. Now, in his second term, he would not only attend the ceremony, but he would have a hand in picking the honorees. And he would appoint himself the evening's host.

When on December 18, 2025, the board of directors of the Kennedy Center had voted unanimously to change the name to "the Donald J. Trump and the John F. Kennedy Memorial Center for the Performing Arts," Trump feigned surprise and humility that the board—which he had personally selected just a few weeks after his second inauguration and of which he was now the chairman—would bestow such an honor.

The renaming was enthusiastically embraced by Sergio Gor, then the head of the presidential personnel office, but later dispatched as ambassador to India. When Gor raised it with Trump months earlier, the President loved it. You're doing all this work for the Kennedy Center, Gor had told him flatteringly. You got the money. You should at least get your name on it with JFK.

The White House quietly ordered the large letters "DONALD J. TRUMP" to be added to the facade well before the board had even rubber-stamped the authorization to rename the building.

Since Trump had taken control, scores of artists had canceled engagements and many more had announced they would refuse to perform in protest. By early November, programming was in trouble and ticket sales had plummeted to catastrophically low levels not seen since the Covid pandemic.

This came during an already turbulent stretch of White House action both overseas and domestically. But Trump's push to put his name on Washington's landmarks—or build new ones in his own image—appeared completely detached from the public interest.

This was just the beginning of a spree of naming.

In early December, as part of his vigorous campaign for the Nobel Peace Prize, and amid dubious claims that he had been the instrument of peace in resolving eight "unendable" conflicts around the world, the administration suddenly announced that the United States Institute of Peace would be renamed "the Donald J. Trump Institute of Peace."

The institute had been conceived of during the Carter administration as an independent, nonpartisan organization created by Congress and it was eventually signed into law by President Reagan.

A White House spokesman explained that the renaming in 2025 was justified because of Trump's prowess as a dealmaker—and also "as a powerful reminder of what strong leadership can accomplish for global stability. Congratulations, world!"

Just before Christmas, the President ordered the creation of a new "golden fleet" of "Trump-class" warships, that would carry his own design touches. He had already launched the "Trump Gold Card," an expedited visa featuring Trump's face and which would grant residency to foreign nationals for the price of $1 million, an effort even some of his own advisors thought was unconstitutional. He would roll out a new program of tax-free investment accounts for children dubbed "Trump Accounts"; he would unveil a website to help people access more affordable prescription drugs that he would call "TrumpRx"; his Treasury Department would announce plans to mint a $1 coin to celebrate the country's 250th anniversary bearing Trump's image on both sides; his face would be emblazoned on national park passes. Later, a giant banner featuring Trump's photo and the words "Make America Safe Again" was hung from the Justice Department's headquarters in

Washington with the agency's seal, a visible reminder of Trump's personal control over the DOJ. For 2026, Trump would try to force Senate Minority Leader Chuck Schumer to support renaming Dulles International Airport and New York's Penn Station for himself, briefly holding hostage the funding for a long-planned and already-appropriated commuter tunnel between New Jersey and New York City to get his way. As part of its "America First" pricing, the Trump administration replaced the free admission to the national parks on Martin Luther King Jr. Day and Juneteenth with brand-new "patriotic" dates, including Trump's birthday; he would tell his staff he wanted the stadium where the Washington Commanders played to be named after him.

In addition to the frenzy of all the naming and renaming, and the palatial ballroom, Trump had begun to obsess over building another immense new monument. Inspired by the Arc de Triomphe in Paris, the President proposed an "Independence Arch" that would stand on Columbia Island in Washington, D.C., across the Arlington Memorial Bridge from the Lincoln Memorial.

He wanted this to be the biggest such arch in the world, and by October he began showing visitors to the Oval Office his various models. The project was already being referred to inside the White House as the "Arc de Trump."

Trump saw himself as a transformational figure in history, one who was already remaking the world in his image, something few leaders ever had the chance to do so definitively.

The original Arc de Triomphe had been commissioned by Napoleon Bonaparte in 1806 to commemorate his victory at the Battle of Austerlitz, a battle that had marked his greatest tactical achievement, briefly establishing French hegemony over Europe. Within a decade he would be undone by hubris and exiled. The triumphal arch—completed long after Bonaparte's death—would take on a more complicated meaning as a symbol of French history and the French people.

The occasion for Trump's arch was ostensibly America's 250th birthday, but when asked by a reporter in October of 2025 who the arch was for, the President had answered: "Me."

The arch in Paris stood at 162.5 feet. The Arch of Triumph in Pyongyang, North Korea, inspired by the Arc de Triomphe and built in the early 1980s to mark the dictator Kim Il Sung's seventieth birthday, was 200 feet high. At 250 feet, Donald Trump's proposed arch would dwarf them both.

As the President showed off his models to a visitor one day in October, he puzzled over the details, including whether the arch should include a platform to take in the view. Privately, he had also been asking confidants what he should have on top of the arch. Should it be, he mused, a large replica of his "Fight, fight, fight!" fist?

Louisiana Governor Jeff Landry, whom the President would appoint as his envoy to promote the acquisition of Greenland, was with him in the Oval Office. As Trump mused over his model arch, Landry shared with the President that back in Louisiana they had a good arch too. Natalie Harp had swiftly printed out photos.

The discussion prompted Trump to phone Louisiana congresswoman Julia Letlow.

"Hi, Julia," he said. "How are you?"

Informing her that the governor was sitting right here with him, Trump told her about his proposed arch and pressed for details about the arch in Louisiana.

"Yeah, we have an arch," the Republican congresswoman said.

"It's a nice arch," the President replied.

He had an aerial photographic map of the National Mall spread out on the Resolute Desk, including the Potomac and the site where he intended to locate his own arch. Bringing out several of his 3D-printed plastic models—small, medium, and supersized, the President's favorite—he placed each at the spot to gauge his guests' responses. Not that the opinions of others would matter, as the biggest was always going to win.

But the Lincoln Memorial across the way was only ninety-nine feet high. "If the arch is 250 feet high, is that a problem?" he asked rhetorically.

There was the other issue too: Should there be an observation deck?

With Letlow still on speakerphone, Trump said to an aide, "Call Emmanuel."

A moment later, the phone on his desk rang. He pushed the flashing button and the French President entered the conversation, also on speakerphone. "Emmanuel? Emmanuel? I'm building a big arch, Emmanuel. I'm trying to figure out if I need a viewing deck. Your arch—do you have—do you have a viewing platform?" Trump asked.

The rooftop viewing terrace on the Arc de Triomphe was a popular tourist spot, offering magnificent views that took in Sacré-Coeur, the Eiffel Tower, and the Champs-Élysées. It was one of the most famous monuments in Paris, standing on the intersection of vast tree-lined boulevards.

"Yes," Macron said, "I have a viewing platform."

"Would you say it's the best view of Paris?" Trump asked. "No? Third best view of Paris. Oh? Eiffel Tower and Notre Dame. Notre Dame, he's done a good job with that. He's done a good job with that. Looks good. Bad fire. Looks really good. What do you think? We have a viewing deck? I don't know. Could be dangerous? People throw bottles and shit off it, right? Do you think they'd throw bottles? Maybe we should have a viewing platform. You can see Arlington Cemetery, it's a great view. I don't know. I don't know, it's dangerous. You can jump off it. What do you think, Emmanuel, do people jump off it? No?"

II

As the fiscal year began on October 1, congressional Democrats had forced a government shutdown over healthcare subsidies under the Affordable Care Act. It would expire at the end of the year, and without it tens of millions of Americans would face extreme increases in their insurance premiums, or would lose coverage altogether.

As the impasse dragged into November and became the longest shutdown in history, nothing much was being done to resolve it.

The tone for the shutdown had been set during the only meeting the President had agreed to with Democratic leadership up to that point in his second term—on September 29—in a wan effort to avert the closure.

During that meeting, the President was flexing his dominance and the conversation quickly took on the air of an extended, elaborate exercise in trolling.

"So, what are we going to do?" Trump said as they all settled into their chairs.

Immediately, Senate Minority Leader Schumer and Speaker Mike Johnson traded sharp disagreements, each calmly but firmly challenging the other over a lack of negotiations and perceived slights going back years.

"Mr. President," Schumer said, "I'm glad we're sitting down. Historically, these have always been bipartisan negotiations, but the Republicans have never sat down with us. This is the first time that I've been here this term, so I'm glad we're sitting down to negotiate."

"That's not true," Johnson said. "It hasn't been bipartisan. You guys never negotiated with us when Biden was in office."

He added, "You didn't talk to us. We always delivered the votes when they were needed. We kept the government open."

Schumer shot back, saying they had always had a meeting of the four congressional leaders. He then launched into his demands—first and foremost, extending the Obamacare subsidies was a must for the Democrats to agree to fund the government.

"Obamacare is shit healthcare," Trump said. "You're talking about premiums for what is bad care. Why don't we just get a better healthcare system? What do you guys think? You like that? What if we just fixed the whole thing?"

Trump had been promising an alternative to Obamacare for a decade, and he had never delivered. The congressional leaders were dumbfounded. Without a funding bill, the government would close in twenty-four hours. And Obamacare was popular, they reminded the President.

"Well, it's all they have. I mean, we could do something better, right?" Trump said. "Don't you think we could do something better? What do you think? Mike? John? What do you guys think?"

"I think that would take a lot of time," Senator Thune said.

"No, I mean, why don't we just do something better?" Trump repeated.

"We have to deal with this now," Schumer said, incredulous.

"I don't know," Trump said. "There's pressure on us right now. So I don't know, I think if there's not pressure on us, we can't get anything done. So why don't you like that? Why don't we just use the pressure to do something better?"

Trump leaned back and smiled. Schumer and House Minority Leader Hakeem Jeffries didn't know what to think. *What is he talking about?*

"Get me a Diet Coke," Trump said. "You all want Cokes? I know John Thune wants a real Coke. You want Cokes?" Everyone was served a drink.

"Now, bring the poison," he said. "I call it poison." An aide hustled in a bowl of candy—Tootsie Rolls, Werther's caramels, Starbursts—and the President proceeded to help himself liberally. He pushed the bowl across the table to Schumer, who leaned over for a look, before carefully removing a caramel.

Trump understood the intractability of the situation and he knew that nothing would come of the meeting. He was content to play games with the Democratic leaders, especially Schumer; it was good sport.

Vice President Vance entered the Oval Office. "Why don't you guys all chat?" Trump said. "Why don't you all talk? JD, I'm going to toss you into this. You'll do good. Why don't you talk to them?"

"Thank you, sir," Vance said. "I'll do that."

When Schumer and the two Republican leaders commenced bickering about the ticking clock and the impending shutdown, Trump leaned back in his chair and shut his eyes. Then, after a few seconds, his eyes opened and he called Harp over to whisper in her ear; he wanted some swag for his guests.

Harp ducked into the side room he called "the Monica Room" to fetch some "Trump 2028" caps. Trump placed them on the Resolute Desk, in front of Schumer and Jeffries. Right away, the White House photographer Dan Torok reentered the room. He leaned in to position the caps, setting up a perfect shot of the Democratic leaders being subjected to Trump's big third-term joke. It was a puerile game that entertained the President.

Schumer didn't react. But Jeffries pointed to the 2028 hat and, gesturing toward Vance, asked, "How does he feel about that?"

"Ah, he's fine. He doesn't care," Trump said. "We're giving him a little more training."

"No comment," Vance said.

Both parties knew exactly what would happen next: The federal government would shut down the following evening.

In the everyday world, far from Washington, partisan political brinkmanship was proving more and more unpopular. Trump's senior staff had known since the summer that he was alienating many of the disaffected and discontented swing voters who had returned him to the White House. And with the Republican hegemony in Washington, they worried the American public would hold the President and his party responsible for the Democrat-led shutdown. It would take forty-two days before the two sides struck a deal to reopen the government.

Trump was becoming frustrated that his message of a return to greatness and flexing of power on the world stage was not hitting the target. The off-year elections in Virginia and New Jersey had gone badly for Republicans, and in numerous state and federal special elections throughout the country, 2025 had seen Democratic candidates over-performing Kamala Harris's 2024 numbers by double digits.

By mid-December, the White House's internal tracking polls told a grim tale. According to Tony Fabrizio's closely held private polling, which was circulated among the inner circle, the American people were judging Trump a failure on the very issues that had elected him President. He had not delivered on one of his most potent and unrealistic campaign promises—to dramatically lower the cost of consumer goods. And given his denial that there was even a problem with affordability, voters were losing faith that he cared.

The numbers were dismal. Overall, 55 percent disapproved of the job Trump was doing, while 42 percent approved. Among "persuadable indies," the all-important bloc of swing voters, it was much worse: 59 percent to 31 percent. On inflation, 59 percent disapproved, while just 37 percent approved. And when asked whether "President Trump's tariffs are causing prices to rise and fueling inflation," 56 percent of respondents said that they were, while only 29 percent said they were not.

Trump's senior staff proposed that he get outside the bubble and start traveling again. But Fabrizio's poll contained some bad news on that score, too. Shortly before the memo was circulated, Trump had given a speech in Pennsylvania billed as a major address on "affordability and the economy."

In the same speech, he called affordability a "hoax" and a "con job"—and then said that "making America affordable again" was his highest priority. It was the kind of contradiction that, delivered by any other politician, would have been a career-defining gaffe. Trump seemed not to notice, or not to care. Neither did the audience. But the voters Fabrizio was polling noticed. Forty-five percent said the speech made them view Trump more unfavorably. Only 22 percent had said it made them think better of him.

It was the same trap that had helped destroy Joe Biden—an insistence that Americans should feel better than they did, delivered with a confidence that read as contempt. Fabrizio's memo made the danger explicit: "Voters remain frustrated with the current economic situation and affordability issues, which contribute directly to their negative feelings toward President Trump and Republicans. If POTUS and the GOP want to gain ground ahead of the midterms, they need to be honest that there is an affordability crisis and confront the issues causing it."

But by the time Fabrizio's memo landed, Trump's focus had shifted even further afield from the national conversation. It was a shift that reinforced yet again that while his constant upheaval of the norms of everyday American life might be wearing thin with the electorate, the President was mainly interested in the next conquest.

III

His mind was now on Venezuela.

Of the thirty-five strikes in the boat-bombing campaign that began in September, twenty-one came as the year ended. The rapid intensification of this opaque operation suggested the bombings themselves were not the endgame. Trump had already begun to openly discuss oil he described as "stolen" from the United States, declaring he intended to get it back.

In March 2025, he had signed an executive order that imposed a 25 percent tariff on any country importing Venezuelan oil, characterizing the nation as "very hostile."

On December 10, the President announced the first physical seizure of a sanctioned oil tanker, the *Skipper*, off the coast of Venezuela. A week later, he ordered a "total and complete blockade" of all sanctioned oil tankers entering or leaving Venezuela. On social media, he demanded Venezuela return oil and assets he said were stolen from the U.S. in 2007 when the Chávez regime had nationalized the oil fields.

As the Trump administration gave shifting explanations for the boat-bombing campaign, and offered scant evidence to bolster claims that drug runners were aboard each boat, the bombings showed Trump at his most unconstrained.

At the same time as he claimed to be focused on stopping drugs from entering the U.S., Trump pardoned the former President and profligate drug trafficker Juan Orlando Hernandez of Honduras. Trump's longtime advisor Roger Stone had advocated relentlessly for the pardon. Trump shrugged off questions about the lack of consistency in his policies given Hernandez had been convicted of helping to smuggle four hundred tons of cocaine into the United States. Stone invoked the familiar pardon formula that had been so effective for others: Hernandez, he told Trump, had been framed by the Biden administration. Unmentioned was the fact that Trump's own lawyer, Emil Bove—installed by Trump in the DOJ and later nominated for a judgeship—was a prosecutor on the Hernandez case.

The drug trafficker's forty-five-year sentence was set aside with the stroke of a pen.

IV

On December 19, the Department of Justice started to release the "Epstein files," as required by law. The administration's panic over the summer at losing control of the Epstein narrative had given way in mid-November to accepting that the bipartisan group pushing for the release of the files finally had the support to force a vote on the House floor.

The bill quickly passed the House and Senate, and Trump, yielding to the inevitable, signed it into law on November 19. The DOJ was now compelled to release the mass of documents from the many disparate investigations involving the dead sex offender within a month.

The legislators who passed the bill had no idea how many files they had mandated to be released. The pages would end up numbering in the millions and the President, his family, or places like Mar-a-Lago would be referenced more than thirty-eight thousand times, according to a *New York Times* analysis.

The entire episode was another flashing light in an era when belief in the American system of justice had corroded to the point of collapse. Raw witness accounts and evidence from incomplete criminal investigations were never meant to be seen by the public. There were long-standing systems in place to protect both the accused and the accuser. The DOJ files basically amounted to a public dump of any document that mentioned Epstein's name, no matter whether the information was confirmed as accurate or not. But so fervent was the belief that the system itself was now complicit in an unimaginable conspiracy that the Epstein Files Transparency Act became possible.

The documents were released with no order or context and they gave an opening to conspiracy-minded sleuths to spend hours affirming their previously held beliefs about the perverts in charge of America.

But it was still a horror story that revealed a hidden strata of society whose business was dense with insider favor-trading, market-moving information, kompromat, and global intrigue. It was a story of depravity and entitlement and shocking indifference to human suffering, all run through with the sickening, clubby banter of rich men and women indulging a pedophile because he hosted entertaining dinner parties and funded their causes or lifestyle.

The released pages named many extraordinarily powerful men. Among them was Epstein's former close friend—now the President of the United States.

In a January 2020 email, a federal prosecutor had told a colleague that Trump had flown on Epstein's private jet far more than anyone knew. Flight records showed at least eight trips between 1993 and 1996, sometimes with his second wife, Marla Maples, sometimes with his children. In January 2024, Trump had declared he had never been on the plane.

What else remained undisclosed? The question would only sharpen as people combed through what was redacted or missing. Among the gaps: records of FBI interviews with a woman who accused Trump of forcing her to perform oral sex on him when she was underage.

There was no "client list." But the documents highlighted Epstein's connections to some of the world's richest and most prominent figures, including Elon Musk and Bill Gates. There were also more than half a dozen senior Trump appointees in the files, including Howard Lutnick. But the documents exposed people on both sides of the political divide: Bill Clinton; Kathryn Ruemmler, Barack Obama's former White House counsel; Brad Karp, chairman of one of the law firms Trump had bullied into providing pro bono services; and the journalist Michael Wolff, who had grown so close to the pedophile that he was secretly advising him on his public relations strategy.

The release of the so-called Epstein files would help Trump in one perverse way; he had long claimed that everyone was corrupt—including and especially his critics—and that he was the only one who was honest about just how dirty the world around him was. Now here was the proof.

Trump would make that point as often as he could. "There are a lot of questions about it," he said, "but nothing on me."

V

For months, the President and his advisors—chiefly Marco Rubio—had been working on a plan to remove Nicolás Maduro from power. Trump had pledged to end wars, not start them—a commitment that was looking shaky, given the boat-bombing campaign in international waters. He was not entirely sure what to do, but he knew one thing: He wanted Venezuela's oil. But, on the other hand, he did not want another quagmire like the invasion of Iraq.

As recently as early November 2025, Trump had been asked during an interview with CBS News if the United States was going to war with Venezuela. Trump had replied, "I doubt it. I don't think so."

But asked if the President of Venezuela's days were numbered, he said, "I would say yeah. I think so."

Earlier in the year, Trump had appointed Ric Grenell, the ambassador to Germany and acting director of national intelligence from his first term, as a special envoy to Venezuela. Grenell was charged with engaging in direct, high-level negotiations with Maduro. In the process, he had secured the release of detained American citizens, negotiated the return of deported Venezuelan criminals, and was working on diplomatic avenues for a peaceful resolution to regional tensions. And he was talking to Maduro about the oil. Maduro indicated he was listening, and he seemed, for a time, to be pliable. It looked as though Maduro might just weather the second Trump term by falling in line.

But Grenell, much to his dismay, was sidelined as a far more aggressive posture took shape and the White House position hardened into a demand for Maduro to leave. He could live a life of luxury in exile, or the United States could take action to force him out.

Trump then turned to at least two highly unconventional emissaries to carry his messages to Maduro; one was a wealthy businessman and another was a controversial media host Trump had known forever.

On November 21, the Brazilian billionaire Joesley Batista, the co-owner of the world's largest meatpacking company, JBS S.A., arrived to meet Trump at the White House. Batista had weathered corruption scandals over the years and had been jailed for obstruction of justice and insider trading. Throughout 2025, he had sought a meeting with Trump, but the President's advisors, leery of the history, had soft-pedaled. Eventually though, because of a friendly relationship Batista had with Melania, he was added to the President's schedule.

Sitting with Trump, the gregarious Brazilian mentioned that he knew Maduro personally and offered suggestions for how to handle him. Trump, seeing an opportunity, summoned Rubio for a conversation with Batista in Spanish, to check out the claims of the rich meat-packer.

When Rubio confirmed that Batista's claims of a connection to Maduro seemed to hold up, an impulsive Trump soon got the Venezuelan dictator on the phone. The conversation was brief, cordial, and apparently confusing to Maduro. Trump's tone was far from threatening, and if he had intended to come off as menacing, the message had not gotten through.

Days later, at Trump's request, Batista secretly traveled to Caracas to meet Maduro and to urge him to resign. Maduro, comfortable in his own authority, immediately refused.

Two weeks later, in mid-December, the President tried again with a very different intermediary, and this time one with more cachet.

Trump asked Tucker Carlson to do him a favor: Would he pass a message to Caracas? The President knew Carlson had an "in" of some sort with the Venezuelan ruler; Maduro had been reaching out to the former Fox host for some time, asking him to come down for an interview.

As bait, Maduro had claimed to Carlson that he could furnish proof U.S. voting machines were tampered with in 2020—a transparently calculated appeal to Trump's unfounded stolen-election grievances—and he had told Carlson he wanted warmer relations with Washington.

"I think our strong preference should be keeping the current government in place," Carlson advised Trump.

"Breaking things is easier than building them," he continued. "It's hard to beat chaos once it takes hold. So you don't want to foment chaos. That's got to be goal one, stability. And you have to give a little in exchange for stability, whether it's your bottom line or your principles. You have to bend in the service of stability."

Trump seemed to share that view, but what he really wanted Carlson to do was scare Maduro into real negotiations. For weeks, the United States had been building up forces in the Caribbean. Multiple warships were on the move, including destroyers and the USS *Gerald R. Ford* aircraft carrier and its associated carrier strike group, as well as the Wasp-class amphibious assault ship USS *Iwo Jima* carrying elements of the 22nd Marine Expeditionary Unit and the Delta Force special mission unit. More than 150 aircraft, including B-1 bombers, F-22 and F-35 fighter jets, and various intelligence, reconnaissance, and surveillance aircraft were sent toward Venezuela. A close advisor said Trump was reluctant to begin such a high-risk military operation if he didn't have to. But he was reaching the point of no return.

The message Trump asked Carlson to share was simple and typical of the President's blustery style, but it had a final sting. In a nutshell, Carlson was to convey to Maduro the following message: *We're going to take over your country. It will be our fifty-first state. And you better start getting real with us. We're very serious about these oil concessions. We located the energy and we took it out of the ground and we built the infrastructure and you stole it. Play ball or you're done.*

Carlson delivered the message to a Maduro confidant, saying, "You know, I'm not a diplomat, but my sense is that the President wouldn't be passing this message to you if he didn't want a negotiation."

Over the next ten days, Carlson and Trump talked several times on the phone. The early indication from Caracas was that Maduro was open to playing ball.

"I think his animal instincts told him that Trump was either an ally or a real threat to him," Carlson would later tell an associate. "He knew Trump was significant and he wanted to reach Trump." Regarding his purported information about voting machines, Carlson would tell the associate, Maduro had something Trump wanted, "and he had a gun to his head."

Within days of Carlson sharing Trump's message to Maduro's ally, Trump took one of his typical spins on Truth Social, posting a confusing demand, showing who was boss, and with a warning:

"America will not allow Criminals, Terrorists, or other Countries to rob, threaten, or harm our Nation and, likewise, will not allow a Hostile Regime to take our Oil, Land, or any other Assets, all of which must be returned to the United States, IMMEDIATELY," Trump wrote. "Venezuela is completely surrounded by the largest Armada ever assembled in the History of South America. It will only get bigger, and the shock to them will be like nothing they have ever seen before—Until such time as they return to the United States of America all of the Oil, Land, and other Assets that they previously stole from us. . . . For the theft of our Assets, and many other reasons, including Terrorism, Drug Smuggling, and Human Trafficking, the Venezuelan Regime has been designated a FOREIGN TERRORIST ORGANIZATION."

The Truth Social post now likely made any deal with Maduro impossible, Carlson would tell the associate. "That got their dander up," Carlson recounted. "It not only offended them, I think that it reduced their latitude, internally. To me, they were like, '*What in the world is that?*' And I said, 'I'm not in charge, man. I'm a podcaster.'"

Rubio, in any case, had thought for some time that the United States' least-bad option was to replace Maduro with his vice president, Delcy Rodríguez.

By Christmas Eve, the new plan was to get Maduro out, either by exiling him to a Muslim country—Qatar, or more likely Turkey—or by arresting him. And then to deal with a Venezuela run by Delcy Rodríguez.

Rubio would tell associates that Rodríguez was corrupt, but a serious person. She worked in tandem with her brother and there was a good likelihood they could keep the country together.

"What we don't want is a series of generals claiming oil fields," Rubio added. "Can't have that. Because that, first of all, defeats the purpose, and second is the migrant crisis. Everything about that is terrible."

Rubio would quietly tell people that the White House had made Maduro a very generous offer that he had declined.

Maduro, he would say, was "going to string us along. And he's got backing from China and Russia and Iran. And he has every incentive to string this out. So we're going with Delcy."

Susie Wiles spent much of the holiday away from Washington at her home in Ponte Vedra Beach, Florida, where the military had set up a secure operations system ahead of the mission.

Trump arrived at Mar-a-Lago for the Christmas holiday with the window for the raid set to open within days. But the President had other business to attend to first. On December 22, he sat down at his private club with Jason Reding Quiñones, the U.S. attorney for the Southern District of Florida, along with Attorney General Pam Bondi and Deputy Attorney General Todd Blanche. Reding Quiñones had just overseen the sentencing of Ryan Routh, the man who had lain in wait with a rifle in the shrubs along the fence of Trump's West Palm Beach golf course. But Trump told advisors he was interested in a more pressing matter: Reding Quiñones's investigation into possible conspiracy charges against a raft of Democratic officials involved in the Russia investigation that had engulfed his first term. The old grievances still came first.

"Holy shit," the President said.

At 2 a.m., Saturday, January 3, 2026, Trump sat in his makeshift SCIF at his Palm Beach estate, staring intently at a monitor, watching the daring and intricate military operation unfold. Fourteen hundred miles away in Caracas, a coordinated attack that had been planned since Thanksgiving and exhaustively rehearsed since then was now underway. A Delta Force extraction team was moving in to seize the Venezuelan dictator.

As the assault unfolded in the middle of the night, there was no guarantee it would go as planned. Visions of another Delta Force mission, the April 1980 operation to rescue fifty-three Americans taken hostage in Tehran—an operation that had failed catastrophically—swirled in Trump's head. Eight American commandos had been killed in Operation Eagle Claw, the country had been humiliated, and President Jimmy Carter himself had been subject to the taunts of the religious fanatic who was the new Iranian head of state, the Ayatollah Ruhollah Khomeini, who declared that the doomed American rescue operation was an act of God Himself. Similarly, a failed mission could make Maduro stronger.

The plan had been set and the team had been ready to go for more than a week and there had been a handful of aborted attempts. On some nights, the weather wasn't optimal. On others, Maduro's whereabouts couldn't be determined with certainty. The CIA had been watching his every move for months, and he was switching up his routine. On a couple of nights, U.S. officials believed that Maduro was out partying and had slept away from his own compound.

"Holy shit," Trump said again. Heavy black curtains enclosed him and his national security nucleus in the SCIF—now a provisional Situation Room—that had been constructed at Mar-a-Lago to allow him to monitor the operation with his team even as his resort home still brimmed with holiday revelers celebrating the new year. Inside the curtain, as the scene unfolded, General Dan Caine narrated the action for the senior officials assembled. Others in the room included CIA Director John Ratcliffe, Marco Rubio, Pete Hegseth, and Stephen Miller.

The U.S. forces reached Maduro's compound at Fort Tiuna in Caracas at 2:01 a.m. local time. Maduro and his wife, Cilia Flores, were captured and on board the USS *Iwo Jima* ninety minutes later. Trump posted a photo of Maduro, cuffed and goggled, wearing a gray Nike tracksuit. By nighttime, Maduro and Flores were in New York.

Trump had told several senior officials in his administration that he now wanted 75 percent of Venezuela's oil profits in perpetuity. In her first public utterances after the operation, Delcy Rodríguez had condemned it as a "foreign-backed attack" and a "kidnapping" by the United States, and asserted that Venezuela "will never be a colony of any nation." She demanded Maduro's immediate release, activated a national defense decree, and declared the country fully mobilized to defend itself.

But the White House was unfazed. Trump's team had received strong private indications that Rodríguez was willing to work with them. On the night of the raid, Rubio spoke to Rodríguez by phone. He said to her: "You have to do two things immediately. You have to bring your country into stability, under control. And you have to prevent mass migration and violence. You have to. That's your number one priority right now. We are willing to begin a new chapter in our relationship."

Just over a week later, Donald Trump posted an image on Truth Social. It was a mock Wikipedia entry for himself, and under his image was the title "Acting President of Venezuela."

The new year had begun.

33

Trump had only a brief window to bask in the glow of the operation to seize Maduro. Already grave trouble was brewing on the domestic front and it was entirely self-inflicted. On the morning of Saturday, January 24, 2026, Alex Pretti, a thirty-seven-year-old intensive care nurse at a Veterans Affairs hospital, was killed by border protection agents on Nicollet Avenue in Minneapolis. They shot at him at least ten times within five seconds while he was already on his knees and pinned down. Some of those bullets struck after he was already motionless.

Pretti's death followed on the heels of the fatal January 7 shooting of another thirty-seven-year-old American citizen, Renee Good. She was a mother of three and a poet, and was shot three times at close range, once in the head near her temple, while trying to drive away from immigration agents who had demanded she get out of her car after she protested the raid by attempting to block their vehicles with her own.

After weeks of uproar, and Trump's false claim that Good had run over an agent, the President was forced to step back, and to announce a de-escalation of federal agents in the city. He suddenly wanted the noise turned down. Trump had been looking for an illegal immigration crackdown—with the spectacle of criminals on the run and of left-wing protesters backing down. Instead, he now had a dead intensive care nurse and a dead local mother broadcast nightly on TV screens, news stories that refused to fade.

Both were white, both were U.S. citizens, and neither remotely fit the intended target of Minnesota's Somali immigrants, a fraction of whom were alleged to have scammed the system for federal benefits. Trump had for weeks portrayed the entire Somali community as "garbage" that should be removed from the country as immigration agents moved their aggressive tactics into the state.

But others in Trump's orbit saw a different kind of opportunity in the Minnesota disaster; specifically a new chance to deploy a sweeping and rarely used legal instrument to intimidate not just protesters, but those on guard to defend the right to protest.

A few days after Pretti was killed, at around nine in the morning, the vice president walked into Susie Wiles's office and took a seat at the end of her long conference table, turning his chair to face the room. It was a regular morning meeting, although the attendance was lighter than usual.

Wiles sat in her customary place in one of the wingback chairs nearest the fireplace, with Deputy Chief of Staff James Blair in the wingback beside her. Karoline Leavitt and Steven Cheung were on the couch. Stephen Miller was at the table to Vance's right, his back to the windows overlooking West Executive Avenue. The staff secretary, Will Scharf, sat at the opposite end of the table from Miller. White House counsel David Warrington was beside the vice president.

Vance got right to the point. He wanted to talk about the situation in Minnesota. In his view they needed to swiftly invoke the Insurrection Act to crush the unrest. It would be painful in the short term, he said, but in the long term it was the right thing to do. The message it would send—that paid agitators could not get away with disrupting the ICE work—would ensure that people wouldn't try it again.

There was no evidence so far that either Pretti or Good were paid activists. But Vance was reviving a subject of repeated discussion for much of 2025 about just when to utilize an extraordinary power in the President's reach. It was a power that Miller and Trump had both itched to use since the first administration, a form of unfinished business for them both.

After Vance made his pitch, Scharf spoke up. He had studied the

Insurrection Act extensively and his research had framed the October 29 confidential memo to Wiles on the subject, although he would not discuss the memo in this meeting. Scharf did not believe the situation in Minnesota warranted invoking the act. His objection was not political. The law, as he understood it, simply did not fit the circumstances on the ground.

Stephen Miller was unusually subdued, offering muted pushback to Scharf. But he suggested that the boundaries of the Insurrection Act had never really been tested. There was a wide range of questions about its scope that remained unanswered.

"That's not true, Stephen," Scharf replied. "It's very prescriptive."

Someone brought up that the last time the Insurrection Act had been invoked was during the Los Angeles riots in 1992. Someone else made the obvious rejoinder that they weren't currently in the middle of anything like the L.A. riots.

Then James Blair weighed in with the political perspective. He thought that using the Insurrection Act would be an overreach and politically ruinous. The scenes of troop deployments in Minnesota already looked chaotic, he said, and the public didn't want more chaos. Escalating would only amplify what people were already recoiling from. Blair put questions to the room that no one could answer: What does the Insurrection Act give us that we don't already have? What changes will there be with the situation on the ground that would be worth the heat? This would backfire and what else could they win that justified the terrible public relations?

David Warrington had previously made the same argument in discussions with others. And now the room was quiet. Nobody had a good response to Blair's questions.

If there was a revealing moment, it was that some in the room just wanted to proceed, even though none could answer the basic question: What power would the act give them that they didn't already have in Minnesota? The Insurrection Act allowed a President to deploy federal troops to execute public safety laws, effectively transferring law enforcement authority to the military—but they could already enforce federal law there without it.

For weeks Wiles had been fielding dozens of calls from elected officials and business leaders about what was happening in Minnesota. After Pretti was killed, she pointedly told colleagues that the reason for going to Minneapolis was "to arrest people who were getting federal benefits wrongly. This is what we went to Minnesota for. And we are so far off that mission." But as was often her way in charged discussions, Wiles said little as the debate in her office continued, giving others the floor.

Cheung weighed in to lay out the public relations challenges of invoking the Insurrection Act. Vance, having heard the arguments, appeared to soften. Perhaps now was not the time.

The meeting ended without resolution—more a vague consensus to keep thinking about it. But the conversation had been clarifying in its own way: Even after the administration's aggressive posture toward protesters had helped escalate tensions, and even with the White House facing intense blowback, the vice president and the President's most powerful policy advisor were still searching for an opportunity to use troops to enforce domestic laws.

But something would have to give to quell the growing public uproar. On March 5, Trump fired Homeland Security Secretary Kristi Noem. Her removal followed two days of bruising congressional hearings and a year of inflammatory public activity, concerns about conflicts of interest in contracts, and a general fixation on showing up for the cameras. For Trump, who shared the limelight with no one, but often gave his cabinet members a long leash, it was the final straw.

Stephen Miller made it clear he was not sorry to see Noem go. In his view, she had done a disastrous job managing DHS. She had brought a trail of problems: constant stories about her travels with Corey Lewandowski, her top advisor; a taste for private jets; and, most significantly for Miller, a poor record of targeting locations effectively for migrant sweeps. None of it surprised him. He had always believed she was the wrong person for the job.

Miller would immediately accuse Renee Good of "domestic terrorism" and call Pretti "an assassin" shortly after he was killed. Trump pointed to the fact that Pretti was carrying a gun, for which, it turned out, he had a permit. Picking up on these attacks, Noem also slapped domestic terrorism labels on both of the dead. Yet shortly after the two shootings, Miller told associates he was furious—not about the overall restrictionist immigration policy or the efforts to shut down liberal protests, which he had driven himself, but about the way it had all been carried out. The immigration agents were supposed to be there to create a "barrier" between protesters and immigration arrest teams, he would say publicly. In private, he laid the blame at the feet of Noem, who for a year had answered not just to the President, but also to Miller.

The legal system was also nearing a breaking point. In July 2025, *The Washington Post* found that in roughly a third of federal lawsuits where judges ruled against the Trump administration, the government was accused of dishonesty with the court, using stall tactics, or defying orders altogether. In February 2026, Reuters found that federal judges had ruled on more than 4,400 occasions that ICE was illegally detaining migrants. Federal officials found themselves straining under conditions the White House had helped create with its demands for large deportation numbers; the DOJ had a severe staff shortage and struggled to attract lawyers willing to work there. Several prosecutors in Minneapolis resigned rather than carry out the administration's crackdown. Shortly after Pretti was killed, one lawyer working at the U.S. Attorney's Office in Minnesota, Julie Le, told a federal judge she was struggling to get ICE to comply with court orders, and said bluntly, "The system sucks. This job sucks. And I am trying every breath that I have so that I can get you what you need."

"Sometimes I wish you would just hold me in contempt, your honor, so that I can have a full 24 hours of sleep," she added.

But even as the legal battles over DHS's crackdowns in Minnesota continued to multiply, and the aggression roiled angry communities, Trump's attention was already focused on another country more than six thousand miles away. When it came to domestic policy, Trump could still be hamstrung in significant ways. Finding quick solutions to inflation and the affordability crisis plaguing many voters was not simple. But on the world stage, which since the 1980s had captured Trump's interest more than the detailed work of domestic policy, he had far greater room to flex the muscle of his imperial presidency.

In pursuit of this next goal, he would widen the fracture in his MAGA coalition, sidestep Congress, and force nations around the world to choose whether they were with him or against him. It was an existential fight that he decided to bet his legacy on.

II

Throughout the 2024 campaign, Iran had made no secret of its desire to kill Donald Trump. Tehran had sworn revenge for the assassination of Quds Force Commander General Qassim Suleimani in a U.S. drone strike in January 2020 and American intelligence had been tracking credible threats against Trump's life ever since. On July 12, 2024, the FBI had arrested Asif Merchant, a Pakistani national who had been trained by Iran's Islamic Revolutionary Guard Corps and dispatched to the United States to hire hit men to kill U.S. politicians, with Trump and Biden among the named targets. Merchant was seized at the airport as he prepared to flee the country.

The following day, Trump was shot in Butler, Pennsylvania, his ear grazed by a would-be assassin. Officials said the Butler gunman appeared to have acted alone, with no connection to Iran. But the timing seemed suspicious to Trump's inner circle, and for Trump it hardly mattered. Iran had just tried to have him killed and then someone else had nearly succeeded. The two events fused in his mind into a single, personal threat.

Nearly two weeks later, now the Republican nominee, Trump met with Benjamin Netanyahu at Mar-a-Lago. He showed off his wound. Netanyahu had come ostensibly to discuss ceasefire negotiations in Gaza, but also to repair his relationship with the potential next President, knowing that Trump remained bitter about Netanyahu's congratulatory call to Biden after the 2020 election. As the meeting wrapped up, Trump offered a confidence: Without mentioning Iran's plot to kill him, Trump nonetheless told Netanyahu that if he returned for a second term, he would take a far harder line on Iran militarily. Often, some on Trump's team heard what they wanted to hear in his private mixed messages, and one close advisor predicted after

Netanyahu's visit that a returned President Trump would lean on sanctions to strangle the Iranian economy and would make no effort to restrain Israel from striking the country directly. But the advisor did not think Trump himself would wage war against Iran.

And yet the serious potential for what would soon unfold was always there. In the immediate aftermath of his election victory, Trump filled his days with lunches and dinners and a steady stream of visitors. When conversations turned to the Middle East, he sounded more hawkish than he had in years. The Palestinians in Gaza who had taken Israeli hostages were "fucking animals," he told one group of guests at Mar-a-Lago in December 2024.

Then he turned to Iran. "We gotta make sure they don't get a bomb in the next five weeks," he said. "Not before January 20. They'll never get a bomb while I'm in charge."

Later, after Midnight Hammer in June 2025, when Trump had declared that Iran's nuclear facilities were "obliterated," he had insisted the destruction was so complete that the Iran problem was now behind them; he believed there was no way Iran's leaders would dare rebuild under the threat of annihilation. And he refused to allow anyone in his administration to suggest that anything less than total "obliteration" had occurred.

But within months it became clear that Iran was intent on rebuilding, and in particular resuming missile production on a significant scale. Trump's advisors sensed that it would not be long before Netanyahu cycled back, to ask Trump to join another Israeli military operation. When the moment came, it was clear the next round would not have such a limited objective: Netanyahu wanted to try to go all the way, to seize the opportunity to achieve his decades-old dream of overthrowing the regime in Tehran, and it seemed not just possible to him, but feasible.

Over the winter of 2025 into 2026, as the Israeli pressure to strike Iran again grew, the CIA director, John Ratcliffe, presented Trump with a range of possible outcomes that could be achieved by a military campaign. These were not forecasts—something that in military terms would depend heavily on the nature and length of a campaign—but more in the vein of: If we do this, then our assessment is that. Ratcliffe had assumed a campaign that would last, at minimum, four to six weeks.

The intelligence painted a grim picture of the potential for regime change. The most probable scenario was also the most dangerous: that militants within Iran's Revolutionary Guard would seize control, sidelining or weakening the clerical establishment—which, for all its rhetoric, tended to be more calculating and less prone to military aggression. A somewhat more optimistic but less likely scenario was that pragmatists within the Revolutionary Guard might seize control. The outcome CIA analysts rated as least likely was a popular uprising overthrowing the government from within. Iranian security forces had recently demonstrated, yet again, a willingness to gun down unarmed protesters in the streets. Any grassroots movement would face brutal and immediate suppression.

None of this meant that a military campaign couldn't succeed on other metrics. CIA analysts thought the U.S. and Israel could significantly degrade Iran's capacity to threaten its neighbors with conventional and nuclear weapons. But for more ambitious goals, the intelligence was sobering. Analysts believed an air campaign alone was highly unlikely to topple the regime. Iran's asymmetric strengths compounded the challenge—particularly its low-cost drone capabilities and its ability to conceal missiles in mountain caves.

Trump didn't buy the pessimistic assessments. He thought a war would be swiftly over. He thought the Iranian regime was pathetically weak—a view solidified the previous June when Iran had responded limply to the devastating waves of American bombing with a series of highly telegraphed symbolic strikes that were easy for the U.S. to swat away. Now, riding the momentum of the Maduro capture, Trump was even more enthralled by the capabilities of the U.S. military. He told aides he would like to see a Venezuela-type situation emerge in Iran—all the benefits of regime change without having to go to the trouble of changing the whole structure of the country. In Trump's view, there was now a new model: Take out the top guy and install a fearful apparatchik who would be deferential to Trump.

But few if any of Trump's advisors believed that Iran, a country of more than 90 million people led by a theocracy for decades, could be another Venezuela. And it seemed implausible that Trump remained ignorant of the realities. The President had been thoroughly briefed by both Ratcliffe and the chairman of the Joint Chiefs of Staff, Dan Caine; the up-to-the-minute intelligence assessments made clear that the Iranian regime had far more depth than Venezuela's, including a powerful religious dimension.

Still, Trump repeatedly told his advisors that he had "a good feeling" about striking Iran and he wanted to go ahead. His take on the eventual outcome ran along the lines of wanting to wipe out the regime and figure out the details later.

III

On Wednesday, February 11, 2026, Benjamin Netanyahu and Marco Rubio met at Blair House, the historic 1824 property that served as the President's official guest residence, to sign Israel's membership in the new entity to rebuild Gaza, the Board of Peace. The two men stood side by side, displaying the signed document for cameras.

From there, Netanyahu was driven the short distance down Pennsylvania Avenue in a black SUV and onto the White House grounds, arriving just before 11 a.m. The air was brisk, the long winter still hanging over Washington. Trump did not greet the prime minister at the West Wing entrance; instead Netanyahu was whisked in through the compound's gates and out of view of the media.

The prime minister had traveled with an entourage that included his military secretary, Major General Roman Gofman, who had been tapped to take over months later as director of Mossad. After a lengthy first meeting in the Cabinet Room, Netanyahu headed downstairs for another. This would be one of the most critical, and entirely secret, meetings of his life—down in the lower level of the White House.

The Situation Room had rarely been visited by a foreign leader in person for such a sensitive meeting. Previous Presidents held virtual meetings with other world leaders from the Situation Room, but aside from occasional tourist-like visits from celebrities, it was traditionally a restricted space. Now Netanyahu joined Trump and a small group of senior advisors, along with intelligence and military officials, all seated around the room's mahogany conference table.

Trump had moved from his usual position at the head of the table to sit in the middle facing the large screens mounted along one wall on the opposite side. Netanyahu sat across from him. Appearing on the screen was David Barnea, the director of Mossad, as well as a number of Israeli officials. It was a powerful image: Netanyahu, the wartime leader, and his trusted team.

Susie Wiles sat at the far end of the table. Rubio had taken his regular seat. Pete Hegseth and Dan Caine, who generally sat together in such settings, were on one side; joining them was John Ratcliffe, the CIA director; Jared Kushner and Steve Witkoff, who had been holding ongoing negotiations with the Iranians in the hopes of averting war, completed the main group.

As the White House had been roiled by national security leaks throughout 2025, this meeting had been kept deliberately small. Neither the energy secretary nor the treasury secretary had been invited. Nor had the commerce secretary, Howard Lutnick, much less the director of national intelligence, Tulsi Gabbard, who was also an outspoken opponent of military interventionism. Also absent, though for a different reason, was the vice president. JD Vance was in Azerbaijan on official business, and the meeting with the Israelis had been scheduled so quickly that he was unable to make it back in time.

Over the course of an hour, Netanyahu made a hard sell about how ripe Iran was to be overwhelmed, and how this could finally be the moment for regime change brought about by a joint U.S.-Israeli assault. At one point, he played a brief video for Trump that included a montage of new leaders who could take over the country if it fell. Among those featured was Reza Pahlavi, the exiled son of Iran's last shah, now a Washington-based dissident who had tried to position himself as a secular leader who could shepherd Iran toward a post-theocratic government.

Netanyahu and his team outlined conditions they portrayed as pointing to near-certain victory. Iran's ballistic missile program could be destroyed within a few weeks; Iran would be so weakened that it could not choke off the Strait of Hormuz; the likelihood that Iran would land blows against U.S. interests in neighboring countries was minimal. Besides, Mossad intelligence indicated that protests inside Iran would begin again and—with the Israeli spy agency helping to foment riots and rebellion—an intense bombing campaign could create the conditions for the Iranian opposition to overthrow the regime. The Israelis also raised the prospect of Iranian Kurdish fighters crossing the border from Iraq to open a ground front in the northwest, further stretching the regime's forces and accelerating its collapse.

Netanyahu delivered his presentation in a confident monotone. It sounded compelling and well-prepared, at least to Trump.

Sounds good to me, the President told the prime minister. To Netanyahu, this signaled a likely green light for a joint U.S.-Israeli operation.

Netanyahu was not the only one who came away with the impression that Trump had all but made up his mind. The President's own advisors could see that Trump had been deeply impressed by the demonstration of what Netanyahu's military and intelligence service could do, just as he had been when the two men spoke ahead of the twelve-day war the previous June.

The prime minister had told Trump that the risks of inaction, now, were greater than the risks of action. He said the price of action would only grow if they delayed striking and allowed Iran more time to rebuild its missile program and create a shield around its nuclear program. Iran had the capacity to build up its missile and drone stockpiles at a far lower cost and much more quickly than the U.S. could build and supply the much more expensive missile interceptors to protect American interests and allies in the region.

Netanyahu had another thing going for him: Distrusted as he was by many of Trump's advisors, he was pushing on an issue close to Trump's own heart. Of all the foreign policy challenges Trump had confronted across two presidencies, Iran stood apart. He regarded the regime in Tehran as a uniquely dangerous adversary and was willing to take great risks to hinder its ability to wage regional wars and to acquire a nuke. Furthermore, Netanyahu's presentation offered Trump an appealing vision: dismantling the Iranian theocracy, which had come to power in 1979, when Trump was thirty-two, and had been a thorn in the side of the United States ever since. Now, he could become the first president since the clerical leadership took over forty-seven years ago to pull off a regime change in Iran.

Netanyahu's presentation set into motion the machinery of American intelligence. Overnight, analysts worked to assess the viability of what Trump had just been shown and the results were shared the following day, February 12, in another meeting in the Situation Room.

Before Trump arrived, two senior intelligence officials briefed the President's inner circle. These officials had deep expertise in U.S. kinetic capabilities and they knew the Iranian system and its players inside out. They had broken down Netanyahu's presentation into four parts: first, decapitation—killing the Ayatollah; second, crippling Iran's capacity to project power and threaten its neighbors; third, a popular uprising inside Iran; and fourth, regime change, with a new secular leader installed to govern the country. The officials assessed that the first two objectives were achievable with American intelligence and military power. They assessed that parts three and four of Netanyahu's pitch, which included the possibility of the Kurds leading a ground invasion into Iran, were detached from reality.

When Trump joined the meeting, Ratcliffe briefed him on the U.S. intelligence assessment of Netanyahu's presentation. The CIA director used one word to describe the Israeli prime minister's regime change scenario: "farcical." At that point, Rubio cut in. "In other words, it's bullshit," he said. Ratcliffe added that given the unpredictability of events in any conflict, regime change could still happen, but it should not be considered an achievable objective.

Several others jumped in, including Vance, just back from Azerbaijan, who also expressed strong skepticism about the prospect of regime change.

The President then turned to the chairman of the Joint Chiefs of Staff, Dan Caine: "General, what do you think?"

Caine replied: "Sir, this is, in my experience, standard operating procedure for the Israelis. They oversell and their plans are not always well-developed. They know they need us and that's why they're hard selling."

Trump quickly weighed the assessment. Regime change, he concluded, would be "their problem." It was unclear whether he was referring to the Israelis or the Iranian people. But the bottom line was that his decision to go to war against Iran would not hinge on whether parts three and four of Netanyahu's presentation were achievable. Trump remained very interested in accomplishing parts one and two: killing the Ayatollah and Iran's top leaders and dismantling the Iranian military.

IV

Dan Caine—the man Trump liked to refer to as "Razin Caine"—had impressed the President years earlier by telling him ISIS could be defeated far more quickly than others projected. Trump rewarded that confidence by elevating the general, who had been an Air Force fighter pilot, to be his top military advisor. Caine was not a political loyalist and he had serious concerns about a war with Iran. But he was very cautious in the way he presented his views to the President.

Caine shared with Trump and members of the cabinet the military assessment that a major campaign against Iran would dramatically deplete stockpiles of American weaponry, with no clear path to quickly replenish. He was deeply worried about both the potential for significant American casualties and the further depletion of munitions and missile interceptors strained after years of support for Ukraine and Israel. He also flagged the enormous difficulty of securing the Strait of Hormuz and the risks of Iran shutting the strait—a scenario Trump dismissed on the assumption that the regime would capitulate before it came to that.

But the munitions question extended well beyond Iran. Without sufficient stockpiles, America's capacity in any future conflict could be seriously compromised. The administration had already pushed major defense contractors to dramatically increase production, but the industrial base simply could not scale up to the speed or volume demanded for such precise, intricate, and complex weaponry.

Trump resisted any public discussion of the munitions shortfall; he viewed any acknowledgment of this serious problem as revealing an

American weakness, though that posture was largely beside the point. America's enemies already had a very detailed picture of what the U.S. had in its stockpile and how quickly it could rebuild.

Caine's role in the lead-up to the war captured a classic tension between military counsel and presidential decision-making. So persistent was the chairman in not taking a stand—repeating that it was not his role to tell the President what to do, but rather to present options along with potential risks and possible second- and third-order consequences—that he could appear to argue all sides of an issue simultaneously. He would constantly ask: "And then what?" But Trump would often hear only what he wanted to hear.

Caine differed in almost every way from the Joint Chiefs chairman in Trump's first administration, General Mark Milley, who had argued vehemently with Trump and who saw his role as stopping the President from taking dangerous or reckless actions.

A close observer noted that Trump seemed to confuse tactical advice from Caine with strategic counsel. In practice, that meant Caine might warn in one breath about the difficulties of one aspect of the operation and in the next note that the U.S. had an essentially unlimited supply of cheap, precision-guided bombs and could strike Iran for weeks once it achieved air superiority. To Caine, these were separate observations. But to Trump, the second likely canceled out the first.

At no point during the deliberations that led to the Iran war did the chairman sit before Trump and all but grab him by the lapels, telling him that war with Iran was a terrible idea—though some of Caine's colleagues believed that was exactly what he thought.

Meanwhile, an influential cadre of power brokers and opinion makers had been pushing Trump to strike Iran. Among their ranks were the retired General Jack Keane, Rupert Murdoch's Fox News, conservative commentators Mark Levin and Marc Thiessen, and Senator Lindsey Graham.

Netanyahu, of course, had been urging action for months. But without the U.S. alongside him, he was ultimately one-armed in a broader conflict. The Israeli prime minister was a student of American media and public opinion and had thought carefully about the optimal channels through which to influence Trump. He coordinated closely with Graham and he benefited from the fact that Trump's information loop in his second term was much tighter than in the first. Trump rarely heard from skeptics. He had largely tuned out his critics and was surrounded by flatterers, both in the White House and even more so on the patio at Mar-a-Lago, where a group of elderly and wealthy Palm Beach residents would cheer on his efforts to join Israel in wiping out Iran's clerical leadership.

Within Trump's cabinet, Hegseth was the biggest proponent of moving forward against Iran.

Marco Rubio, the secretary of state, was privately skeptical; he did not believe the Iranians would agree to a deal, but his preference was to continue a campaign of maximum pressure rather than launch a full-scale military operation. Rubio did not forcefully argue his case in front of Trump, and after the war began he delivered the administration's justification with full conviction: "If you tell the President of the United States that if we don't go first, we're going to have more people killed and more people injured, the President's going to go first. That's what he did."

Susie Wiles had concerns about what a new conflict overseas could entail, but she did not tend to weigh in hard on military matters in larger meetings; rather, she encouraged advisors to share their views and their concerns with the President in those settings. Wiles would exert influence on many other issues, but in the room with Trump and the generals, she sat back. Those close to her said she did not view it as her role to share her concerns with the President on a military decision in front of others. And she believed that the expertise of advisors like Caine, Ratcliffe, and Rubio was more significant for the President to hear.

Still, Wiles had been worried about being dragged into another Middle East war. An attack on Iran carried with it the potential to set off soaring gas prices just months before midterm elections that would decide whether the final two years of Trump's second term would be years of accomplishment or subpoenas and a possible impeachment led by House Democrats.

Trump was already very unpopular; polls showed voters now preferred his predecessor, Joe Biden, whose record Trump had spent a year trying to erase. But in the end, Wiles was on board with the operation.

V

Nobody in Trump's inner circle was more worried about the Iran war—or did more to try to stop it—than the vice president.

JD Vance had built his political career opposing precisely the kind of military adventurism now under consideration. He had described a war with Iran as "a huge distraction of resources" and "massively expensive."

He was not, however, a dove across the board. In January, when Trump publicly warned Iran to stop killing protesters and promised help was on its way, Vance had privately encouraged the President to enforce his red line. What Vance was pushing for was a limited, punitive strike, something closer to the model of Trump's 2017 missile attack against Syria to register his disapproval of President Bashar al-Assad's use of chemical weapons against his own people.

Vance believed a regime-change war with Iran would be a disaster. His preference was no strikes at all. But knowing that Trump was likely to intervene in some fashion, he tried to steer him toward more limited actions. If the President was set on going in, Vance argued, he should do so with overwhelming force, in the hope of achieving his objectives quickly.

In front of his colleagues, Vance had warned Trump that a war against Iran could break apart his political coalition and would be seen as a betrayal by many voters who had bought into the promise of no new wars. Vance raised other concerns, too. As vice president, he was aware of the scope of America's munitions problem. A war against a regime with enormous will for survival could leave the U.S. in a far worse position to fight conflicts for some years to come.

The potential for U.S. casualties and regional chaos was immense, he told colleagues, and no amount of military insight could truly gauge what Iran would do in retaliation when survival of the regime was at stake. A war could easily go in unpredictable directions. Moreover, there seemed little chance of building a peaceful Iran in the aftermath.

Beyond all of this was perhaps the biggest risk of all: Iran held the advantage when it came to the Strait of Hormuz. If this narrow waterway, which carried vast quantities of oil and natural gas, was choked off, the domestic political consequences in the U.S. would be incalculable, starting with higher gasoline prices.

Tucker Carlson, another prominent skeptic, had come to the Oval Office several times over the previous year to warn Trump that a war with Iran would destroy his presidency. A couple of weeks before the war began, Trump, trying again to suppress the concerns, attempted to reassure him over the phone. "I know you're worried about it, but it's going to be okay," Trump said. Carlson asked how he knew. "Because it always is," Trump replied.

In the final days of February, the U.S. and the Israelis discussed a piece of fresh and incomparable intelligence that would dramatically accelerate their timeline. The Ayatollah would be meeting above ground with other top officials of the regime—in broad daylight and wide open for an air attack. It was a fleeting chance to strike at the heart of Iran's leadership, the kind of target that might not present itself again.

Trump had effectively made up his mind for an attack weeks earlier, advisors said. But he had not yet decided exactly when. Now Netanyahu urged him to move fast.

That same week, Jared Kushner and Steve Witkoff called from Geneva after the latest talks with Iranian officials. Over three rounds of negotiations in Oman and Switzerland, the two had tested Iran's willingness to make a deal. At one point, they offered the Iranians free nuclear fuel for the life of their program—a test of whether Tehran's insistence on enrichment was truly about civilian energy or about preserving the capability to build a bomb. The Iranians rejected the offer, calling it an assault on their dignity.

Kushner and Witkoff laid out the picture for Trump. They could probably negotiate something resembling an Obama-era deal, maybe even slightly better, they said, but it would take months. The Iranians were not looking to move quickly; it seemed likely they were trying to wait out the Trump presidency. If Trump was asking whether they could look him in the eye and tell him they could solve the problem, it's going to take a lot for us to get there, Kushner told him, because they're playing games with us all over the place. Everything rode on the assessment of Kushner and Witkoff, two men who shared the broader Trump team's contempt for subject-matter experts inside the U.S. government. They both had little patience for the traditional bureaucracy in nation-to-nation negotiations. But the negotiations served another purpose: They gave Trump time to move military assets into the region, to prepare for war.

On February 23—five days before the war began—the warnings Dan Caine had delivered to the President behind closed doors spilled into public view. *Axios* broke the news that the chairman had cautioned Trump about the risks of entanglement and significant U.S. casualties. The report described Caine as a "reluctant warrior" on Iran. *The Washington Post* followed with a similar account, reporting that Caine had warned of critical munitions shortfalls and the lack of allied support.

Caine was distressed by the reports and told those around him that he had never experienced anything like it. He was concerned about his position being politicized. "This isn't my role," he told associates. Trump moved quickly to shut down the narrative, posting on Truth Social that Caine did not oppose the war and believed it would be "something easily won" if necessary. Caine had said nothing of the sort.

The Iran war would crack open the movement Trump had built. Former allies on the populist right—those who cheered "America First" as a rallying cry against foreign interventions—were about to witness the America First President enter a new war in the Middle East. By February 2026, the automatic deference from Republicans that had defined Trump's first year back in power was beginning to erode.

The White House press secretary, Karoline Leavitt, sometime later acknowledged that Trump had gone to war based on "a good feeling that the Iranian regime was going to strike the United States assets and our personnel in the region." But with the exception of the vice president, nobody on the senior team—not his secretary of state, not his chairman of the Joint Chiefs, not his chief of staff—had made a real effort to talk him out of it.

And—as with Midnight Hammer, as with the seizure of Maduro—Trump made no effort to build the public case for war beforehand; he preferred to maintain total ambiguity around his intentions to the point of admonishing anyone who tried to offer clarity. When he finally acted, the shift was jarring. The attack on Iran would come not even three months after his administration released a national security strategy proclaiming: "the days in which the Middle East dominated American foreign policy in both long-term planning and day-to-day execution are thankfully over . . ."

VI

On Thursday, February 26, around 5 p.m., the final go/no-go meeting got underway in the Situation Room. By now the positions of everyone in the room had crystallized. Everything had been discussed in prior meetings; everyone knew everyone else's stance. The President was the President, and they would back his decision. There were no presentations, no paperwork—just a discussion that would last an hour and a half. It had been a tense week.

Trump was in his usual place at the head of the table. To his right sat the vice president; next to Vance was Susie Wiles, then John Ratcliffe, then David Warrington, and Steven Cheung. Across the table from Cheung was Karoline Leavitt; to her right, Dan Caine, then Pete Hegseth, then Marco Rubio.

The war-planning group had been kept so tight that the two key officials who would need to manage the largest supply disruption in the history of the global oil market—Treasury Secretary Scott Bessent and Energy Secretary Chris Wright—were still not in the loop, one day before the launch of the war. Nor was the director of national intelligence, Tulsi Gabbard.

Trump opened the meeting: Okay, what have we got? Hegseth and Caine ran through the sequencing of the attacks. Then Trump said he wanted to go around the table and hear everyone's view.

They started with the vice president. Vance, whose disagreement with the whole premise was well established, addressed Trump: You know I think this is a bad idea, but if you want to do it I'll support you.

Wiles told the President that if he felt he needed to proceed for America's national security, then he should go ahead.

Ratcliffe offered no opinion on whether to proceed, but he discussed the stunning new intelligence that the Iranian leadership was about to gather in the Ayatollah's compound in Tehran. The CIA director told the President that regime change was possible depending on how this was defined. "If we just mean killing the Supreme Leader we can probably do that," he said.

When called on, Warrington, the White House counsel, said it was a legally permissible option in terms of how the plan had been conceived by U.S. officials and presented to the President. He did not offer a personal opinion, but when pressed by the President to provide one, he said that as a Marine veteran he had known an American service member killed by Iran years earlier. This issue remained deeply personal. He told the President that if Israel intended to proceed regardless, the United States should join them.

Cheung laid out the likely public relations fallout: Trump had run for office opposed to further wars. Voters had not voted for conflict overseas. The plans ran contrary, too, to everything the administration had said after Midnight Hammer. How would they explain away eight months of insisting that Iranian nuclear facilities had been totally obliterated? Cheung gave neither a yes or no but said that whatever decision Trump made would be the right one.

Leavitt told the President that this was his decision and the press team would manage the fallout as best they could.

Hegseth adopted a narrow position; they would have to take care of the Iranians eventually, so they might as well do it now. He offered technical assessments as well: They could run the campaign in a certain amount of time with a given level of force.

Caine was sober, laying out the risks and what the campaign would mean in terms of munitions depletion. He offered no opinion; his position was that if Trump ordered the operation, the military would execute. Both of Trump's top military leaders previewed how the campaign would unfold and the capacity of the U.S. to degrade Iran's military capabilities.

When it was his turn to speak, Rubio told the President: If our goal is regime change or an uprising, we shouldn't do it. But if the goal is to destroy Iran's missile program, that's a goal we can achieve.

In essence, everyone had deferred to Trump's instincts. "I think we need to do it," the President told the room. He said they had to make sure Iran could not have a nuclear weapon, and they had to make sure Iran could not just shoot missiles at Israel or throughout the region.

Caine told Trump he had some time yet; he did not need to give the final go-ahead until 4 p.m. the following day.

On the afternoon of Friday, February 27, at 3:38, and while en route to an event in Texas, Trump gave the final order. It had been a quiet flight. In the early hours of the following morning, Operation Epic Fury began—a joint U.S.-Israeli military campaign against the Islamic Republic of Iran, and the most consequential military decision of either of Trump's presidencies.

It was also the most significant American military operation since the 2003 invasion of Iraq. It was an air and naval campaign against a major regional power, launched without a vote in Congress, without the support of NATO, and over the private concerns of the vice president, the chief of staff, and the chairman of the Joint Chiefs of Staff.

The President announced the war not with an address to the nation or a briefing to congressional leadership, but with a post on Truth Social at 2:30 a.m., with an eight-minute video that concluded with a direct message to the Iranian people: "The hour of your freedom is at hand."

Epilogue

Washington was under a tornado watch on the afternoon of Monday, March 16, 2026. Rain lashed the windows and wind whipped through the trees on the North Lawn as we made our way into the West Wing.

When we were ushered into the Oval Office, walking past a stone-faced Walt Nauta standing a few feet from the door, we were not entirely sure what to expect. We had been trying for nearly two months to get the President to agree to sit down with us so we could give him a chance to respond to our reporting, and do some fact-checking. After initially being told he was not interested, Trump had recently changed his mind.

We had war-gamed the way the interview would go, given Trump was notoriously difficult to keep on subject and there was limited time. He had already tried to throw us off balance the Friday before, posting on Truth Social a screed against Maggie and a warning that she and "some of her 'associates'" might be added to his pending lawsuit against *The New York Times*.

A few aides were stationed near the Resolute Desk as we waited for the President: Press Secretary Karoline Leavitt, Communications Director Steven Cheung, and, off to the side, the most devoted of all, Natalie Harp.

Trump entered the Oval Office from the corridor connected to his private dining room. He was in smiling-salesman mode. "Nice to see you," he said, gesturing for us to sit down opposite him at the desk. He wore a spotted saffron tie with the usual navy suit.

It was the seventeenth day of his war with Iran. Thirteen American service members had already been killed and more than two hundred had been wounded. Thousands of Iranians were dead, including the Ayatollah Ali Khamenei. The Pentagon had already spent more than $15 billion and the Strait of Hormuz was largely closed, sending global oil prices surging. The day before, Trump had made a demand for an international coalition of warships to secure the waterway, but few nations seemed interested in helping. This was hardly surprising. Trump had spent the previous year mocking NATO, bypassing the United Nations, and making clear that alliances were, in his view, either protection rackets or obstacles. The nations he was now calling on for help were the same ones he had bullied with tariffs, threatened with territorial claims, and cut out of major decisions—like the one he had just made to wage war against Iran.

As he greeted us, the war seemed the furthest thing from Trump's mind. On the Resolute Desk, instead of a map of the Middle East, were printouts of maple trees.

"I'm ordering trees for the White House," Trump told us. "I know how to buy good trees. Maples."

The problem, the President said, was that nurseries cut these maples from the bottom so that they could fit in the trucks. Uncut, they were much more beautiful.

Trump held another printout. The headline screamed "339 billion all-time views" of Trump TikToks. "Can you believe it?" the President asked us.

Cheung added: "The numbers are out of control after the operation."

The "operation" in question was Operation Epic Fury, the title Trump had given his war with Iran. The conflict, it seemed, had been good for online engagement, and the White House digital team had spent the previous two weeks creating viral clips that spliced together footage of American air strikes with pumping music and video game graphics.

"That's some number, huh?" Trump said, pointing at the TikTok sheet. "Can you believe? I guess that's why it's worth a lot of money, right?"

Then Trump showed us two final printouts, renderings from different angles of the grand ballroom he was building on the White House grounds. He was in a convivial mood. The structure would have ten columns on one facade, he said, modeled on the Roman style, and the other side would be inspired by Athens. He noted, with evident satisfaction, that the columns were larger than those of the Supreme Court.

Behind the scenes, some of his aides had told us they wished Trump was more anxious about the dangers he was courting, and about his plunging poll numbers. The discontent was palpable beyond the polling. In an internal memo circulated to roughly a dozen Trump advisors later in the month, the President's pollster, Tony Fabrizio, summarized findings from two nights of focus groups conducted earlier in March; the first fell on the very same day we sat looking at Trump's maple tree printouts in the Oval Office. The results were bracing: The war in Iran was unpopular, poorly understood, and seen as a broken campaign promise that was distracting the President from the economy and healthcare. The military action lacked a clear rationale, and voters saw negative economic consequences downstream of the conflict, compounding the affordability crisis that was already their top concern about the Trump presidency. Perhaps most distressing for the Trump team: The Epstein files came up consistently in focus groups and were "a real negative with some of these voters." The silver lining, only eight months before the midterm elections, was that voters still distrusted Democrats, "but we need to get things under control on the world stage," the memo stated, and focus on voters' concerns about affordability.

But Trump was uninterested in such feedback. To the extent he still cared about polling at all, he was seeing far fewer polls than during his first term. His advisors knew he was not receptive to being briefed on harsh realities. In his second term, unlike his first, he was willing to take breathtaking risks, risks that could throw not only his presidency but the Republican Party and the entire world into chaos and carnage. More than ever before as President, he was operating on pure gut instinct.

It would take a combination of mind reader and psychologist to explain fully why Trump was willing to gamble so much more recklessly now. There were the obvious theories: He was term-limited and no longer had to worry about reelection; he had immunity confirmed by the Supreme Court and no longer had to worry about prosecutions; he was more confident in his instincts; he had already served a presidential term and had felt vindicated so often; and there was the fact that he was a walking moral hazard, rarely saddled for long with the costs or consequences of his risk-taking and rule-breaking. Now was his moment to try things, like military adventures and overthrowing the global trade system.

The interview lasted for around an hour. We had come with a long list of detailed questions about the events and decisions we had been reporting on—about Iran and Israel and Venezuela, about tariffs and deportations and the attorney general and the men and women who served him. Through it all, Trump was digressive, boastful, charming, combative, veering from subject to subject with an energy that made it, as we had anticipated, nearly impossible to hold him on any one topic for long. He talked about the McDonald's stunt that had charged up his 2024 campaign. He praised the doctors at Walter Reed. He paid an unusual compliment to Netanyahu; when asked about their up-and-down relationship, Trump said, "We're better under war." As a wartime partner, he added, "He's been very good. He—because he's not afraid of war." He described his "love affair" with Venezuela, born of his years owning the Miss Universe pageant and the beautiful women who represented that country. He marveled at the speed and violence of the Maduro raid. He expressed a wish that his attorney general would move faster "with respect to things." He defended his tariffs, recounting the way he had imposed one escalation after another on China—10 percent here, 20 percent there, a little extra for fentanyl—until one day he looked at the total and said, in disbelief, "A hundred and forty-five?" Even the President seemed momentarily startled by his own appetite.

We had hoped to prompt Trump on how he viewed his own power and his position in relation to history and we planned to ask as soon as there was an opportunity. How would he rank himself among the club of forty-four other men to become President since the founding? We had no doubt he would be quick to respond, and likely he would say number one. Nevertheless, we wanted to hear his perspective; he had just launched a war and had been bragging that he was afraid of nothing. A President with no sleepless nights on going to war was worth exploring.

Trump had said recently, "No other President could do some of the shit I'm doing." Noting this, and seeing if he would go further, we asked whether he thought there had ever been an American President as powerful as he was now. It was the same question he had posed to Tucker Carlson in February 2025.

"As powerful as I am?" Trump mused. Instead of answering directly, he embarked on a strange story.

"There's a great golfer named Gary Player," he said. "Did you ever hear of him?" Player, Trump explained, was a friend and one of the greatest golfers of all time. He had recently turned ninety and Trump had played with him to mark his birthday. "And he shot a seventy-one, which is pretty tough."

But the point of the story was not about golf. It was about a friend of Player's, a man Trump described as "a historian." They had attended an event honoring Player, Trump said, and the historian—whose name Trump could not immediately recall, dispatching Harp to find it—had gotten up to speak. "And he said, 'I'd like to say something about the President.'"

Trump gestured for Harp to bring us copies of the two-page document. He began reading from it, reciting the names of some of history's most powerful figures, explaining how each fell short of his own power as U.S. President. Alexander the Great, the Caesars, William the Conqueror—"They didn't have airplanes, right? You couldn't travel around." Genghis Khan. Attila the Hun. Tamerlane. "Napoleon," he said with relish. "Hitler. Mao. Stalin."

These leaders "maintained power through fear," he said. "Who would ever do a thing like that? Right?"

Trump lingered on the document's central argument: that each leader, however fearsome in his day, had no global reach. Their power was local. But his was not.

"I never thought of it in terms of that," Trump said. "It's very interesting, the power." Then he added: "But when I read it, I said, 'He's right.'"

Harp gave copies to each of us, and Trump rolled on.

The document's opening line was the mesmerized citation of an acolyte: "Donald Trump is, without question, the most powerful man that the planet has ever known—by a long way." It went on over the two pages. Genghis Khan and Attila the Hun were "butchers" and "terrorists—and more like the Taliban than people with real power." It concluded with a flourish on William the Conqueror, who had come up in a conversation between Trump and the author during a round of golf: "If President Trump is the American Eagle, then William the Conqueror was merely a sparrow."

"You can't talk about your power," Trump told us. "Oh, I'm so powerful. You can't do that. Doesn't come off well." He was content to let someone else make the case on his behalf, and he wanted to make sure we left with a copy.

Later, Harp would text us the author's name. He was not actually a historian, but rather had been Gary Player's caddy and personal confidant for decades. When Jonathan tracked him down later for an interview, he said he had spent a lifetime studying history on his own, outside any university or academic framework or institution. He had first shared his assessment of Trump's power with Player and later explained it directly to Trump over golf in Florida. Afterward, he had written it up and sent it to the President's office.

And yet, if the source seemed peculiar, the issue was not frivolous: that Trump was an American President willing to deploy the full range of the nation's economic and military power without the inhibition that had characterized many of his predecessors, eradicating whatever systemic checks he could and often ignoring the ones that remained. This was a phenomenon that serious analysts of the presidency had also observed, albeit using very different language. What was revealing was not really that Trump agreed with the thesis but the way he inhabited it: the evident pleasure he took in the company of Mao, Hitler, and Stalin, masters of state control through murder, torture, and detention, and Napoleon—and the untroubled ease with which he accepted a place among men who had reshaped the world through conquest and fear. He drew no distinction between those who built and those who destroyed, between those who liberated and those who enslaved. What mattered was that they had had huge power—and that he had more.

Embellishing this idea, Trump then surprised us by articulating one of the central arguments we had made in the introduction to our book, though from his own peculiar vantage point:

"It's very interesting, the power," he said. "The election was rigged. If it weren't, my presidency could never have been as powerful in the second term as it has been in the third. Or even close."

Whether the 2020 election was "rigged" was not a matter of debate for any serious person. It was not rigged. Trump had lost. But the underlying point he made—that if he had served a consecutive second term beginning in January 2021, he would never have accumulated the power he now wielded—matched our own analysis.

The indictments, the conviction, the assassination attempts, the four years of exile that allowed him to shed the restraining forces of his first term, to assemble a team of true loyalists who had spent years studying the levers of government and plotting how to seize them—all of it had, paradoxically, made Trump stronger, more ruthless, and more commanding than he could have been otherwise: the most powerful President of our lifetimes.

There was another dimension to Trump's power that the caddy's document did not capture but was no less significant: Trump was the first modern President to govern as though the international system simply did not exist. His predecessors, even the most hawkish among them, had operated within a web of treaties, institutions, and norms—NATO, the United Nations, the World Trade Organization—that shaped and constrained how American power was exercised. Trump did not merely buck against these constraints, as other Presidents had; he ignored them entirely, and in doing so demonstrated that they had no mechanism to stop him. He had reduced funding to the UN and created his own forum of strongmen. He had waged war without a coalition. He had imposed tariffs as instruments of personal leverage. He had discarded international law with a single sentence: "I don't need international law."

And the system, it turned out, had no answer. The system was only real if the world's great superpower bought into it. By the spring of 2026, the pretense was over. Nobody—not the diplomats in Brussels, not the generals at NATO headquarters, not the delegates at the United Nations—believed the old order was coming back. In making this argument, the political commentator John Judis had compared Trump to one of the philosopher Hegel's "world-historical individuals"—figures who, without fully understanding what they were doing, demolished one era and ushered in another.

As the interview wound down, Trump offered a parting shot—one directed, in particular, at Maggie, whom he had already attacked in his post three days earlier. "Remember this," he said. "I know your book will be critical, but remember this: People are tired of your bullshit. Always criticizing."

He invoked his political comeback and 2024 victory. "They illegally indicted me, they impeached me, they did everything—they shot me, I guess you could say. But I won the election in a landslide. Nobody else could've done it," he added. "And there's only one thing you can say about me that anybody believes, and you know what that is.

"Essentially I won every fucking time," he said.

Maggie told him she hoped he would read the book, that we thought it captured his presidency quite well.

Trump wasn't finished. "And I'm tired of winning and winning and winning and just getting bad fucking press. It's about time that you tell the truth. Okay?"

Maggie replied, "Thank you for having us, Mr. President."

Trump ushered us out before beginning a public signing of executive orders. He said he wasn't sure exactly what orders he was being handed, but he was unable to resist a quick slap at Biden before we left: "I actually do my own signings."

We gathered our things and walked out. The rain had eased, though a heavy gray still hung over the capital.

Debts

This book has been the hardest thing either of us has ever done professionally and it was very much a team effort. We pushed ourselves to the physical brink over the past nearly three years and our families bore the brunt of our commitment. Our spouses in particular worked miracles during our absences and we will be paying off those debts for years to come.

Jonathan Jao, our editor at Simon & Schuster, gave this book more of himself than we had any right to expect, and more than we will ever fully know how to repay. He stitches where you can't see the stitches, and the book you are holding is as much a product of his vision as of our reporting. We are deeply grateful to him, as well as to Priscilla Painton, Jonathan Karp, Sean Manning, Julia Prosser, Rebecca Rozenberg, Irene Kheradi, Nancy Tan, Jonathan Evans, Rob Sternitzky, Amanda Mulholland, Ruth Lee-Mui, Elisa Rivlin, Michael Burke, Dominick Montalto, Chris Milea, Laura Ogar, Lisa Erwin, Beth Maglione, Jackie Seow, and Jennie Miller.

We are grateful to our agents, Matt Latimer of Javelin (Maggie) and Pilar Queen of UTA (Jonathan). Thank you for believing in us and for zealously defending our interests.

Evelyn Duffy was a vital partner on research. We employed two fact-checkers to review every word and line, and they were exceptional: Cameron Peters, who also helped with research, and Julie Tate.

We are profoundly grateful to *The New York Times*. A. G. Sulzberger is devoted to journalism and shares our feeling that our profession is a calling and a great responsibility. His leadership of the *Times* during an extraordinarily challenging period for the news industry has been a source of confidence and pride for those of us in the newsroom. Similarly, we owe a huge debt of gratitude to David McCraw and the *New York Times* legal team, as does most of journalism.

We have a very long list of people to thank at the *Times* and, with anticipatory apologies, our list is surely incomplete. The paper's leaders have been extraordinarily patient and supportive of us throughout this project. Thank you especially to Meredith Kopit Levien, Joe Kahn, Carolyn Ryan, Dean Baquet, Matt Purdy, Sam Dolnick, Matea Gold, David Halbfinger, and Manny Fernandez. Thank you to Dick Stevenson, one of the finest editors we've ever known, for his resolute leadership of the Washington bureau; and to the galvanizing and big-hearted Elizabeth Kennedy for showing us the way on the White House team. Thank you to all of our politics team colleagues from 2024 (and especially our partners on Trump stories: the wickedly talented Shane Goldmacher, Michael Bender, and Michael Gold), as well as Kathleen Hennessy, Liz Johnstone, Paul Volpe, and Zach Jonck; our ride-or-die colleagues on the White House beat (Zolan Kanno-Youngs, Katie Rogers, Erica Green, Peter Baker, David Sanger, Luke Broadwater, Tyler Pager, Shawn McCreesh, Anton Troianovski, and alum-for-life Michael Shear); and other generous colleagues: Ben Protess, Willy Rashbaum, Jonah Bromwich, Julian Barnes, Michael Schmidt, Mark Mazzetti, Annie Karni, Ken Vogel, Ronen Bergman, Thomas Friedman, Maureen Dowd, Andrew Ross Sorkin, David Leonhardt, Elizabeth Bumiller, Ezra Klein, Adam Rasgon, Carl Hulse, Adam Entous, Eric Schmitt, Matt Flegenheimer, Jessica Dimson, Adam Nagourney, Nestor Ramos, Pat Healy, Helene Cooper, Greg Jaffe, Adam Goldman, Devlin Barrett, Glenn Thrush, Alan Feuer, Nick Corasaniti, Katie Glueck, Lisa Lerer, Reid Epstein, Katie Rosman, Jacob Bernstein, Nicholas Fandos, Ben Oreskes, Ben Weiser, Rebecca Davis O'Brien, Teddy Schleifer, Brooks Barnes, David McCabe, Alan Blinder, Andrew Trunsky, Lisa Friedman, Coral Davenport, Charlie Stadtlander, Emily Cochrane, Farnaz Fassihi, Jeff Burgess, David Fahrenthold, Jason Reich, Jim Rutenberg, Jonathan Weisman, Kate Kelly, Katie Benner, Nick Confessore, Jeremy Peters, Ruth Igielnik, Ryan Mac, Kate Conger, Nick Nehamas, Steven Ginsberg, Kate Christobek, Dana Rubenstein, Justin Scheck, Jessica Green-Silverberg, Matt Goldstein, Russ Buettner, Mike McIntire, Susanne Craig, Matt Apuzzo, Eric Lipton, Adam Liptak, Jodi Kantor, Megan

Twohey, Kitty Bennett, Robert Draper, Hamed Aleaziz, Michael Crowley, Edward Wong, Noah Weiland, Jeanna Smialek, Colby Smith, Alan Rappeport, Jim Tankersley, Andy Duehren, Natalie Kitroeff, Michael Barbaro, Rachel Abrams, Anatoly Kurmanaev, Eileen Sullivan, Julie Davis, Catie Edmondson, David Yaffe-Bellany, Isabel Kershner, Vivian Nereim, and Marisa Schwartz Taylor. And thank you to the magnificent Margaret Goldberg, Shawn Bower, and Sarah Kate Thomas, who went above and beyond for us.

Our colleague Charlie Savage was our partner on our comprehensive *Times* reporting series, through 2023 and 2024, that investigated the plans and stakes of Trump's second-term agenda. The series became the basis for this book.

Doug Mills is the GOAT of White House photographers and has the eye of a great reporter. He is also a cherished friend and has been the most generous colleague we could ever hope for.

We would like to recognize the work of longtime Trump White House beat reporters and competitors, who made us tear our hair out when we were scooped and also made us better: Kaitlan Collins, Jonathan Karl, Josh Dawsey, Robert Costa, Rebecca Ballhaus, Alex Leary, Alex Isenstadt, Marc Caputo, Meridith McGraw, Ashley Parker, Asawin Suebsaeng, Tim Alberta, and Alayna Treene. And a big thank you to Jake Sherman and John Bresnahan of *Punchbowl News* for helping us think through Trump's relationship with Congress.

—MAGGIE HABERMAN
JONATHAN SWAN

Thank you to Betsy, to whom I proposed marriage on our first date ten years ago. She said no, but it wasn't a hard no. So I tried again the next day. Betsy is a brilliant journalist who understood exactly what this book would demand and chose to support it anyway. She solo-parented through toddler birthday parties and family holidays, lived with a husband who was even more monomaniacal than usual—which is saying something—and read every page of every draft, marking them up by hand. She did much of this while pregnant, and almost never complained, though she has informed me she never wants to hear about another book ever again. She is the best thing that ever happened to me.

Thank you to Esther and Sam for bringing me laughter and light every day. Thank you to my dad, Norman Swan, an inspiring brilliant journalist, who worked so hard to give us a better childhood than he had. And to my mum, Lee Sutton (she would never forgive me if I used the American "mom"), a devoted doctor, who in many ways sacrificed even more. She was and is the best mum a boy could ever hope for. I am grateful to have sisters who are also my dear friends—Anna and Georgia—and to have a loving extended family across two continents: the Swans, the Suttons, the Woodruffs, and "The" Gibbs (singular).

Thank you to Tara Leigh Anglin, a true mensch who gracefully handled any challenge or curveball thrown her way. And to Juanita Powell-Brunson for taking such good care of us.

Thank you to my brilliant and steadfast agent Pilar Queen. To Walter Isaacson, Jon Meacham, Sally Quinn, Bob Woodward, and Evan Thomas for your generosity and wisdom; to Jesse Olson for keeping me on my toes; to godfathers Doug and Greg; and to my Aussie crew: Sproats, Farruge, Coe, Keeble, Brenton, Doyle, Haigh, Laws, Max, Cassie, and Mary.

Thank you to the people who took chances on me when others wouldn't: to Rose Herceg for enlarging my dreams; to Jock Cheetham, who helped get me in the door at *The Sydney Morning Herald*; to Bob Cusack, who gave me my first job in American journalism; and to Jim VandeHei, Mike Allen, and Roy Schwartz, who let me ride a few years on the *Axios* rocket ship. Thank you to Carolyn Ryan for sharing my enthusiasms and for her genius, and to David Halbfinger for persuading me to join the *Times*. And thank you to Perri Peltz, Matt O'Neill, and Beth Morrissey; I will always be proud of the work we did together.

Pam Williams's impact on my life as a journalist has been singular. When I first started out as a rookie reporter in Sydney, I was in awe of Pam's long-form investigations in the *Australian Financial Review*. They seemed like journalism magic, with a glittering tiny jewel or a major revelation—usually both—on every page. I cold-emailed her, asking if she'd have coffee with me. She's been my hero, mentor, and cherished friend ever since, guiding me through every significant moment in my career. I don't know where I'd be without Pam, but for sure it would not be here.

Thank you to Maggie for running through walls, and most of all for your friendship and loyalty.

—JONATHAN SWAN

An additional thanks to Matt Latimer for a steady hand that rivals Leonardo DiCaprio's in *The Departed*, for his patience, and for his faith in me no matter what, as well as his colleagues Keith Urbahn and Matt Carlini. Thank you to John Ellis for being an invaluable font of wisdom. Thank you to Michael O'Connor for nearly two decades of support. Thank you to John Harris, Jim VandeHei, Danielle Jones, and Kim Kingsley for bringing me on at *Politico* in 2010, and then to Carolyn Ryan for hiring me at the *Times*. A massive thank-you to Juanita Powell-Brunson, Natoria Carey, and Tara Leigh Anglin for the hand-holds and help. Thank you to my dears Lauren, Kerri, Cathie, Stefan, Dinny, Amanda, Kate, Lisa, Sara, and John for being there, always.

Thank you to Gregg Birnbaum and David Seifman, who trained me early in covering government; and to the late Wayne Barrett and Tom Robbins, as well as Tim O'Brien of Bloomberg Opinion, all of whom forged a path that many, many of us have walked on the perennial Trump beat. And to Sasha Issenberg, who taught me how to write a book.

To my former and current CNN folks—Jeff Zucker, Jamie Zahn, Mark Thompson, Amy Entelis, Virginia Moseley, Rebecca Kutler, Rebecca Schatz, Jake Tapper, Anderson Cooper, Dana Bash, John Berman, Phil Mattingly, Wolf Blitzer (and Kaitlan again)—thank you for everything. A non-CNN note of thanks to Joe Scarborough and Mika Brzezinski, Nicolle Wallace, Alex Wagner, Kara Swisher, Abby Livingston, and John Heilemann for support over many years.

To my husband, and my three children, who are all my heart, I am so grateful. Deep love to my brother, Zach, and my sister, Emma; to my father, Clyde, the hardest-working and best journalist I ever saw; to my mom, Nancy, a single mom who raised us to never be cowed; and to my stepmom, Kathy, who loved us as her own.

Lastly, endless thanks to Jonathan Swan for nearly ten years of friendship and for coming to the *Times*, for being an incredible, meticulous journalist and a loyal colleague. And thank you as well for the gift of Pam Williams in my life.

—MAGGIE HABERMAN

Notes

Prologue

Liptak, Kevin. "A Very Mar-a-Lago New Year's Eve." CNN, December 31, 2025.

Yourish, Karen, and Charlie Smart. "How Trump Used 10 Emergency Declarations to Justify Hundreds of Actions." *New York Times*, August 22, 2025.

Introduction

Associated Press. "US Pays About $160M Towards Nearly $4Bn in UN Dues." February 20, 2026.

Barrett, Wayne. "Like Father, Like Son: Anatomy of a Young Power Broker." *Village Voice*, January 15, 1979.

Blair, Gwenda. "How Norman Vincent Peale Taught Donald Trump to Worship Himself." *Politico Magazine*, October 6, 2015.

Broadwater, Luke, and Tripp Mickle. "Trump Announces Additional $100 Billion Apple Investment in U.S." *New York Times*, August 6, 2025.

Eder, Steve. "Did a Queens Podiatrist Help Donald Trump Avoid Vietnam?" *New York Times*, December 26, 2018.

Hounshell, Blake, and Daniel Lippman. "POLITICO Playbook: Assange Arrested in London as Mueller Report Looms." *Politico*, April 11, 2019.

Judkis, Maura. "The New Don Jr.–Connected D.C. Club Has Been a Mystery. Here Are the Details." *Washington Post*, June 9, 2025.

Lerman, Rachel. "Trump Remains Banned from Twitter, Facebook. Here's How His Messages Could Still Get Through." *Washington Post*, May 6, 2021.

Lucas, Ryan. "Where the Jan. 6 Insurrection Investigation Stands, One Year Later." NPR, January 6, 2022.

Neustadt, Richard E. *Presidential Power: The Politics of Leadership*. John Wiley & Sons, 1960.

Peters, Jeremy W. "How Murdoch Runs Fox News, in His Own (Often Terse) Words." *New York Times*, March 9, 2023.

Protess, Ben, Andrea Fuller, Sharon LaFraniere, and Seamus Hughes. "The S.E.C. Was Tough on Crypto. It Pulled Back After Trump Returned to Office." *New York Times*, December 14, 2025.

Sanger, David E., Tyler Pager, Katie Rogers, and Zolan Kanno-Youngs. "Trump Lays Out a Vision of Power Restrained Only by 'My Own Morality.'" *New York Times*, January 8, 2026.

Swan, Jonathan, Maggie Haberman, and Shane Goldmacher. "How Trump Uses the Power and Imagery of His Presidency." *New York Times*, February 5, 2024.

Swan, Jonathan, and Zachary Basu. "Trump's War with His Generals." *Axios*, May 16, 2021.

Chapter 1

Allen, Mike, and Sara Fischer. "Exclusive: Meta Kills DEI Programs." *Axios*, January 10, 2025.

Bennett, Kate. "Trumps' Snub of Bidens Historic in Its Magnitude." CNN, January 18, 2021.

ESPN. "Pat Summerall Dies at 82." April 16, 2013.

Goldstein, Matthew, and Ryan Mac. "Trump's Truth Social Is Poised to Join a Crowded Field." *New York Times*, February 18, 2022.

Gomez Licon, Adriana, and Michelle L. Price. "Trump Calls It the 'Center of the Universe.' Mar-a-Lago Is a Magnet for Those Seeking Influence." Associated Press, December 31, 2024.

Haag, Matthew, and Jacey Fortin. "Vanessa Trump, Donald Trump Jr.'s Wife, Files for Divorce." *New York Times*, March 15, 2018.

Isaac, Mike, Jonathan Swan, Maggie Haberman, and Theodore Schleifer. "Mark Zuckerberg Meets with Trump at Mar-a-Lago." *New York Times*, November 27, 2024.

Isenstadt, Alex. "Trump Claims Zuckerberg Plotted Against Him During the 2020 Election in Soon-to-Be Released Book." *Politico*, August 28, 2024.

Kelly, Stephanie. "Trump Shakes Hands with Pence, Engages Obama at Carter Funeral." Reuters, January 9, 2025.

Klepper, David. "Music to Trump's Ears: Whitewashing Jan. 6 Riot with Song." Associated Press, April 21, 2023.

Martin, Jonathan. "Biden White House Is Discussing Preemptive Pardons for Those in Trump's Crosshairs." *Politico Magazine*, December 4, 2024.

McCreesh, Shawn. "Trump's Latest Photo Book Offers Gossip, Boasting and a Threat." *New York Times*, September 9, 2024.

McGraw, Meridith, and Natalie Allison. "Trump 'Felt the Bullet Ripping Through the Skin' During Apparent Assassination Attempt." *Politico*, July 13, 2024.

Nelson, Louis. "Bill Clinton: Trump Knows How to Get 'Angry, White Men to Vote for Him.'" *Politico*, December 19, 2016.

Schwartz, Brian, Dana Mattioli, and Rebecca Ballhaus. "The Week CEOs Bent the Knee to Trump." *Wall Street Journal*, December 13, 2024.

Chapter 2

Associated Press. "Vance Says Jan. 6 Participants Who Committed Violence 'Obviously' Shouldn't Be Pardoned." January 12, 2025.

Baker, Peter. "For Trump, a Vindication for the Man and His Movement." *New York Times*, January 20, 2025.

Barrett, Devlin. "Senate Confirms Trump Attorney Todd Blanche as No. 2 Justice Dept. Official." *New York Times*, March 5, 2025.

Blair, Chad. "Gabbard Met Assad Twice for a Total of Two Hours." *Honolulu Civil Beat*, February 8, 2017.

Demirjian, Karoun. "Hegseth Won't Say Whether Sexual Assault, Drinking or Adultery Is Disqualifying." *New York Times*, January 14, 2025.

Isenstadt, Alex. "Corey Lewandowski Cuts Deal on Charge Stemming from Alleged Unwanted Sexual Advances." *Politico*, September 28, 2022.

Jakes, Lara, and Michael Crowley. "With an Eye on 2024, a Rarely Bashful Pompeo Grows More Combative." *New York Times*, March 29, 2021.

Rascoe, Ayesha. "For 1st Time in 150 Years, Outgoing President Doesn't Attend Inauguration." NPR, January 20, 2021.

Rucker, Philip, Josh Dawsey, Shane Harris, and Ashley Parker. "Aides Weigh Resignations, Removal Options as Trump Rages Against Perceived Betrayals." *Washington Post*, January 7, 2021.

Sentner, Irie. "Here's the Schedule for Trump's Inauguration Day." *Politico*, January 20, 2025.

Slattery, Gram, and Helen Coster. "JD Vance Once Compared Trump to Hitler. Now, He Is Trump's Vice President–Elect." Reuters, November 6, 2024.

Thrush, Glenn. "Pam Bondi Is Trump's New Choice for Attorney General. Here's What to Know About Her." *New York Times*, November 21, 2024.

Chapter 3

Barstow, David, Susanne Craig, and Russ Buettner. "Trump Engaged in Suspect Tax Schemes as He Reaped Riches from His Father." *New York Times*, October 2, 2018.

Guerrero, Jean. *Hatemonger: Stephen Miller, Donald Trump, and the White Nationalist Agenda*. William Morrow, 2020.

Kliff, Sarah, and Noah Weiland. "Payment System That Provides Medicaid Funding to States Stops Working, Officials Say." *New York Times*, January 28, 2025.

Messerly, Megan, Josh Gerstein, Kyle Cheney, and Nahal Toosi. "Trump Fires Independent Inspectors General in Friday Night Purge." *Politico*, January 25, 2025.

Shear, Michael D. "Judge Stays Trump's Federal Funding Freeze, but Disruption to Medicaid Sows Fear." *New York Times*, January 28, 2025.

Chapter 4

Cho, Kelly Kasulis, Tobi Raji, Kim Bellware, Kyle Melnick, and Helier Cheung. "What We Know About the Plane and Military Helicopter Crash in D.C." *Washington Post*, January 30, 2025.

Collins, Eliza. "Trump: I Consult Myself on Foreign Policy." *Politico*, March 16, 2016.

Diamond, Jeremy, and Nicole Gaouette. "Donald Trump Unveils Foreign Policy Advisers." CNN, March 21, 2016.

Entous, Adam. "The Separation: Inside the Unraveling U.S.-Ukraine Partnership." *New York Times*, December 30, 2025.

Hussein, Fatima, and Lolita C. Baldor. "Trump Selects Longtime Adviser Keith Kellogg as Special Envoy for Ukraine and Russia." Associated Press, November 27, 2024.

Osborn, Andrew, and Polina Nikolskaya. "Russia's Putin Authorises 'Special Military Operation' Against Ukraine." Reuters, February 24, 2022.

RFE/RL Ukrainian Service. "Designated U.S. Envoy for Ukraine Says Trump Wants Equitable End to War." Radio Free Europe/Radio Liberty, January 9, 2025.

Washington Post. "The Lives Lost in the D.C. Plane-Helicopter Crash." February 25, 2025.

Chapter 5

Bidgood, Jess. "Why the White House Car Show Mattered to Musk." *New York Times*, March 12, 2025.

Butler, Desmond, Jonathan O'Connell, Hannah Natanson, and Aaron Gregg. "DOGE Has the Keys to Sensitive Data That Could Help Elon Musk." *Washington Post*, June 30, 2025.

Conger, Kate, and Lauren Hirsch. "Elon Musk Completes $44 Billion Deal to Own Twitter." *New York Times*, October 27, 2022.

Doan, Laura, and Julia Ingram. "Elon Musk Makes Baseless Claim About Large Number of Dead People on Government Payroll." CBS News, February 27, 2025.

Fernandez, Madison. "In Arizona Speech, Trump Jokes Musk Is 'Not Going to Be President.'" *Politico*, December 22, 2024.

Haberman, Maggie, Jonathan Swan, and Ryan Mac. "How Elon Musk Has Planted Himself Almost Literally at Trump's Doorstep." *New York Times*, December 30, 2024.

Isaacson, Walter. *Elon Musk*. Simon & Schuster, 2023.

Kolodny, Lora. "Elon Musk Says It's Time for Trump to 'Sail into the Sunset.'" CNBC, July 12, 2022.

Lipton, Eric, and Kirsten Grind. "Elon Musk's Business Empire Scores Benefits Under Trump Shake-Up." *New York Times*, February 11, 2025.

Roulette, Joey. "Trump, Musk Watch SpaceX Launch Starship, Booster Misses Landing." Reuters, November 20, 2024.

Rubin, Alissa J. "Islamic State Camps Pose a Dangerous Problem for Syria's Leaders." *New York Times*, December 10, 2025.

Solomon, Erika, Ben Hubbard, and Lara Jakes. "Despite Waivers, U.S. Funding Freeze Sows Doubt About Camp Holding ISIS Members." *New York Times*, February 6, 2025.

Swan, Jonathan, Maggie Haberman, Nicholas Nehamas, Theodore Schleifer, and David A. Fahrenthold. "A Subdued Musk Backs Away from Washington, but His Project Remains." *New York Times*, April 23, 2025.

Swan, Jonathan, Theodore Schleifer, Maggie Haberman, et al. "How Elon Musk Executed His Takeover of the Federal Bureaucracy." *New York Times*, February 28, 2025.

Tanis, Fatima. "U.S. Puts Virtually All Foreign Aid on 90-Day Hold, Issues 'Stop-Work' Order." NPR, January 24, 2025.

Toh, Michelle, and Juliana Liu. "Elon Musk Says He's Cut About 80% of Twitter's Staff." CNN, April 12, 2023.

Vanity Fair. "Elon Musk and Y Combinator President on Thinking for the Future." October 8, 2015.

Chapter 6

Aleaziz, Hamed. "The Trump Administration Will Deport People Seeking Asylum in the US to Guatemala Without Them Seeing a Lawyer First." *BuzzFeed News*, November 20, 2019.

Associated Press. "Rubio Says El Salvador Will House Deportees from U.S., Including Americans." February 4, 2025.

Collins, Ben, and Anna Schecter. "Stephen Miller Planted Anti-Rubio Stories in Breitbart During 2016 Campaign, Leaked Emails Show." NBC News, November 19, 2019.

Correal, Annie. "El Salvador Police Say Quotas and Rumors Fueled Bukele's Mass Arrests." *New York Times*, June 27, 2025.

Crooks, Nathan, and Rita Devlin Marier. "Marco Rubio Says No Thanks to 'Dictator' Maduro's Invitation." *Bloomberg News*, October 17, 2017.

Dixon, Matt, Henry J. Gomez, and Allan Smith. "Trump Elevates Marco Rubio as a Potential Successor—and as a 2028 Rival to Vance." NBC News, May 8, 2025.

Hansler, Jennifer. "Rubio: 'Zero-Tolerance' Immigration Is What Trump Campaigned On." CNN, June 22, 2018.

Holland, Steve, Jeff Mason, and Dmitry Antonov. "US Frees Jailed Cybercrime Boss After Russia Releases Teacher Marc Fogel." Reuters, February 12, 2025.

Leary, Alex. "Rise and Stall: The Political Trajectory of Marco Rubio." *Tampa Bay Times*, March 3, 2016.

LeVine, Marianne. "How Marco Rubio Went from Rival to One of Donald Trump's VP Finalists." *Washington Post*, June 19, 2024.

Mascaro, Lisa. "What Marco Rubio's Foray into the 2013 Immigration Overhaul Push Revealed." *Los Angeles Times*, December 11, 2015.

Miller, John J. "Rubio Rising." *National Review*, September 7, 2009.

Narea, Nicole. "Trump's Agreements in Central America Are Dismantling the Asylum System as We Know It." *Vox*, September 26, 2019.

Nawaz, Amna, Teresa Cebrián Aranda, and Julia Galiano-Rios. "Thousands of Innocent People Jailed in El Salvador's Gang Crackdown." *PBS NewsHour*, February 13, 2024.

Pannell, Alfie. "The 'World's Coolest Dictator' Heads to the White House." NPR, April 14, 2025.

Parker, Ashley, Michael Scherer, and Nick Miroff. "The Wrath of Stephen Miller." *The Atlantic*, January 7, 2026.

Roig-Franzia, Manuel. *The Rise of Marco Rubio*. Simon & Schuster, 2012.

Rubio, Marco. *An American Son: A Memoir*. Sentinel, 2013.

Savage, Charlie, Maggie Haberman, and Jonathan Swan. "Sweeping Raids, Giant Camps and Mass Deportations: Inside Trump's 2025 Immigration Plans." *New York Times*, November 11, 2023.

Chapter 7

Baum, Gary. "Wrongful Death Lawsuit Hits L.A. Rehab Center Following THR Investigation." *Hollywood Reporter*, August 17, 2013.

Burke, Mack. "Witkoff, Mubadala Get $615M Refinance on Park Lane Hotel." *Commercial Observer*, June 6, 2019.

Chance, Matthew, and Katharina Krebs. "Russian Artist Reveals Mystery Trump Portrait Gifted by Putin to the US President." CNN, April 22, 2025.

DeYoung, Karen, Shira Rubin, and Gerry Shih. "An Unlikely Team of U.S. Negotiators Wrestled Israel and Hamas to a Ceasefire." *Washington Post*, January 18, 2025.

D'Souza, Charlotte. "Historic Manhattan Hotel with Checkered Past Changes Hands." PERE, October 11, 2023.

The Economist. "The Education of Steve Witkoff." September 18, 2025.

Farrell, Maureen. "He Helped 'Break' the Bank of England. Now He May Run the U.S. Treasury." *New York Times*, November 26, 2024.

Haberman, Maggie, Zolan Kanno-Youngs, and Anton Troianovski. "Trump Says Call with Putin Is Beginning of Ukraine Peace Negotiations." *New York Times*, February 12, 2025.

Kirkpatrick, David D. "Steven Witkoff Keeps Adding to His Office-Space Empire." *Wall Street Journal*, September 9, 1998.

Leonard, Devin. "Steve Witkoff's Nine Lives: Tough Guys Don't Fold—They Crawl Back from the Abyss." *New York Observer*, December 6, 1999.

Maynes, Charles. "U.S. and Russia Discuss Ending Ukraine War, Without Kyiv." NPR, February 18, 2025.

Richards, Zoë. "Trump Says Ukraine 'Should Have Never Started' War in Ukraine." NBC News, February 18, 2025.

Stanley-Becker, Isaac. "Trump's Real Secretary of State." *The Atlantic*, May 14, 2025.

Starcevic, Seb. "Putin Prayed for Trump After Assassination Attempt, Top Envoy Says." *Politico*, March 21, 2025.

Stoddart, Michelle, and Alexandra Hutzler. "Vance, Zelenskyy Meet on Ending Russia-Ukraine War as Administration Sends Mixed Messages." ABC News, February 14, 2025.

Varenikova, Maria. "Treasury Secretary Makes Trip to Kyiv." *New York Times*, February 12, 2025.

Chapter 8

Associated Press. "Trump Slams Israel's Netanyahu for Congratulating Biden." December 10, 2021.

Baker, Peter, and Maggie Haberman. "As Protests and Violence Spill Over, Trump Shrinks Back." *New York Times*, May 31, 2020.

Broadwater, Luke. "What to Know About the 'Massive' Military Bunker Beneath Trump's Ballroom." *New York Times*, April 2, 2026.

Edwards, Jonathan, and Dan Diamond. "White House Begins Demolishing East Wing Facade to Build Trump's Ballroom." *Washington Post*, October 20, 2025.

Estrin, Daniel. "Trump Has a Deal for Netanyahu When They Meet Tuesday. Will He Take It?" NPR, February 3, 2025.

Falconer, Rebecca, and Sareen Habeshian. "Trump Says Gaza 'Could Be Better than Monaco' Once It's Rebuilt." *Axios*, October 8, 2024.

Kershner, Isabel. "Netanyahu Arrives in Washington at Critical Juncture for Mideast." *New York Times*, February 2, 2025.

McGann, Laura. "Melania Trump's Changes to the White House Rose Garden, Explained." *Vox*, August 22, 2020.

Qiblawi, Tamara, Eliza Mackintosh, Wayne Chang, et al. "Israel Concealed Explosives Inside Batteries of Pagers Sold to Hezbollah, Lebanese Officials Say." CNN, September 27, 2024.

Swan, Jonathan, and Maggie Haberman. "Inside Trump's Hastily Written Proposal to 'Own' Gaza." *New York Times*, February 5, 2025.

Swan, Jonathan, Maggie Haberman, Mark Mazzetti, and Ronen Bergman. "How Trump Shifted on Iran Under Pressure from Israel." *New York Times*, June 17, 2025.

Taub, Amanda. "What International Law Says About Trump's Proposal to Remove Palestinians from Gaza." *New York Times*, February 11, 2025.

Chapter 9

Conger, Kate, Eileen Sullivan, and Christina Jewett. "Musk Says Government Workers Must Detail Their Workweek or Lose Their Jobs." *New York Times*, February 22, 2025.

Lotz, Avery. "Russia Gloats About Shift in U.S. Relations with Ukraine." *Axios*, March 2, 2025.

Chapter 10

Cameron, Chris. "Reeling from $450 Million Penalty, Trump Hawks $400 Shoes." *New York Times*, February 18, 2024.

Carlson, Michael. "Ivana Trump Obituary." *The Guardian*, July 15, 2022.

Donnan, Shawn. "How Trump's Tariffs Aim a Wrecking Ball at the Economy of the Americas." *Bloomberg News*, February 2, 2025.

Editorial Board. "The Dumbest Trade War in History." *Wall Street Journal*, January 31, 2025.

Flatley, Daniel, and Erik Schatzker. "Bessent on Tariffs, Deficits and Embracing Trump's Economic Plan." *Bloomberg News*, August 11, 2025.

Johnson, Jenna. "Trump Lives in the Jet Set, and He's Not Afraid to Show It." *Washington Post*, February 27, 2016.

Judkis, Maura. "The Growing Legend of the Missing Oval Office Ivy." *Washington Post*, March 18, 2025.

Swan, Jonathan, Maggie Haberman, and Ana Swanson. "Trump's Unwelcome News to Auto Chiefs: Buckle Up for What's to Come." *New York Times*, March 17, 2025.

Swanson, Ana, and Jack Ewing. "Trump to Pause Auto Tariffs for One Month as Other Levies Continue." *New York Times*, March 5, 2025.

Wagner, James. "Mexico Deploys 10,000 National Guard Members to U.S. Border: What to Know." *New York Times*, February 4, 2025.

Weisman, Jonathan. "Trump Praises Tariffs, and William McKinley, to Power Brokers." *New York Times*, September 5, 2024.

Wichter, Zach. "America's Tariff Men: Connecting McKinley to Trump." *New York Times*, December 6, 2018.

Chapter 11

Alfred, Tsehai, Surina Venkat, Daksha Pillai, Miranda Lu, and Aiyana St. Hilaire. "Palestinian Activist Mahmoud Khalil, SIPA '24, Detained by Immigration and Customs Enforcement, Lawyer Says." *Columbia Spectator*, March 9, 2025.

Associated Press. "Exxon, Conoco Refuse to Sign Venezuela Deal." June 26, 2007.

Barnes, Julian E., Tyler Pager, and Maria Abi-Habib. "Trump Calls Off Diplomatic Outreach to Venezuela." *New York Times*, October 6, 2025.

Barrett, Devlin. "White House Denies Homan Took Bag of Cash in F.B.I. Inquiry." *New York Times*, September 22, 2025.

Barrett, Devlin, Glenn Thrush, Alan Feuer, Maggie Haberman, and Hamed Aleaziz. "Trump Justice Dept. Closed Investigation into Tom Homan for Accepting Bag of Cash." *New York Times*, September 20, 2025.

Bolton, John. *The Room Where It Happened: A White House Memoir*. Simon & Schuster, 2020.

Eaton, Collin. "How Chevron Secured Its Place as Venezuela's Largest Foreign Investor." *Wall Street Journal*, December 20, 2025.

Ellsworth, Brian. "Chavez Drives Exxon and ConocoPhillips from Venezuela." Reuters, August 9, 2007.

Herrero, Ana Vanessa. "After U.S. Backs Juan Guaidó as Venezuela's Leader, Maduro Cuts Ties." *New York Times*, January 23, 2019.

Kanno-Youngs, Zolan, and Hamed Aleaziz. "Inside Trump's Crackdown on Dissent: Obscure Laws, ICE Agents and Fear." *New York Times*, March 12, 2025.

Miroff, Nick. "Trump Loves ICE. Its Workforce Has Never Been So Miserable." *The Atlantic*, July 10, 2025.

Miroff, Nick. "Trump's Top Border Adviser Says He Will Bring Back Family Detention." *Washington Post*, December 26, 2024.

New York Times. "Trump Alarms Venezuela with Talk of a 'Military Option.'" August 12, 2017.

Puko, Timothy. "What Is Willow? How an Alaska Oil Project Could Affect the Environment." *Washington Post*, April 22, 2023.

Rabinowitz, Hannah, Ella Nilsen, and Laura Paddison. "The Trump Admin Is Suing Four States to Stop Them from Holding Fossil Fuel Giants Accountable for Climate Damage." CNN, May 2, 2025.

Raymond, Nate. "Trump Administration Unlawfully Ended Venezuelans' Legal Status, US Court Rules." Reuters, January 29, 2026.

Rein, Lisa. "Meet the Man the White House Has Honored for Deporting Illegal Immigrants." *Washington Post*, April 27, 2016.

Renshaw, Jarrett, and Trevor Hunnicutt. "Trump Pushes Energy Dominance Agenda in Meeting with US Oil Executives." Reuters, March 19, 2025.

Robles, Frances, Julie Turkewitz, and Zolan Kanno-Youngs. "U.S. Botched a Deal to Swap Venezuelans Held in El Salvador for Americans." *New York Times*, July 8, 2025.

Romero, Simon. "Chávez Takes Over Foreign-Controlled Oil Projects in Venezuela." *New York Times*, May 2, 2007.

Chapter 12

Hill, Meredith Lee. "The Private GOP Panic over the Slash-and-Burn DOGE Firings." *Politico*, February 20, 2025.

Hilton, Isabel. "Taiwan Makes the Majority of the World's Computer Chips. Now It's Running Out of Electricity." *Wired*, October 5, 2024.

Manfredi, Lucas. "Elon Musk Praises 'Smart, Hardworking' People in China, Sees 'Complacency,' 'Entitlement' Growing in America." Fox Business, August 2, 2020.

Scott, Rachel, Will Steakin, Katherine Faulders, and Sarah Beth Hensley. "Trump Tells Cabinet Members That They're in Charge, Not Musk: Sources." ABC News, March 6, 2025.

South China Morning Post. "TSMC Extends Dominance of Semiconductors with 56% Share of Global Lithography Systems." November 13, 2024.

Steakin, Will. "While Musk Is Leaving the White House, He'll Continue as Unofficial Adviser, Official Says." ABC News, May 29, 2025.

Sullivan, Eileen, and Maggie Haberman. "Trump Moves to Restrain Elon Musk." *New York Times*, March 6, 2025.

Swan, Jonathan, and Maggie Haberman. "Inside the Explosive Meeting Where Trump Officials Clashed with Elon Musk." *New York Times*, March 7, 2025.

Swanson, Ana. "Congress Is Giving Billions to the Chip Industry. Strings Are Attached." *New York Times*, August 3, 2022.

Chapter 13

Caputo, Marc. "Scoop: Musk vs. Bessent Dispute Erupted into West Wing Shouting Match." *Axios*, April 23, 2025.

Chapman, Michelle. "Airlines, Rattled by Trade War and Spending Pullback, Continue to Cut Flights, Pull Outlooks." Associated Press, April 24, 2025.

Cox, Jeff. "Jamie Dimon Says a Recession Is 'Likely Outcome' from Trump's Tariff Turmoil." CNBC, April 9, 2025.

Donnan, Shawn. "Bessent Defiant on Tariffs as He Rejects a US Recession." *Bloomberg News*, April 6, 2025.

Fox News. "Treasury Secretary Bessent Says Trump Will Keep Insisting on Fair Trade for the American People." March 31, 2025.

Hu, Bei. "Dalio Sees Once-a-Lifetime Collapse in Economic, Political Order." *Bloomberg News*, April 9, 2025.

Jett, Jennifer, and Peter Guo. "China Hits Back at Trump with 34% Tariff on U.S. Imports." NBC News, April 4, 2025.

Mena, Bryan. "Key Takeaways from Trump's 'Liberation Day' Tariffs." CNN, April 2, 2025.

Nam, Rafael. "U.S. Stocks Soar in an Incredible Rally after Trump Pauses Many of His Tariffs." NPR, April 9, 2025.

New York Times. "No Jurors Picked on First Day of Trump's Manhattan Criminal Trial." April 15, 2024.

Pager, Tyler, Maggie Haberman, Ana Swanson, and Jonathan Swan. "From 'Be Cool!' to 'Getting Yippy': Inside Trump's Reversal on Tariffs." *New York Times*, April 9, 2025.

Reuters. "S&P 500 Loses $2.4 Trillion in Market Value, Biggest One-Day Loss Since 2020." April 3, 2025.

Reuters. "Sudden Selloff Shakes US Bond Market." April 8, 2025.

Shepardson, David, Jarrett Renshaw, and David Lawder. "Trump Officials Eye Tariff Relief for USMCA-Compliant Products, Lutnick Says." Reuters, March 5, 2025.

Singh, Rajesh Kumar. "Delta Air Lines Pulls Financial Forecast, Saying Trump Tariffs Hit Demand." Reuters, April 9, 2025.

Tully, Shawn. "Are Trump's Tariffs as Bad as the Smoot-Hawley Act, Which Is Blamed for Deepening the Great Depression? They're Actually Worse." *Fortune*, April 3, 2025.

Weisset, Will. "Trump Says High Tariffs May Have Prevented the Great Depression. History Says Different." Associated Press, April 8, 2025.

Chapter 14

Barnes, Daniel. "Major Law Firm Strikes Preemptive Deal with White House." *Politico*, March 28, 2025.

Bender, Michael C. "The Harvard-Trained Lawyer Behind Trump's Fight Against Top Universities." *New York Times*, August 11, 2025.

Bender, Michael C., Alan Blinder, and Jonathan Swan. "Inside Trump's Pressure Campaign on Universities." *New York Times*, April 14, 2025.

Binkley, Collin, and Michael Casey. "Judge Reverses Trump Administration's Cuts of Billions in Research Funding to Harvard." Associated Press, September 3, 2025.

Brooks, Brad, and Kanishka Singh. "Harvard at Risk of Losing $9 Billion in Federal Funds as US Launches Review." Reuters, March 31, 2025.

Gold, Michael. "'I'm Not Going to Have Time for Retribution,' Trump Says at Town Hall." *New York Times*, January 11, 2024.

Haberman, Maggie, and Eric Schmitt. "Trump Revokes Security Detail for Mark Esper, Former Defense Secretary." *New York Times*, February 5, 2025.

Rashbaum, William K., Ben Protess, and Jonah E. Bromwich. "Trump Is Guilty of 'Numerous' Felonies, Prosecutor Who Resigned Says." *New York Times*, March 23, 2022.

Savage, Charlie. "The Four Trump Criminal Cases: Strengths and Weaknesses." *New York Times*, August 28, 2023.

Schmidt, Michael S., and Michael C. Bender. "Trump Officials Blame Mistake for Setting Off Confrontation with Harvard." *New York Times*, April 18, 2025.

Schmidt, Michael S., Matthew Goldstein, Jessica Silver-Greenberg, and Ben Protess. "How a Major Democratic Law Firm Ended Up Bowing to Trump." *New York Times*, March 21, 2025.

Shear, Michael D. "Miles Taylor, a Former Homeland Security Official, Reveals He Was 'Anonymous.'" *New York Times*, October 28, 2020.

Taylor, Miles. "Opinion: I Am Part of the Resistance Inside the Trump Administration." *New York Times*, September 5, 2018.

Chapter 15

Allison, Natalie, and Abigail Hauslohner. "Conflict in Mideast Causes Battle Within MAGA Ranks—Stay Out or Fight?" *Washington Post*, June 18, 2025.

Associated Press. "An Appeals Court Throws Out a Massive Civil Fraud Penalty Against President Trump." August 21, 2025.

Barnes, Julian E. "Head of National Security Agency and Cyber Command Is Ousted." *New York Times*, April 3, 2025.

Brockell, Gillian. "Donald Trump's Father Was Arrested, Too. Twice." *Washington Post*, April 4, 2023.

Bromwich, Jonah E. "Trump Official Scrutinizes N.Y.'s Attorney General Over Real Estate." *New York Times*, April 16, 2025.

Bromwich, Jonah E., and Ben Protess. "Trump Fraud Trial Penalty Will Exceed $450 Million." *New York Times*, February 16, 2024.

Chappell, Bill. "'I'm the Only One That Matters,' Trump Says of State Dept. Job Vacancies." NPR, November 3, 2017.

Craig, Susanne, and Benjamin Weiser. "What to Know About Trump's Cash as He Faces Penalties of $537 Million." *New York Times*, March 1, 2024.

The Economist. "Mike Waltz's Demotion Is a Loss for Defence Hawks." May 1, 2025.

Goldberg, Jeffrey. "The Trump Administration Accidentally Texted Me Its War Plans." *The Atlantic*, March 24, 2025.

Haberman, Maggie, Jonathan Swan, and Ken Bensinger. "Trump Fires 6 N.S.C. Officials After Oval Office Meeting with Laura Loomer." *New York Times*, April 3, 2025.

Lowell, Hugo, and Joseph Gedeon. "Trump Fires Six National Security Staffers After Meeting with Far-Right Activist Laura Loomer." *The Guardian*, April 3, 2025.

McGraw, Meridith. "Ivanka Trump Would Be 'Dynamite' as UN Ambassador, According to Her Dad." ABC News, October 9, 2018.

Meko, Hurubie. "Letitia James Ran on a Platform of Holding Trump to Account." *New York Times*, October 9, 2025.

Prokop, Andrew. "The Trump Administration Attack Dog You Should Pay Attention To." *Vox*, July 29, 2025.

Rashbaum, William K., and Danny Hakim. "New York Attorney General Opens Investigation of Trump Projects." *New York Times*, March 11, 2019.

Reisman, Nick. "Letitia James Pursued Trump. Then She Was Indicted." *Politico*, October 9, 2025.

Scott, Rachel, Benjamin Siegel, Katherine Faulders, and John Santucci. "Trump Picks Rep. Mike Waltz, a Former Green Beret, as National Security Adviser." ABC News, November 12, 2024.

Chapter 16

Balk, Tim. "Judge Blocks Deportations of Venezuelans Under Wartime Law." *New York Times*, March 15, 2025.

Broadwater, Luke, Albert Sun, Annie Correal, and Chris Cameron. "A Judge Ordered Deportation Planes to Turn Around. The White House Didn't Listen." *New York Times*, March 17, 2025.

Feuer, Alan, Hamed Aleaziz, and Abbie VanSickle. "Supreme Court, for Now, Blocks Deportation of Migrants Under Wartime Law." *New York Times*, April 18, 2025.

Holpuch, Amanda. "What Is Habeas Corpus, the Basic Right That Trump Officials Are Talking About Suspending?" *New York Times*, May 20, 2025.

Hudson, John. "El Salvador Offers to Jail 'American Criminals,' Including U.S. Citizens." *Washington Post*, February 3, 2025.

Kanno-Youngs, Zolan, Hamed Aleaziz, and Eileen Sullivan. "Trump Starts Immigration Crackdown, Enlisting the Military and Testing the Law." *New York Times*, January 20, 2025.

Kellerman, Ben. "ICE Has Detained a Growing Share of People with No Criminal Record or Charge." Reuters, February 27, 2026.

Loller, Travis, John Seewer, and Marc Levy. "Kilmar Abrego Garcia Freed from Immigration Detention After Judge Orders His Release." Associated Press, December 11, 2025.

Rosenberg, Mica, Perla Trevizo, Melissa Sanchez, et al. "Trump Administration Knew Vast Majority of Venezuelans Sent to Salvadoran Prison Had Not Been Convicted of U.S. Crimes." *ProPublica / Alianza Rebelde Investiga / Cazadores de Fake News*, May 30, 2025.

Sacchetti, Maria, and Carol D. Leonnig. "ICE Declares Millions of Undocumented Immigrants Ineligible for Bond Hearings." *Washington Post*, July 14, 2025.

Scharf, Will. *This Week with George Stephanopoulos*. Interview by George Stephanopoulos. ABC News, June 2, 2024.

Chapter 17

Axelrod, Tal, and Zachary Basu. "Ben Shapiro, Laura Loomer Lead Rare MAGA Backlash to Trump's Qatari Jet." *Axios*, May 13, 2025.

Chang, Brittany. "See Inside the Luxurious Boeing 747 Qatar Is Giving to Trump to Serve as Air Force One." *Business Insider*, May 21, 2025.

Gold, Michael. "Senate Democrats Seek Inquiry into Bondi's Role in Gift of Qatari Jet to Trump." *New York Times*, May 21, 2025.

Karl, Jonathan, and Katherine Faulders. "Trump Administration Poised to Accept 'Palace in the Sky' as a Gift for Trump from Qatar: Sources." ABC News, May 11, 2025.

Pager, Tyler, and Eric Schmitt. "Trump Could Begin Flying on Jet Donated by Qatar by Summer." *New York Times*, January 22, 2026.

Regalado, Francesca, Luke Broadwater, and Yan Zhuang. "Air Force One Turns Back with Trump After Electrical Issue." *New York Times*, January 20, 2026.

Strobel, Warren P., Alex Horton, and Abigail Hauslohner. "Navigating Iran Crisis, Trump Relies on Experience over Star Power." *Washington Post*, June 19, 2025.

Swan, Jonathan, Kate Kelly, Maggie Haberman, and Mark Mazzetti. "Kushner Firm Got Hundreds of Millions from 2 Persian Gulf Nations." *New York Times*, March 30, 2023.

Wilson, Tom, Tom Bergin, Lawrence Delevingne, and Michelle Conlin. "Insight: How the Trump Family Took Over a Crypto Firm as It Raised Hundreds of Millions." Reuters, March 31, 2025.

Yaffe-Bellany, David. "At a Dubai Conference, Trump's Conflicts Take Center Stage." *New York Times*, May 1, 2025.

Chapter 18

Barnes, Julian E., Mark Mazzetti, and Maggie Haberman. "In New Assessment, C.I.A. Chief Says U.S. Strikes 'Severely Damaged' Iranian Program." *New York Times*, June 25, 2025.

Beauchamp, Zack. "The GOP's Antisemitism Crisis." *Vox*, October 27, 2025.

Béchard, Deni Ellis. "Why This Is the Only Bomb That Could Destroy Iran's Nuclear Bunker—Under 300 Feet of Rock." *Scientific American*, June 18, 2025.

Bertrand, Natasha, Katie Bo Lillis, and Zachary Cohen. "Exclusive: Early US Intel Assessment Suggests Strikes on Iran Did Not Destroy Nuclear Sites, Sources Say." CNN, June 24, 2025.

Churchwell, Sarah. "The 'American Dream'? 'America First' Eclipses It." *Washington Post*, September 9, 2022.

Cooper, Helene, Eric Schmitt, and Samuel Granados. "Iran's Best-Protected Nuclear Site Is Deep Underground." *New York Times*, June 16, 2025.

Keating, Joshua. "Iran Had a Plan to Fight Israel and the US. It All Collapsed After October 7." *Vox*, March 4, 2026.

Lamothe, Dan, and Alex Horton. "JD Vance's Marine Buddies Back His Service over His Politics." *Washington Post*, August 4, 2024.

Mac, Ryan, and Theodore Schleifer. "How a Network of Tech Billionaires Helped J.D. Vance Leap into Power." *New York Times*, July 17, 2024.

RFE/RL Radio Farda. "UAE Delegate Delivers Letter from Trump to Khamenei, Iran Says." Radio Free Europe/Radio Liberty, March 12, 2025.

Sanger, David E. "Iran Complies with Nuclear Deal; Sanctions Are Lifted." *New York Times*, January 16, 2016.

Scherer, Michael. "Trump Says He Decides What 'America First' Means." *The Atlantic*, June 14, 2025.

Swan, Jonathan, Maggie Haberman, Mark Mazzetti, and Ronen Bergman. "How Trump Shifted on Iran Under Pressure from Israel." *New York Times*, June 17, 2025.

Vaez, Ali. "The Iranian Nuclear Deal's Sunset Clauses: Why They Are Not a Path to a Bomb." *Foreign Affairs*, October 3, 2017.

Vance, J. D. *Hillbilly Elegy: A Memoir of a Family and Culture in Crisis.* Harper Press, 2016.

Vance, J. D. "Opioid of the Masses." *The Atlantic*, July 4, 2016.

Chapter 19

Bunch, Lonnie G., III. *A Fool's Errand: Creating the National Museum of African American History and Culture in the Age of Bush, Obama, and Trump*. Smithsonian Books, 2019.

Hernández, Javier C., and Maggie Haberman. "Touring Kennedy Center, Trump Mused on His Childhood 'Aptitude for Music.'" *New York Times*, March 19, 2025.

Jackson, Christine. "Ai Weiwei's Portraits of Dissidents Debut at the Hirshhorn Wednesday." *Washingtonian*, June 27, 2017.

Judkis, Maura. "She Told Trump the Smithsonian Needs Changing. He's Ordered Her to Do It." *New York Times*, April 12, 2025.

McGlone, Peggy. "Lonnie Bunch, the Smithsonian's First Black Leader, on the Challenge of Making It 'a Place That Matters.'" *Washington Post*, June 30, 2019.

Pogrebin, Robin. "Amy Sherald Cancels Her Smithsonian Show, Citing Censorship." *New York Times*, July 24, 2025.

Pogrebin, Robin, and Graham Bowley. "Smithsonian Museum Director Trump Said He Fired Decides to Step Down." *New York Times*, June 13, 2025.

Pogrebin, Robin, Graham Bowley, and Zachary Small. "Smithsonian's Reaction to Trump's Firing of Its Museum Director: Silence." *New York Times*, June 3, 2025.

Chapter 20

Badger, Emily, David A. Fahrenthold, Alicia Parlapiano, and Margot Sanger-Katz. "How Did DOGE Disrupt So Much While Saving So Little?" *New York Times*, December 23, 2025.

Caputo, Marc. "Scoop: Trump's $2 Billion Fundraising Binge." *Axios*, November 5, 2025.

Colvin, Jill, Lisa Mascaro, and Hannah Fingerhut. "Pressure on Iowa Senator Shows Consequences for Republicans Who Oppose Trump." Associated Press, December 12, 2024.

Freedlander, David. "Chris LaCivita, the Swiftboater Coming for Biden." *New York*, February 22, 2024.

Garrett, Luke. "Tipped Workers Expect Tax Boon This Year, but Not a Long-Term Fix." NPR, February 25, 2025.

Grisales, Claudia. "Sen. John Thune, Once a Political Enemy of Trump, Emerges as a Key Ally." NPR, July 2, 2025.

Haberman, Maggie, Jonathan Swan, and Carl Hulse. "Trump Endorses Mike Johnson to Continue as House Speaker." *New York Times*, December 30, 2024.

Isenstadt, Alex. "Trump's 5-Step Push to Keep GOP Control of the House in '26." *Axios*, May 27, 2025.

Karni, Annie, and Jonathan Swan. "Trump, with More Honey than Vinegar, Cements an Iron Grip on Republicans." *New York Times*, March 10, 2025.

Massoglia, Anna. "Million-Dollar Donors Flooded Trump's Second Inauguration." Brennan Center for Justice, July 1, 2025.

Mayer, Jane. "Pete Hegseth's Secret History." *New Yorker*, December 1, 2024.

Megerian, Chris, and Darlene Superville. "Trump's Rose Garden Club Is a Lavish New Hangout for Political Allies and Business Elites." Associated Press, September 24, 2025.

Reese, Reagan. "EXCLUSIVE: Hegseth Confirmation Battle Heats Up with New Ad Targeting Joni Ernst." *Daily Caller*, December 6, 2024.

Schleifer, Theodore, and Shane Goldmacher. "Trump, Raking in Cash, Expands His Power in the G.O.P. Money World." *New York Times*, May 10, 2025.

Sherman, Jake, and Anna Palmer. *The Hill to Die On: The Battle for Congress and the Future of Trump's America.* Penguin Random House, 2020.

Walsh, Steve. "Pete Hegseth's Views About Women and Military Standards." NPR, January 22, 2025.

Wu, Ashley, Doug Mills, Junho Lee, et al. "'He's a Maximalist': Inside Trump's Gilded Oval Office." *New York Times*, December 23, 2025.

Chapter 21

Brown, Julie K. "Alan Dershowitz Suggests Curbing Press Access to Hearing on Jeffrey Epstein Sex Abuse." *Miami Herald*, March 1, 2019.

Bruck, Connie. "Alan Dershowitz, Devil's Advocate." *New Yorker*, July 29, 2019.

Ellison, Sarah. "How MAGA Influencers Put Pressure on Trump, Bondi over Epstein." *Washington Post*, July 19, 2025.

Hill, James. "What Virginia Giuffre Has Said About Trump and Jeffrey Epstein." ABC News, November 12, 2025.

Hill, James, and Aaron Katersky. "Discredited Claims About Clinton, Trump Mentioned in Latest Batch of Epstein Docs." ABC News, January 9, 2024.

Hutzler, Alexandra. "What Trump Has Said About Jeffrey Epstein over the Years, Including on 2024 Campaign Trail." ABC News, July 16, 2025.

Khadeeja, Safdar, and Joe Palazzolo. "Jeffrey Epstein's Friends Sent Him Bawdy Letters for a 50th Birthday Album. One Was from Donald Trump." *Wall Street Journal*, July 17, 2025.

Mehrotra, Dhruv. "The FBI's Jeffrey Epstein Prison Video Had Nearly 3 Minutes Cut Out." *Wired*, July 15, 2025.

Popli, Nik. "Amid Campaign, Trump Kept Epstein Issue at Arm's Length. His Allies Did Not." *Time*, July 17, 2025.

Roberts, Sam. "Virginia Giuffre, Voice in Epstein Sex-Trafficking Scandal, Dies at 41." *New York Times*, April 25, 2025.

Thomas, Landon, Jr. "Jeffrey Epstein: International Moneyman of Mystery." *New York*, October 28, 2002.

Chapter 22

Appelbaum, Binyamin. "Stock Market Rout Has Trump Fixated on Fed Chair Powell." *New York Times*, December 23, 2018.

Bender, Michael C., Rebecca Ballhaus, Peter Nicholas, and Alex Leary. "Trump Steps Up Attacks on Fed Chairman Jerome Powell." *Wall Street Journal*, October 23, 2018.

Casselman, Ben. "Lisa Cook Broke Ground at the Fed, Before Attack by Trump." *New York Times*, August 23, 2025.

Condon, Christopher. "Fed Says It Was 'Honored' by Trump's Tour of Building Site." *Bloomberg News*, July 25, 2025.

Cook, Nancy, Ben White, and Victoria Guida. "Mnuchin Pushing Trump to Pick Jerome Powell for Fed." *Politico*, October 11, 2017.

Cox, Jeff. "Trump Lays into the Federal Reserve, Says He's 'Not Thrilled' About Interest Rate Hikes." CNBC, July 19, 2018.

Dickler, Jessica. "Why Fed Chair Powell Wears Purple Ties—'It's Not That We Are Bipartisan, We Are Nonpolitical.'" CNBC, April 7, 2025.

Gangitano, Alex. "5 Takeaways from Trump's Visit to the Federal Reserve." *The Hill*, July 24, 2025.

Grossman, Matt. "Who Is Kevin Warsh, Trump's Fed Chair Pick?" *Wall Street Journal*, January 30, 2026.

Guida, Victoria. "Trump Formally Nominates Warsh to Chair the Fed." Politico Pro, March 4, 2026.

Guida, Victoria. "Trump Housing Official Brings New Allegation Against Fed's Cook." *Politico*, August 29, 2025.

Haberman, Maggie, and Colby Smith. "Trump Has Draft of Letter to Fire Fed Chair. He Asked Republicans If He Should Send It." *New York Times*, July 16, 2025.

Jacobs, Jennifer, Saleha Mohsin, and Margaret Talev. "Trump Discusses Firing Fed's Powell After Latest Rate Hike, Sources Say." *Bloomberg News*, December 21, 2018.

Klein, Betsy. "'The Best Poles Anywhere in the Country': Trump Installs Gigantic US Flags at the White House." CNN, June 18, 2025.

Liptak, Adam. "A Brief from Every Living Former Fed Chair Could Sway the Justices." *New York Times*, January 21, 2026.

Oprysko, Caitlin. "Trump Asks If Fed's Powell or China's Xi Is the 'Bigger Enemy.'" *Politico*, August 23, 2019.

Rappeport, Alan, and Colby Smith. "Fed Governor Steps Down Early, Giving Trump Opportunity to Shape Central Bank." *New York Times*, August 1, 2025.

Reuters. "Trump Still Wants Negative Interest Rates, but Says Fed Chair Has Improved." May 13, 2020.

Roytburg, Eva. "Another 'Central Casting' Central Banker: Trump's Pick of Kevin Warsh Fits a Well-Established Pattern." *Fortune*, January 30, 2026.

Schaffer, Michael. "Is Trump Using an Obscure Architecture Board to Fire Jerome Powell?" *Politico Magazine*, n.d.

Sherman, Mark. "Supreme Court Lets Lisa Cook Remain as a Federal Reserve Governor for Now in Unsigned Order." Associated Press, October 1, 2025.

Shimkus, Ben. “A Peek Inside the Fed’s Renovations That Are Now at the Center of a DOJ Probe.” *Business Insider*, January 12, 2026.

Siegel, Benjamin. “Why the White House Is Attacking Jerome Powell over the ‘Taj Mahal on the National Mall.’” ABC News, January 12, 2026.

Smialek, Jeanna. *Limitless: The Federal Reserve Takes on a New Age of Crisis.* Penguin Random House, 2023.

Smith, Colby. “Former Fed Official Violated Trading Rules, Disclosures Show.” *New York Times*, November 15, 2025.

Smith, Colby. “Trump Criticizes the Fed in a Private Meeting with Powell.” *New York Times*, May 29, 2025.

Smith, Colby, Alan Rappeport, and Tony Romm. “Powell Fact-Checks Trump on Cost of Fed Renovations.” *New York Times*, July 24, 2025.

Smith, Colby, Jonathan Swan, and Maggie Haberman. “Risk of Financial Panic Tempers Trump on Firing Powell.” *New York Times*, April 18, 2025.

Swan, Jonathan, Maggie Haberman, Jeanna Smialek, and Alan Rappeport. “After Flurry of Cabinet Picks, Trump Rethinks Candidates for Treasury Secretary.” *New York Times*, November 17, 2024.

Swanson, Ana, and Binyamin Appelbaum. “Trump Announces Jerome Powell as New Fed Chairman.” *New York Times*, November 2, 2017.

Thrush, Glenn, and Colby Smith. “Federal Prosecutors Open Investigation into Fed Chair Powell.” *New York Times*, January 11, 2026.

Timiraos, Nick. “If Trump Tries to Fire Powell, Fed Chair Is Ready for a Legal Fight.” *Wall Street Journal*, November 10, 2024.

Timiraos, Nick. *Trillion Dollar Triage: How Jay Powell and the Fed Battled a President and a Pandemic—and Prevented Economic Disaster.* Little, Brown and Company, 2022.

Walsh, Joe. “Trump Says He Has ‘No Intention of Firing’ Federal Reserve Chief Jerome Powell.” CBS News, April 22, 2025.

Chapter 23

Allen, Mike, and Jim VandeHei. “Behind the Curtain—Jensen vs. Dario: ‘There Will Be More Jobs.’” *Axios*, July 14, 2025.

Mickle, Tripp. “How Nvidia’s Jensen Huang Persuaded Trump to Sell A.I. Chips to China.” *New York Times*, July 17, 2025.

Mickle, Tripp, and Ana Swanson. “How Trump and Nvidia’s C.E.O. Became Partners on the International Stage.” *New York Times*, November 19, 2025.

Mickle, Tripp, and Ana Swanson. “Trump Clears Sale of More Powerful Nvidia A.I. Chips to China.” *New York Times*, December 8, 2025.

Mickle, Tripp, and Cade Metz. “Nvidia Comes Out Swinging as Congress Weighs Limits on China Chip Sales.” *New York Times*, September 9, 2025.

Oremus, Will. “How Tech’s Bold Bid to Curb AI Laws Fell Apart.” *Washington Post*, July 1, 2025.

Schreckinger, Ben. “‘Oh, No’: The Day Trump Learned to Tweet.” *Politico*, December 20, 2018.

Steakin, Will. “Inside MAGA’s Growing Fight to Stop Trump’s AI Revolution.” ABC News, November 24, 2025.

Whelan, Robbie, Amrith Ramkumar, Lauren Thomas, and Josh Dawsey. “Inside Intel’s Tricky Dance with Trump.” *Wall Street Journal*, August 24, 2025.

Witt, Stephen. *The Thinking Machine: Jensen Huang, Nvidia, and the World’s Most Coveted Microchip.* Penguin Random House, 2025.

Chapter 24

Associated Press. "What to Know About Gregory Bovino and His Role in Trump's Immigration Crackdown." January 27, 2026.

Barr, William P. *One Damn Thing After Another: Memoirs of an Attorney General.* HarperCollins, 2022.

Cancryn, Adam, Priscilla Alvarez, and Zachary Cohen. "Stephen Miller Takes Center Stage in Trump's Crime and Military Crackdown." CNN, October 11, 2025.

Esper, Mark T. *A Sacred Oath: Memoirs of a Secretary of Defense During Extraordinary Times*. Harper-Collins, 2022.

Flynn, Meagan, and Martin Weil. "D.C. Mayor Bowser Says She Had 'Great Meeting' with Trump at Mar-a-Lago." *Washington Post*, December 31, 2024.

Frontline. "Timeline: What Led to the Tiananmen Square Massacre." June 5, 2019.

Grynbaum, Michael M. "Stephen Miller Cited 'Plenary Authority,' Then Paused. Conspiracy Theories Started Flying." *New York Times*, October 8, 2025.

Hermann, Peter, Sarah Pulliam Bailey, and Michelle Boorstein. "Fire Set at Historic St. John's Church During Protests of George Floyd's Death." *Washington Post*, June 1, 2020.

Hill, James, and Armando Garcia. "Border Patrol Commander Admitted He Lied About Tear Gas Incident, Judge Says, as She Restricts Use of Force by Immigration Agents in Chicago." ABC News, November 7, 2025.

Hill, Jim. "'Power Picnics' Bring Former Presidents to Bakersfield." CNN, October 24, 1993.

Jenkins, Jack. "In Chicago, Clergy and Faith-Based Protesters Say ICE Is Threatening Their Religious Freedom." Religion News Service, October 8, 2025.

Luna, Jackeline. "Video Shows Bovino Giving Orders to Federal Agents in Los Angeles." *New York Times*, January 29, 2026.

Magpayo, Genesis. "What Is the Insurrection Act? Here's What Trump Has Said About Using It." PBS News, October 27, 2025.

Marcus, Ruth. "Clinton Rejects Call for Guard in D.C." *Washington Post*, October 25, 1993.

McCarthy, Bill. "White House's Chicago 'Chaos' Video Uses Footage from Other Cities." AFP Fact Check, October 14, 2025.

Nehamas, Nicholas, and Campbell Robertson. "Trump Threatens Federal Takeover of Washington After Member of DOGE Is Assaulted." *New York Times*, August 5, 2025.

Nguyen, Alex, Marijke Friedman, and Paul Cobler. "Greg Abbott Authorizes Trump to Deploy Texas National Guard to Other States." *Texas Tribune*, October 5, 2025.

Plaskin, Glenn. "The 1990 Playboy Interview with Donald Trump." *Playboy*, March 1, 1990.

Polansek, Tom, and Ted Hesson. "Trump Administration Says It Launches ICE Crackdown in Illinois." Reuters, September 9, 2025.

Queally, James, and Brittny Mejia. "Attacks on ICE up 1,000%? Trump Administration Claim Not Backed Up by Court Records." *Los Angeles Times*, December 1, 2025.

Regalado, Francesca, Jin Yu Young, Ali Watkins, and Mark Walker. "What We Know About the Shooting of National Guard Troops in Washington." *New York Times*, November 26, 2025.

Rogers, Katie. "Trump Takes Control of D.C. Police, Citing 'Bloodthirsty Criminals.' But Crime Is Down." *New York Times*, August 11, 2025.

Savage, Charlie, Jonathan Swan, and Maggie Haberman. "Deploying on U.S. Soil: How Trump Would Use Soldiers Against Riots, Crime and Migrants." *New York Times*, August 17, 2024.

Spagat, Elliot. "Gregory Bovino, Head of Los Angeles Campaign, Shows How Immigration Agents Rack Up Arrests." Associated Press, September 4, 2025.

Spagat, Elliot. "In His Words: How Gregory Bovino Became a Face of Trump's Mass Deportations and Ended His Career." Associated Press, March 17, 2026.

Stelter, Brian. "Dr. Phil Was Embedded with ICE During Controversial Los Angeles Immigration Raids." CNN, June 9, 2025.

Sullivan, Tim. "In Chicago, an Immense Show of Force Signals a Sharp Escalation in White House Immigration Crackdown." Associated Press, October 21, 2025.

Tareen, Sophia. "Using Helicopters and Chemical Agents, Immigration Agents Become Increasingly Aggressive in Chicago." Associated Press, October 6, 2025.

Treisman, Rachel. "How Long Can Trump's D.C. Takeover Last? Here's What to Know." NPR, August 20, 2025.

Chapter 25

Harwell, Drew. "The White House Wants You to Laugh at Its Deportation Memes." *Washington Post*, June 14, 2025.

Kanno-Youngs, Zolan, Hamed Aleaziz, and Arijeta Lajka. "Trump's Immigration P.R. Campaign Enters a New Militarized Phase." *New York Times*, June 12, 2025.

Poniewozik, James. "The Trump Administration's Department of Homeland Publicity." *New York Times*, April 5, 2025.

Chapter 26

Altus, Kristen. "Former President Trump Calls the 'Enemy from Within' More Dangerous than Any Foreign Entity." Fox News, October 13, 2024.

Andrews, Natalie. "Friendship with Charlie Kirk Helped Propel JD Vance to Vice Presidency." *Wall Street Journal*, September 12, 2025.

Babb, Carla. "More Troops Suspended Pending Investigations into Kirk-Related Posts." *Military Times*, September 24, 2025.

Barrett, Devlin. "The Battle in Virginia Over an Activist Who Protested Stephen Miller." *New York Times*, November 3, 2025.

Barrett, Devlin. "Justice Dept. Official Pushes Prosecutors to Investigate George Soros's Foundation." *New York Times*, September 25, 2025.

Bernstein, Joseph. "When Did Cancel Culture Become 'Consequence Culture'?" *New York Times*, September 18, 2025.

Bodroghkozy, Aniko. "Assassination Videos Used to Be Something We Were Spared." *Time*, September 20, 2025.

Bogel-Burroughs, Nicholas. "Texts from Suspect in Charlie Kirk Shooting Offer Insight into a Motive." *New York Times*, September 16, 2025.

Bogel-Burroughs, Nicholas, and Bernard Mokam. "A Broad Wave of Firings Followed Charlie Kirk's Assassination." *New York Times*, September 26, 2025.

Burns, Dasha. "Vance to Escort Charlie Kirk's Body Back to Phoenix." *Politico*, September 11, 2025.

Childers, Andrew. "State Department Warns Immigrants Not to Mock Kirk's Death." *Axios*, September 11, 2025.

Demirjian, Karoun. "In Their Own Words: Trump and Top Officials Change Tone on Free Speech." *New York Times*, September 18, 2025.

Demissie, Hannah, and Alexandra Hutzler. "Vance Says 'Left-Wing Extremism' Helped Lead to Charlie Kirk's Killing." ABC News, September 15, 2025.

Draper, Robert. "How Charlie Kirk Became the Youth Whisperer of the American Right." *New York Times Magazine*, February 10, 2025.

Fausset, Richard, Sheera Frenkel, and Aric Toler. "The Police Found Messages After Kirk's Killing. What They Mean Is Unclear." *New York Times*, September 13, 2025.

Gamio, Lazaro, Ashley Wu, and Allison McCann. "Maps, Video and Photos: Where and When Charlie Kirk Was Fatally Shot." *New York Times*, September 10, 2025.

George, Olivia. "She Protested at Stephen Miller's Home. Now Police Are Investigating." *Washington Post*, January 18, 2026.

Gomez Licon, Adriana, and Bill Barrow. "How Charlie Kirk Helped Shape a Conservative Force for a New Generation." Associated Press, September 11, 2025.

Healy, Jack, and Anna Griffin. "A Note, a Gun and a Mother's Conscience Led to an Arrest in Kirk's Killing." *New York Times*, September 17, 2025.

Matthews, Alex Leeds, and Brian Stelter. "Timeline: Jimmy Kimmel's Suspension and Planned Return to ABC." CNN, September 22, 2025.

Mediaite. "Trump Treasury Secretary Says Far-Left Organizations Being Treated Like Terror Suspects 'After 9/11.'" October 15, 2025.

Perez, Evan, Zachary Cohen, Natasha Bertrand, Kylie Atwood, and Kristen Holmes. "Exclusive: Secret Service Ramped Up Security After Intel of Iran Plot to Assassinate Trump; No Known Connection to Shooting." CNN, July 16, 2024.

Robertson, Noah, and Tara Copp. "Hegseth's Sprawling Hunt for Charlie Kirk Critics Spans Nearly 300 Investigations." *Washington Post*, October 8, 2025.

Rogers, Katie, and Zolan Kanno-Youngs. "White House Plans Broad Crackdown on Liberal Groups." *New York Times*, September 15, 2025.

Sanger, David E. "Trump Downplays Violence on the Right and Says the Left Is the Problem." *New York Times*, September 12, 2025.

Scherer, Michael, Missy Ryan, and Ashley Parker. "Top Trump Officials Are Moving onto Military Bases." *The Atlantic*, October 30, 2025.

Sentner, Irie. "Vance, White House Promise to 'Go After' Left-Leaning Organizations." *Politico*, September 15, 2025.

SPLC Hatewatch. "Antisemitic Conspiracy Theories Claim Israel, Mossad to Blame for Kirk Killing." October 28, 2025.

Tanner, Courtney. "'I Heard That Bullet': Charlie Kirk's Security Chief Recounts the Fatal Shooting and What Happened Next." *Salt Lake Tribune*, November 19, 2025.

Treisman, Rachel. "33 Hours: A Timeline of Charlie Kirk's Shooting and the Search for a Suspect." NPR, September 12, 2025.

Walker, Mark, Alan Blinder, and Anushka Patil. "Security at Kirk Event Seemed Light to Those Who Attended." *New York Times*, September 11, 2025.

Chapter 27

Barrett, Devlin, Glenn Thrush, and Alan Feuer. "Grand Jury Indicts Longtime Trump Target, Former F.B.I. Director James Comey." *New York Times*, September 25, 2025.

Barrett, Devlin, Glenn Thrush, and Jonah E. Bromwich. "New York Attorney General Letitia James Is Indicted After Trump's Pressure Campaign." *New York Times*, October 9, 2025.

Barrett, Devlin, Glenn Thrush, and Minho Kim. "John Bolton Indicted over Handling of Classified Information." *New York Times*, October 16, 2025.

Dawsey, Josh, Sadie Gurman, and Aruna Viswanatha. "Inside the Justice Department Where the President Calls the Shots." *Wall Street Journal*, October 8, 2025.

Rabinowitz, Hannah. "Attorney General Bondi Orders Prosecutors to Start Grand Jury Probe into Obama Officials over Russia Investigation." CNN, August 4, 2025.

Richer, Alanna Durkin, and Michael Kunzelman. "Justice Department Fails Twice to Re-Indict New York Attorney General James, AP Source Says." Associated Press, December 11, 2025.

Smith, Dave. "Meet Lindsey Halligan, the 36-Year-Old Former Miss Colorado Hopeful Who Only Worked 3 Federal Cases Before Trump Promoted Her to U.S. Attorney." *Fortune*, September 25, 2025.

Thrush, Glenn, Alan Feuer, Devlin Barrett, and Maggie Haberman. "Trump's 'Russia Hoax' Grievance." *New York Times*, August 5, 2025.

Thrush, Glenn, Maggie Haberman, Alan Feuer, and Tyler Pager. "Inside the Trump Administration's Push to Prosecute James Comey." *New York Times*, September 27, 2025.

Chapter 28

Barnes, Julian E., and Charlie Savage. "Video of Boat Strike Shows Survivors Waving Before Fatal Follow-Up Attack." *New York Times*, December 5, 2025.

Barnes, Julian E., Tyler Pager, and Eric Schmitt. "Inside 'Operation Absolute Resolve,' the U.S. Effort to Capture Maduro." *New York Times*, January 3, 2026.

Bertrand, Natasha, and Avery Schmitz. "Here's What the US Military Has Positioned as Trump Pressures Venezuela." CNN, October 19, 2025.

Cooper, Helene, Maggie Haberman, Charlie Savage, and Eric Schmitt. "Trump Directs Military to Target Foreign Drug Cartels." *New York Times*, August 8, 2025.

Esper, Mark T. *A Sacred Oath: Memoirs of a Secretary of Defense During Extraordinary Times*. HarperCollins, 2022.

Fitzpatrick, Sarah, and Missy Ryan. "The Pentagon's Lawyers Are Now Under Review." *The Atlantic*, March 12, 2026.

Gasparino, Charles. "'Donroe Doctrine' Ousted Maduro—and It's a Smash Hit for Investors of Venezuelan Bonds." *New York Post*, January 9, 2026.

Goodin, Emily. "Trump Threatens to Expand Drug War to Land After Deadly Strike in the Pacific." *Miami Herald*, October 22, 2025.

Hegseth, Pete. *The War on Warriors: Behind the Betrayal of the Men Who Keep Us Free*. Broadside Books, 2024.

Horton, Alex, and Samuel Oakford. "U.S. Special Operations Helicopters, B-52s near Venezuela Expand Caribbean Mission." *Washington Post*, October 16, 2025.

Khardori, Ankush. "Remember the Torture Memos? The Boat Strike Memos May Be Worse." *Politico Magazine*, December 11, 2025.

Madhani, Aamer, and Regina Garcia Cano. "U.S. Carried Out Strike on Drug-Carrying Vessel That Left from Venezuela, Trump Says." Associated Press, September 2, 2025.

Mazzei, Patricia. "Powerful Venezuelan Lawmaker May Have Issued Death Order Against Rubio." *Miami Herald*, August 17, 2017.

Mellen, Riley. "Satellite Data Reveals How the U.S. Navy Is Deployed Near Venezuela." *New York Times*, November 21, 2025.

Nicas, Jack, and Helene Cooper. "Mexico Winds Down Search for Survivor of U.S. Boat Strike." *New York Times*, October 31, 2025.

Pager, Tyler, Anatoly Kurmanaev, and Julian E. Barnes. "Why Trump Refused to Back Venezuela's Machado: Fears of Chaos, and Fraying Ties." *New York Times*, January 5, 2026.

Patil, Anushka. "A Timeline of Trump's Strikes on Vessels He Says Are Smuggling Drugs." *New York Times*, February 17, 2026.

Rodriguez, Sabrina. "How Marco Rubio Runs Trump's Latin America Policy." *Politico*, August 3, 2020.

Savage, Charlie. "Trump Team Calls Maduro a 'Cartel' Boss. That Word Doesn't Mean What You Think." *New York Times*, November 18, 2025.

Schmitt, Eric. "Alvin Holsey, Admiral Who Oversaw Boat Strikes Off Venezuela's Coast, Retires." *New York Times*, December 12, 2025.

Schmitt, Eric, and Tyler Pager. "Head of the U.S. Military's Southern Command Is Stepping Down, Officials Say." *New York Times*, October 16, 2025.

Siniawski, Natalia, and Raul Cortes. "Mexico's Sheinbaum Says US Military Intervention Ruled Out After Talks with Trump." Reuters, January 12, 2026.

Swan, Jonathan, Maggie Haberman, Charlie Savage, and Emiliano Rodríguez Mega. "Trump Wanted to Fire Missiles at Mexico. Now the G.O.P. Wants to Send Troops." *New York Times*, October 3, 2023.

Turse, Nick. "U.S. Attacked Boat Near Venezuela Multiple Times to Kill Survivors." *The Intercept*, September 10, 2025.

Wee, Sui-Lee, and Camille Elemia. "For Duterte, Signs of a Reckoning Years After He Ordered a Deadly Drug War." *New York Times*, March 10, 2025.

Wong, Edward, Tyler Pager, Charlie Savage, Julian E. Barnes, and Maria Abi-Habib. "How Oil, Drugs and Immigration Fueled Trump's Venezuela Campaign." *New York Times*, December 27, 2025.

Chapter 29

Associated Press. "Israel's Netanyahu Says He Has Nominated Trump for a Nobel Peace Prize. What Happens Next?" July 8, 2025.

Fassihi, Farnaz. "In Major Breakthrough, U.N. Security Council Adopts U.S. Peace Plan for Gaza." *New York Times*, November 17, 2025.

Holliday, Shelby, Michael R. Gordon, Lara Seligman, and Summer Said. "How Israel Used Ballistic Missiles from the Red Sea to Carry Out Its Audacious Qatar Attack." *Wall Street Journal*, September 12, 2025.

Karni, Annie. "Jared Kushner's Mission Impossible." *Politico Magazine*, February 11, 2017.

Kershner, Isabel. "Israelis Rally for Hostages in Gaza, Hoping It Will Be the Last Time." *New York Times*, October 11, 2025.

Kingsley, Patrick, Rawan Sheikh Ahmad, Yan Zhuang, Aaron Boxerman, and Michael Levenson. "Israel Resumes Strikes on Gaza, Killing Hundreds, as Cease-Fire Breaks Down." *New York Times*, March 18, 2025.

Kirkpatrick, David D., and Kate Kelly. "Before Giving Billions to Jared Kushner, Saudi Investment Fund Had Big Doubts." *New York Times*, April 10, 2022.

Mazzetti, Mark, Adam Rasgon, Katie Rogers, and Luke Broadwater. "How Fury over Israel's Qatar Attack Pushed Netanyahu on Gaza." *New York Times*, October 3, 2025.

Mills, Andrew, Jana Choukeir, Ahmed Elimam, and Jeff Mason. "Israel Attacks Hamas Leaders in Qatar, Trump Says He's 'Very Unhappy' About Strike." Reuters, September 9, 2025.

Nereim, Vivian. "What Are the Abraham Accords, Trump's 2020 Mideast Deals?" *New York Times*, October 13, 2025.

Nissenbaum, Dion, and Summer Said. "Jared Kushner's Deal-Making Career Off to Sluggish Start." *Wall Street Journal*, August 18, 2023.

Nissenbaum, Dion, and Summer Said. "Saudi Arabia, Qatar Near Deal to End Gulf Dispute, Officials Say." *Wall Street Journal*, December 4, 2020.

Pesoli, Mike, and Michelle L. Price. "Trump's Quest for the Nobel Peace Prize Falls Short Again Despite High-Profile Nominations." Associated Press, October 10, 2025.

Rasgon, Adam, and Isabel Kershner. "What Drove Israel's Brazen Attack on Hamas in Qatar?" *New York Times*, September 11, 2025.

Rasgon, Adam, Vivian Nereim, and Ronen Bergman. "Israel Attempts to Kill Hamas Leadership in Airstrike on Qatar, a Gaza War Mediator." *New York Times*, September 9, 2025.

Ravid, Barak. "Direct Meeting Between Trump Envoys and Hamas Leaders Sealed Gaza Deal." *Axios*, October 13, 2025.

Ravid, Barak. "Netanyahu Apologizes to Qatar for Violating Sovereignty with Airstrike." *Axios*, September 29, 2025.

Ravid, Barak, and Marc Caputo. "Tony Blair and Jared Kushner Brief Trump on Gaza Post-War Plans." *Axios*, August 27, 2025.

Reuters. "Kushner's Affinity's Assets Jump to $4.8 Billion After Gulf Cash Injection." March 28, 2025.

Rogers, Katie, and Tyler Pager. "How Jared Kushner, a Self-Described 'Deal Guy,' Helped Broker a Gaza Breakthrough." *New York Times*, October 9, 2025.

Rowlands, Lyndal. "Indonesia, Morocco, Kosovo Among 5 Countries to Send Troops Under Gaza Plan." *Al Jazeera*, February 20, 2026.

Schwartz, Felicia, Eli Stokols, Nicholas Vinocur, and Hans von der Burchard. "Trump Promises Arab, Muslim Leaders He Won't Let Israel Annex the West Bank." *Politico*, September 24, 2025.

Scribner, Herb. "Trump's Board of Peace Debuts: Who's In, Who's Out, Who Could Join Next." *Axios*, February 19, 2026.

Swan, Jonathan, Kate Kelly, Maggie Haberman, and Mark Mazzetti. "Kushner Firm Got Hundreds of Millions from 2 Persian Gulf Nations." *New York Times*, March 30, 2023.

Chapter 30

Ball, Molly. "Trump Is Losing Political Ground on Immigration." *Wall Street Journal*, June 20, 2025.

Barrett, Devlin, and Tyler Pager. "Trump Said to Demand Justice Dept. Pay Him $230 Million for Past Cases." *New York Times*, October 21, 2025.

Grynbaum, Michael M. "Trump Refiles His $15 Billion Defamation Lawsuit Against *The New York Times*." *New York Times*, October 17, 2025.

Harbison, Judy. "The Blue Room: Restored Again to Its 1817 Style." *New York Times*, January 7, 1973.

Mahler, Jonathan, and Jim Rutenberg. "How Rupert Murdoch's Empire of Influence Remade the World." *New York Times*, April 3, 2019.

Mangan, Dan. "Trump Dined with Rupert Murdoch Despite Suing Him for $10B over Epstein Letter: Report." CNBC, October 22, 2025.

Robertson, Katie. "Trump Sues *Wall Street Journal* for Article on Note to Epstein." *New York Times*, July 18, 2025.

UPI. "Murdoch Becomes U.S. Citizen, Can Buy TV Network." September 4, 1985.

Chapter 31

Anderson, Jess. "Why 'Chelsea's Trophy' Is in the US President's Office." BBC Sport, August 20, 2025.

Ballhaus, Rebecca, Josh Dawsey, and C. Ryan Barber. "Inside the New Fast Track to a Presidential Pardon." *Wall Street Journal*, December 23, 2025.

Ballhaus, Rebecca, Josh Dawsey, Patricia Kowsmann, and Angus Berwick. "Trump Pardons Convicted Binance Founder." *Wall Street Journal*, October 23, 2025.

Ballhaus, Rebecca, Dana Mattioli, and Annie Linskey. "How the Trumps Turned an Election Victory into a Cash Bonanza." *Wall Street Journal*, February 13, 2025.

Berwick, Angus, Patricia Kowsmann, and Rebecca Ballhaus. "How a Billionaire Felon Boosted Trump's Crypto Company En Route to a Pardon." *Wall Street Journal*, October 29, 2025.

Buettner, Russ, Susanne Craig, and Mike McIntire. "Long-Concealed Records Show Trump's Chronic Losses and Years of Tax Avoidance." *New York Times*, September 27, 2020.

Dale, Brady. "Trump's Promises to Bitcoin Conference: 'Fire' SEC Chair, Build 'Strategic Bitcoin Stockpile.'" *Axios*, July 27, 2024.

Duehren, Andrew, and Alan Feuer. "Justice Dept. Struggles to Respond to Trump's Suit Against I.R.S." *New York Times*, March 31, 2026.

Editorial Board. "How Trump Has Pocketed $1,408,500,000." *New York Times*, January 20, 2026.

Judkis, Maura. "The New Don Jr.-Connected D.C. Club Has Been a Mystery. Here Are the Details." *Washington Post*, June 9, 2025.

Kamin, Debra, and Bradley Hope. "Where Mideast Envoy Pitched Peace, His Son Pitched Investors." *New York Times*, September 26, 2025.

Kang, Cecilia, Tripp Mickle, Ryan Mac, David Yaffe-Bellany, and Theodore Schleifer. "Silicon Valley's Man in the White House Is Benefiting Himself and His Friends." *New York Times*, November 30, 2025.

Kessler, Sam, Rebecca Ballhaus, Eliot Brown, and Angus Berwick. "'Spy Sheikh' Bought Secret Stake in Trump Company." *Wall Street Journal*, January 31, 2026.

Khan-Mullins, Kyle. "How 19-Year-Old Barron Trump Is Worth $150 Million." *Forbes*, October 6, 2025.

Kirkpatrick, David D. "The Number." *New Yorker*, January 31, 2026.

Kirkpatrick, David D. "Trumps Profiteering Hits $4 Billion." *New Yorker*, January 31, 2026.

LaFraniere, Sharon. "Trump Says He Has No Issue with His Family's Foreign Business Deals." *New York Times*, January 8, 2026.

LeVine, Marianne, Liz Goodwin, and Dan Lamothe. "Kristi Noem Is Living Rent-Free in Home Used by Coast Guard Commandant." *Washington Post*, August 15, 2025.

Lipton, Eric, and David Yaffe-Bellany. "Trump's Cryptocurrency Surges to Become One of the World's Most Valuable." *New York Times*, January 19, 2025.

Lipton, Eric, David Yaffe-Bellany, and Ben Protess. "Secret Deals, Foreign Investments, Presidential Policy Changes: The Rise of Trump's Crypto Firm." *New York Times*, April 29, 2025.

Loizos, Connie. "David Sacks and the Blurred Lines of Government Service." *TechCrunch*, July 19, 2025.

Rogers, Katie. "In Trump's Administration, Military Housing Is Becoming a Hot Commodity." *New York Times*, March 21, 2026.

Roush, Ty. "Trump Pardons Billionaire Binance Founder—And His Crypto Ally—Changpeng Zhao." *Forbes*, October 23, 2025.

Swan, Jonathan, Kate Kelly, Maggie Haberman, and Mark Mazzetti. "Kushner Firm Got Hundreds of Millions from 2 Persian Gulf Nations." *New York Times*, March 30, 2023.

Swetlitz, Ike. "Donald Trump, Bad Science, and the Vitamin Company That Went Bust." *STAT News*, November 4, 2015.

Trump, Donald J. "Rona Barrett's 1980 Interview of Donald Trump." Interview by Rona Barrett. *Washington Post*, October 6, 1980.

Yaffe-Bellany, David. "At a Dubai Conference, Trump's Conflicts Take Center Stage." *New York Times*, May 1, 2025.

Chapter 32

Ainsley, Julia. "'No Expense Has Been Spared': Inside a Luxury Jet DHS Wants to Buy for Deportations." NBC News, February 19, 2026.

Ali, Idrees, Phil Stewart, Shariq Khan, and Marianna Parraga. "Trump Orders 'Blockade' of Sanctioned Oil Tankers Leaving, Entering Venezuela." Reuters, December 17, 2025.

Andrews, Travis M., Jeremy B. Merrill, and Shelly Tan. "Kennedy Center Ticket Sales Have Plummeted Since Trump Takeover." *Washington Post*, October 31, 2025.

Ballhaus, Rebecca, Josh Dawsey, and C. Ryan Barber. "Inside the New Fast Track to a Presidential Pardon." *Wall Street Journal*, December 23, 2025.

Bazail-Eimil, Eric, and James Bikales. "US Seizes Cuba-Bound Venezuelan Oil Tanker, Ramping Up Pressure on Maduro." *Politico*, December 10, 2025.

Blum, Howard. "Trump: Development of a Manhattan Developer." *New York Times*, August 26, 1980.

Bose, Nandita, and Courtney Rozen. "Trump Puts His Own Name on US Institute of Peace Ahead of Rwanda-Congo Peace Deal." Reuters, December 4, 2025.

Bromwich, Jonah E. "A Pardon and a Prosecution in New York Show Trump's Personal Geopolitics." *New York Times*, January 3, 2026.

Brown, Julie K., and Emily Goodin. "Epstein Files Reveal His Obsession with Trump." *Miami Herald*, November 14, 2025.

Buck, Ivy, and Anastasia Tsioulcas. "Here's Who's Canceled Their Kennedy Center Performances Since Trump Took Over." NPR, March 2, 2026.

Cameron, Chris. "Presidential History, According to Trump." *New York Times*, December 17, 2025.

Cameron, Chris, and Maxine Joselow. "Trump Administration Will Raise Prices for Foreign Visitors at National Parks." *New York Times*, November 25, 2025.

Caputo, Marc. "Scoop: The Letter Behind Trump's Pardon of Honduras' Ex-President for Drug Trafficking." *Axios*, December 1, 2025.

Castro-Root, Gabe. "National Parks Drop Free Entrance on M.L.K. Day and Juneteenth." *New York Times*, December 8, 2025.

Crane, Emily. "Trump Taunts Dems with 'Trump 2028' Hats During Failed Government Shutdown Negotiations." *New York Post*, October 1, 2025.

Eder, Steve, Michael C. Bender, and David Enrich. "How Trump Appears in the Epstein Files." *New York Times*, February 1, 2026.

Enrich, David. "Federal Prosecutor Was Surprised by Trump's Flights on Epstein's Jet." *New York Times*, December 23, 2025.

Friedman, Amanda, and Doug Palmer. "Trump Threatens a 25 Percent Tariff on Countries That Buy Oil and Gas from Venezuela." *Politico*, March 24, 2025.

Gamio, Lazaro, Martín González Gómez, Malika Khurana, et al. "Maps, Videos and Photos: How Maduro's Capture Unfolded." *New York Times*, January 4, 2026.

Gold, Michael. "Epstein Alleged in Emails That Trump Knew of His Conduct." *New York Times*, November 12, 2025.

The Guardian. "Trump Says Maduro's Days Are Numbered but 'Doubts' US Will Go to War with Venezuela." November 2, 2025.

Kelly, John. "Next up in the 'Blame Nixon?' Game: Jackie Kennedy's Plaques." *Washington Post*, March 21, 2010.

Kurmanaev, Anatoly, Mariana Martínez, and Tyler Pager. "The Fall of a Strongman: Inside Maduro's Last Days in Power." *New York Times*, February 25, 2026.

Lalljee, Jason. "Trump 'Walk of Fame' Trolls Biden with Autopen Signature in Place of Portrait." *Axios*, September 24, 2025.

Linskey, Annie, Jessica Toonkel, Josh Dawsey, and Dave Michaels. "Behind Trump's Push to Remake the Kennedy Center in His Own Image." *Wall Street Journal*, February 10, 2026.

McFadden, Robert D. "Jacqueline Kennedy Onassis Dies of Cancer at 64." *New York Times*, May 20, 1994.

Pellish, Aaron, Dasha Burns, and Alec Hernandez. "Trump and Republicans Admonish Others for Their Election Losses." *Politico*, November 5, 2025.

Schmidt, Samantha, Peter Jamison, and Maria Sacchetti. "Trump to Send Venezuelans Back to Maduro's Repressive State." *Washington Post*, February 1, 2025.

Van Natta, Don Jr., and Adam Schefter. "Sources: Trump Wants Commanders' New D.C. Stadium Named for Him." ESPN, November 8, 2025.

Chapter 33

Aleaziz, Hamed, Zolan Kanno-Youngs, and Ernesto Londoño. "New ICE Operation Is Said to Target Somali Migrants in Twin Cities." *New York Times*, December 2, 2025.

Bender, Michael C., Michael Gold, Hamed Aleaziz, Maggie Haberman, and Zolan Kanno-Youngs. "Trump Announces He Is Replacing Noem with Oklahoma Senator." *New York Times*, March 5, 2026.

Bogel-Burroughs, Nicholas, Ann Hinga Klein, and Dan Simmons. "Who Was Renee Good, the Woman Killed by an ICE Agent in Minneapolis?" *New York Times*, January 10, 2026.

Bosman, Julie. "Private Autopsy Shows Renee Good Was Shot at Least 3 Times, Lawyers Say." *New York Times*, January 21, 2026.

Cameron, Chris. "What Is the Insurrection Act That Trump Says He's Considering?" *New York Times*, November 6, 2025.

Erden, Bora, Devon Lum, Helmuth Rosales, et al. "Timeline: A Moment-by-Moment Look at the Shooting of Alex Pretti." *New York Times*, January 24, 2026.

Fassihi, Farnaz, Adam Rasgon, Eric Schmitt, and Michael Levenson. "Trump Says 'Time for Peace' After Iran Gives Warning Before Firing on U.S. Base." *New York Times*, June 23, 2025.

Garip, Patricia, and Eric Martin. "Brazil Billionaire Flew to Venezuela to Urge Maduro to Step Down." *Bloomberg News*, December 3, 2025.

Hudson, John, and Tara Copp. "Trump's Top General Foresees Acute Risks in an Attack on Iran." *Washington Post*, February 23, 2026.

Jimison, Robert. "Rubio Walks Back Suggestion That Israel Forced U.S. Hand in Iran Strikes." *New York Times*, March 3, 2026.

Jouvenal, Justin. "Trump Officials Accused of Defying 1 in 3 Judges Who Ruled Against Him." *Washington Post*, July 21, 2025.

Kanno-Youngs, Zolan. "Trump Called for 'De-Escalation' in Minneapolis. It Didn't Last Long." *New York Times*, January 30, 2026.

Kanno-Youngs, Zolan. "We Pressed Trump on His Conclusion About the ICE Shooting. Here's What He Said." *New York Times*, January 8, 2026.

Kanno-Youngs, Zolan, and Hamed Aleaziz. "Kristi Noem Survived Many Crises. Then She Crossed a Trump Red Line." *New York Times*, March 6, 2026.

Kanno-Youngs, Zolan, and Shawn McCreesh. "Trump Calls Somalis 'Garbage' He Doesn't Want in the Country." *New York Times*, December 2, 2025.

Kavi, Aishvarya, and David E. Sanger. "Trump Suggests He Will 'De-Escalate' in Minneapolis, Without Offering Details." *New York Times*, January 27, 2026.

Knickmeyer, Ellen, Michelle L. Price, and Stephany Matat. "Trump Meets with Israeli Prime Minister Netanyahu at Mar-a-Lago." Associated Press, July 26, 2024.

Knoll, Corina, Julie Bosman, and Maia Coleman. "Alex Jeffrey Pretti Knew He Wanted to Help Others." *New York Times*, January 24, 2026.

Londoño, Ernesto. "How Fraud Swamped Minnesota's Social Services System on Tim Walz's Watch." *New York Times*, November 29, 2025.

Lum, Devon, and Haley Willis. "Videos Show Moments in Which Agents Killed a Man in Minneapolis." *New York Times*, January 24, 2026.

Mazzetti, Mark, Julian E. Barnes, Tyler Pager, et al. "How Trump Decided to Go to War." *New York Times*, March 2, 2026.

McSwane, J. David. "Two CBP Agents Identified in Alex Pretti Shooting." *ProPublica*, February 1, 2026.

Nerozzi, Diana, and Eli Stokols. "Vance Was 'Skeptical' Voice in White House on Iran Strikes." *Politico*, March 13, 2026.

Perez, Evan, Zachary Cohen, Natasha Bertrand, Kylie Atwood, and Kristen Holmes. "Exclusive: Secret Service Ramped Up Security After Intel of Iran Plot to Assassinate Trump; No Known Connection to Shooting." CNN, July 16, 2024.

Ravid, Barak, and Marc Caputo. "Trump's Top General Warns of Iran Strike Risks." *Axios*, February 23, 2026.

Raymond, Nate, Kristina Cooke, and Brad Heath. "Courts Have Ruled 4,400 Times That ICE Jailed People Illegally. It Hasn't Stopped." Reuters, February 14, 2026.

Sakellariadis, John. "Iran Has a Hit List of Former Trump Aides. The U.S. Is Scrambling to Protect Them." *Politico*, October 11, 2024.

Schmitt, Eric. "Trump's Frustration with Generals Resulted in an Unconventional Pick." *New York Times*, February 23, 2025.

Stein, Robin, Devon Lum, Dmitriy Khavin, et al. "Video Analysis of ICE Shooting Sheds Light on Contested Moments." *New York Times*, January 15, 2026.

Stephanopoulos, George. *The Situation Room: The Inside Story of Presidents in Crisis*. With Lisa Dickey. Grand Central Publishing, 2024.

Epilogue

Judis, John B. "Trump as Alexander the Great: A Theory That Explains Iran (And Everything Else)." *NOTUS*, March 15, 2026.

Knoll, Corina, Christina Morales, Pooja Salhotra, Jacey Fortin, and Susan C. Beachy. "These American Service Members Died in the Iran Conflict." *New York Times*, March 14, 2026.

Metz, Sam, Will Weissert, Julia Frankel, and Cara Anna. "Trump Says That He's Asked 'About 7' Countries to Join Coalition to Police Iran's Strait of Hormuz." Associated Press, March 16, 2026.

Romm, Tony. "White House Seeks $1.5 Trillion for Defense in New Budget Request." *New York Times*, April 3, 2026.

Sanger, David E., Tyler Pager, Katie Rogers, and Zolan Kanno-Youngs. "Trump Lays Out a Vision of Power Restrained Only by 'My Own Morality.'" *New York Times*, January 8, 2026.

Index

Abbott, Greg, 282
ABC, 139–40, 143, 158, 166, 196, 232, 303
Abraham Accords, 61, 193, 329, 330, 340
Abrego Garcia, Kilmar, 164–68
Abu Dhabi, 188, 328
Ackman, Bill, 121
ActBlue, 301
Adams, Cindy, 342
Adams, John, 208
Adams, John Quincy, 208
Affinity Partners, 329
affordability, 347, 349, 374–75, 389, 409
Affordable Care Act (Obamacare), 45, 218, 371–72
Afghanistan, xvii, xxiii, xxiv, 14
Africa, xvii, 322, 323
AI (artificial intelligence), 256–67, 354
  Biden administration and, 256, 258, 259, 263
  ChatGPT, 256–58, 286
  chips in, 111–13, 258–67
  dangers of, 261–63
  data centers for, 257, 258, 259, 260, 262, 263, 353
  deepfakes, 257
  job loss from, 262
Air Force, Department of, 181, 359 397
Air Force One, 49, 80, 120, 181, 183
Air Force Two, 297, 299
airlines, 38, 122
air traffic controllers, 108–9
Alaska, 105
Alexander the Great, 411
Al Hol detention camp, 50
Alien Enemies Act, 162–64, 166
Al-Qaeda, 304, 321, 325
Altman, Sam, 256
Amazon, 6, 99, 359, 364
America First doctrine, 36, 72–73, 83, 194, 197, 316, 347, 369, 402
America First Legal, 28
American Bitcoin, 354–55
American Civil Liberties Union, 163
American Revolution, 160
antifa, 280, 299
antisemitism, 136–38, 186, 298
ANUFH (Arlington Neighbors United for Humanity), 300
Apple, xxvi, 6, 288
Apprentice, The, 86
Araghchi, Abbas, 188–89, 190, 191
Arc de Triomphe, 369–71
Arc de Trump (Independence Arch), 344, 369–71
artificial intelligence, *see* AI
Aryam Investment 1, 352
AsiaSat, 153
Assad, Bashar al-, 13, 400
Associated Press, 276
Atlantic, The, 154, 194
Attila the Hun, 411
Austerlitz, Battle of, 369
Australia, 343
automobile industry, 91–92, 113, 115, 116, 121, 177
Axios, 218, 402

Bahrain, 329
Baier, Bret, 127, 196
Bailey, Andrew, 306
Bank of England, 66
Bannon, Steve, xx, xxiii, 22, 66, 185, 219, 260, 262–63, 356
Barnea, David, 394

Barr, William, xxiv, 18, 274
Barra, Mary, 91–93
Barrett, Wayne, xxvii
Bartiromo, Maria, 264
Batista, Fulgencio, 56
Batista, Joesley, 379–80
Bay of Pigs, 56
Benny Show, The, 223
Beria, Lavrenti, 254
Bessent, Scott, 133, 174, 241, 329, 354
  Epshteyn and, 133–34
  Iran and, 403
  Kirk assassination and, 304
  Musk and, 123–24
  Powell and, 245, 246
  tariffs and China and, 90, 93, 116–20, 122, 123, 178–80
  Ukraine and, 36, 38, 66–67, 80–81, 83
Bezos, Jeff, 6–8, 358–60, 364
Bezos, Lauren Sánchez, 8
Biden, Hunter, xxiii, 4, 5, 20
Biden, Jill, 21, 75, 76
Biden, Joe, xxi, 5, 10, 24, 30, 31, 59, 61, 75, 76, 105, 152, 153, 170, 172, 211, 222, 227, 244, 253, 311, 320, 327, 336, 361, 372, 375, 376, 390, 399, 414
  Afghanistan and, xvii
  AI and, 256, 258, 263
  Bragg and, 310
  chip sales and, 259, 260, 265
  in election of 2020, xvii–xx, xxiii, 3–7, 10, 69, 74, 128, 129, 133, 151, 157, 163, 390
  in election of 2024, 3, 4, 10, 142, 144, 256
  Homan and, 98
  immigration policies of, 53–54, 95, 98, 99
  Musk and, 42
  Netanyahu and, 69
  presidential library of, 360
  presidential pardons of, 20–21
  Putin and, 65
  Trump's call to Zelensky about, xxiii–xxiv
  Trump's inauguration and, 19–21
  Trump's legal problems and, 148, 149
  Trump's meeting with, 3–5, 20–21
  Ukraine and, 36, 37, 39, 82–84
  Wong and, 152–53
"Big Balls" (Edward Coristine), 271–72, 275
Big Beautiful Bill, 104, 211–13, 219–20, 221, 262
Binance, 355–56
bin Laden, Osama, 227
Black Hawk raid, 281, 282
Black Lives Matter, 301
Blair, James, 104, 174, 216–17, 252, 386, 387
  Epstein files and, 224, 228, 229, 235, 236
  Federal Reserve and, 247–50
Blair, Tony, 330–32
Blair House, 393
Blanche, Todd, xiv–xv, 18, 29, 164, 291, 305, 307–12, 382
  Epstein files and, 224, 228, 231, 232, 234–38, 240, 309
Bloomberg Law, 361
Bloomberg News, 91
Blue Origin, 359
Board of Peace, xxvi, 340–41, 393
Boasberg, James, 163–64, 167
boat-bombing campaign, 320–26, 346, 375, 376, 378
Boehler, Adam, 59
Bolton, John, 128, 156, 311
Bondi, Pam, 18, 58, 101, 104, 182, 240, 271, 272, 275, 291, 306, 307, 310, 311, 382
  Epstein files and, 222, 224–25, 228–32, 235, 236, 309
  Kirk assassination and, 296, 303
  Trump's complaints about, 305, 309
  Trump's Truth Social message to, 307, 308, 310
bond market, 119, 123, 251
Bongino, Dan, 223, 224, 231–34, 306
Border, The, 276
Bove, Emil, 376
Bovino, Gregory, 275–77, 281, 290
Bowser, Muriel, 275
Bradley, Frank M., 324
Bragg, Alvin, xxi, 131, 148–49, 310
Breitbart, 57, 169
Brennan, John, 152, 311
Brockman, Greg, 257–58
Brooks, Rebekah, 344
Brown v. Board of Education, 132
Bryan, Zach, 290
Buckley, William F., Jr., 57
Budowich, Taylor, 11, 228, 232, 235, 236, 293–97
Bukele, Nayib, 52–55, 162–63, 165
Bunch, Lonnie G., III, 198–200, 202, 203, 205–9
Burchett, Tim, 214–15
Burgum, Doug, 258

Buria, Ricky, 323
Bush, George H. W., 272, 283, 343
Bush, George W., 9, 161, 169–70, 196, 304, 325, 343
Butler, PA, xxii, 9, 63, 390

Cadence Design Systems, 264–66
Caine, Dan, 174, 320, 383, 393, 394, 396–98, 402–4
California, 27, 150, 276–77, 283, 355
Canada, 103, 360, 363
  tariffs and, 89, 91–93, 113, 115
  United States–Mexico–Canada Agreement, 92, 115
Cantor Fitzgerald, 353, 355
Cape Canaveral, 358
Caracas, 380, 381, 383, 384
Caribbean, 320
  boat-bombing campaign in, 290, 320–26, 346, 375, 376, 378
  warships in, 380–81
Carlson, Tucker, 34, 73–75, 156, 185, 193–94, 298
  AI and, 262
  Epstein files and, 222, 224, 228
  Iran and, 401
  Maduro and, 380–82
Carpenter, Sabrina, 289
Carr, Brendan, 303
Carroll, E. Jean, 135, 139–40
Cartel of the Suns, 322
Carter, Jimmy, 10, 368, 383
Casino, 28
Castro, Fidel, 56
CBS, 28, 70, 122, 141–43, 378
CCP (Chinese Communist Party), 53, 111, 152–54, 261–62
CECOT (Terrorism Confinement Center), 52, 55, 162–65, 167
CENTCOM (U.S. Central Command), 50, 184, 323
Center for Renewing America, 274
Cernovich, Mike, 229
Charlie Kirk Show, The, 304
ChatGPT, 256–58, 286
Chávez, Hugo, 102, 103, 376
Chavez-DeRemer, Lori, 362
Cheney, Dick, 78
Cheung, Steven, 71, 72, 174, 228, 235, 236, 285–89, 291, 294, 386, 388, 403, 404, 407, 408
Chevron, 100, 102–5
Chicago, IL, 273, 281, 282
China, xxvi, 39, 63–64, 177–80, 304, 325, 355
  American technology and, 261
  Board of Peace and, 340–41
  chips and, 111–13, 260–64, 266
  Covid pandemic and, 178, 179
  drugs and, 179, 317, 320
  human rights abuses in, 178–79, 272
  Iran and, 63–64, 189
  Musk and, 111, 113
  rare earths and magnets exports of, 177, 179
  Taiwan and, 111, 112, 178
  Tan's ties to, 264, 266, 267
  tariffs and, 89, 90, 93, 112, 114, 121, 122, 177–79, 410
  Tiananmen Square protests and massacre in, 272–73
  Venezuela and, 103, 105, 382
  Wong family and, 152–54
Chinese Communist Party (CCP), 53, 111, 152–54, 261–62
chips (semiconductors), 111–13, 178, 179, 258–67
CHIPS and Science Act, 112, 265, 266
Churchill, Winston, 83
CIA (Central Intelligence Agency), 13, 65, 71, 152, 174, 190, 311, 316
  Iran and, 392, 396
  Maduro and, 322, 383
Citizens for Responsibility and Ethics in Washington (CREW), 310
civil rights movement, 276, 283
Civil War, 88, 160, 283
Clapper, James, 152
climate change, 101
Climate Superfund, 101
Clinton, Bill, 5, 10, 76, 273, 328, 378
Clinton, Hillary, xxi, xxiv, 5, 76, 227
CNN, 24, 165, 196, 348
Coast Guard, U.S., 320, 362, 363
cocaine, 320, 321, 324, 326, 376
Cohen, Michael, 134, 147, 240, 310
Cohn, Roy, xxv, 15, 157, 287
Colbert, Stephen, 143
Collins, Doug, 109
Collins, Kaitlan, 165, 167
Colombia, 321, 324
Columbia University, 95, 137
Comer, James, 235, 239

Comey, James, xxiv, 152, 234, 305–8, 312
  "86 47" post of, 306
  indictment of, 310–11
Comey, Maurene, 234
Commerce Department, 89, 265
Congress, xx, xxii, xxv, xxvii, 48, 49, 134, 213, 243, 248, 278, 367, 368, 390
  Big Beautiful Bill and, 211–12
  boat-bombing campaign and, 326
  Cuban Caucus in, 104
  Epstein files and, 228, 376
  Foreign Emoluments Clause and, 182
  habeas corpus and, 159–61
  House of Representatives, 57, 89, 104, 116, 156, 201, 217, 218, 235, 236
  Iran war and, 405
  monetary policy and, 243
  monuments and, 366
  Senate, xxiv, 14, 57, 110, 134, 154, 201, 217–20, 248, 254, 275
  Trump's relationship with, 211, 213–20
  war declarations and, 321, 405
ConocoPhillips, 100, 102, 105
Conservative Political Action Conference, 127
Constitution, U.S., 45, 94, 152, 321, 356
  Fifth Amendment to, 146
  First Amendment to, 303
  Foreign Emoluments Clause of, 182
  habeas corpus and, 159, 160, 167
  monetary policy and, 243
Cook, Lisa, 253–55
Cook, Tim, xxvi, 6
Coristine, Edward ("Big Balls"), 271–72, 275
Corporate Sustainability Due Diligence Directive (CSDDD), 101
Costa Rica, 59
Cotton, Tom, 154, 264, 267
Council of Economic Advisers, 118
Covid pandemic, xvii, xviii, xxiii, xxv, 53, 94, 178, 179, 251, 256, 258, 278, 368
Covington & Burling, 130, 132, 136
Cox, Spencer, 294
CREW (Citizens for Responsibility and Ethics in Washington), 310
crime, 272, 273
  criminal justice system, 136
  drug, *see* drugs, illicit
  immigrants and, 55, 99, 163–66, 281
  National Guard and, 272, 273, 276–78
  in Washington, D.C., 278
cryptocurrency, 44, 181, 260, 354
  Trump family and, xxii, xxvii, 181, 351–57
CSDDD (Corporate Sustainability Due Diligence Directive), 101
Cuba, 56, 57, 317
Cuban Caucus, 104
Cuban Missile Crisis, 326
currency notes, 216
Cybersecurity and Infrastructure Security Agency, 129

Dalio, Ray, 122
Dan Bongino Show, The, 223
Daniels, Stormy, xx, 128, 148
data centers, 257, 259, 260, 262, 263
Davidson, Warren, 216
Declaration of Independence, 135
  250th anniversary of, 206, 208, 216, 218, 368, 369
deep state, xxiv, 13, 28, 30, 223, 315
Defense Department, xxiv, 14, 50, 71, 97, 139, 182, 195, 274, 316, 319, 323, 359
  Kirk assassination and, 303
  social media and, 289
DEI (diversity, equity, and inclusion) policies, 7, 24, 95, 109, 138, 198, 199
Delaney, John, 32
Dell, 111
Delta Air Lines, 122
Delta Force, 380, 383
Democracy Forward, 163
Democrats, xvii, xxi, 4, 10–11, 14, 42, 49, 53, 61, 98, 102, 130, 144, 145, 150, 152, 166, 218, 240, 278, 291, 298, 304, 306, 307, 324, 374, 409
  cities and states run by, 272, 279, 280
  Epstein files and, 225, 234–36
  Federal Reserve and, 242
  fundraising by, 301
  government shutdown and, 371–74
  Iran and, 399
  national convention of, 281–82
  Russia investigation and, 383
  Vance's comment about, 348
demonstrations, *see* protests and riots
De Oliveira, Carlos, xx
Depression, Great, 94, 117, 121
Dermer, Ron, 72, 176, 331, 334, 336, 337
DeSantis, Ron, 15, 33, 58, 61, 151, 262, 288

Detroit, MI, 283
Dhillon, Harmeet, 291
DHS, *see* Homeland Security, Department of
Díaz-Balart, Mario, 104
Dimon, Jamie, 122
Diplomatic Club, 188
Disney, 140–42
Dmitriev, Kirill, 40–41, 62
DOGE (Department of Government Efficiency), 8, 24, 26, 44–51, 52, 107–11, 124, 155, 212
  Coristine ("Big Balls") at, 271–72, 275
  Musk's "What did you do last week" email, 79–80, 110
Dogecoin, 44
Doha, 62
  Israeli strike on, 331–34, 336, 337
DOJ, *see* Justice Department
Domestic Policy Council, 207
Dominican Republic, 59
Dominion Voting Systems, 74
Donroe Doctrine, xxvii, 325
Dorr, Kaelan, 287–89
Dorsey, Jack, 6
Dough, 352
Dow Jones Industrial Average, 93, 119
Draino, DC, 229
drugs, illicit, 89, 317, 320, 321
  boat-bombing campaign and, 320–26, 346, 375, 376, 378
  China and, 179, 317, 320
  cocaine, 320, 321, 324, 326, 376
  fentanyl, 89, 92, 94, 286, 287, 289, 317, 319, 320, 410
  Mexico and, 316–17, 319, 320
  opioids, 320
drugs, prescription, 357, 368
Duffy, Sean, 108–9
Dulles International Airport, 215, 369
Duterte, Rodrigo, 317, 320

Eagle Claw operation, 383
Economic Club of Chicago, 244
Economic Club of New York, 88
economy, 89, 90, 122, 244, 260, 409
  affordability and, 291, 347, 349, 374–75, 389, 409
  Federal Reserve and, *see* Federal Reserve
  Great Depression, 94, 117, 121
  inflation, xvii, 177–78, 244, 246, 374
  national debt, 42, 212
  Panic of 1893, 89
  stock market, 93, 119
  see also trade
Education, Department of, 138, 139
Egypt, 72, 338
Eisenhower, Dwight D., 283, 367
Electoral College, 9
Elias, Marc, 130
Elkann, John, 91–92
Ellis, Jenna, xx
Ellison, David, 142, 143
Ellison, Larry, 142, 143
El Salvador, 52–55, 59, 162–65, 167
Emancipation Proclamation, 345
emergency powers, xiv, xxv, 89, 94–95
Engoron, Arthur, 146, 147, 310
EPA (Environmental Protection Agency), 109
Epic Fury operation, 402–5
  see also Iran war
Epshteyn, Boris, 129, 132–36, 140, 142, 158, 308–9, 364
  Bessent and, 133–34
Epstein, Jeffrey, 225–26
  death of, 221–22, 231–32
  Trump's friendship with, 225–27, 342, 377
Epstein files, 221–40, 285, 298, 309, 409
  DOJ and, 221–22, 224, 225, 229–34, 236, 238, 239
  DOJ's release of, 376–78
  Epstein Files Transparency Act, 236, 377
  FBI and, 221–24, 228, 230, 231, 233, 378
  Maxwell and, 228, 234–35, 237, 240
  Ransome deposition and, 237–38
  Russiagate and, 239, 240
  website for, 236, 238
Equal Employment Opportunity Commission, 49
Ernst, Joni, 219
Esper, Mark, xxiv, 103, 129, 274
Esquire, 87
Europe, 39, 246, 316, 340, 369
European Union (EU), 38, 101, 112–13
EUV (extreme ultraviolet lithography), 111
ExxonMobil, 100–102

Fabrizio, Tony, 216, 224, 349, 374, 375, 409
Facebook, xx, 6, 7, 288, 289

Face the Nation, 28
Fahey, John, 204
Farley, Jim, 91–92
FBI (Federal Bureau of Investigation), 20, 150, 232, 290, 300, 305, 306, 309, 311, 362, 390
  Epstein files and, 221–24, 228, 230, 231, 233, 378
FCC (Federal Communications Commission), 142, 143, 303
federal deficit, 44
federal employees and bureaucracy, 29, 30, 43, 44, 47
  DOGE and, *see* DOGE
  Schedule F and, xxv
federal government shutdown, 371–74
Federal Housing Finance Agency, 149, 251
Federal Reserve, 241–55
  Board of Governors, 242, 253–55
  building renovations, 248–52
  Cook at, 253–55
  Federal Reserve Act, 243, 254
  interest rates set by, 120, 242–44, 246–48, 251
  Powell as chairman of, 119, 241–48, 250–54
Federal Rules of Criminal Procedure, 234
Feinberg, Steve, 359
fentanyl, 89, 92, 94, 286, 287, 289, 317, 319, 320, 410
FHFA (Federal Housing Finance Agency), 149
FIFA (Fédération Internationale de Football Association), 360–62
Fifth Amendment, 146
First Amendment, 303
Flag Day, 215
Flores, Cilia, 384
Florida, 32–34, 56, 58, 104, 140, 311, 318, 357–58
Florida Department of Transportation, 249
Floyd, George, 162, 273–74, 276
Fogel, Marc, 41, 59, 62, 63
Folkman, Zachary, 352, 353
Fool's Errand, A (Bunch), 200
Forbes, 352, 355
Ford, Gerald, 366
Ford Foundation, 302
Ford Motor Company, 91–92
Foreign Corrupt Practices Act, 360–61
Fortune 500 companies, 217, 261
Fox & Friends, 272
Fox & Friends Weekend, 14
Fox Business, 264, 324
Fox News, xiii, xx, 9, 14, 36, 73, 74, 127, 186, 192, 193, 196, 229, 252, 275, 300, 304, 343, 344, 347, 398
Fox News Sunday, 21
France, 189, 369
Franklin, Benjamin, 75
free speech, 95, 303
Fridman, Lex, 44, 222
Friedman, Milton, 121
Fuentes, Nick, 186

Gabbard, Tulsi, 13–14, 174, 239–40, 311, 394, 403
Gaetz, Matt, 18, 20, 219
Gaiser, T. Elliot, 319
Gallagher, Eddie, 14
Gang of Eight, 57
Garber, Alan, 138
Garden City Hotel, 144
Garland, Merrick, 21
Gates, Bill, 378
Gateway Pundit, 169
gay marriage, 132
Gaza, 20, 61, 62, 71–74, 137, 186, 189, 293, 328, 330–35, 339–41, 390, 391, 393
General Motors, 91–92
General Services Administration, 138
Genghis Khan, 411
Gensler, Gary, 354
Gerald R. Ford, USS, 380
Germany, 189
  Nazi, 64–65, 160
Gibson, Mel, 287
Gilded Age, 88
Gill, Brandon, 216
Giménez, Carlos, 104, 199, 202–5, 207
Giuffra, Robert, 135, 136
Giuffre, Virginia, 237
Giuliani, Rudy, xiii, 278
globalists, 91
globalization, 90
Godfather, The, 287
Gofman, Roman, 393
Goldberg, Jeffrey, 154
Golsteyn, Mathew, 14
Good, Renee, 385–86, 388
Goodell, Roger, 360
Google, 6, 288

Gor, Sergio, 80, 151–55, 174, 208, 367
Gorbachev, Mikhail, 273
Government Accountability Office, 49
Government Gangsters (Patel), 306
Graham, Lindsey, 298, 398, 399
Grant, Ulysses S., 283
Great Depression, 94, 117, 121
Greene, Marjorie Taylor, 223, 235
Greenland, 103, 370
Greer, Jamieson, 115
Grenell, Richard, 104, 199, 379
Guaidó, Juan, 103
Guantánamo Bay, 31, 161
Guatemala, 53, 59

habeas corpus, 158–62, 166–68, 284
Haley, Nikki, 61, 156
Haley, Vince, 206–7
Halligan, Lindsey, 201, 206, 208–9, 307–12
Hamad bin Jassim bin Jaber Al Thani, 181
Hamas, 20, 62, 70, 184, 327, 330, 331, 333–35, 337–40
Hannity, 118
Hannity, Sean, 301
Harp, Natalie, 33, 88, 114–15, 169, 186, 212, 271, 295, 370, 373, 407, 411, 412
Harris, Kamala, 10, 277
 in presidential election, 4, 9, 53, 128, 141, 144, 256, 277, 374
 60 Minutes interview of, 141, 142
Harvard Corporation, 137–38
Harvard University, 136–39
hate speech, 303
Haugh, Timothy, 152
Hawaii, 13, 161
Hawley, Josh, 262
Health and Human Services, Department of, 138, 363
healthcare, 409
 government shutdown and, 371–74
 Medicaid, 24, 211–12, 220
 Medicare, 24
 Obamacare (Affordable Care Act), 45, 218, 371–74
HealthCare.gov, 45
Hegel, Georg Wilhelm Friedrich, 413
Hegseth, Pete, 14–15, 18, 29, 103, 174, 196, 214, 219, 275, 278–80, 318–19, 338, 384
 boat-bombing campaign and, 320, 321, 325
 bombing videos and, 322–23
 book by, 318
 Iran and, 394, 399, 403, 404
 Signal app and, 154, 279–80
 social media and, 290
 Ukraine and, 36, 38
Heritage Foundation, 45
Hernandez, Juan Orlando, 376
Herro, Chase, 352, 353
Hezbollah, 184
 pager attack against, 70, 73–74
Hillbilly Elegy (Vance), 187
Hiroshima, 239
Hitler, Adolf, 17, 411, 412
Hodgetwins, 223
Hoffman, Reid, 301
Holsey, Alvin, 325
Homan, Tom, 95–98, 286
Homeland Security, Department of (DHS), xiv, xxv, 15, 97, 99, 100, 129, 139, 162, 211, 227, 301–3, 388
 social media and, 289, 290
 Tren de Aragua and, 281
Homeland Security Council (HSC), 279, 316, 319
homelessness, 278
Home Rule Act, 278
Honduras, 53, 376
Hong Kong, 153, 178
Hoover, Herbert, 117, 366
Hortman, Melissa, 304
House of Representatives, 57, 89, 104, 116, 156, 201, 217, 218, 235, 236
Houthis, 154
HPE, 111
HP Inc., 111
Huang, Jensen, 258–62, 267
Huang, Lori, 260
Hur, Robert, 31
Hurricane Hugo, 283

IBM, 111
ICC (International Criminal Court), 317
ICE (Immigration and Customs Enforcement), xiv, 54, 95–97, 99, 162, 164, 168, 280–82, 301, 386, 389
 Good shot by officer of, 385–86, 388
 masks worn by officers of, 301
 McGraw and, 276

ICE (*cont.*)
  mug shots of immigrants arrested by, 286
  National Guard and, 274
  protesters and, 276, 281, 290–91, 385–89
  social media and, 289, 290
  violence against officers of, 301
IEEPA (International Emergency Economic Powers Act), 89
Illinois, 277, 281–82
immigrants, immigration, xxv, 7, 15, 43, 53–54, 89, 92, 95–100, 128, 158–68, 284, 298, 307, 316, 319, 349
  Alien Enemies Act, 162–66
  apprehended at the border versus arrested within the country, 168
  asylum seekers, 53, 54, 95, 168
  Biden administration and, 53–54, 95, 98, 99
  birthright citizenship and, 29–30
  border security and, xxv, 53–54, 89, 94–97, 99–100, 211, 273, 281, 290, 349
  in California, 27
  criminals, 55, 99, 163–66, 281
  detentions and deportations, 31, 54–55, 95–100, 159, 162–68, 274, 286, 289, 291, 349, 389, 410
  family separation policy, 97
  Gang of Eight and, 57
  habeas corpus rights and, 158–62, 166–68, 284
  H-1B visas, 262, 298
  ICE and, *see* ICE
  "invasion" rhetoric and, 95, 162, 163
  Kirk assassination and, 303
  National Guard and, 277
  protests and, 276, 281, 290–91, 385–89
  sanctuary cities and, 53, 281
  self-deportation of, 289, 291
  shootings by immigration agents and, xvi, 385–86, 388–89
  social media and, 285–87, 289, 291
Independence Arch (Arc de Trump), 344, 369–71
India, 37, 112, 114, 367
Indonesia, 340
industry and manufacturing, 90–91, 259, 261
Infantino, Gianni, 360–62
inflation, xvii, 177–78, 244, 246, 374
Instagram, xx, 6, 180, 289
Insurrection Act, 162, 274–76, 282–84, 386–88
Intel, 111, 263–67
Intercept, The, 324
interest rates, 120, 242–44, 246–48, 251
International Criminal Court (ICC), 317
Iran, 129, 154, 156, 188–97, 325, 363, 390–91
  China and, 63–64, 189
  hostage crisis in, 383
  Iran-Contra affair, 234
  nuclear program of, 70, 71, 175, 176, 184–86, 188–91, 194–97, 211, 330, 391, 392, 395, 401, 404
  Obama and, 175, 189, 190, 401
  protests in, 395, 396, 400
  Revolutionary Guard in, 390, 392
  Russia and, 63–64, 185
  shah of, 394
  Trump targeted by, 295–96, 390
  Venezuela and, 103, 382
Iran war (2026), xxvi, 74, 75, 156, 175–76, 183–86, 190–97, 211, 239, 298, 327, 330, 349, 391–405, 407–10, 413
  Kurds and, 395, 396
  lack of popular support for, 409
  munitions depletion from, 397–98, 400, 402, 404
  Operation Epic Fury begins, 402–5
  regime change as goal in, 186, 194, 196, 391–97, 399, 400, 403, 404
  Strait of Hormuz in, 395, 397, 400–401, 408
  Trump's Truth Social posts on, 402, 405
Iraq, 14, 57, 103, 194, 196, 321, 324, 378, 395, 405
IRS (Internal Revenue Service), 47, 123, 304, 364
Isaacman, Jared, 358, 359
ISIS (Islamic State), 50, 397
Israel, xxv, 61–62, 69–74, 137, 155–56, 185–86, 192, 298, 333, 336, 337, 347, 397, 410
  Abraham Accords and, 61, 193, 329, 330, 340
  Doha strike by, 331–34, 336, 337
  Gaza and, 20, 61, 62, 71–74, 137, 186, 189, 293, 328, 330–35, 339–41, 390, 391, 393
  Hamas and, 20, 62, 70, 184, 327, 330, 331, 333–35, 337–40
  Hezbollah pager attack by, 70, 73–74
  Iran and, *see* Iran war
  State of Israel established, 338
Iwo Jima, USS, 380, 384

Jacobs, Jay, 144
James, Letitia, xxi, 144–50, 251, 305, 307, 308, 310–12, 364
January 6 U.S. Capitol attack, xviii, xix, 6–7, 11, 16–17, 20–22, 213, 297, 309, 343, 356, 364
Japan
  Hiroshima bombing, 239
  Pearl Harbor attack, 83, 161
JBS S.A., 379
JCPOA (Joint Comprehensive Plan of Action), 189
Jeffries, Hakeem, 373
Jimmy Kimmel Live!, 303
jobs, 90, 109, 178, 244, 246, 261, 262
John F. Kennedy Center for the Performing Arts, 199, 361–62, 367–68
Johnson, Benny, 223
Johnson, Lyndon, 283
Johnson, Mike, 210–14, 372
Joint Chiefs of Staff, xxiv, 18, 128, 174, 274
Joint Special Operations Command, 324
Jones, Alex, 222
Jordan, 72
JPMorgan Chase, 122
judges, federal, 162, 167
  see also Supreme Court, U.S.
Judis, John, 413
Juneteenth, 369
Justice Department (DOJ), xxiv, xxvi, 5, 18–21, 29, 30, 95, 97, 129–30, 150, 153, 157, 232, 240, 302, 305–7, 311, 312, 319, 353, 362, 363, 376
  banner on headquarters of, 368–69
  corruption cases and, 361
  Epstein files and, 221–22, 224, 225, 229–34, 236, 238, 239
  Epstein files released by, 376–78
  Homan investigated by, 98
  immigration policies and, 160, 164, 167, 168, 389
  National Institute of Justice, 302
  Powell and, 252
  social media and, 289, 291
  Soros investigated by, 304
  Trump's claim against, 364

Kaplan, Roberta, 135
Karni, Annie, 214
Karp, Brad, 131–32, 135–36, 378
Kash's Corner, 223
Kavanaugh, Brett, 153
Kazakhstan, 340
Keane, Jack, 398
Kellogg, Keith, 35–41, 65, 67, 82
Kelly, John, xxiii
Kelly, Megyn, 224
Kelly, Sharon Pratt, 273
Kennedy, Jacqueline, 77, 345, 365, 366
Kennedy, John F., 49, 56, 262, 283, 365–67
Kennedy, Robert F., Jr., 14, 214
Kennedy Center for the Performing Arts, 199, 361–62, 367–68
Kent, George, xxiv
Kerry, John, 216
KGB, 63
Khalil, Mahmoud, 95
Khamenei, Ayatollah Ali, xxvi, 183, 188, 396, 397, 401, 403, 407
Khanna, Ro, 236, 285
Khardori, Ankush, 325
Khomeini, Ayatollah Ruhollah, 383
Kim Il Sung, 370
Kim Jong Un, 188, 287
Kimmel, Jimmy, 303
King, Martin Luther, Jr., 283, 369
King, Rodney, 283
Kirk, Charlie, 15, 185, 186, 191, 219, 289, 292–93, 297–98
  assassination of, 292–304, 310
  Epstein files and, 222–25
  left-wing groups and, 301
  memorial for, 359
  Miller and, 295, 300, 301
  Vance and, 292, 294, 295, 297, 299, 302
Kirk, Erika, 297
Kissinger, Henry, 40
Kraft, Robert, 131
Krebs, Chris, 129
Kudlow, Larry, 66
Kuiper satellite project, 359
Ku Klux Klan, 161, 283
Kurilla, Michael, 50, 184
Kushner, Charles, 356
Kushner, Jared, 34, 61, 171, 328–40, 352, 353, 394, 401–2

LaCivita, Chris, 216, 218
Lafayette Square, 274
Lamar, Kendrick, 290

Lammy, David, 236
Lance, Ryan, 105–6
Landry, Jeff, 370
Latin America, 52–57, 59, 320, 321
  see also specific countries
Lavizzo-Mourey, Risa, 203
Lavrov, Sergey, 68, 86
Le, Julie, 389
Leavitt, Karoline, 24, 71, 87, 167, 173, 174, 180–81, 344, 407
  Epstein files and, 228, 235, 236
  Iran and, 386, 402–4
  Kirk assassination and, 294
  protesters and, 290–91
Lebanon, Hezbollah pager attack in, 70, 73–74
Letlow, Julia, 370
Levenbach, Stuart, 249
Levin, Mark, 186, 398
Lewandowski, Corey, 15–16, 388
Lewinsky, Monica, 76
Lex Fridman Podcast, 44, 222
Liberation Day, 92–93, 113, 115–21, 150–51, 179, 244, 245
Libs of TikTok, 223
Libya, 103
Lightcap, Brad, 256–57, 258
Limbaugh, Rush, 27
Lincoln, Abraham, 160, 161, 283, 345, 365
Lincoln Memorial, 217, 344, 369, 370
Little Rock, AR, 283
Loomer, Laura, 150–55, 157, 182, 223, 233, 309
Lorance, Clint, 14
Los Angeles, CA, 275–77, 279, 281, 283, 290, 387
Low, Jho, 61
Luna, Anna Paulina, 215, 251–52
Lutnick, Howard, 12, 44, 92, 93, 121, 124, 130, 151, 174, 263, 293, 353–55, 358, 378, 394
  Tan and, 265
  tariffs and, 101, 114–18, 120–23
  at technology conference, 111–13
  Ukraine minerals deal and, 80–82

Machado, Maria Corina, 317
Macron, Emmanuel, 370–71
Maduro, Nicolás, xiv, xvi, xxvi, 57, 103–4, 317, 318, 320, 322, 378–84, 385, 392, 402, 410
MAGA coalition, xiii, xv, xviii, 22, 30, 115, 151, 170, 171, 175, 180, 185–87, 214, 219, 260, 298, 306, 311, 345, 390
  AI and, 262–63
  Bondi and Blanche targeted by, 309
  Epstein files and, 222, 225, 228, 229, 231, 233, 236, 238
  infighting in, 298
  Kirk and, 297, 298, 303
Magna Carta, 160
Mailman, May, 30–31, 138–39
Make Autorail Great Again Act, 215–16
Manafort, Paul, 134, 240, 308, 356
manufacturing and industry, 90–91, 111–13, 259, 261, 265, 267
Mao Zedong, 411, 412
Maples, Marla, 377
Mar-a-Lago, xx, 9, 33, 36, 45, 46, 69, 77, 133, 149, 170, 214, 241, 260, 275, 357, 382, 383, 390, 391, 399
  cabinet selection meeting at, 12–17, 46
  dinner for tech CEOs at, 6–8
  document storage and, 128, 158, 364
  Epstein files and, 226, 237, 377
  Musk at, 46
  New Year's celebration at, xiii–xvi
Marine One, 214
Markarova, Oksana, 86
Marshall, Thurgood, 132
Martin, Margo, 151
Martin Luther King Jr. Day, 283, 369
Mashal, Khaled, 331
Massie, Thomas, 219–20, 235, 236, 285
Mattis, James, xxiii, 103
Maxwell, Ghislaine, 228, 234–35, 237, 240
Mayer, Jane, 285
McCain, John, 158, 218
McCarthy, Joseph, 143
McCarthy, Ryan, 18
McConnell, Mitch, 11, 213
McDaniel, Ronna, 364
McDowell, Addison, 215
McDowell, Ches, 356
McEntee, John, xxiv
McGraw, Phil, 276
McGurk, Brett, 61, 62
McKinley, William, 88–89
McMahon, Wendy, 142
Medicaid, 24, 211–12, 220
Medicare, 24
Medvedev, Dmitry, 86
Merchan, Juan, 310

Merchant, Asif, 390
Meta, 6, 7, 262
Metrorail, 216
Mexico, 113, 290, 319–20, 360
  drug cartels in, 317, 319, 320
  tariffs against, 89–93, 115
  United States–Mexico–Canada Agreement, 92, 115
MGX, 355–56
Middle East, 40, 59, 61, 69, 141, 155, 183–85, 196, 316, 322, 323, 327–41, 352, 357, 358, 391, 403
  Abraham Accords and, 61, 193, 329, 330, 340
  Trump's trip to, 180, 183, 190, 250, 261
  see also specific countries
Midnight Hammer operation, 195, 391, 402, 404
midterm elections, 217, 291, 350, 359, 375, 399, 409
Midway Blitz operation, 281
military justice system, 14
Miller, Katie, 23, 26, 45, 79, 271, 300, 363
Miller, Stephen, xiv, xxv, 12, 15, 16, 23–32, 34, 36, 46, 98, 129, 132, 138, 159, 162, 174, 271–72, 291, 300–301, 306, 315–16, 318, 319, 358, 384
  Covid pandemic and, 94
  early life of, 27, 28
  executive orders and, 23, 24, 30
  federal troops and, 273–76, 278, 280, 282–84
  foreign policy as viewed by, 316
  fossil fuels and, 100–102
  Homeland Security Council and, 279, 316, 319
  immigration policies and, 27–30, 54, 57, 96–100, 159–62, 164–68, 281, 289, 300, 316, 386, 387
  job titles of, 23
  Kirk and, 295, 300, 301
  Lance and, 105–6
  military housing and, 363
  Musk and, 45
  National Joint Terrorism Task Force and, 304
  Noem and, 388, 389
  nonprofit launched by, 28
  OMB memo and, 23–25, 31
  physical appearance of, 27, 28
  protests against, 300, 304
  Rubio and, 57
  Scharf and, 159
  secrecy of, 315–16
  tariffs and, 89–90, 116
  in Trump's 2016 campaign, 27, 28
Milley, Mark, xxiv, 18, 128, 152, 274, 398
Minnesota, xv, xvi, 279, 304, 385–89
Minnesota Star Tribune, The, 279
Miss Universe pageant, 37, 410
MIT (Massachusetts Institute of Technology), 109, 265
Mithril Capital, 187
Mizelle, Chad, 29
Mnuchin, Steven, 242, 251
Modi, Narendra, 37
Mohammed bin Abdulrahman bin Jassim Al Thani, 329, 332, 333, 338
Mohammed bin Salman (MBS), 41, 62, 68, 328, 329, 360
Monaco, 72
monetary policy, 122, 243
Monroe, James, 345
Monroe Doctrine, xxvii, 325
Moran, Terry, 166
Mornings with Maria, 264
Morocco, 329, 340
mortgage fraud, 150, 253–54, 308
Moss, Ben, 204
Mossad, 70, 393–95
Mount Rushmore National Memorial, 215, 252
MS-13, 163, 164, 166
Munich Security Conference, 67
Murdoch, James, 343
Murdoch, Rupert, xx, 190, 227, 342–47, 398
  Trump's lawsuit against, 226–27, 342–44
Musk, Elon, 8, 42–49, 73, 74, 155, 219, 257, 258, 271, 363, 378
  Bessent and, 123–24
  Biden administration and, 42
  Big Beautiful Bill and, 212, 221
  China and, 111, 113
  at DOGE, 8, 24, 26, 44–51, 107–11, 124, 272
  Duffy and, 108–9
  end of government role of, 110, 123, 358
  Epstein files and, 221, 222
  federal judges and, 167
  IRS and, 123
  at Mar-a-Lago, 46
  Rubio and, 80, 107–8
  SpaceX, 42, 358–60
  at technology conference, 111–12
  Tesla, 111, 212
  trade wars and, 121

Musk, Elon (*cont.*)
Trump's reconciliation with, 359
Trump's split with, 221
Trump's 2024 campaign and, 42–44
USAID and, 49–51, 80, 107
"What did you do last week" email of, 79–80, 110
White House presence of, 48–49, 110
Wiles and, 48, 79, 80, 107
X and, 7, 42–44, 47, 48
Musk, X (Elon's son), 49
Muslim travel ban, 25

NAFTA (North American Free Trade Agreement), 113
Napoleon I, 369, 411, 412
NASA (National Aeronautics and Space Administration), 358, 359
Nash, John, 76
Nation, The, 302
National Archives, 157
National Capital Planning Commission (NCPC), 248–52
National Cultural Center, 367
National Geographic, 204
National Guard, 272, 273, 274, 276–80, 282, 284, 285, 290
National Institute of Justice, 302
National Institutes of Health (NIH), 139, 216
National Joint Terrorism Task Force, 303–4
National Museum of African American History and Culture, 200
National Museum of American History, 203
National Museum of Asian Art, 203
national parks, 368
National Portrait Gallery, 198–99, 203–6
National Postal Museum, 201
National Review, 57
National Security Presidential Memorandum/NSPM-7, 303–4
National Zoo, 202
NATO (North Atlantic Treaty Organization), xxv, xxvi, 405, 408, 413
Ukraine and, 65, 67, 82
Nauta, Walt, xx, 171–72, 407
Navarro, Peter, xx, 115–16, 118, 119, 179
Navy, U.S., 316
Nazi Germany, 64–65, 160
NBC, 364
NCPC (National Capital Planning Commission), 248–52
Netanyahu, Benjamin, xv, xxv, 62, 69–74, 175, 176, 183–86, 188, 190–93, 197, 327, 330–39, 390–91, 393–99, 401, 410
Netanyahu, Sara, xv, 70
Netherlands, 37, 200
Never Trumpers, 152, 187, 295
New Jersey, 200, 360, 369, 374
News Corp, 227, 343, 344
Newsom, Gavin, 276, 277, 291, 347
New York (magazine), 226
New York, NY, 87, 278, 342, 366, 369
New York Daily News, 342
New Yorker, The, 285
New York Post, 190, 325, 342, 344
New York State, 101, 145, 147
New York Times, The, 129, 196, 214, 286, 324, 354, 355, 366, 377, 407
New York Times Co. v. Sullivan, 140
Nexstar, 303
NFL (National Football League), 360
NFTs (non-fungible tokens), 354
NIH (National Institutes of Health), 139, 216
9/11 terrorist attacks, 78, 227, 304, 316, 321, 324, 325
Nixon, Pat, 76, 365
Nixon, Richard, 39–40, 76, 243, 279, 365
Nobel Peace Prize, 327, 341, 362, 368
Noble, Wendy, 152
Nocella, Joseph, 361
Noem, Kristi, xiv, 15–16, 29, 99, 100, 278, 362, 363, 389
firing of, 388, 389
social media and, 286
nonprofit groups, 28, 40, 301, 302
North Korea, 118, 179, 188, 370
NSA (National Security Agency), 152, 154
NSC (National Security Council), xxiv, 40, 50–51, 152–55, 173, 182
nuclear weapons, 53, 239
Hiroshima bombing, 239
Iran and, 70, 71, 175, 176, 184–86, 188–91, 194–97, 211, 330, 391, 392, 395, 401, 404
Nvidia, 258–63, 266, 267

Obama, Barack, xxiv, 10, 57, 152, 169–70, 200, 227, 311, 378
Gabbard's allegations against, 240

immigration policies and, 53–54, 96
Iran and, 175, 189, 190, 401
Nobel awarded to, 327
Obama, Michelle, 204–5
Obamacare (Affordable Care Act), 45, 218, 371–73
O'Brien, Robert, 17
O'Brien, Tim, 287
Office of Foreign Assets Control (OFAC), 322
Office of Legal Counsel (OLC), 30, 319, 325
oil and gas, 94, 100–106
Strait of Hormuz and, 400–401, 408
in Venezuela, 322, 375–76, 378, 379, 381, 382, 384
Olympic Games, 363
Oman, 188–89, 401
OMB (Office of Management and Budget), 23–25, 31, 46, 247, 248
One Big Beautiful Bill, 104, 211–13, 219–20, 221, 262
OpenAI, 256–57
Open Society Foundation, 302
Operation Eagle Claw, 383
Operation Epic Fury, 402–5
see also Iran war
Operation Midnight Hammer, 195, 391, 402, 404
Operation Midway Blitz, 281
opioid crisis, 320
O'Rourke, Meredith, 217
Owens, Bill, 142
Owens, Candace, 298

Pahlavi, Reza, 394
Palestinians, 71, 72, 95, 331, 391
Palestinian Authority, 340
see also Gaza
Palihapitiya, Chamath, 43
Panama, 59
Panic of 1893, 89
Paoletta, Mark, 24, 31, 248, 249
Paramount Global, 142, 143
Paris, 75, 339, 345
Arc de Triomphe in, 369–71
Paris Agreement, 101
Park Lane Hotel, 61
Parnell, Sean, 194, 195
Patel, Kash, 20, 29, 271, 306, 310, 362–63
book by, 306
Epstein files and, 223–24, 228, 231–33, 235, 236
Kirk assassination and, 296, 299
social media and, 290
Paul, Rand, 324
Paul, Weiss, Rifkind, Wharton & Garrison, 130–32, 134–36
Peale, Norman Vincent, xix
Pearl Harbor attack, 83, 161
Pelosi, Paul, 304
Peltz, Nelson, 43
Pence, Mike, 17, 61
Penn Station, 369
Pentagon, xxv, 14, 39, 71, 103, 128, 194, 223, 275, 318, 321–23, 326, 357, 359, 407–8
Perkins Coie, 130
Perry, Scott, 151
Peskov, Dmitry, 86
Peters, Gary, 204
Philippines, 161, 317
Pichai, Sundar, 6
Pirro, Jeanine, xiii, 252, 344
Playboy, 272–73
Player, Gary, 411, 412
Politico, 325
Pomerantz, Mark, 131, 135, 148
Pompeo, Mike, 17, 129, 179
Poniewozik, James, 286
Poole, Keith, 344
populism, xvii, xviii, 347, 402
Portland, OR, 279–80
Posobiec, Jack, 219
Posse Comitatus Act, 277
Potomac River midair collision, 38
Powell, Jerome, 119, 241–48, 250–54
prescription drugs, 357, 368
presidential election of 1896, 88–89
presidential election of 2004, 9, 216
presidential election of 2016
Rubio in, 55, 57
Russian interference in, xviii, 10–11, 13, 18, 150, 157, 239, 240, 305–8, 311, 364, 383
Trump's campaign in, xx, 9, 15, 27, 28, 34, 35, 55, 74, 289, 293
Trump's victory in, 5, 8–9, 145, 342
presidential election of 2020, xvii–xx, xxiii, 3–7, 9, 16, 33, 69, 329
Biden in, xvii–xx, xxiii, 3–7, 10, 69, 74, 128, 129, 133, 151, 157, 163, 390
as stolen, xviii–xx, 3–7, 10, 16, 74, 128, 129, 133, 151, 157, 163, 304, 319, 380, 412

presidential election of 2024, 7–10, 172, 297, 364
Biden in, 3, 4, 10, 142, 144, 256
CBS coverage of, 141
Harris in, 4, 9, 53, 128, 141, 144, 256, 277, 374
Iranian plots during, 295–96
Kirk and, 294
Musk and, 42–44
Republicans in, 17, 151, 215, 217, 225, 298
swing voters in, 291, 374
Trump's campaign in, xxi, xxii, 40, 69, 74, 88, 93, 104, 127, 128, 148, 149, 151, 157, 213–17, 222, 273, 277, 287–88, 294–96, 390, 410
Trump's victory in, 9, 64, 69–70, 83, 117, 170, 180–81, 199, 241, 282, 291, 304, 350, 374, 391, 414
Vance in, 187, 346, 348
presidential election of 2028, 58, 277, 291, 350, 373
Rubio and, 58, 345–48
Vance and, 58, 83, 186, 299, 345–48, 373
Presidential Emergency Operations Center, 78
presidential immunity, xxii, 11, 134, 158, 240, 317, 357, 409
presidential pardons, 356
by Biden, 5, 20–21
by Trump, 11, 14, 22, 157, 169, 235, 309, 355–57, 376
Presidential Personnel Office, xxiv, 80, 169, 208, 367
President's Council of Advisors on Science and Technology, 258
Presler, Scott, 223
Pretti, Alex, 385–86, 388–89
Price, Tom, 363
Pritzker, JB, 277, 281–82
Project 2025, 45
protectionism, 91
protests and riots, xxiv, 95, 137, 280, 283, 293, 301, 387
George Floyd, 162, 273–74, 276
immigration agents and, 276, 281, 290–91, 385–89
Insurrection Act and, 162, 274–76, 386–88
National Guard and, 277, 280
as organized and paid, 301, 302, 386
Vance and, 278
Proud Boys, 304
Pulte, Bill, 149–51, 157, 251–53, 307, 308
Putin, Vladimir, 4, 35, 36, 38, 40, 62–65, 82, 84, 111, 175–77

Qatar, xxvi, 61, 62, 180, 181, 182, 194, 197, 329, 331, 332, 334, 335, 338–39, 353, 361
Israeli strike on Doha, 331–34, 336, 337
Trump gifted luxury jet by, 181–82, 360
Qatar Investment Authority, 329
Qualcomm, 111

race and cultural institutions, 200–201
Raichik, Chaya, 223
Ramaswamy, Vivek, 43
Ransome, Sarah, 237–38
Ratcliffe, John, 13, 65, 174, 320, 384, 391–93, 396, 399, 403
Reagan, Ronald, 33, 210, 283, 343, 368
Reconstruction, 161
Reding Quiñones, Jason, 382–83
Red Scare, 301
Redstone, Shari, 142
regulations, 43, 44, 100–102
Republicans, 14, 28, 32, 42, 43, 61, 63, 116, 153, 187, 275, 291, 295, 327, 350, 353, 359, 374, 375
AI and, 260, 262–63
Big Beautiful Bill and, 211–12, 262
boat-bombing campaign and, 324
Cuban Caucus, 104
DOGE and, 109
Epstein files and, 224, 225, 235
Federal Reserve and, 242, 254
foreign policy and, 49–50, 156
government shutdown and, 372, 373
Israel and, 185, 186, 192
Kirk and, 298
National Committee of, 217, 364
in presidential election of 2024, 17, 151, 215, 217, 225, 298
Rubio and, 55, 57
tariffs and, 88, 91
Trump and, xviii, xix, xxii, xxiii, 6, 9, 11, 14, 15, 27, 55, 61, 63, 74, 88, 91, 127, 149, 151, 211, 213–20, 243, 298, 350, 402, 409
universities and, 137
Venezuela and, 104
Reuters, 389
riots, *see* protests and riots
Roberts, John, 201, 203, 205, 207

Robinson, Tyler, 299, 301
Rodrigo, Olivia, 289
Rodriguez, Delcy, 382, 384
Rogan, Joe, 225, 236, 237
Ronald Reagan Washington National Airport, 38, 108
Roosevelt, Franklin Delano, xiii, 64, 75, 83, 94, 161
Rose Garden, 77, 153, 170, 218
Rose Garden Club, 218
Routh, Ryan, 382
Rubenstein, David, 199
Rubio, Marco, 16, 55–59, 104, 154, 155, 174, 187, 191, 295, 317, 329, 330, 338, 344
  background of, 56
  boat-bombing campaign and, 320, 322, 346
  El Salvador and, 52–55, 59, 162
  in Gang of Eight, 57
  immigration policies and, 54–57
  Iran and, 71, 188, 191, 192, 196, 393, 394, 399, 403, 404
  Miller and, 57
  Musk and, 80, 107–8
  national security advisor role of, 157, 174, 317, 318
  at New Year's celebration, xiii–xiv
  political career of, 56
  presidential campaign of, 55, 57
  presidential election of 2028 and, 58, 345–48
  Republican Party and, 55, 57
  secretary of state role of, 12, 16, 58, 157, 174, 317, 318, 348
  as senator, 317, 318
  tariffs and, 90
  Trump's vice president selection and, 57–58
  Ukraine and, 36, 38, 40–41, 65, 68, 176
  USAID and, 50, 51, 107, 157
  Vance and, 58, 348
  Venezuela and, xiv, 56–57, 104, 317–18, 320, 378, 379, 382, 384
  Wiles and, 58, 317
  Zelensky and, 86
Ruemmler, Kathryn, 378
Rugg, Collin, 229
Russia, 40, 189, 257, 273, 304, 316, 325
  Board of Peace and, 340–41
  economy of, 40
  election interference investigation, xviii, 10–11, 13, 18, 150, 157, 239, 240, 305–8, 311, 364, 383
  Fogel released by, 41, 59, 62, 63
  Iran and, 63–64, 185
  Ukraine's war with, 3, 35–41, 59, 62, 64–68, 82–86, 111, 176–77, 185, 189, 323, 327, 328, 349, 359, 397
  U.S. business deals with, 63–65
  Venezuela and, 103, 382
  Witkoff and, 40, 41, 59, 62–65
Ryan, Paul, 213

Sacks, David, 258, 260, 262, 354, 359
Saddam Hussein, 324
St. John's Episcopal Church, 19, 274
St. Jude Children's Research Hospital, xv
Sajet, Kim, 198–99, 204–5
Sajwani, Hussain, xv
Salazar, Maria Elvira, 104
Salisbury, Anthony, 279–80
Sanders, Sarah Huckabee, 262
S&P 500, 119
San Francisco Museum of Modern Art, 205
Saudi Arabia, 37, 41, 67, 71, 180, 329
  Trump's visit to, 183, 261
Sauer, D. John, 361
Save America (Trump), 5–6
Scavino, Dan, xiii, 37, 169, 174
Scharf, Will, 130, 158–61, 162, 166, 168, 249–50, 283, 284, 297, 308, 386–87
Schedule F, xxv
Scherer, Michael, 194
Schiff, Adam, 150, 307
Schumer, Chuck, 369, 372–73
Schwartz, Arthur, 297
Scott, Rick, 32, 58
Secret Service, 13, 146, 223, 300, 306
Securities and Exchange Commission, U.S., 354
Selma to Montgomery marches, 283
semiconductors (chips), 111–13, 178, 179, 258–67
Semisonic, 289
Senate, xxiv, 14, 57, 110, 134, 154, 201, 217–20, 248, 254, 275
September 11 terrorist attacks, 78, 227, 304, 316, 321, 324, 325

Sessions, Jeff, 18, 27, 57
1789 Capital, 357
Sheinbaum, Claudia, 89, 92, 319–20
Sherald, Amy, 204–6
Siebert, Erik, 307–9
Signal, 154, 279–80, 292–95
Sims, Cliff, 297
Sinclair Broadcast Group, 303
Situation Room, 227, 393–94
60 Minutes, 141, 142
Skadden, Arps, Slate, Meagher & Flom, 136
Skipper, 375
Skydance Media, 142, 143
slavery, 200, 208
Smith, Jack, 130, 133
Smithsonian Institution, 198–209
  Board of Regents, 201–5
  Executive Committee, 207, 209
  National Museum of African American History and Culture, 200
  National Museum of American History, 203
  National Museum of Asian Art, 203
  National Portrait Gallery, 198–99, 203–6
Smoot-Hawley Tariff Act, 91, 117
Snoop Dogg, 354
social media, 285–91
  Facebook, xx, 6, 7, 288, 289
  Instagram, xx, 6, 180, 289
  Kirk assassination and, 296–97
  memes on, 286, 287, 289
  TikTok, 179, 288, 289, 292, 296, 408
  Trump banned on, xx, 6, 42
  Truth Social, *see* Truth Social
  White House communications, 285–91
  X (Twitter), xx, 6, 7, 42–44, 47, 48, 121–22, 150–51, 186, 197, 212, 221, 225, 241, 285, 288–91, 293, 296
Social Security, 24
Social Security Administration, 47
Somalia, xxiv, 323
Somali immigrants, xv, 386
Soros, George, 66, 120, 302, 304
Souza, Pete, 227
space program, 262, 358–60
SpaceX, 42, 358–60
Special Report, 196
Spectrum News, 144
Stalin, Joseph, 254, 411, 412
Starlink, 359
Starmer, Keir, 172, 230
State Department, xxiv, 29, 39, 51, 71, 107–8, 155, 174, 303, 316
Statue of Liberty, 204–6
Stellantis, 91–92
Stephanopoulos, George, 139–40
Steube, Greg, 215–16
stock market, 93, 119, 259
Stone, Roger, 13, 15, 134, 149–51, 157, 240, 356, 376
Strait of Hormuz, 395, 397, 400–401, 408
Suleimani, Qassim, 129, 390
Sullivan & Cromwell, 135
Summerall, Pat, 4
Super Bowl, 360
Supreme Court, U.S., 11, 201, 282, 361, 408
  Brown v. Board of Education, 132
  Federal Reserve and, 242, 251, 254
  habeas corpus and, 159–61
  immigration policies and, 159–61, 164–66
  New York Times Co. v. Sullivan, 140
  Trump v. United States, xxii, 11, 134, 158, 240, 357, 409
Surabian, Andy, 292–95
Sweeney, Sydney, 358
Swift Boat campaign, 216
Syria, xxiv, 13, 50, 103, 323, 400
Syrian Democratic Forces, 50

Taft, William Howard, 87–88
Tahnoon bin Zayed Al Nahyan (TBZ), 41, 352–53, 355–56
Taiwan, 111–12, 178
Taliban, 411
Tamerlane, 411
Tan, Lip-Bu, 263–67
Tapper, Jake, 24
tariffs, xxv, 44, 88–93, 94, 101, 112, 113, 114–23, 129, 244, 245, 375, 410, 413
  Canada and, 89, 91–93, 113, 115
  China and, 89, 90, 93, 112, 114, 121, 122, 177–79, 410
  Liberation Day, 92–93, 113, 115–21, 150–51, 179, 244, 245
  Mexico and, 89–93, 115
  prices and, 177, 246, 374
  Smoot-Hawley, 91, 117
taxes, 89, 112, 128, 131, 139, 211
  Climate Superfund and, 101
  Internal Revenue Service, 47, 123, 304, 364

Taylor, Miles, 129
Tea Party movement, 32, 56
technology, xxvii, 5–8, 90, 258, 262
  AI, *see* AI
  semiconductors in, 111–13, 178, 179, 258–63
  Technology CEO Council, 111–13
Tegna, 303
Tenney, Claudia, 215
terrorism, 330, 381
  bombings of suspects, 322–23
  Cartel of the Suns and, 322
  domestic, 301–4, 389
  drug smugglers and, 321, 326
  interrogations of suspects, 325
  National Joint Terrorism Task Force, 303–4
  redefinition of, 321
  September 11 attacks, 78, 227, 304, 316, 321, 324, 325
  war on, 304
Tesla, 111, 212
Thiel, Peter, 187, 301
Thiessen, Marc, 398
This Week, 158, 196
Thomson, Robert, 227
Thune, John, 192, 213–14, 372–73
Tiananmen Square protests and massacre, 272–73
TikTok, 179, 288, 289, 292, 296, 408
Tillerson, Rex, 58
Tillis, Thom, 220
Time Life Inc., 204
Torok, Dan, 373
Toyota, 116
trade, 57, 115, 409
  free, 91, 121
  NAFTA, 113
  tariffs and, *see* tariffs
  U.S. trade deficits, 94–95, 118
  World Trade Organization, xxvi
Treasury Department, 47, 50, 78, 90, 304, 364
  Office of Foreign Assets Control, 322
  special coin to be minted by, 368
  Trump's lawsuit against, 364
Tren de Aragua, 55, 104, 163, 281, 321, 323
Truman, Harry, 29
Trump, Barron, 294, 352
Trump, Donald
  age and health issues of, 172–73
  assassination attempts against, xxii, 9, 13, 43–44, 63, 172, 293–95, 382, 390, 413, 414
  assassination plots against, 295–96, 390
  authors' meeting with, 407–14
  birthday of, 369
  books by, 5–6, 151
  cataract surgery of, 172
  cultural interests of, 199
  decision-making of, 174
  document storage by, xx, xxi, 76, 128, 158, 171, 364
  in election of 2020, xvii–xx, xxiii, 3–7, 9, 10, 16–18, 33, 74, 128, 129, 133, 151, 157, 163
  fundraising of, 217–19
  gold as signature of, 87, 88, 208, 210–11, 348
  hearing loss of, 173
  impeachments of, xviii, xxiii–xxiv, 135, 199, 215, 218, 399, 414
  legal cases against, xx–xxii, 43, 127–28, 130–31, 133, 135, 139–40, 144–49, 158, 163, 171, 310, 413, 414
  as night owl, 76, 172
  portrait of, 198–99
  power as viewed by, 410–13
  presidential library of, 140–42, 181, 182, 217, 357–58, 360
  real estate and, 144–46, 180, 351, 365–66
  social media bans on, xx, 6, 42
  speakerphone calls of, 311
  tax returns of, 364
  tributes to, 215–16
  TV watching of, 77, 171, 264
  wealth of, 351–52
Trump, Donald, first term of, xviii, xix, xxiii, xxv, 13, 17, 25, 26, 32, 35, 39, 45, 53, 57, 58, 104, 129, 134, 157, 171–73, 175, 186, 200, 216, 223, 256, 259, 273, 316–18, 320, 328–30, 343, 353, 363–64, 366, 367, 413
  cabinet selection in, 16, 46
  CBS coverage of, 141
  Congress and, 213, 214
  election, *see* presidential election of 2016
  end of, 215, 366
  Federal Reserve and, 241, 242, 251
  inaugural address in, 19
  social media in, 285, 288, 289

Trump, Donald, second term of
cabinet selection in, 12–19, 133, 219
conflicts of interest and, 353, 357, 388
election, *see* presidential election of 2024
executive orders in, xiv, 20, 23, 24, 30, 50, 89, 94, 97, 129–32, 136, 201, 263, 271, 272
inauguration, 6, 9–11, 19–22, 36, 100, 117, 162, 217, 259, 360
meetings in, 169–71, 173–74, 315
naming and renaming during, 365–69
pardons in, 355–57, 376
polls and approval ratings in, xviii, 224, 349, 374, 375, 399
presidential immunity and, xxii, 11, 134, 158, 409
retribution campaigns during, 127–43, 144, 148–50, 158–59, 174, 305–12, 342
transition in, 12, 16, 21, 29, 30, 36, 42, 44, 133, 241, 242, 275, 297, 318, 329, 355, 364
vice president selection in, 57–58
White House officials' relocation to military bases during, 363
Trump, Donald, Jr., xxii, xxvii, 11, 15, 34, 86, 120, 181, 219, 222, 225, 292–94, 330, 352, 354, 356, 357
Trump, Eric, xiii, 132, 147, 181, 330, 352, 354–55, 357–58, 360, 364
Trump, Fred, xxvii, 102, 131, 147–48, 199, 365
Trump, Ivana, 87, 342
Trump, Ivanka, 148–49, 156, 329, 339, 353
Trump, Lara, xiii
Trump, Melania, xiii, xvi, 19, 21, 48, 69, 76–78, 148–49, 210–11, 214, 345, 379
documentary on, 364
Trump Accounts, 368
Trump-class warships, 368
Trump Derangement Syndrome (TDS) Research Act, 216
Trump Digital Trading Cards, 354
Trump family, 26, 102, 131, 132, 145, 295, 357–58
crypto ventures of, xxii, xxvii, 181, 351–57
Trump Gold Card, 368
Trump Organization, xx, 131, 145, 353, 364
TrumpRx, 368
Trump Tower, 87, 140, 171
Trump v. United States presidential immunity case, xxii, 11, 134, 158, 240, 357, 409
Truth Social, 6, 65, 79, 95, 110, 122, 143, 169, 182, 192, 194–96, 224, 225, 235, 245, 253–54, 258, 263–64, 280, 310
boat-bombing campaign and, 323, 326
Trump's Iran war posts on, 402, 405
Trump's message to Bondi on, 307, 308, 310
Trump's posts and comments about Maggie on, 407, 413–14
Trump's Venezuela posts on, 381–82, 384
TSMC, 111–12
Tucker, Emma, 226–27
Turkey, 71, 338, 382
Turning Point USA, 185, 224–25, 289, 292
Twain, Mark, 88
Twitter, *see* X

UAE (United Arab Emirates), 41, 62, 71, 180, 181, 188, 261, 328, 329, 352, 353, 355
UFC (Ultimate Fighting Championship), 287, 288, 363
Ukraine, 37, 38, 64, 65, 67
Biden administration and, 36, 37, 39, 82–84
NATO membership for, 65, 67, 82
Russia's war with, 3, 35–41, 59, 62, 64–68, 82–86, 111, 176–77, 185, 189, 323, 327, 328, 349, 359, 397
U.S. minerals deal with, 66, 67, 80–83, 85
Zelensky's White House visit and, 80–86
United Kingdom, 189, 236
United Nations, xxvi, 340, 408, 413
General Assembly, 332–34
Security Council, 340
Ukraine war and, 176
U.S. ambassadors to, 156
United States Capitol Building, 250
January 6 attack on, xviii, xix, 6–7, 11, 16–17, 20–22, 213, 297, 309, 343, 356, 364
United States history, 200–201, 204, 206
slavery in, 200, 208
250th anniversary, 206, 208, 216, 218, 368, 369
United States Institute of Peace, 368
University of Alabama, 283
University of Mississippi, 283
USAID (United States Agency for International Development), 49–50, 80, 107, 157
U.S. Cyber Command, 152
U.S. Digital Service, 45
USD1, 181, 356

USMCA (United States–Mexico–Canada Agreement), 92, 115
USTR (Office of the United States Trade Representative), 115
Utah Valley University, 292
Uyghurs, 178

Vance, Cyrus, Jr., 131
Vance, JD, 12, 15, 21, 31, 34, 46, 71, 83, 151, 155, 156, 174, 191, 278, 292, 299, 301, 338, 344, 346, 348–50, 386, 394, 396
  Big Beautiful Bill and, 220
  early life of, 187
  Epstein files and, 222, 225, 228–29, 234–38
  Federal Reserve and, 252
  government shutdown and, 373
  Iran and, 394, 396, 400, 403
  Israel and Iran and, 185, 186, 191, 192, 195–97
  Kirk and, 292, 294, 295, 297, 299, 302
  left-wing groups and, 302
  memoir of, 187
  political career of, 187, 295
  Powell and, 246
  presidential election of 2028 and, 58, 83, 186, 299, 345–48, 373
  protesters and, 278
  on Rogan podcast, 127
  Rubio and, 58, 348
  Smithsonian and, 198, 201, 203–5, 207
  social media and, 290
  as Trump's running mate, 187, 346, 348
  Ukraine and, 36–38
  Zelensky's White House visit and, 83–86
Vance, Usha, 82, 297, 299, 344
Vanilla Ice, xiv, 289
Venezuela, 55–57, 102–5, 167, 392–93, 410
  boat-bombing campaign and, 320–26, 346, 375, 376, 378
  Maduro in, xiv, xvi, xxvi, 57, 103–4, 317, 318, 320, 322, 378–84, 385, 392, 402, 410
  military operation against, 380–81
  oil in, 322, 375–76, 378, 379, 381, 382, 384
  Tren de Aragua in, 55, 104, 163, 281, 321, 323
  Trump's Truth Social posts about, 381–82, 384
Vermont, 101
Versailles, 250
veterans, 14, 109, 136, 140
Veterans Affairs, Department of, 109, 385
Vietnam War, xxii
Village Voice, The, xxvii
Vindman, Alexander, xxiv
Virginia, 150, 259, 307–8, 374
Virgin Islands, 283
Vision 2030 agenda, 328
Von, Theo, 222
Vought, Russell, xxv, 24, 31, 34, 45–46, 207, 274
  Federal Reserve and, 247–49, 252
Vulcan Elements, 357

Walczak, Paul, 357
Wall Street Journal, The, 91, 226, 235, 329, 352, 353, 356
  Trump's lawsuit against, 226–27, 342–44
Walter Reed National Military Medical Center, 173, 410
Waltz, Mike, 13, 36, 37, 40, 59, 63–65, 68, 71, 72, 153–56, 188, 329, 340
  appointment as UN ambassador, 156
  Loomer and, 153–55
  Signalgate and, 153–54
  Zelensky and, 83, 86
War, Department of, 318
Warner Bros. Discovery, 122
War on Warriors, The (Hegseth), 318
Warrington, David, 21, 134, 159, 164, 181–82, 228, 235, 357, 386, 387, 403, 404
War Room, 22, 262–63
Warsh, Kevin, 241–42
Washington, D.C., 128, 217, 250, 252, 366
  crime and homelessness in, 278
  federal takeover of, 275
  National Guard in, 272, 273, 278–79, 284
Washington, George, 210, 366
Washington Commanders, 369
Washington Dulles International Airport, 215, 369
Washington Metropolitan Area Transit Authority (WMATA), 215–16
Washington Monument, 345, 366
Washington Post, The, 6–8, 389, 402
Watergate scandal, 18, 279, 307
weapons of mass destruction, 321, 324
Weaver, Patrick, 279–80
Weisselberg, Allen, 131
Wheeler, Liz, 229
Whistler, James McNeill, 203
White House Communications Office, 229, 230
  social media and, 285–91

White House decor and renovations, 75–78, 87–88, 170, 171, 183, 208, 210–11, 218, 345, 347–48, 365, 366
  ballroom, xxvii, 77–78, 170, 208, 217, 344, 349, 369, 408
  maple trees, 408, 409
  Rose Garden, 77, 170, 218
White House Situation Room, 40, 80, 186, 227, 232–39, 240, 383, 393–94, 396, 403
white supremacy, 161, 186, 299, 304
Whitney Museum of American Art, 205
Wiles, Susie, xiv, xx, 4, 12, 21, 31–34, 40, 71, 104, 135, 151, 152, 157, 170, 173, 174, 191, 216, 218, 249, 265, 283, 309–11, 329, 335, 344, 357
  Bowser and, 275
  Epstein files and, 224, 228, 232–33, 235, 236, 238
  immigration policies and, 158, 164, 166, 386–88
  Iran and, 394, 399, 403
  Kirk assassination and, 294, 295, 297
  Musk and, 48, 79, 80, 107
  Newsom and, 277
  Powell and, 245
  Rubio and, 58, 317
  Venezuela and, 382
  Waltz and, 155
William the Conqueror, 411
Willow project, 105–6
Wilson, Joe, 216
Wilson, Pete, 27
Windsor, Edie, 132
Wirth, Mike, 102, 105
Witkoff, Alex, 352, 354
Witkoff, Andrew, 60
Witkoff, Steve, 40, 41, 59, 60–61, 135, 174, 181, 334, 352, 360
  crypto and, 352, 353, 354, 355
  Iran and, 394, 401–2
  Kushner and, 329–34, 335, 336–37, 338, 339
  Middle East and, 40, 59, 61–62, 70, 72, 175, 185, 188–92, 327–28, 329–39, 353
  Putin and, 176–77
  real estate investments of, 60, 61
  Russia and, 40, 41, 59, 62–65
  son's death and, 60
Witkoff, Zach, 181, 352, 354–56
WMATA (Washington Metropolitan Area Transit Authority), 215
"woke" ideology, 24, 50, 137, 199, 201, 319, 342
Wolff, Michael, 378
Wong, Alex, 152–54
Wong, Candice, 152
Woods, Darren, 101
Woodward, Stanley, 228
working people, 90
World Cup, 360, 361
World Liberty Financial (WLF), 181, 352–53, 355–56
World Trade Organization, xxvi, 413
World War II, xxv, 64–65, 83, 160, 161, 163, 194, 239
Wray, Christopher, 362
Wright, Chris, 403
writ of habeas corpus, 158–62, 166–68, 284
Wyden, Ron, 134

X (Twitter), xx, 6, 7, 42–44, 47, 48, 121, 150–51, 186, 197, 212, 221, 225, 241, 285, 288–91, 293, 296
xAI, 271
Xi Jinping, 4, 111, 121, 174, 177, 179, 180, 244, 287, 317

Yeary, Frank, 264
Yemen, 323
Yoo, John, 325
Youngkin, Glenn, 300

Zeldin, Lee, 109
Zelensky, Volodymyr, 37, 38, 65–68
  Trump's call to, about Bidens, xxiii
  White House visit of, 80, 82–86, 208
Zhao, Changpeng, 355–57
Zhukova, Elena, 344
Zuckerberg, Mark, 6–8